# Bitumen

# Bitumen

## THE PEOPLE, PERFORMANCE AND PASSIONS BEHIND ALBERTA'S OIL SANDS

---

CANADA 150

*Peter McKenzie-Brown*

© 2017 Peter McKenzie-Brown
ISBN: 1546452303
ISBN-13: 9781546452300

## To Bernie

*For six years as I researched and wrote this book, you encouraged me when things went well and cheered me on when they were tough. Thank you.*

This history has received a Government of Canada license to use the Canada 150 logo, which celebrates the Confederation of the provinces in 1867.

# Contents

# Foreword

---

## By Earle Gray

*Bitumen* is a powerful addition to the corpus of writing about Canada's petroleum industry. But it is more than history: it is an account of current challenges and visions of future possibilities. While he focuses on the vast oil deposits in the Alberta oil sands, McKenzie-Brown also sheds wide-ranging light on other aspects of the Canadian petroleum industry's history.

He has weaved his story from an impressive array of diverse sources, as well as intensive and extensive research. The result is a must-read for anyone interested not only in the history of the Canada's oil business, but perhaps more importantly, Canada's economic history.

The author of eight books, Earle Gray was editor of *Oilweek* magazine for nearly 20 years and, in the 1970s, public affairs director for a consortium that planned and researched a multi-billion dollar gas pipeline from Alaska's Prudhoe Bay and the Northwest Territories to southern Canada. He has contributed to the *Canadian Encyclopedia*, *Maclean's*, *Financial Post*, *Toronto Star*, *Canadian Business*, and others. He is the recipient of numerous writing awards, a lifetime achievement award from the Petroleum History Society and the Samuel T. Pees Keeper of the Flame Award from the US Petroleum History Institute.

For the oil sands, it has been a history of eight decades of formidable challenge, big hopes and plans, tenacious perseverance, scientific and technical study, and repeated failures until sustained commercial oil production was finally achieved in 1967. The challenges facing the oil sands today are no less formidable, including economic, environmental, technical, regulatory, and competition from lower-cost oil production from tight formations, induced by "fracking" and horizontal drilling.

Vociferous critics of oil sands development are entirely correct in their profound concerns about how oil sands production, with its heavy emissions of carbon dioxide, contribute almost as much as coal to the rise of global warming, and its existential threat.

Yet some critics too often forget a few things. The clamour for non-carbon fuels sometimes seems to lose sight of the fact that large-scale development will require decades. The world does need to curb its appetite for fuel, and reduce the role of fossil fuels in the energy mix, but large volumes of oil and gas will still be needed for as long as the future can reasonably be anticipated. And the oil sands offer availability insurance.

It is easy to forget that, starting in the early 1960s, billions of dollars, in today's money, were invested to develop commercial oil sands before there was any generally understood concern or awareness of the impending risks of global warming. Global warming was not an issue before the 1980s. More than just financial gain motivated leaders who risked more than just investments in efforts to develop commercial production. Yes, as McKenzie-Brown points out, there were frauds and con artists in early years, such as Alfred Hammerstein and A.F.A. Coyne.

Yet not just industry leaders, but virtually the whole country viewed the development of this energy as a boon to both national and North American interests. None were more motivated by a concept of a North American common interest than J. Howard Pew, the patriarch of the family that controlled Sun Oil Company. Other Sun Oil directors saw more assured and profitable opportunity, under then-existing conditions, in developing oil production in Venezuela. Pew made it clear that if the company's board did not agree to finance the first commercial oil sands venture, he would finance it himself. He saw the oil sands as key to North American energy concern, and was clearly motivated by that as well as by commercial opportunity.

It is too easy to take for granted, to forget how virtually every aspect of modern life is dependent on oil and gas, not merely for fuel but for everything made of plastic, the asphalt shingles on our roofs, the carpets on our floor, untold thousands of other items we use virtually every hour of every day, not to mention the food we eat. Eight barrels of crude oil and equivalent natural gas, 283 U.S. gallons, was required in 2003 to raise a 1,250-pound champion steer, perhaps three-quarters of a gallon for every pound of butchered beef. It is too easy to ignore how long it will take and how much it will cost to replace even a meaningful portion of the trillions of dollars of facilities that make it possible to supply the world with 90 million barrels of crude oil every day. Oil sands may supply only a small element of the world's oil demand, but it looms large in the North American context, and even the knowledge that much greater quantity can be made available is important to energy security.

It is too easy to forget how much the prosperity of every economically advanced country depends on oil and none more so than Canada. The oil sands have become cornerstones of the economy. Any cutback in oil sands production would be a blow to the economy, and even a slowdown in the pace of development could send tremors. Yet the risk of this cannot be discounted.

In a 2013 forecast the Canadian Association of Petroleum Producers foresaw a tripling of oil sands production during the 19-year period to 2030, rather than cutbacks. That would have boosted oil sands production from 1.8 million to 5.2 million barrels a day, and total Canadian oil output to 6.8 million barrels a day, two-and-a-half times as much as Canadians now consume. With little increase anticipated in domestic consumption, Canada would have to increase its net oil exports by some three million barrels a day to achieve the CAPP forecast. The only export market now available is the United States, which seems in no need for any additional imported oil. Indeed, the U.S. Energy Information Office recently ruminated briefly about difficulties in absorbing all the oil supplies now available, including imports from Canada. CAPP has since backed off that forecast.

Long-term and even medium-term forecasts of oil supply, demand and prices, by industry, government, and academics, have been mostly useless, or worse. Almost all have been far off the mark. This book recounts the record of erroneous oil forecast in the early decades of the industry's history, as reported in Ida Tarbell's seminal *History of the Standard Oil Company*. But the trend has been sustained throughout the industry's history of almost 160 years. When Prime Minister Pierre Trudeau and Alberta Premier Peter Lougheed drank champagne on September 1, 1981 to celebrate an Alberta-Canada revenue sharing agreement, it was based on a predicted steady rise in oil prices from $45 to $80 per barrel. Instead of rising, oil prices were already heading steadily down, to $19 over an eight-year period. A trio of once widely acclaimed 21st century end-of-oil-type forecasts are the latest to get it wrong, including *Hubbert's Peak: The Impending World Oil Shortage,* by Kenneth S. Deffeyes, in 2001; *The End of Oil: On the Edge of a Perilous New World,* by Paul Roberts, in 2004; and *Why Your World is About to Get a Whole Lot Smaller: Oil and the End of Globalization,* by Canadian economist Jeff Rubin, in 2009.

The ink was hardly dry on the last of these books before the extent of a profound revolution in both oil and gas supply, wrought by directional drilling and hydraulic fracturing of tight oil and gas formations, was fully apparent. Instead of falling off a cliff, the world's estimated remaining oil reserves increased over a 20-year period by 440 per cent, to 1,688 billion barrels at the end of 2013. Nothing, as an old saying has it, is as difficult to predict as the future.

By far the most dramatic change in oil supplies has been in the United States, where oil production had been in what seemed like an inexorable decline, falling, for example, from 8.4 million barrels a day in 1994 to 6.7 million in 2008. But the trend was reversed the next year, climbing to 10 million barrels a day in 2013, with a further increase to 12 million barrels a day in 2015 anticipated by the U.S. Energy Information Agency. A country that has increased its oil production by 5.3 million barrels a day hardly looks like an assured bet to buy an addition three million barrels a day from Canada, or from anyone else. Sustained development of additional oil sands production – or perhaps even maintaining the existing production rate – would seem to require sales to China, India or elsewhere.

Nothing is likely to impact oil sands development more than government regulation to curb emissions of global-warming carbon dioxide. As this is written, long anticipated federal government regulations are still awaited. Regardless of what these may entail, carbon pricing seems almost certain to ultimately emerge as a key element of global effort to curb global warming. Critics like to call this a tax, but it is not. Carbon pricing means including some element of the cost of mostly $CO_2$-induced global warming in the price of fossil fuels. This would set the price closer to the full cost of production and consumption. The greater the $CO_2$ content, the greater the external cost, and the greater the carbon price for any fuel.

Carbon pricing appears to be the government mechanism most acceptable to the oil industry. More importantly, it is seen by crucial global agencies – the International Energy Agency, the World Bank, the International Monetary Fund, the Intergovernmental Panel on Climate Change, and the 34-nation Organization for Economic Cooperation and Development – as the main element of any effort to combat global warming. "Credible and consistent carbon pricing must be the cornerstone of government actions to tackle climate change" by stimulating energy conservation and development of non-carbon fuels, an OECD statement exclaims. ExxonMobil, British Petroleum, Shell, Chevron, ConocoPhillips and 24 other major corporations have already incorporated carbon pricing in planning future operations and investments, the *New York Times* reports.

How much might carbon pricing cost? Don't be surprised at a carbon pump price of $1 a litre, based on the carbon content of today's gasoline. That would bring the North American price to about what most Europeans already pay. And it will not be as painful as you might expect. The U.S. government has already mandated an almost two-fold increase in the average fuel economy of new cars and trucks, to 54.5 miles per U.S. gallon (more than 60 mpg for the more Canadian-familiar Imperial gallon) by 2025. If cars travel twice as far on a gallon or litre of gasoline, a carbon price is unlikely to pinch motorists, assuming that the carbon price is introduced over an appropriate period of time. The American mandate for motor fuel economy will perforce become the Canadian mandate, unless Canada acts to set its own standards. Canada stands to become a follower, not a leader, in this and all aspects of carbon pricing, if it is not prepared to act on its own. What happens here would be determined in Washington and elsewhere if Canada is not proactive.

Carbon pricing might just turn out to be more opportunity than threat for the oil sands. Ultimately, the long-run viability of the oil sands hangs on the industry's ability to reduce $CO_2$ emission, as well as the use of water and other resources. Carbon pricing will give the oil sands industry a greater incentive, and perhaps the ability, to pursue and invest in those goals much more aggressively. Such high-cost, non-carbon fuels as cellulosic ethanol could emerge as the market competition facing the oil sands, and the lower the $CO_2$, the greater the ability to compete. Absent some form of carbon pricing, alternative government actions to curb global warming might slowly squeeze the life out of the oil sands, as they are now squeezing the life out of coal-fuelled thermal electric power plants in the United States.

But what if carbon pricing is the impetus that, after 90 years of promise and frustration, unlocks the potential of firefloods to cut in half the $CO_2$ emissions in producing the 80 per cent of the bitumen in the Athabasca oil sands that can be recovered only *in-situ*, as opposed to mining? Burning underground 10 per cent of the bitumen to separate 90 per cent from the sand would confer other major environmental advantages in addition to cutting $CO_2$ emissions. What if using super-hot heat buried deep under the surface is used to generate electricity and steam, rather than burning gas? What if carbon pricing results in the capture and underground storage of virtually all the $CO_2$ emissions not only from the production and upgrading of bitumen, but also the enormous amount of $CO_2$ emitted by Alberta's coal-fired thermal electric power plants?

Will such things be accomplished with carbon pricing? Will they slash carbon dumping enough to make the oil sands competitive with non-carbon fuels? I have no idea. But they at least hint at the possibilities.

If the possibilities are there, so is the vision. McKenzie-Brown quotes oil sands leaders, such as Clement Bowman, who share progressive views on contentious issues of energy and environment. Bowman, a leader in the development of oil sands technology that minimizes not just cost but the use of resources and environment impact, sees Canada's energy resources as an integrated system embracing oil sands, coal, hydro, nuclear and renewable energy. Bowman argues that we must learn how to use our nation's gift of energy resources "without using the environment as a dump for waste products." He says, "Canada has an opportunity to provide global leadership in addressing the collision between [petroleum fuels] and the environment, the dominant issue facing our planet in this century."[1]

# Introduction

_____

*"At its heart, participating in the oil sands
industry is a journey of constant tests."*

— DEBORAH JAREMKO, 2014.

OIL AND NATURAL GAS VIRTUALLY created a second industrial revolution — one more far-reaching by orders of magnitude than the century-long event that began in Britain in the mid-1700s.[2]

There are two main reasons for this. The first is that liquid hydrocarbons fuelled a revolution in the technologies used for transportation and manufacturing. One result was a sharp rise in standards of living within the countries fortunate enough to own the resources and develop infrastructure to exploit them. In many regions, notably Western Canada, governments were the primary owners of these resources, and the resources themselves are vast. Thus, their development requires close cooperation among government, industry and the scientific communities.

Within this context, a cacophony of information about the oil sands has come out in traditional form, and the numbers are growing. Four oil sands books came out in the late 1970s and 1980s – to a large degree as a celebration of the anticipated start-up of the giant Syncrude plant.

Earle Gray first released one of those volumes – *The Great Canadian Oil Patch: The Petroleum Era from Birth to Peak* – in 1970, and a thoroughly revised edition 34 years later. Each version was a comprehensive look at Canada's petroleum sector at time of publication.

In 1993, David Breen released his magisterial study of Alberta's petroleum industry and its regulator. A decade later, Paul Chastko's *Developing Alberta's Oil Sands: from Karl Clark to Kyoto* came out; it covers the period 1920-1997. A third volume is Joyce Hunt's massive, *Local Push Global Pull: The Untold History of the Athabaska Oil Sands 1900-1930*. It primarily covers the first three decades of the 20th century.

In 2009, Satya Das – an engineer with an oil sands background – published a book called *Green Oil: Clean Energy for the 21st Century?* In that tome he argues that the oil sands can be developed as a green commodity. Other recent contributions include *The Future of Oil: A Straight Story of the Canadian Oil Sands* by Sanjay Patel, another petroleum engineer; Alistair Sweeney's *Black Bonanza*; and *Ethical Oil: The Case for Canada's Oil Sands* by right-wing commentator Ezra Levant.

A recent development has been the publication of popular books focused on global warming, and zeroing in on oil sands development as a threat to humanity. One such came from the pen of a prolific Montréal-based writer, William Marsden. It's title? *Stupid to the Last Drop: How Alberta is bringing environmental Armageddon to Canada (and doesn't seem to care)*. Not to be outdone, Andrew Nikiforuk released *Tar Sands: Dirty oil and the future of a continent* in the same year, 2010.

Before continuing this story, it is worth putting the Marsden and Nikiforuk books in perspective. A 2012 report compares greenhouse gas emissions from the 36 sources of oil used in the United States. According to economist Jackie Forrest, if you factor extraction, processing, transportation and consumption as fuel into the equation – that is, if you use the "well-to-wheels" approach in making GHG calculations – emissions from oil sands are in 14th place on the table. If you add Canadian well-to-wheels calculations into the mix, the number rises to ninth place.[3] Put another way, the environmental enthusiasm of the writers seems to have interfered with the accuracy of their research.

## CHALLENGE AND METHOD

The book you are holding in your hands provides balance and perspective to help the reader navigate the seemingly endless debates about the financial viability and environmental costs of oil sands development. It draws from a wide range of documents to provide a current, informed and accessible account of the industry's evolution, achievements and drawbacks.

Like a living thing, the manuscript grew over several years. My sources included numerous books and reports – some originally published in the 19th century. Much of this nourishment came from the Glenbow Archives and from Alberta's Provincial Archives.

My keen interest in the oil sands began with my work as coordinator and one of six interviewers for the Petroleum History Society's Oil Sands Oral History Project. Access to those transcribed interviews gave me insights into the thinking of many industry leaders and government officials. So did interviews I undertook in my day job, which involved writing petroleum-related articles for a number of magazines.

The Calgary-based Petroleum History Society's oral histories were another source of valuable information. It was a privilege to have been on the team which interviewed those pioneering men and women, and to have had early and easy access to the transcripts.

In my view, these oral histories were a particularly valuable resource. As Victorian writer Thomas Carlyle wrote, history is "the essence of innumerable Biographies." He added, "but if one Biography, nay our own Biography, study and recapitulate it as we may, remains in so many points unintelligible to us; how much more must these million, the very facts of which, to say nothing of the purport of them, we know not, and cannot know!"[4] If this is true of a single biography, would an industrial history covering three centuries be more unmanageable still?

Perhaps the answer to Carlyle's dilemma can be found in an idea presented by another 19th century thinker, American philosopher William James. According to his "great man" theory of history, "sporadic great men come everywhere." In the context of this history, scientific investigation of petroleum and of the oil sands began in Canada in the 19th century, with European records of early interest in the commodity dating back three full centuries.

"But for a community to get vibrating through and through with intensely active life, many geniuses coming together in rapid succession are required,"

James said. "This is why great epochs are so rare. Blow must follow blow so fast that no cooling can occur in the intervals. Then the mass of the nation grows incandescent, and may continue to glow by pure inertia long after the originators of its internal movement have passed away."[5] Surely that pattern describes the increasing interest in and development of the oil sands during the last 90 years.

The stories of those who found, explored and helped develop the oil sands are an integral part of Canada's history, but primarily because politics, governments, regulators, corporations and scientific institutions enabled their efforts to prosper or – in more cases than we care to remember – caused them to fail. Especially in the early years, those pioneers were exploring and investigating areas in which simple survival was a fundamental feature of daily life – to a large extent because of great distances, and the bitterness of winter in Alberta's northern forests. When fast-flowing rivers were clear of ice, navigating scows full of equipment and supplies to the nearest railway was another, sometimes deadly, challenge.

## THE PLAYERS

The players include people from Ottawa, the Alberta government, the private sector, the scientific community, First Nations and NGOs. This has not always been so, however. Between 1875 and 1918 the federal government was the principal actor, as an unpublished study by William Wylie explains – "at first from a sense of responsibility for regional development." Near the end, it was because of "strategic considerations."

"In the 1920s, the government of Alberta became the major force, in part in order to assert its claim to control provincial resources. In the 1930s, two private companies showed signs of promise and the two governments pulled back in deference to private development and in order to cut costs," he wrote. "The 1940s were years of increased involvement on the part of both levels of government due partially to strategic considerations, and to the power struggle between them. In the 1950s, the conventional oil boom in the province took attention away from the oil sands and delayed their development until the 60s and 70s when the long run decline of the conventional reserves was finally anticipated. When commercial development occurred, private industry was the major agency, but with considerable governmental backing as well."[6]

Released in 1990, Wylie's study coincided with industry/government negotiations that led to a new stage of oil sands development. Since 1992, financial responsibility for oil sands development has lain entirely with the private sector. The signal for this development began during the new Ralph Klein government, when the stars aligned for deregulation of the petroleum industry along free-market lines. Alberta dramatically reduced its royalties, and the federal and Alberta governments withdrew financial support from the OSLO oil sands plant and other petroleum projects. The era of government-funded loan guarantees and tax and royalty concessions was over. Since that time government has provided regulation and an improved fiscal regime for oil sands development, but no cash. Industry has taken the risks and benefitted from the rewards.

During this period, the sector developed important new production technologies. "At its heart, participating in the oil sands industry is a journey of constant tests," said Deborah Jaremko, editor of the industry's trade magazine. "At first, it was that the technology was unproven. Then it was that low oil prices severely challenged the economics. Then, with rising oil prices and new technology, came the whirlwind of a boom coloured by the new visibility brought by the oil sands' presence on the world stage."[7]

By overcoming continual challenges, the industry has benefitted the people of Canada – a reality that seems obvious, given the size of this resource. At 168 billion barrels of recoverable reserves, these deposits represent the third-largest oil reserves in the world, after those of Saudi Arabia and Venezuela.

According to the Canadian Energy Research Institute (CERI), almost every community in Canada has been touched by oil sands development through its impact on job creation and economic growth. Every dollar invested in the oil sands creates about $8 worth of economic activity. One-third of that value creation takes place outside Alberta – in other provinces, the U.S. and around the world.

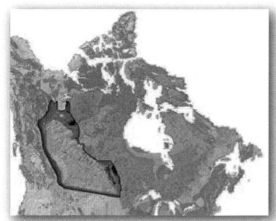

At this writing, Alberta collects some $4.5 billion in oil sands royalties each year. As importantly, oil sands development and operations provide economic stimulus – $21 billion in 2012 and direct employment for 20,000 – many of whom fly in from across Canada for their 8-days-on, 10-days-off shifts. In real terms, investment related to the oil sands would generate an anticipated $79.4 billion in government revenues between 2012 and 2035.[8]

## THE RESOURCE BASE AND CLIMATE CHANGE

As one of the world's great sources of petroleum, the Western Canada Sedimentary Basin – it stretches along the U.S. border from Manitoba to the Rockies, thence up to Yukon and the Northwest Territories – contains the lion's share of Canada's hydrocarbon wealth.

The graphic shows its outline in black. It is worth putting the basin into geographical and geological context.

According to one view, Earth has two energy super-provinces – one in the Old World,[i] the other in the New. The New World super-province stretches south from northern Alaska and the Beaufort Sea, through Yukon and the Prairie Provinces. The basin continues through most of the major petroleum-producing American states and the Gulf of Mexico down to Venezuela's Orinoco heavy oil belt. From there, it underlies numerous petroleum basins within the vast land mass between South America's Atlantic coast and the eastern Andes.[9]

---

i The Old World super-province reaches from Nigeria and North Africa through the Middle East into Siberia. Rich with conventional oil and natural gas, it is the source of most of the petroleum traded on global markets.

Besides its immense petroleum resources, Alberta has enormous coal resources. The province burns twice as much coal as do all the other provinces combined, and mines this hydrocarbon for export and to generate electricity. Although the province's coal-burning power plants are being phased out, the province will continue to export the commodity. The result of this resource wealth is that, although Alberta has some 11 per cent of Canada's population, the province produces 40 per cent of her greenhouse gases.

Per capita, Canadians would probably be among the world's largest emitters of greenhouse gases even if the west did not encompass one of the world's great hydrocarbon basins. After all, the country is rich, cold and vast. Canadians drive long distances in cars and trucks, both for work and pleasure. We consume large volumes of fuel oil and natural gas to heat our homes, offices and factories. And we are frequent flyers.

In an effort to deal with greenhouse gases, in 2009 Alberta created the Carbon Capture and Emissions Management Corporation (CCEMC) as a not-for-profit Delegated Administration Organization (DAO). The provincial government establishes DAOs – the other one is for reclamation of "orphaned" wells – to regulate the collection of funds for specific activities. Remitting those funds to independent DAO boards secures the independence of investment decision-making.

Despite its reputation as something of an environmental pariah within the confederation, in 2007 Alberta became the first Canadian province (and well ahead of any US state) to enact a carbon pricing mechanism. The Specified Gas Emitters Regulation charged industrial emitters $15 per tonne of $CO_2$ for emissions that are beyond a 12 per cent reduction from an established baseline. The programme's basic design was deliberatively punitive. From the beginning, its goal was to reduce emissions by large emitters, rather than emissions from transportation and agricultural practices, for example.

"We are the only technology fund supported with regulations like Alberta's," said CCEMC's managing director, Kirk Andries. "In this province, large-scale industrial emitters have three compliance options. They can reduce greenhouse gases by continuous improvement; they can buy offsets or emission performance credits from other emitters; they can pay into the fund; or they can do all these things. It's up to the emitter to decide how they want to pay the bill. There is no 'silver bullet' in the world of managing greenhouse gas emissions.

It is a multifaceted and complex area in which to operate. We need to deal with all sources of greenhouse gas emissions."[10]

Those emissions include carbon dioxide ($CO_2$) and methane ($CH_4$). A third GHG – nitrous oxide ($N_2O$) has nearly 300 times the ability of carbon dioxide to trap heat in the atmosphere. In western Canada, nitrogen fertilizers used by farmers across the prairies are the main source of nitrous oxide emissions.

This funding is possible because Alberta's largest emitters – those who discharge at least 100,000 tonnes of carbon equivalent per day – are responsible for most of the province's industrial emissions. Big emitters pay $15 per tonne for their output of greenhouse gas emissions – to be increased by 2018 to $30 per tonne. Those funds are the source of CCEMC investments in experimental technologies that will reduce Alberta's GHG emissions.

Elsewhere, this history covers the ideas of Clement Bowman and others who argue that Canada can become an energy superpower while successfully managing the greenhouse gases associated with hydrocarbon combustion. Indeed, they argue, the creation of Canada involved many such vast projects: The Canadian Pacific Railway, for example; the James Bay generating facilities; Syncrude.

## EARLY INTEREST

I became interested in the oil sands in 1978, when I worked for Gulf Oil Canada – at the time, one of the owners of the giant Syncrude project. I visited the project just before it opened, accompanying Gulf's board of directors at the behest of my boss, Brock Hammond. From the primitive Fort McMurray airport we took a large tour bus to the site. The driver, who had a flair for impressing visitors, drove the front half of the bus into the bucket of one of the draglines then used for oil sands mining.

The immensity of the facility was extraordinary. Syncrude soon became, and remains, Canada's largest source of oil production. The visit encouraged me to stay current in what I saw as an exciting area of industrial development.

The first historian I read was Joseph Fitzgerald, whose background with the resource ran broad and deep. He was part of the team developing Great

Canadian Oil Sands (GCOS), the commercial oil sands plant which preceded Syncrude. So deep was the animosity between conventional oil and the oil sands in the early days that in 1962 he nearly got the boot from Calgary's exclusive Petroleum Club. He had gone there for lunch with a friend, who had left the table for a few minutes.

As Fitzgerald tells the story, he sat alone until a man went to the table, "asking if I was indeed 'one of those guys from the tar sands.' Assuming he was curious about our work, I assured him that I indeed was one of them. With that he demanded proof of my membership in the Petroleum Club, or one of its affiliates. I explained that I was a guest. 'Where was my host?'" Fitzgerald went on to explain that he was not sure where his host had gone, but that he would be back soon.

"My visitor sought out the nearest waiter, and demanded that I be asked for proof of membership or confirmation of guest status." The harassment continued until "the man returned, with the club manager in tow. This was too much for me to believe. Now the manager was demanding some evidence that I was better than a 'tar sands miner.' Had my host not returned at the right moment, I am sure I would have been promptly thrown out of the Petroleum Club." Fitzgerald's tormenter later returned and said he would "move a resolution to see that I, 'and none of your kind' would ever enjoy privileges at the club, or any over which the fraternity had control."[11] One way to look at Fitzgerald's story is from the perspective that antagonism to the oil sands has a long and interesting history.

The point of this book, however, is that Thomas Carlyle – the Victorian historian – got it just right. The oil sands reflect the achievements of innumerable biographies – many of them remarkable by almost any standard. One of those stories was the extraordinary determination of J. Howard Pew, the chairman of Sun Oil Company. Sun, which designed and constructed the Great Canadian Oil Sands (GCOS) plant, was one of the world's largest publically traded oil companies, and employed 70,000. A great company had taken a bold step, and had done so in the still-rural province of Alberta.

In those days the notion of building an oil sands project was so exotic that only a visionary would have taken it on. Alberta was a have-not province, with modest prospects. Oil was cheap on world markets, and Alberta producers received only $2.45 per barrel for light crude oil. To secure optimal production from its reserves, the province's regulatory body – then known as the Oil and Gas Conservation Board – restricted the volumes coming out of the ground. This "prorationing" involved calculations of the maximum rate at which each oil reservoir could be produced without impairing ultimate production. At the time of the Leduc discovery, some oil states still lacked regulatory policies to avoid such waste. Alberta, however, had one of the world's best conservation regimes because of the experience at Turner Valley.

Conventional wisdom held that the oil sands sector would be marginally profitable, but would flood existing petroleum markets, throwing the balance sheets of Canada's conventional oil producers into the red. Yet with the hindsight of history, the construction of that northeastern Alberta plant – small and rickety by today's standards – was the most significant business event of the year. GCOS led to the creation of Suncor Ltd., which would become the largest energy company in Canada, and her second-largest corporation. For its part, Alberta became an economic powerhouse chafing at the bit to begin exporting its crude oil bounty overseas.

An investment anomaly, it had world-class, undeveloped hydrocarbon resources, a stable political environment and the greatest concentrations of engineering expertise on the planet. Competitors from around the world have invested in the province's rich resources – especially the oil sands.

The construction of the first commercial oil sands plant reflected the imagination and efforts of a long line of people and institutions: explorers and traders going back to the 18th century; government in the 19th; industry and provincial regulators in the 20th. By the time GCOS project pumped its first barrel, scientists and technical specialists had been experimenting with the oil sands for more than half a century; entrepreneurs had been active since the 1920s; business leaders since the late 1940s.

When the petroleum industry first emerged, it was a marginal "snake oil" business. By the time this plant started up, petroleum was a cornerstone of the global economy. It was, and is, the primary source of the transportation and heating fuels, electric power and petrochemicals we consume virtually every moment of every day. This book tells many of the stories behind the creation of an industry now central to our lives and well-being. Going from lighter to heavier hydrocarbons, petroleum generally falls into five categories: natural gas, natural gas liquids, light and medium crude oil, heavy oil and bitumen.

Canada's oil sands deposits are in Alberta, although the Athabasca and Cold Lake deposits dip across the Saskatchewan border. In addition, the country's "heavy oil belt" lies in a string of reservoirs along the Saskatchewan-Alberta boundary. Lloydminster is its buckle.

## Words, words, words

When Shakespeare's Polonius became concerned about Hamlet's mental state, he asked the Danish prince, who had a book in hand, "What do you read, my Lord?" Famously, Hamlet replied: "Words, words, words."[12]

At this point in the oil sands tale, it is time to clarify the use of a few words which will frequently follow. The term "tar sands" is less common today than "oil sands," but the words mean the same thing. In common use, these word pairs serve as adjectives – for example, "an oil sands company" or "tar sands research."

People who oppose development of this resource seem to feel they are tarring the industry, as it were, by using the older term. However, such important pioneers as Karl Clark and Sidney Ells used the term tar sands in their scientific work. So did many government- and industry-sponsored studies. For that reason, this book accepts the terms as synonymous. Less common but technically accurate is the expression "bituminous sands."

The expressions "the oil sands" and "the tar sands" are collective nouns. To clarify, other collective nouns include a flock of geese and a herd of cattle. When you refer to the oil sands or the tar sands, you are referring to Alberta's oil sands or tar sands deposits as a group.

The oil sands originated through the migration of lighter forms of petroleum upward through Earth into a geologic conglomerate of sand and rock, where various processes transformed them into the tarry substance we know as bitumen.

•

The word petroleum encompasses a wide range of substances. All are molecular compounds of hydrogen and carbon. They form a spectrum of materials from light gases through liquids to heavy, gummy, near-solids. The differences derive from the varying proportions of hydrogen and carbon making up the petroleum molecules. At the light end, natural gas contains a high ratio of hydrogen to carbon atoms. At the heavy end, tarry bitumen contains a much lower hydrogen-to-carbon ratio. These petroleum mixtures usually contain sulphur and traces of other elements and compounds.

The oil sands deposits in northern Alberta underlie 77,000 square kilometres of mostly boreal forest. Collectively, they contain about 1.7 trillion barrels of bitumen – dwarfing the oil reserves of the Middle East. One deposit alone, the Athabasca, is the world's largest known single oil resource. However, the need for often complex and expensive production techniques means that, although the bitumen and heavy oil resources are vast, only a fraction is likely to see the inside of a refinery. The size of that fraction is a function of economics and technology, however, and it has grown rapidly since about 1990, but not only in Canada: oil sands and heavy oil deposits are found in 70 countries, with the largest deposits in Venezuela and Canada. Canada's three main oil sand deposits are located in sandstone reservoirs in northern Alberta, with the major reservoirs named Athabasca, Cold Lake and Peace River.

Bitumen also exists in carbonate reservoirs in many places around the world. Again, the difference for Canada is order of magnitude: 96 per cent of the world's bitumen carbonates are in Alberta. Fanciful mapping of the bitumen carbonates across northern Alberta – deposits that are deeper than the oil sands – led to its description as a "carbonate triangle."

Unlike the sandstone reservoirs common to most of Alberta's bitumen deposits, the triangle's reservoirs rocks consist of limestone (a calcium carbonate) and dolomite (a magnesium and calcium carbonate, and contain an estimated 450 billion barrels of this black, immobile gunk – 96 per cent of the world's supply. Seventy-one per cent of that total (318 billion barrels) is in the Grosmont formation – a massive structure underlying much of the Athabasca oil sands deposit. There are another 65 billion barrels in the Nisku carbonate, which is associated with the Grosmont. In Alberta's Peace

River region, the bitumen-saturated carbonates also contain about 65 billion barrels.[13]

There have been some important experiments with these resources, but they are not yet a significant source of energy. According to Glen Schmidt of Laricina Energy, "the reservoir and geology are well defined. We have a lot of oil in place. You have relatively high porosity, which means it can be recovered thermally and the basic principle of mobilizing bitumen and draining it is what we are seeing demonstrated in our pilot....So the science is simple."[14] A pioneer in developing this huge resource, during preparation of this book the company underwent a radical restructuring in the face of potential bankruptcy.

## JEVONS AND HIS PARADOX

Canadians sometimes seem embarrassed by the large role that resources play in the national economy. One wonders, "Why?"

It is not true that resource economies require employees with lower skills, as many people believe. The towns created by felling trees, mining, and hydrocarbon production are not necessarily low-skill communities. "The exploitation of natural resources is increasingly a high-skill and capital-intensive process," according to one report. "To achieve higher productivity, firms in the resource-based sector continually update their capital stock, which embodies new knowledge and advanced technology. Trade in natural resource-based goods and services, therefore, can also support high real incomes."[15]

This is particularly true for oil and gas, which is a capital-intensive industry. To get these hydrocarbons out of ground, you need more capital than labour. To explore, develop and produce petroleum you need to spend on equipment and facilities, goods and services. The industry's technologies and processes change rapidly because, in the petroleum industry more than most, new technologies and the application of new geological and engineering ideas drive costs down.

No resource extraction industry illustrates this better than the oil sands. In some ways, it is the embodiment of a concept known to history as the Jevons Paradox. The originator was William Jevons, a mathematician and logician, and his Victorian prose expressed the concept eloquently. "It is wholly a confusion of ideas to suppose that the economical use of fuel is equivalent to a diminished consumption," he said. "The very contrary is the truth."[16]

A Brit, Jevons presented his idea during an era – the latter 1800s – when coal was the principal fuel firing the Empire's industry, ships and railways. Coal "stands not beside but entirely above all other commodities," he said. "It is the material energy of the country – the universal aid – the factor in everything we do. With coal almost any feat is possible or easy; without it we are thrown back into the laborious poverty of early times."

In his brief book, Jevons presented many arguments that echoed through the years, and have their parallels today. "The duration of our present cheap supplies of coal cannot but excite deep interest and anxiety wherever or whenever it is mentioned." Coal was "the sole necessary basis of our material power [and] gives efficiency to our moral and intellectual capabilities." England's "manufacturing and commercial greatness" was at stake, he said. "Nor can we be sure that material decay may not involve us in moral and intellectual retrogression. And as there is no part of the civilized world where the life of our true and beneficent Commonwealth can be a matter of indifference, so, above all, to an Englishman who knows the grand and steadfast course his country has pursued to its present point, its future must be a matter of almost personal solicitude and affection."[17]

The concept is that technological progress increases the efficiency with which we use fuels. As fuels used more efficiently become cheaper per unit of output, output and consumption both increase – in a sense, the opposite of what you would expect.

That is why the oil sands, once an economically marginal resource, are now seeking global markets. Indeed, the oil sands are the latest antidote to a hundred years of pessimism about future sources of hydrocarbons: in 1914 America's Bureau of Mines famously forecast that US reserves would gone within a decade, and 25 years later its Interior Department predicted that they only had 13 years to go.

As the 21st century stole in, thoughtful geologists and other thinkers again argued that the time really was ripe for oil supplies to begin their inevitable and terminal decline. Therefore, the rate of discovery, which initially increases quickly, must reach a maximum and decline. Named after American geophysicist M. King Hubbert, who created a method of modelling the production curve given an assumed ultimate recovery volume, it was the topic of several books published at the beginning of the 21$^{st}$ century – notably two by Princeton University professor Kenneth Deffeyes, who popularized the concept of a "Hubbert's Peak" in oil production.[18] The irony is that, as I complete this document, the world is awash with oil and natural gas and prices range from low to awful. Petroleum economics have alternated between boom and bust for a century and a half.

In a sense, that takes me back to my early years in Canada's petroleum industry. I had recently joined the Canadian Petroleum Association when, on October 28, 1980, Ottawa introduced the National Energy Program. That disastrous policy played a key role in the story you are holding in your hands. Based as it was on flawed energy supply, demand and pricing forecasts, the NEP caused damage throughout the industry. As the damage deepened, CPA president Ian Smyth would say "prediction is very difficult, especially about the future." As oil prices declined and then collapsed, we simplified our take on such prophecies. "If you forecast oil prices," we would say, nodding wisely, "you will be wrong."

Those years affected me profoundly. Having found myself caught up in a geopolitical maelstrom, I took it on myself to begin recording the petroleum industry's history – in the early years, with the moral and intellectual support of the late Hans Maciej. Maciej seemed to know everything about the oil industry, and his name appears often in these pages.

This is one of a number of books I have written or co-authored, and each has somehow touched upon the petroleum sector's past. Collectively, they help explain how Alberta became a petroleum giant, and they touch on the industry's importance to Canada.

CHAPTER 1

# Revolution

———

*A Certain Gum or pitch that runs down the river..."*

— *James Knight, 1715*

MODERN INDUSTRY BEGAN WITH BRITAIN'S industrial revolution, an event which ultimately led, in real terms, to an average 1,000 per cent increase in wealth for every man, woman and child on the planet.[19] Then came "the development of the key managerial institutions of modern capitalism in the United States during this long period of world industrial dominance," historian Michael Bliss explained. "Canadian business history, by contrast ... is an account of the attempt by enterprising spirits to create wealth in the sprawling, thinly populated northern part of the North American continent."[20]

"Development of Alberta's oil sands has been a great Canadian achievement and is a tribute to those with the foresight, perseverance, and ability to overcome immense challenges," wrote Chuck Collyer, himself an important player in the oil sands but also an amateur historian. In the early 1970s Collyer was in charge of project development for Syncrude, one of the great oil sands megaprojects. "The early explorers and fur traders travelling on the Athabasca River had no way of knowing that the bitumen outcroppings were evidence of one of the world's largest oil reserves," he continued.[21] Indeed, for much of the three centuries since a Hudson's Bay Company (HBC) employee first saw evidence of these deposits, oil had few uses and little value.

Still, during those years colourful explorers observed and speculated on the oil sands. Their journal entries provided fascinating descriptions of the sands and the bitumen leaking out of them. Some wondered about the commercial possibilities of this mysterious substance, and to extract it for trade. This led to expeditions and drilling as the Dominion government began investigating their economic potential. Of course, historic times in western Canada are quite recent. In archaeological terms, interaction between humankind and the oil sands go much farther back.

For long distances along the Athabasca and Clearwater Rivers the oil sands lie exposed, so Canada's First Nations certainly knew about bitumen from the time they began to navigate those rivers. When did that occur? The first people to encounter the oil sands were probably Aboriginals migrating to North America across the Bering Strait between present-day Russia and Alaska, 13,000-14,000 years ago. During that brief window of time, toward the end of the last ice age, an ice-free corridor opened up east of today's Rocky Mountains, enabling Pleistocene hunters to migrate from Asia to the more southerly areas of North America. This idea gained common currency with the work of C. Vance Haynes in the 1960s. Although recent scholarship suggests that this thinking in this area is incomplete,[22] Haynes' notion is a convenient way to think of the time and place when humanity first viewed the oil sands.

The earliest historical record of the oil sands came 300 years ago, when James Knight made a seminal observation in his diary. On June 27, 1715 he had learned from Cree "Home Guard" Indians, local trappers and factory provisioners "abt the Great River it runs into the Sea on the Back of this Country & they tells us there is a Certain Gum or pitch that runs down the river in Such abundance that they cannot land but at certain places & that it is very broad and flows as much water."[23] In English, at least, this is the first written reference to the Alberta oil sands which, in terms of bitumen in place, rank among the world's largest petroleum deposits.

Knight was the governor of York Factory (a British settlement and trading post on the southwestern shore of Hudson Bay, in present-day Manitoba). The "sea" beyond the headwaters of the Churchill River which the Aboriginal traveller had told him about was Lake Athabasca, which today straddles northeastern

Alberta and northwestern Saskatchewan, at the edge of the Precambrian Shield. Located on the southwestern shore of Hudson Bay and founded in 1684, York Factory is today a national heritage site at the mouth of the Hayes River, approximately 120 kilometres south-southeast of present-day Churchill, Manitoba. The settlement served as the Hudson's Bay Company's northern headquarters from 1821 to 1873, and operated as a fur trading post for more than 270 years, until 1957.

Earlier references to petroleum in North America go much farther back. The earliest came from the Hernando de Soto expedition to the Americas. The expedition of this Spanish conquistador used seep oil for ship repair along the Gulf Coast in 1543, and published a report describing this use 14 years later.[24] Other early reports, which go back to 1656 and possibly as early as 1627, describe the Cuba oil spring in what is now western New York State.[25] "The Swan was one of the chiefs in a party of Cree Indians who met Governor James Knight in council at York Fort in 1715," Neatby said. "Knight sent the Swan with a party mustering 25 canoes to establish friendly relations with the Indians who dwelt between the source of the Churchill and the 'West Seas' (Lake Athabasca). The Swan returned two years later" and reported a friendly reception from "the natives" (probably Beaver Indians of the Athabasca Valley). Swan brought with him "a quantity of beaver skins which excited the admiration of Knight by their 'Goodness & Largeness.'"[26]

According to Harold Innis, who in the 1920s wrote a landmark interpretation of Canada's economic development, "The economic history of Canada has been dominated by the discrepancy between the centre and the margins of Western civilization. [People's] energy has been directed toward the exploitation of staple products and the tendency has been cumulative. [Raw material] supplied to the mother country stimulated manufacturers of the finished product and also of the products which were in demand in the colony."

He contended that "large-scale production of raw materials was encouraged by improvement of techniques of production, of marketing, and of transport as well as by improvement in the manufacture of the finished product." Therefore people in the colonies, as they were then, "directly and indirectly" focused on developing staple commodities – what we today would call resources. This was how Canadians became directly involved "in the production of the staple and indirectly in the production of facilities promoting production" he wrote. The result is that "agriculture, industry, transportation, trade, finance, and governmental activities tend to become subordinate to the production of the staple for a more highly specialized manufacturing community."[27] This book later returns to Innis's notion of a "staples economy," and its impact on Canada as an industrial power.

The region now known as Western Canada had an economy almost entirely dominated by the beaver trade when York Factory's boss, Henry Kelsey, made a famous entry into his log. York Factory was a settlement and trading post located on the southwestern shore of Hudson Bay in what today is northeastern Manitoba. On June 12, 1719, Kelsey wrote that "Captain Swan" (Wa-Pa-Sun) had brought him a sample "of that Gum or pitch that flows out of the Banks of the River."[28] The way Kelsey wrote about this delivery may suggest frequent discussions about its existence – a notion consistent with Knight's journal entry four years earlier.


## PETER POND AND ALEXANDER MACKENZIE

The first westerner to report seeing the oil sands in their natural state was Yankee fur trader Peter Pond. "Born in 1739, son of a Connecticut shoemaker and descendant of an old colonial line of military men, Pond eagerly took up arms for King George III, fighting against French forces at Ticonderoga, Fort Niagara, and Montréal," said historian Barry Gough in a concise portrayal of his life. "His military campaigning led Pond to take a favorable view of Canada and its prospects at the Peace of 1763....Of industrious habits, and with a good common education, he was a feisty, roistering, self-directed man who took to trading with the native people as easily as he campaigned in wilderness military forays." The "peace" Gough refers to involved King George III's Royal Proclamation of 1764, which enabled Britain to administer North American lands which France had ceded the previous year. Language used in the proclamation established the constitutional framework for treaties with Aboriginal communities as "First Nations."

Pond was "of a violent temper and perhaps morose and quarrelsome disposition," Gough said. It is alleged that "he committed or plotted murder or manslaughter against other traders. Both times he ran free in a wild world where the writ of the Crown in Canada had only paper authority."[29]

In a journal he wrote toward the end of his life, Pond described in idiosyncratic spelling his participation in the 1760 victory of the British Empire over France. "We then left a garrison and descended the river til we reacht Montreal the ondly plase the French had in possession in Canaday. Hear we lay one night with our armes. The next day the town sranderd to Gineral Amharst."[30]

As a fur trader, he was active throughout present-day Minnesota and Wisconsin. Through business, he became acquainted with Alexander Henry the younger, Simon McTavish and the brothers Thomas, Benjamin and Joseph Frobisher. They formed the Montréal-based North West Company, which became a fierce competitor to HBC. In search of new fur resources, Pond explored west of the Great Lakes. In 1776–1778 he founded and wintered at a fur post at the junction of the Sturgeon River and North Saskatchewan River. During his explorations, he travelled down the Clearwater River to the Athabasca.

There is little doubt that Pond saw the oil sands. What is in doubt, however, is whether he was actually the first non-native to view and report on their presence – and if he was, in what words. Even the great Canadian historian Harold Innis attributed a passage in French to this marginally literate man: «*Ce qu'il y a de certain, c'est que le long des bords de cette rivière et du Lac Arabosca [Athabasca], on trouve des sources de bitume qui coulent sur la terre.*» [ii] Given Pond's appalling written English, it is impossible to credit him with fluency in French.[31]

Oil sands historian Joseph Fitzgerald offers a reasonable explanation. He believes the quote originated with a Frenchman named Saint Jean de Crèvecœur, who had visited the Athabasca country in 1785. According to Fitzgerald's account, Crèvecœur took notes on Pond's speculations about the country, and this famous sentence appeared in a biography of the Frenchman, published in 1883.

Consistent with this explanation is that Northwestern fur traders developed a language of their own. Citing a journey that began almost 100 years after

---

ii "It is sure that along the banks of that river [the Peace] and Lake Athabasca there are sources of bitumen, which flows along the ground."

Peter Pond's, Juliette Champagne quoted expedition leaders Viscount William Milton and Dr. Walter Cheadle as saying "Our conversation was carried on in Canadian French, for [the guides'] knowledge of English was very imperfect. Amongst themselves, they used a mixed patois of French and Indian, for a long time perfectly incomprehensible to us."

Language played a key role in the work of missionaries, according to Champagne. French missionaries had such a high success rate among the indigenous peoples of the Upper North-West because the people there spoke a pidgin or creole of French, Dené and Cree, giving Francophones access to the native languages.

A missionary at Fort Good Hope, Father Henri Grollier – he died in 1864, aged 38 – was adamant that the people there should not speak to him in any other language than French. There was to be no mixture of languages for him. However his superior, Bishop Grandin, disagreed with this amateurish point of view and saw the advantages of learning aboriginal languages. Anglophone missionaries did not have the linguistic advantage of those who spoke French and thus had a handicap when it came to communicating with the Indigenous peoples. This contributed to the lesser success of those who tried to convert aboriginals to Anglicanism and other Reformation creeds. It also helped that the word was out among those of French/Indian mixed blood that the Catholic faith was the true one, and that all the others were doomed.[32]

At least partly because of his association with the murder of fellow fur traders Jean-Etienne Waddens and John Ross, in the latter 1770s Pond's "star rapidly faded."[33] A decade later, though, he drew a map of the general outline of the Mackenzie River basin, and prepared other maps based on his explorations and on information provided to him by First Nations peoples. While his business was the fur trade – in 1779 he came out of the Chipewyan country with 80,000 prime beaver pelts – it was his eye-witness report on the presence of bitumen and his map-making that secured for Pond a place in the oil sands chronicles.

His understanding of the geography of the west played a sinister role in Canadian history, however. According to David Thompson, a contemporary of Pond and the greatest map-maker of the era, Pond used his knowledge of western North America to have an undue portion of the continent allocated to the newly independent United States. "A boundary line through the middle of Lake Champlain, and thence due west would have been accepted in the United States for it was more than they could justly claim, had a gentleman of abilities been selected on the part of Great Britain, but at that time North America was held in contempt," he wrote.

> To the United States commissioners Mr. Pond designated a boundary line passing through the middle of the St. Lawrence to Lake Superior, through that lake and the interior countries to the northwest corner of the Lake of the Woods; and thence westward to the head of the Missouri [Mississippi], being twice the area of the territory the States could justly claim. This exorbitant demand the British commissioners accepted, and it was confirmed by both nations. Such was the hand that designated the boundary line between the dominions of Great Britain and the territories of the United States.[34]

In the 1500s, Portugal and Spain had taken control of the sea routes to Asia and claimed sovereignty over Latin America. The British (and French) response was to claim and begin settling North America. Also, Britain sought a Northwest Passage to gain access to Asian markets. This context helps explain the activities of Alexander Mackenzie, whom the Montréal-based North West Company sent west to become Pond's successor. From Pond he learned that, according to Aboriginals, local rivers flowed to the northwest and he got fired up with the idea of going on this northern expedition. Pond impetuously left the company the following year, perhaps because he wanted to devote his final years to exploration.

Before he left for Montréal, Pond had been the victim of back-stabbing of the metaphorical variety – notably from Mackenzie himself, who outwardly maligned the idea of following the great river north. However, it is worth remembering that Pond was the original proponent of the notion of seeking the North West Passage by this route. In 1790 Pond sold his interest in the Northwest Company for £800, and then returned to Milford, Connecticut.

Innis speculates that his retirement may have been prompted by news of Mackenzie's voyage, which disproved his theory about the Northwest Passage. In 1807 he died in poverty.

## RICHARDSON AND FRANKLIN

Mackenzie had full authority to manage the North West Company's local affairs, and to reorganize "the posts of the area, and complete freedom to undertake his mission into unknown parts. Free of the pressing executive obligations that had pinned him down for a decade, [Mackenzie] was released to pursue the Northwest Passage." Mackenzie's star "glowed ever brighter."[35]

The notion that the tributaries of that area gathered into a great river possibly flowing to the Northwest Passage had fired him up, and after Pond returned to Montréal the Scottish-born adventurer followed the river to its mouth. This basin provides access by canoe to the lands that eventually became Western Canada.[iii]

In 1792, Mackenzie set out again to find a route to the Pacific. This time he took a series of tributaries to the Peace River, wintering in what became known as Fort Fork. The following year he crossed the Great Divide, then reached an inlet to the Pacific Ocean. He had thus commanded two epochal expeditions: the first by a European from the interior of the continent to the Arctic and the first expedition across North America north of Mexico.

In published reports of his two expeditions, Mackenzie provided a great deal of information about the Aboriginal People he encountered, including their dress and customs – frequently deriding the "superstitions" of the locals.

---

iii Although map-makers named the river after Mackenzie, he was not the first European to explore it. Between 1754-5 HBC adventurer Anthony "Henday" canoed from York Factory on Hudson Bay to present-day Alberta. He was on a trading expedition, and the paying guest of a party of Assiniboine and Cree Indians. He almost certainly saw bitumen deposits on his travels, but made no reference to them in his journals. His descriptions of Aboriginal life and game hunting, however, are fascinating. According to an annotated release of his journal (1973), his surname was almost certainly Hendry, not Henday. One irony of this is that is Anthony HendayDrive is under construction as a ring road in the Edmonton metropolitan area.

His lively account also presents detailed descriptions of geographical features he chanced upon during his ground-breaking adventure. His lively report presented a wealth of information about his travels and sold well in Britain and America's eastern seaboard. Today, the most widely quoted passage from his book has to do with the oil sands. "At about twenty-four miles from the Fork, are some bitumenous fountains; into which a pole of twenty feet long may be inserted without the least resistance," he wrote. "The bitumen is in a fluid state, and when mixed with gum or the resinous substance collected from the Spruce Fir, serves to gum the canoes. In its heated state it emits a smell like that of Sea Coal. The banks of the river, which are there very elevated, discover veins of the same bitumenous quality."[36]

It is primarily in liberal societies that science emerges as a force for understanding reality, according to science historian Timothy Ferris. In a compelling book, Ferris noted that science did not become a significant force at all until the late 1700s, as the Enlightenment developed in Britain and France, and the United States declaimed its Declaration of Independence.[37] It is therefore not surprising that serious research into the oil sands did not begin until the 19th century.

In their expeditions (1819-22 and 1825-27), Dr. John Richardson, Royal Navy Captain John Franklin and Captain George Back diarized and later published reports on every feature of the new land they were charting. Of these three men, Franklin has the distinction of having been the greatest explorer in North American waters. His efforts contributed greatly to the Victorian world's understanding of the continent's shape, and provided support for British sovereignty over those lands.

On their way to explore the Arctic coast east of the Mackenzie delta, Franklin described "pure sulphur deposited by springs and smelling very strongly." For his part, Richardson noted the "sulphurous springs" and "bituminous salt" in this region.[38] He also observed a "peaty bog, whose crevices are filled with petroleum, a mineral which exists in great abundance in this district. We never observed it flowing from the limestone, but always above it, and generally agglutinating the beds of sand into a kind of pitchy sandstone. Sometimes fragments of this stone contain so much petroleum as to float down the stream."[39]

Their reports on the follow-up expedition contained further detailed information about the region. In his 130-page appendix to Franklin's massive report, Richardson described sandstone cliffs "about twenty miles below Fort Good Hope." Some of the sandstone "beds contain small pieces of bituminous shale; and they are interstratified with thin layers of bituminous flinty-slate, and of flinty slate passing into bituminous shale."[40]

In an engaging profile of Sir John Richardson, who was knighted in 1846, Stewart Houston summarized his achievements. He "achieved fame as a surgeon and naturalist (as part of) the two arctic land expeditions led by John Franklin in 1819-22 and 1825-27. A true generalist, Richardson was competent in geology, mammalogy, ichthyology, and botany – including the difficult field of lichenology – and soon became knowledgeable in ornithology."[41]

At the beginning of the Great Depression, Dr. David Alexander Stewart gave Richardson high praise before the combined annual meetings of the British and Canadian Medical Associations in Winnipeg. As part of a longer commentary, he said "His was perhaps a life of industry more than a life of genius, but it was a full, good life, and in many ways even a great life. It is not every day that we meet in one person – surgeon, physician, sailor, soldier, administrator, explorer, naturalist, author, and scholar, who has been eminent in some roles and commendable in all."[42]

Richardson kept careful notes of each day's activities. On the matter of the oil sands, he wrote that "The limestone is immediately covered by a thin stratum of yellowish-white earth which from the fineness of its grain appears at first sight to be a marl or clay. It does not, however, effervesce with acids, is harsh and meagre, and, when examined with the microscope, is seen to be chiefly composed of minute fragments of translucent quartz, with a greyish basis in form of an impalpable powder. This seam follows the undulations of the limestone; but the beds of the superincumbent bituminous shale, or rather of sand charged with slaggy mineral pitch, are horizontal." Richardson continued, "About 30 miles below the Clear-water [sic] River…the limestone beds are covered by a bituminous deposit upward of one hundred feet thick, whose lower member is a conglomerate, having an earthy basis much stained with iron and colored by bitumen." His comments were an excellent study of the surface geology of the region. "A copious spring of mineral pitch issues from a crevice in a cliff composed of sand and bitumen," he said. "It lies a few hundred yards back from the river in the middle of a thick wood. Several small birds were found suffocated in the pitch."[43]

A national hero in Britain, Franklin was knighted in 1829 and served as governor of Van Diemen's Land (now Tasmania) from 1836 to 1843. His final expedition departed England in 1845. In command of two ships, HMS *Erebus* and HMS *Terror*, which carried 128 officers and men, he sought the fabled Northwest Passage through the Arctic Islands and guided his vessels to the top of Victoria Strait. "There, on the threshold of success, the battle-scarred and toil-worn old veteran died on his ship," wrote Leslie Neatby. "His crews perished in the ice, but not before winning for themselves and their late commander the title of discoverers of the Northwest Passage."[44]

"When the return of John Franklin's third and final attempt to find the Northwest Passage, this time by ship, was overdue," Houston said, "Richardson and fellow doctor John Rae in 1848 made the fastest canoe trip on record, leaving Sault Ste. Marie on 3 May and arriving at the mouth of the Mackenzie on 3 August. After a month of futile search along the familiar arctic shore, Richardson, now 60, kept up with the younger men on the 15-day overland march back to Great Bear Lake."[45] *En route*, he observed outcrops of bitumen along the Slave and Mackenzie rivers "about 19 miles below Fort McMurray," and commented on burning oil shale along the cliffs at Cape Bathurst. "The air was hot from the burning shale and from it alum had been formed."[46]

They found some relics, including the graves of three crewmen, and heard from Inuit that "a party of white men, amounting to about 40, were seen travelling southward over the ice and dragging a boat with them," according to Rae's report. "At a later date the same season... The bodies of some 30 persons were discovered on the continent, and five on an island near it. ...From the mutilated state of many of the corpses and the contents of the kettles, it is evident that our wretched countrymen had been driven to the last resource – cannibalism – as a means of prolonging existence."[47] Starvation, exposure and scurvy had all contributed to the failure of the expedition. As the news trickled in, the Victorian press wrote lurid and spellbinding stories about Englishmen resorting to cannibalism.

Thanks to a campaign waged by Lady Franklin (and supported by novelist Charles Dickens), Rae's refusal to retract the information he had received from the Inuit brought many mapmakers and others to ignore his achievements. One of these was his 1854 discovery that King William Land was an island, separated from Boothia Peninsula by a channel that remained open for months each year. Rae "realized that this waterway, which connected points accessible by sailing ship, constituted the missing north-south link in the Northwest Passage," Ken McGoogan said. He was unable to prove this discovery, however, so he said little about it. "But when, half a century later, the Norwegian Roald Amundsen became the first explorer to sail through the passage, he not only used that channel but acknowledged its discoverer by naming it Rae Strait."[48]

Other adventurers participated in the search for Franklin and his crew — there were 30 expeditions in all — and, in the spirit of the times, published narratives about their expeditions. Captain Charles Francis Hall, a Yankee, became an authority on arctic survival. Historian George Swinton described him as a "high school dropout, blacksmith, engraver, stationer, journalist, incipient publisher, explorer and indefatigable enthusiast (who) conducted three strange and adventurous Arctic expeditions," and gave his greatest achievement as "his belief and his proof that in order to survive in the Arctic one had to live as an Eskimo."[49]

Interest in the high Arctic continued, and 1926 was a year of high exploration in the area. *The New York Times* reported that six or more expeditions were preparing to hop off for the pole. "Some are 100 per cent one nationality or another in personnel, while the others are mixed," wrote the reporter. Thus, "the question of what flag will fly over new lands which may be discovered takes on new importance," according to the newspaper. "If the nationality of the actual discoverer is to govern future sovereignty of lands in the Far North, difficult and embarrassing problems might arise within the mixed national groups." However, the newspaper noted a principle that "discovery must be backed up by bona fide utilization of new lands to afford a basis for claims of sovereignty which would be recognized by all nations."[50]

In October 2014, Parks Canada announced the discovery of the sunken remains of *Erebus*. In part, the search for the vessels was to reinforce Canada's claim to sovereignty in the high Arctic – a claim disputed by Russia. With the Arctic ice melting, the region's abundant supplies of oil, gas and minerals had become more accessible, as had shortened shipping routes and open water for commercial fishing. This set off a global competition for influence and economic opportunities far beyond the nations that border the Arctic. An illustration of the increasing importance of the Arctic is that the Arctic Council – composed of Canada, Denmark, Finland, Iceland, Norway, Russia, Sweden and the United States – in 2013 granted observer status to China, India, Italy, Japan, Singapore and South Korea.[51]

## SNAKE OIL

Among European settlers in North America, the earliest records of the oil sands were roughly coincident with the American Revolutionary War – a convulsion followed in short succession by such upheavals as the rebellions of 1837–38 in Upper and Lower Canada. John George Lambton, Earl of Durham, had just been appointed Governor General with special powers as high commissioner of British North America. Durham mediated these rebellions and, so doing, strengthened the foundations of what would become Canada.

His *Report on the Affairs of British North America* – commonly known as the Durham Report – was a key document in the early history of Canada as it was elsewhere in the British Empire. Britain's North American colonies had employed legislative assemblies for several decades, but Lambton gave them more power. Before his reforms, the assemblies could only offer advice to the governor general (or lieutenant governor) and his appointed council, and the man in charge frequently rejected that advice. Under a 1741 reform, the executive was responsible to the assembly, and British North America, like Britain itself, enjoyed responsible government. The Durham Report formalized the creation of a "liberal society" in the northern colonies. As we observed earlier, Ferris argues that liberal society – "a state that guarantees human rights to its citizens, who elect their leaders"[52] – is essential for the nurture of science.

The first page of Durham's report proclaimed that "While the present state of things is allowed to last, the actual inhabitants of these Provinces have no security for person or property – no enjoyment of what they possess – no stimulus to industry." He returned to that theme again and again, and made numerous observations about life in Upper and Lower Canada – so named because they were farther up or lower down from the mouth of the St. Lawrence River. Durham's report also contains the famous assessment that Canada, with both Francophone and Anglophone residents, consisted of "two nations warring within the bosom of a single state."[53] His solution was to take steps, unsuccessfully, to eliminate the use of French.

A new political entity, Canada developed the world's first serious petroleum industry. While Americans had found earlier uses for oil, those uses had nothing to do with the petroleum industry we know today. As muckraking journalist Ida Tarbell described in her famous 1904 history of the Standard Oil Company, the first use of oil was based on the efforts of entrepreneurs who gathered it from seeps along streams and rivers, then bottled and sold the stuff as medication. "By the middle of the century it was without doubt the great American medicine," she said, and it was first known in the eastern United States as Seneca Oil, after one of the rivers where it was collected. "While it was admitted to be chiefly a liniment, it was recommended for cholera morbus, liver complaint, bronchitis and consumption, and the dose prescribed was three teaspoonfuls three times a day!"[54] The term Seneca Oil became "snake oil"; the expression "snake oil salesman," a synonym for a quack, charlatan, or fraud.

The purveyors of snake oil were unaware, perhaps, that a thirsty army of new machines was powering the Industrial Revolution. By 1850, industrial demand for lighting fuel and lubricants exceeded conventional supplies, and household and commercial demand for illuminating fuel was also on the rise. In the beginning, commercial whaling met these needs by boiling whale blubber into illuminating oil. However, with growing prosperity on both sides of the Atlantic, whale populations declined precipitously and the price of whale oil climbed sharply. Efforts to distil illuminating fuels from oil shales and bitumen deposits, though making progress, failed to meet demand.

There were also efforts to distill liquid fuels from coal, but they were "probably smelly," historian Earle Gray wrote. However, "gas distilled from coal was generally not."[55] Indeed, coal gas, or manufactured gas, was a big industry for more than 150 years, until largely displaced by lower-cost natural gas, which also has higher energy content. In 1790, William Murdoch in Scotland first distilled coal gas commercially. That gas soon became commonplace for lighting streets, factories, and even some homes in London and other centres.

Even after the advent of electric lighting, coal gas continued to be used for space heating – in Britain, well into the 1960s, after which natural gas supplies from the North Sea gradually replaced it.[iv] Coal gas is still an important source of energy in many parts of the world, and a petrochemical feedstock in India and China, for example.

In Canada, too, it still plays a role. In recent years Canadians have used *in-situ* coal gasification and constructed an experimental integrated gasification combined cycle power plant, for example. It is a minor source of energy, however, because it is not necessary. Canada has so many other petroleum and petroleum gas resources that she does not need a large-scale coal gas industry.

## ABRAHAM GESNER

Given this environment, fuels changed dramatically – especially in the areas of North America where there were easily accessible supplies of oil. Indeed, the first efforts to process a tar-like substance took place in what today are Canada's Atlantic Provinces. In the 1840s Abraham Gesner developed a refining process which transmuted bitumen and oil into kerosene. However, Gesner's first efforts were focused on producing gas for lighting from bitumen. Only in the 1850s did he focus on producing what he termed kerosene as a liquid lamp fuel – a fuel that became the world's principal source of light until Edison developed his electric

---

iv The term natural gas is relatively new. The petroleum industry began using the expression in the latter 1800s to distinguish it from coal gas. Until the completion of the Westcoast and TransCanada pipelines in the late 1950s, gas utilities at such major centres as Vancouver, Winnipeg, Toronto, and Montreal supplied their customers with low-cost coal gas.

light bulb. Of equal importance, he helped found the world's first substantial refinery to extract a liquid fuel, kerosene, from coal. In the move from whale oil lamps to petroleum lighting, this was a critical development. And until the First World War, most refined oil simply burned in lamps. Gesner's work thus lit homes and factories throughout the world.

By Gesner's reckoning, in the two decades from about 1846 he had conducted some 2,000 experiments, all of them aimed at converting bitumen-like substances into a lighting fuel. Bituminous experiments were only one of countless endeavours by this largely self-educated man. He was "surely one of the last Renaissance men," according to Gray: "farmer, physician, geologist, chemist, inventor, author of some 20 books and reports, the most popular lecturer in the Maritimes, an advocate for the rights and welfare of the Mic Mac Indians who were his guides on field trips, and a proponent of scientific farming practices."

He was the first geologist appointed by a British colony, and made geological surveys of both New Brunswick and Prince Edward Island, and "his inventions included one of the first electric motors driven by a voltaic battery, briquettes made from compressed coal dust, a machine for insulating electric wires, a wood preservative, and a process for using asphalt to pave highways." He also founded the first science museum in Canada – a collection of 2,000 preserved animals and other artifacts. Today, that collection is a cornerstone of New Brunswick's provincial museum.

Gesner first encountered bitumen when he was working as a deckhand on a voyage to the West Indies. He returned to Nova Scotia with "no money but a boat load of rocks, minerals, shells, curios, and a pile of bitumen from the pitch lake in Trinidad." However, on his geological surveys he found a bitumen deposit in New Brunswick's Albert County – hence the name "albertite," erroneously classed as coal. About 1843, Gesner began to experiment with the pitch he had brought from Trinidad a quarter of a century earlier. He had already noted that it melted when hot and burned with a steady flame. At temperatures below 427°C (800°F), he distilled from it a liquid he called kerosene oil. At higher temperatures, it released gas, which he called kerosene gas.

In his lively account of Gesner's achievements, Earle Gray said he "attempted to lease and mine albertite, but in a dispute that involved a suspicion of skullduggery by a rival, an armed standoff at the prospective mine site, and a celebrated legal case, he lost the right to mine the bitumen. He sought a franchise to provide Halifax with manufactured gas from bitumen, rather than coal, only to again lose out to his rivals" in a highly publicised trial.[56]

Convinced that kerosene's future lay elsewhere, in 1853 Gesner moved to New York City, and received U.S. patents 11,203, 11,204, and 11,205 for "Improvement in kerosene burning fluids." As Loris Russell explained, the three patents were essentially the same in text, but covered respectively what Gesner called A, C, and B kerosene. "'A' kerosene was the lightest fraction, and [was subsequently renamed] gasoline. Less volatile 'B' kerosene had as its primary use mixing with the other grades. 'C' kerosene was the lamp fuel, and soon became known as coal-oil. Under Gesner's guidance the Asphalt Mining and Kerosene Gas Company set up a factory on Long Island, Russell adds. "Modern engineers have admired the efficient design shown in the published plans." The company became the North American Kerosene Gas Light Company, with John and George Austen – they were brothers – serving as sales agents. The company prospered, and "Gesner lived comfortably in Brooklyn, N.Y., a prominent figure in the local church and community."[57]

Both of Canada's two petroleum pioneers worked with bitumen, and Gray's brief history covered both. "The coal oil refiners in the 1850s did everything to create the oil industry except find crude oil," he wrote. "They created the product, a lamp fuel; developed and improved the technology to produce it from bituminous materials; built the refineries; gave rise to improved oil lamps; and created the marketing facilities and market demand. All that was then needed was a supply of crude oil, which could greatly cut the cost of making lamp fuel from solid bitumen."[58]

## Charles Nelson Tripp

As Gesner's business in the US flourished, Charles Nelson Tripp recovered bitumen in Enniskillen Township on the north shore of Lake Erie. Tripp's dabbling in the "gum beds" of that locale in 1851 led to the incorporation of Canada's first oil company. Parliament chartered the International Mining and Manufacturing

Company in 1854, with Tripp as president. The charter empowered the company to explore for asphalt beds and oil and salt springs, and to manufacture oils, naphtha, paints, burning fluids, varnishes and related products.

According to Gray, the chemist Thomas Sterry Hunt, who was also a geologist with the Geological Survey of Canada, first drew attention to these bitumen deposits in the GSC's annual report for 1849. In his analysis of a sample of that bitumen, "Hunt pointed to potential commercial uses: *to build roads, to pave the bottom of ships, to manufacture gas for lighting, for which it is eminently suited.*" At that point, Charles Nelson Tripp, "an energetic and visionary prospector and promoter" invested six years in trying to develop the resource into a business. Tripp and his brother Henry worked in a remote forest in one of the last areas in Canada West to be settled. "It was an area of seasonal swamp, a shin-busting tangle of fallen trees, with no roads or railway and more than 20 miles from the nearest water transportation, at Sarnia."[59]

Hunt's report preceded by some years the famous tests conducted by Yale chemistry professor Benjamin Silliman in 1855. The most important difference is that Silliman established that fractional distillation of crude oil could create a number of useful liquid products, one of which (he called it "camphene") was 11 times brighter than a candle when burned in a mechanical lamp. It was about one third brighter than "best sperm oil," and less expensive. "It is worthy of note that my experiments prove that nearly the whole of the raw product [crude oil] may be manufactured without waste, and this solely by a well-directed process which is in practice one of the most simple of all chemical processes" – namely, distillation.[60]

Fractional distillation was a game changer in its day. It separated oil into component parts, or fractions, by heating the oil to temperatures at which its various fractions vapourize, then recovering those fractions through condensation. Each fraction contains different hydrocarbons; the heaviest are the last to reach their boiling point. Half a century later, the Burton-Humphreys process laid the groundwork for the modern refining and petrochemical to develop. We'll turn to that transformation in chapter three.

Although encouraged to develop the bitumen for street lighting, Tripp focused instead on mining the bitumen and then boiling it in open pots to produce a paving material. "His paving material won a prize at the 1855 Universal Exhibition in Paris, and he also won an order for asphalt to help pave the streets of Paris. But he was already going broke, with judgments piling up for unpaid bills, including money owed to James Miller Williams for the purchase of wagons." A carriage maker, Williams and several associates acquired Tripp's properties and refined some kerosene from the bitumen in 1857. However, his first product probably smelled, and he did not seem to have a commercial product until he found crude oil. That discovery took place in 1858, when he ordered a well dug a few yards down an incline from Tripp's former asphalt plant. At a depth of 60 feet, the well struck free oil instead of water. It was the first commercial oil well in North America, remembered as Williams No. 1 at Oil Springs.

Williams later bought out his partners and formed J.M. Williams & Company – re-organized four years later as the Canadian Oil Company, in which he held a one-third interest. In 1857 he built a refinery on Coal Oil Inlet in Hamilton, to distill and refine the bitumen, although there is no record that he succeeded. The next year, however, the Hamilton refinery began producing fuel from the light oil crude oil found while digging for water. This operation was "North America's first crude oil refinery," Gray wrote. "With later expansion and much modification, it remained in operation for more than three decades, until 1891."[61] Other productive fields went on stream around the town of Petrolia, north of Oil Springs. As a result, nearby London, Ontario also became a refining centre.

## TRADE IN TAR

The first known reference to trade in bitumen comes from a letter from W.L. Hardisty of the Hudson's Bay Company at Fort Simpson. Dated 1872 and addressed to Mr. Gaudet at Fort Good Hope, the letter said "I shall require 5 kegs of good clean tar from you, for Fort Simpson, and 1 keg for Peels River, to be sent down by the spring boat."[62] To drive from Fort Simpson to Fort McMurray is a 1,637-kilometre, 19-hour drive along the McKenzie Highway. This gives a sense of the strength and resilience of early traders making their living in Canada's North.

There are other records of bitumen trade from that era. For example, Juliette Champagne – a historian who specializes in French-language material – cites an 1878 letter from Bishop Henri Faraud, who wanted what he described as "a barrel or two of the tar that could be obtained from the fine tar sands beyond Fort McMurray." Faraud's headquarters were in Lac la Biche, so he did not have easy access to bitumen. His mission used the Athabasca River to bring freight to the North, and larger canoes needed tar to stay afloat.

The minor bitumen deposits near his headquarters "were very sandy and would take weeks of boiling in special kettles to purify," she wrote. "Tar was always in short supply for use on the barges, and year after year the same requests occur" because bitumen was essential for boats and barges. In exchange for the little favours, "Faraud usually sent a little gift which would please, but that year he lacked a small barrel to send wine."[63]

Two years later, according to Champagne, when he was "returning from his Northern Missions, he managed to collect some tar from the 'spring on the way', but lost it and other supplies when they cracked their canoe in rapids south of Fort MacMurray [sic]." She added that they were paddling a *canot du maître* [master canoe], which George Simpson once had used. It was "rather amazing that it could have lasted so many years, as Simpson had retired at least 30 years before."[64]

Bishop Alexandre Taché had descended the river in 1856 in a *canot du nord* [a northern canoe, which was smaller than the canot du maître], but these small vessels were clearly not for serious freighting. In 1864, Bishop Faraud had a boat built and christened Aurora. It was their first.

The HBC had not used the Athabasca since losing two fully loaded and manned canoes many years before and considered the river impassable. But in 1864 the company "sent a boat fully loaded with 25 barrels of salt along with the Aurora from Fort Chipewyan to test the waters, so to speak," Champagne wrote. The two boats were to return together, but there was a delay on the part of the mission. The Hudson Bay Company's boatmen became increasingly agitated about the lowering of the water level in the La Biche River, so they left on July 22nd.

For its part, Aurora finally left August 3rd, making the return trip alone. "The boat scraped her keel while passing some rapids, giving the passengers a good scare, and their trip took 18 days." The HBC eventually lent the mission a carpenter to build boats on site.[65]

In a book based on Jesuit Father Joseph Le Treste's memoirs, Juliette Champagne brings some humour to the oil sands story when she describes a run-in with the oil sands the priest had during the war. In 1915, Le Treste used a small boat with an outboard motor to take Bishop Gabriel Breynat to Fort McMurray from the Nativité Mission at Fort Chipewyan. Along the way they lost the boat's propeller in the Athabasca River, but managed to find a replacement. On his return to Fort Chipewyan, Le Treste stopped to collect tar, because "the brothers of the mission of the Nativité Mission much wanted some to caulk their skiffs and boats."

"I had no difficulty in filling a vessel with four gallons of tar," he wrote. "But I had no tools, so I used my hands like spades," without concern for what would follow. "Coated with a thick layer of tar, my hands became massive and my fingers inseparable." To extricate himself, Le Treste scrubbed himself with "water and sand, but in vain. My position got a bit comical, and greatly amused my companion," he wrote.

Fortunately, need is the mother of invention. "Remembering that we had gasoline, I asked Victor to pour some on my hands, thinking it might be the specific cure for this embarrassing case. I was not mistaken…that thick tarry layer broke away and disappeared completely. Again I could row and move freely."[66]


## SCIENCE BEGINS

The earliest scientific research into the oil sands came through the Geological Survey of Canada (GSC). Created in 1841, when the Province of Canada – it then included both Ontario and Québec – approved funding to conduct a geological survey of the province. The following year the Survey began to fulfill its mandate. It is Canada's oldest scientific organization.

"The decision to undertake a geological survey of the fledgling nation was based on the realization that the development of an industrial economy in Canada – an economy that could compete with those in Europe and the United

States – would depend to a considerable extent on a viable mining industry," according to Christy Vodden. "The question was: did the Province of Canada have the resource base to support such an industry? The answer would depend for the most part on a thorough geological assessment of the landmass."

Like other such disciplines of the early 19ᵗʰ century, hard-rock geology was still an infant science. "At the time, many viewed the proposed survey as a short-term way to stimulate the mining industry, thereby enriching the provincial coffers," Vodden continued. "As events unfolded, however, the Province of Canada became the Dominion of Canada, eventually stretching 5,514 kilometres between its Atlantic and Pacific coasts, and 4,634 kilometres from the south to the very top of Ellesmere Island. Canada now also has a vast offshore. With this growth in territory came a commensurate increase in work for the Survey."[67]

The Survey helped determine the route for a transcontinental railway that would link East and West and also helped identify the natural resources available in this mostly unexplored territory.


## INTRIGUE AT THE GSC

Surveyors included John Macoun, Robert Bell, G. M. Dawson, R. G. McConnell and Joseph B. Tyrrell, who in August 1884 discovered the skull of the first Albertosaurus, a species of tyrannosaur, from the badlands near Drumheller.

"I was climbing up a steep face about 400 feet high," Tyrell explained. I stuck my head around a point, and there was this skull leering at me, sticking right out of the ground. It gave me a fright." Dinosaur Provincial Park, as the area is now known, is home to the world's largest concentration of Cretaceous period fossils.[68] Albertosaurus received its name in 1905, to commemorate the province's new status as a province.

The Dominion Land Survey began dividing Western Canada into one-square-mile sections for agriculture and other purposes. The surveyor most closely associated with the oil sands is William Ogilvie, who in 1883-1884 led teams that surveyed the fifth meridian from Edmonton to the Athabasca River, the Peace River from Chipewyan to Dunvegan, and the Athabasca River from

Slave River to Athabasca Landing. Another Dominion surveyor, Otto Klotz, wrote a prophetic diary entry in 1887. "At the present moment Manitoba and the whole Northwest is greatly interested in the so called Hudson's Bay Route, i.e., a railroad to Hudson's Bay & then by steamer to Liverpool, the practicality of which is by the most believed and by the rest earnestly desired," he said. "It appears that the salvation of the country depends upon the feasibility of this scheme."[69] Just such a railway – to Churchill, Manitoba – reached Hudson Bay in 1929.

The GSC's John Macoun had fled Ireland's potato famine for Canada in 1850. Although his education was middling, his mind was quick and he had a consuming interest in botany. By 1868 he was a professor of botany and geology at St. Albert's College in Belleville, Ontario. Sanford Fleming, then chief engineer for the proposed Canadian Pacific Railway, recruited him to participate in his 1872 expedition to the Pacific. In total, Macoun participated in five separate surveying expeditions in the Northwest, and his work contributed to the largely political decision to lay track along a southerly route across the prairies for the Canadian Pacific Railway. Like Confederation itself, this would discourage Yankee incursions into the Northwest Territories.

Macoun's reports attracted the notice of Alfred Richard Cecil Selwyn, director of the Geological Survey of Canada. In an 1875 expedition, Macoun described the presence of the oil sands on a voyage up the Clearwater River. "The first indications of 'tar' were in the form of pebbles composed of sand and tar, formed above and carried down by the ice," he wrote. "From this time forward, we continued to see deposits of tar wherever we came near the river margin....The tar was frequently observed, sometimes forming a bed two feet thick. Early in the afternoon, we came upon the shale beds which produce the tar and sailed past them all the evening....That there must be enormous quantities, I am quite satisfied, on account of having seen the tar along the bank for over one hundred miles."[70]

While his autobiography stressed the inconveniences, dangers and risks of his expeditions, a well-known passage in his report to the GSC talked about "the not-far distant future, where other sounds than these would wake up the silent forest; when the white man would be busy, with his ready instrument, steam, raising the untold wealth which lies buried beneath the surface, and converting the present desolation into a bustling mart of trade."[71]

In 1879, acting on the initiative of the minister of customs, the government took the unprecedented step of hiring Macoun permanently as its explorer in the northwest. He was named Dominion botanist to the GSC in November 1881 and the following year moved with his family to Ottawa. In 1883 the deputy minister of the interior, his boss, described him as "a good specialist and honest fool outside of that."[72] In 1887 he was appointed the survey's naturalist and one of its assistant directors. He remained with the Survey for 31 years.

The University of Saskatchewan's Bill Waiser, who wrote about a number of important GSC figures, called Macoun's colleague Dr. Robert Bell "Canada's greatest exploring scientist." Bell named more than 3,000 geographical features, and his colleagues called him "the father of Canadian place-names."[73] Of particular note, he participated in numerous explorations of Canada, including one specifically undertaken to study the Athabasca oil sands area. Bell identified the "asphaltic sands" as Lower Cretaceous in age, and proposed that the bitumen originated in the Devonian strata.

Bell examined the oil sands in 1881 and 1884 and was the first to suggest they might represent a resource with great commercial potential. "The enormous quantity of asphalt, or thickened petroleum, in such a depth and extent of sand indicates an abundant origin. It is hardly likely that the source from whence it came is exhausted. The whole of the liquid petroleum may have escaped in some parts of the area below the sandstone, while in others it is probably still imprisoned in great quantities and may be found by boring."[74] He described the behaviour of bitumen when it came in contact with river water in these words: "In flowing, with a rolling movement, over the beach of the river, the sandy pitch incorporates the pebbles and boulders, which, in some places, become a large proportion of the mixture, and when this is flattened by the pressure of the passing ice it forms a natural asphaltic pavement."[75]

Bell was an important player in respect to the oil sands, but his colleagues were not generous in their assessment of his personality. As Waiser put it, "Bell was never satisfied with his position at the Geological Survey. He continually plotted against director Alfred Richard Cecil Selwyn and then George Mercer Dawson."[76]

Pleasantly interspersed with free verse, Dawson's memoirs provided frank insights into the rivalry between Bell and himself for the director's job. "In naming him here," he wrote, "I make it clear that this memoir must not be published...until after my death." He then described the competition between the two men and took satisfaction in his own victory. After learning of Dawson's appointment, he wrote, Bell had written to Canada's new Prime Minister, Sir Mackenzie Bowell. He complained "of a terrible injustice, which he took as a 'most undeserved slur after a lifetime spent in faithful services to the country.'"[77]

Although he had less direct involvement with the oil sands than Bell, Dawson had the bigger vision. "We find ourselves possessed in Canada of a country vast in its dimensions, but of which the population is as yet comparatively small," he wrote in 1894. "If, therefore, we have good reason to believe that the natural resources of our territory are in any respect commensurate with its area, we may look forward with confidence to a great future. But in order that this may be realized properly and soon, we must devote ourselves to the exploration and definition of our latent wealth...."[78]

Using material provided by GSC researchers, a Survey chemist, Christian Hoffmann, experimented with hot water applied to the sand and bitumen samples. Notably, he found that hot water causes the oil to separate from the sand grains which held it. "Should it be deemed more expedient to separate the bitumen," he observed, "this may be affected by simply boiling or macerating the material with hot water, when the bituminous matter, entering into fusion, will rise as a scum to the surface, and may be removed by skimmers while the sand falls to the bottom of the vessel."[79] While bitumen is generally heavier than water, boiling expands the material, enabling it to float.

## FOUNDING FORT McMURRAY

Fort McMurray was founded by a Hudson's Bay Company employee named Henry "John" Moberly. In 1879, Moberly set out from the company's factory at Fort Chipewyan to establish a new trading post farther south. "A blizzard for the last three days of the trip made travelling anything but pleasant, but as the wind was fair we carried on and landed, in a foot of snow, at the mouth of the

Clearwater River," he said, describing the founding of the outpost. "I chose a site for the fort in a thick poplar wood and the weather having turned fine we began clearing the ground."[80] He named the new outpost Fort McMurray after his boss, William McMurray, who was the factor at Fort Chipewyan and had specified the location for the new site. Tom Morimoto, who moved to Fort McMurray as a toddler in 1920, observed in his memoirs that Moberly generally gets credit for naming the town, and suggested that Moberly simply did not want to share the glory. He "did not even mention McMurray in his memoirs, saying only that 'it was named after a Chief Factor, one of my oldest friends.'"[81]

It is difficult to overstate the importance of this village, which eventually became one of Alberta's largest population centres. Located in the heart of the oil sands, around that location bitumen is closest to the surface and in some places seeps into the river. Virtually all the earliest field tests took place there. In the 20th century it became a gathering-place for scientists and inventors who saw potential wealth in the oil sands, and sought ways to make serious money from it. Until the 1960s, the village changed little.

One 20th century scientist, Sidney Ells, described his first visit to this simple community. The year was 1913, and "McMurray consisted of a dozen primitive log cabins, a bug infested hovel proudly referred to as the 'hotel' and during the summer months many Indian teepees and tents. Everywhere starving train dogs roamed at will and the greatest care for the protection of food and other supplies was essential," he wrote. "The community depended solely on the fur trade and this was conducted by the Hudson's Bay Company and two 'free-traders' in small log cabins. There was no telegraphic communication, but theoretically a mail service operated from Athabasca four times a year, by water in summer and by dog train in winter."[82]

"The climate was a lot colder in those days than it is now," said Tom Morimoto. "There were days that it would never get above -40°. Everybody burned wood. That was the fuel they used instead of coal because it was too expensive to bring coal in from Edmonton. So, most people burned wood and you could see the smoke going straight up. On cold days, it would get down to -65°F [-54°C] and it stayed cold for months on end." The villagers were primarily Métis, and there was essentially no cash economy. The fur trade still ruled. Trappers traded furs for goods, although the Bay no longer had a monopoly. "There were a lot of independent store-keepers there, too, and other fur buyers. Especially at Christmas time, all the Indians would come in on dog teams.... It used to be great for us kids, because the dogs would get into fights and there would be dog teams all tangled up in their harness and people trying to separate them."

Morimoto recalled trading for muskrats as a teenager with a resident named Alec McIvor. He was a partner with store-owner Sam Kushner. "Kushner would take a scow loaded with provisions and dry goods to trade for muskrats. I think it was '36 when the Athabasca River flooded and the ice jammed during break up. It jammed and it flooded for miles. The water rose about 40 feet. So, we were following the ice down. It would jam and we'd have to wait until the ice broke and then we'd go a few more miles until we got down to the Athabasca Delta." Traders went to Lake Athabasca because "that's where all the muskrats were," he continued. "The trappers would get hundreds of muskrats each spring. I think the season ended in March or April. [We would trade for them but] Kushner went around to the various trappers and bought his muskrats."[83]

## THE MATTER OF RESERVES

As the GSC surveys of western Canada reported in, policy makers became interested in the matter of the volumes of oil available in the west. This was a matter of commercial interest, given the growing demand for oil in a world which increasingly needed oils to lubricate machinery and to power growing armies of oil-fired internal combustion engines.

At an 1888 committee meeting in Canada's Senate, the GSC's R.G. McConnell provided the first creditable estimate of the oil sands' potential. He used three assumptions based on field and lab work to come up with his calculations. First, he said, there were at least 1,000 square miles of bitumen-saturated sand in the area. Second, the sands were 150 to 225 feet thick. Third – and this result came from laboratory tests that involved boiling oil sand samples – the bitumen content averaged 12 per cent by weight. Therefore there were about 30 million "long tons" of bitumen in place – roughly speaking, 220 million barrels.

At this writing, the estimate of recoverable oil sands reserves is three orders of magnitude greater. Of course, McConnell's number was an estimate of resources in place. It was not what today is known as a "reserves estimate." At that time the concept of recoverable reserves – hydrocarbons that are economically producible at current prices using existing technology – was unknown. No one had any idea how to calculate what percentage of oil in the ground would ever see the inside of a pipeline. The problem of calculating oil sands reserves bedevilled the petroleum industry for another 120 years, as this document explains later on.

"The Tar sands must have consisted originally of almost unconsolidated sands and soft sandstone, ranging in texture from a fine silt to a coarse grit, but have been cemented into a coherent tarry mass, 200 feet thick, by the heavy constituents from the underlying Devonian limestone," McConnell said. "It is also possible that the sands at their outcrop may by the deposition of tarry substances be plugged tightly enough to prevent further egress."[84]

The Geological Survey's Dr. George Dawson told the same inquiry that "the pitch found along the Athabasca may probably be of considerable value in the future; but in the meantime was most important as giving reason to believe that extensive deposits of petroleum existed in the country in which it occurred. The quantity appears to be practically inexhaustible."[85]

## PELICAN

Parliament voted $7,000 for drilling in 1894 and the Dominion Government commissioned the Geological Survey of Canada to drill for oil along the Athabasca River. The Survey probably hoped to find free oil at the base of the sands, as drillers had in the gum beds of southern Ontario a few decades earlier. Drilling started on August 15 at a site near Athabasca. According to McConnell's estimates, drillers would encounter oil sand at depths of 1200 to 1500 feet. The hole didn't reach this depth, however, because the drillers "ran out of hole" as successively smaller diameters of casing reduced the size of the hole until further progress was impossible. Neither did later drilling find free oil at that location. However, drilling three years later at a second site struck gas.

Spudded in the early summer of 1897, before winter the Pelican Rapids well reached a depth of 820 feet and then blew wild. According to drilling contractor A.W Fraser, "The roar of the gas could be heard for three miles or more. Soon it had completely dried the hole, and was blowing a cloud of dust fifty feet into the air. Small nodules of iron-pyrites, about the size of a walnut, were blown out of the hole with incredible velocity, they came out like bullets from a rifle. [The workers] could not see them going, but could hear them crack against the top of the derrick. It was impossible to do anything with the bore that day, so they were forced to let it stand just as it was. There was danger that the men would be killed if struck by these missiles."[86] Fraser's crew unsuccessfully tried to kill the well by casing it, so they packed up and headed home. They returned the following year to finish the job, failed again and abandoned it.

The flow of gas was ignited from time to time, making the area a source of great wonder and a favourite winter campsite for aboriginals. Natural gas flowed from the well at a rate of some 8,500,000 cubic feet per day until 1918. In that year a crew led by geologist S.E. Slipper and oilman Charles W. Dingman finally shut it in.

A final early commentary on the oil sands came from Charles Mair, who viewed the Athabasca area in 1899. In his day one of Canada's best-known poets, Mair served as secretary for a federal survey party determining boundaries for Treaty Eight – an agreement signed on behalf of Queen Victoria with various First Nations in the Lesser Slave Lake area. In a book on the expedition, Mair provided a graphic description of the oil sands. "We are now traversing perhaps the most interesting region in all the north," he wrote. "In the neighborhood of McMurray there are several tar wells, so called, and there, if a hole is scraped in the bank, it slowly fills in with tar mingled with sand. This is separated and is used, in its native state, for gumming canoes and boats"[87] – thus confirming this practice a century after Alexander McKenzie made a similar diary entry.

The others on that survey party also saw the oil sands, of course, but were not enamoured of their economic merits. In their report they noted that "The country along the Athabasca River is well-wooded, and there are miles of tar-saturated banks. But as far as our restricted view of the Lake Athabasca and

Slave River Country enabled us to judge, its wealth, apart from possible mineral development, consists exclusively in its fisheries and furs."[88]

Where these people saw fish and fur, others began testing the Athabasca deposit in hopes of finding free oil. Although the fur trade still dominated Canada's north, perhaps bitumen also had commercial potential — one day, but not yet. How could it get to market? How could a producer extract it, given climatic and technological limitations? While they noted the existence and potential of the oil sands, the official position of the Ottawa and its Geological Survey was that the resource deserved a note on the inventory of Canada's resources. Development, however, would come much later.

# CHAPTER 2

# The war to end war

———

*"This remarkable series of Bituminous Shales and Limestones, of such*
*thickness and of such richness contains the material from which a*
*vast amount of petroleum might be generated and might pass into an*
*overlying porous rock. It is admirable as an oil generating formation."*

— *T.O. BOSWORTH, 1914*

DURING THE 19TH CENTURY, BRITAIN began converting its fleet to hydrocarbons, and the other maritime powers soon followed. Hydrocarbons had been powering steam engines for more than a century, and had been a key driver behind Britain's Industrial Revolution. In the beginning, there had been doubts about using coal or oil for shipping. Indeed, in 1838 Dionysius Lardner, an Irish-born professor of natural philosophy, told the British Association for the Advancement of Science that "Men might as well project a voyage to the Moon, as attempt to employ steam navigation against the stormy North Atlantic Ocean."[89]

The context is that one of Lardner's contemporaries, the highly successful mechanical and civil engineer with the grand name Isambard Kingdom Brunel, had proposed to build the steamship Great Western for the transatlantic passage from the British Isles to New York. The irony is that experiments in such an undertaking had begun nearly two decades earlier. The first ship to cross the Atlantic using a coal-powered engine was the USS Savannah, which in 1819 sailed from New York to the coast of Ireland in 23 days. "What made the Savannah a memorable vessel," Simon Winchester wrote, "is that although she had the usual three masts of a seagoing clipper, she also had a funnel – bent at the top, like a drinking straw – and below, amidships, a 72-horsepower engine."[90]

In September 1833, *SS Royal William*, the first ship to cross the Atlantic under steam power alone, docked at Gravesend on the Thames. Built at Cape Blanc, Québec, it had carried a load of coal and seven passengers on a 25-day voyage from Pictou, Nova Scotia. The principal investor in the wooden-hulled paddle wheeler was Sam Cunard, from Nova Scotia, who in 1840 launched the trans-Atlantic steamship company that became the Cunard Line – famous for its *Queen Elizabeth* and *Queen Mary* ships, among many others.

One new-fangled naval vessel never used coal or fuel oil. Developed separately in France and Germany, the earliest submarines used kerosene, and soon switched to diesel-electric. Their development didn't alarm Britain much at first, since submarines could "only" sink ships, and most states were signatories to a variety of treaties which ensured that "passenger ships should never be attacked; that the crews of merchant ships should be placed out of harm's way before their vessel was plundered and sunk…; and that formal warnings had to be given before an attack."[91]

On the surface there didn't seem much likelihood of war. Even so, in 1910 Canada's federal government issued new regulations governing petroleum development in Canada. One of those regulations specified that supplies could be pre-empted if needed to fuel the Royal Navy. This was the work of Winston Churchill's predecessor in the Admiralty, Reginald McKenna, who argued for the budget to build four new Dreadnoughts and four contingent ships, to be laid down later. Churchill had vehemently opposed the expenditure.

Converting the Royal Navy to oil had been a risky venture. Switching a coal-shovelling navy to fuel oil meant foregoing the security of British coal supplies and its system of fueling stations and supply ships to a reliance on oil. The major sources of that commodity were outside the British Empire, in the United States, Persia (Iran), Russia and Mexico, so it was clearly in the Britain's interest to diversify its supplies. Accordingly, in 1913 Canada's Department of Mines asked Sidney Clarke Ells, a McGill-educated engineer, to investigate Alberta's oil sands. Ells had become interested in the science of oil exploration through his father Robert, a long-time member of the Geological Survey of Canada, who had studied New Brunswick's oil shales.

Another noteworthy researcher from this period was University of Alberta chemistry professor Adolph Lehman. Before the war, Lehman had begun conducting research into the oil sands, wondering whether bitumen molecules could be the basis for a chemical industry, much as coal tar had done in the 19th century. During the war, his lab work focused on whether bitumen contained molecules helpful for the manufacture of explosives.

Given that his assignment to the oil sands was prompted by the prospect of war, it is ironic that Ells cut short his early research by signing up for the military. However, he did prepare a brief paper before going overseas. Published in 1914, it suggested using the oil sands ore as a paving material. Ells signed up for military service, but received orders to do further research on the oil sands. During 1915-16, according to Mary Clark Sheppard, his research "took him back to Fort McMurray for further field work, to Edmonton where he oversaw a demonstration of how the raw tar sand could be turned into a road surfacing material, to the United States on a fact-finding tour principally in Kentucky and California and finally to the Mellon Institute in Pittsburgh, where he spent several months analyzing the oil sand and considering ways of possible separation."[92] For reasons now lost, the oil sands effort was then abandoned. Ells rejoined his unit and departed for Europe, remaining there until year-end 1919.

Before his transfer overseas, Ells published a report on the oil sands titled *Notes on Certain Aspects of the Bituminous Sands in the Province of Alberta*. Oil sands scholar Barry Glen Ferguson described it as "a huge, two-volume unpaginated tome" which, with its 23 appendices, "reflected all the ungainly energy and enthusiasm associated with Ells himself."[93] This document received an uncharitable review from Karl Clark, who found it to be derivative and disorganized, and Ells soon found that Clark and other researchers were excluding him from investigating the most important oil sands issues – to a large extent because of his overpowering and frequently tactless personality

As the war began it was clear that Alberta was prospective for both oil and gas. The most spectacular single event in those early years was the Calgary Petroleum Products #1 discovery, which began disgorging wet gas at Turner

•

Valley, southwest of Calgary on May 15, 1914.<sup>v</sup> More significant in the context of the war, Canada changed the regulations governing development of the oil sands. Of particular interest, companies developing oil in Canada needed to be British or Canadian – "at all times British subjects."[94] In respect to light oil production, American firms found ways around this, but not for the oil sands.

## COUREURS DES BOIS

Canada's petroleum industry developed quite differently from that of the United States. Simply put, the patterns of petroleum industry development in the two countries paralleled their respective patterns of settlement.

The US takes up the best temperate lands along the eastern seaboard, and there are no major barriers to settlement between New York and San Francisco. The Cordillera is a problem, but settlement in the far west was still not seriously hindered – especially after the construction of the transcontinental railways. That pattern exactly reflects the development of the US petroleum industry. In the US there are many sedimentary basins – smallish, but regularly spaced across the country. Once Colonel Edwin Drake drilled his historic well in 1859, the American petroleum industry developed in these basins as people moved across the country.

Canada has quite a different geography. Settlement was difficult in this country because the Canadian Shield provided barriers in many ways. Trapped between the Shield and the Cordillera, the Western Canada sedimentary basin is far bigger than the on-shore basins in the US. Because of the Shield, it is well separated from the small basins in eastern and central Canada. The Shield and

---

v Today, the industry describes this hydrocarbon – so light and clean that automobile engines could use it directly from the well – as natural gas condensate. On discovery day, a staff reporter for *The Calgary Daily Herald* wrote that a laboratory had pronounced it to be "the most remarkable [oil] ever discovered in the history of the world....It is not a remote possibility that great quantities of this enormously profitable gasoline oil may be found beneath the hills stretching southwest of Calgary."

its northern latitudes created the *coureurs des bois* model of how the Canadian industry developed.

*Coureurs des bois* ("runners of the woods") were fur traders who earned their livelihoods with the aid of canoe transport along Canada's mostly northward-flowing rivers, and played a big role in the country's creation. For example, from remote northern locations they brought information about resource potential to political and commercial centres. Partly because of their efforts, Canada's earliest hydrocarbons were found in outposts of settlement. For example, the Oil Springs discovery near present-day Sarnia, Ontario was contemporaneous with Colonel Drake's 1859 well. Based on investigation into the well-known gum beds near Black Creek, the Oil Springs discovery took place on the north shore of Lake Erie – in an area without roads, but along the transportation and trading system afforded by the Great Lakes. Fur traders were the first Europeans to see the oil sands.

A successful *coureur des bois* had to develop many skills, including those of businessman and expert canoeist. To survive in the Canadian wilderness, they had to be competent in many skills, including fishing, snowshoeing and hunting. Venturing into the wilderness might involve thousands of kilometres of travel by canoe; living off corn and bear fat for a year or more, and sleeping in bark or branch shelters. Physically arduous and illegal, to succeed was difficult and bore with it a high mortality rate. The promise of profit, adventure and freedom, however, drew many into the outback.

Typically, these traders left Montréal in the spring (usually in May), as soon as the rivers and lakes were clear of ice. Their canoes loaded with supplies and goods for trading, they took the course west to the richest beaver lands - usually by way of the Ottawa and Mattawa rivers. Such travel involved numerous overland portages to cross waterfalls, for example, and to reach new watersheds.

Packing a canoe for such a trip was difficult, as more than thirty articles were considered essential for survival and business. Trade goods included broadcloth, linen and wool blankets; firearms and ammunition; such metal goods as pots, knives and hatchets; and liquor. For maximum success, these goods needed to take up most of the space in the canoe. The food these traders consumed *en route* included local game and non-perishable grain and pemmican.[95]

## SEMINAL EVENTS

Two important petroleum-related events took place in early 1914. For one, oil fever swept Calgary. Investors lined up outside makeshift brokerage houses to get in on exploration activity triggered by a wet gas discovery at Turner Valley. So great was the excitement that in one 24-hour period promoters formed more than 500 "oil companies." Although incorporated in 1913, the Calgary Stock Exchange was unable to control the unscrupulous practices that relieved many Albertans of their savings.

Calgary Petroleum Products #1, the well behind this speculative flurry, was near the crest of the great structure that underlies Turner Valley. Using an American-style cable-tool drilling rig, the tools hung from the longest manila drilling line ever used.

Spudded in January 1913, the well came in with a roar on May 14, 1914. It found the reservoir at about 2,000 feet and soon produced 4 million cubic feet of gas per day from a Cretaceous sandstone horizon. The gas dripped with smelly naphtha, a light oil condensate – pure enough to burn in automobiles without further refining. Fame and success greeted Bill Herron, William Elder and Archibald Dingman as well as the other partners in the syndicate that created the Calgary Petroleum Products Company.

The other seminal event from that year was a field expedition along the Mackenzie River by British geologist T. O. Bosworth. Two Calgary businessmen, F. C. Lowes and J. K. Cornwall, commissioned Bosworth's journey. They wanted to investigate the petroleum potential of northern Alberta and beyond, and to stake the most promising claims. Bosworth did not disappoint. His confidence that the north was highly prospective is apparent on almost every page of his 69-page report. Bosworth's own words suggest how ambitious the expedition was. Bosworth discounted Alberta's light oil prospects, which from the perspective of hindsight was a blunder. Seen strictly as a study of Canada's northerly geological prospects, however, his expedition and the resulting report was a *tour de force*.

"The undertaking was planned in March 1914," he wrote, "prior to the recent finding of light oil near Calgary and the 'oil boom' occasioned thereby.... In April I consulted with the officers of the Government Geological Survey and other Departments in Ottawa and gathered from them all available information; maps and literature bearing on the subject…" He continued, "At the beginning of May, I journeyed from London to Canada accompanied by three assistant geologists and surveyors, and on May 19th, the expedition set out from Edmonton to travel northwards in the Guidance of the Northern Trading Company. We returned to Edmonton September 24th."

During that period, the Bosworth expedition covered great distances, and according to his report there were "excellent exploration prospects in three general regions: The Mackenzie River between Old Fort Good Hope and Fort Norman; the Tar Springs District on the Great Slave Lake; and in the Tar Sand District on the Athabasca River." His report offered concise, well-written geological descriptions of rocks, formations and structures. It also included chemical reports on both rocks and oil from seepages in the area. "Near Old Fort Good Hope (lat. 67 30') in the banks of a tributary stream, the shales are well exposed," he wrote. "From the fossils it is evident that the shales are of Upper Paleozoic Age and probably belong to the Upper Devonian…."

In a description of what Bosworth called the Tar Springs District, he said "*This remarkable series of Bituminous Shales and Limestones*, of such *thickness* and of such *richness* contains the material from which *a vast amount of petroleum* might be generated and might pass into an overlying porous rock. *It is admirable as an oil generating formation.*"Elsewhere, he added that "The porous dolomite is saturated with fluid petroleum which is seeping out into [Lake Athabasca] all along the coast for several miles, so that distinct films of oil are ever on the water at most parts of the shore. There are also little springs on the shore where oil is ascending more copiously and causing small pools in among the rocks."

In a discussion of the evidence of good reservoir rock, Bosworth pointed to a nearby occurrence of gray clay shales and shaley sandstone, and to another of greenish shaley sandstone containing occasional fossils – corals, chenetes and rhynconella. Both of the formation rocks Bosworth speculated upon lay above the Devonian shales.

The recommendations in the Bosworth report reflected the mood of the times. "To avoid all competition, I strongly advise that you form a controlling company or syndicate containing the most influential men," he wrote. "I recommend particularly that you arrange matters in such a way that it would be to the obvious advantage of every oilman to join you, and that you freely provide the opportunity so that the Company may include every man who wishes to venture anything in the exploitation of the oilfields of the North. By this means alone can you hope to avoid competition and the unfortunate results which must follow." One of the ironies of these comments, of course, is that they came barely three years after the US Supreme Court ordered the Standard Oil Trust dismantled for its anti-competitive practices.

In his report Bosworth noted that he had investigated the discovery at Turner Valley. Fifteen months in the drilling, the wet gas discovery had come in on May 14, 1914 – just before Bosworth left Edmonton on his expedition. Within 20 years, Turner Valley would be recognized as the largest oilfield in the British Empire. Bosworth, however, was not impressed. In his view, the real potential was in the North. Believing Turner Valley would ultimately disappoint, he wrote that "...there are a number of oil companies in Western Canada who have capital in hand which must be spent on drilling wells. At this moment they are faced with failure [at Turner Valley], and might gladly turn to any region where there is a genuine reason to expect oil. Any such companies might become associated with your controlling company to the obvious advantage of all parties, on terms which can be mutually arranged.

Bosworth advised his clients to secure control of these resources (he had staked for them the best prospects he found), and then to protect their interests. In his view, the business conglomerate that they created "would also provide for the transportation; the necessary railroads; the pipe lines, the refineries, and, what is more important than all the rest, and which would give you complete command of the whole situation, all of the oil produced in the region would pass through your hands to be marketed by you." He added, "If you could succeed in promoting a great scheme on some such lines as these, no smaller rival group could hope to compete against you, and you might eventually be in the position to control the great oil fields of the North."[96] The practical value of his advice may be seen in the fact that seven decades elapsed before oil from the Norman Wells oilfield actually began flowing to southern markets.

By the time Bosworth returned from his expedition, the First World War had begun. An event that affected every aspect of life in the province, the first years of the Great War were a struggle among three European cousins – King George V of Britain, Czar Nicholas III of Russia and Kaiser Wilhelm II of Germany. Improbably, in response to a tangled web of alliances among Europe's powers and the assassination of a European aristocrat, Canada – which at the beginning of hostilities only had 3,007 men in its army – mobilized large armies to serve in Western Europe. Ultimately, Canadian participation in the war led to sweeping social change within Canada herself.

## TECHNOLOGICAL SHIFT

Two scientists working for Standard Oil of Indiana inadvertently played a key role in the Allies' First World War victory, and developed a technology which would create the petrochemical industry and make the oil sands a practical business. Both men had earned PhDs in chemistry from Johns Hopkins University. One of those men was Robert Humphreys; the other was his boss, William Burton. Generally known to history as the Burton process, the technology they developed should more fairly be known as the Burton-Humphreys process, since both men played key roles in its development.

To understand the importance of their work, it is important to appreciate the state of petroleum refining before they began. Until the end of the 1890s, gasoline was a by-product of fractional distillation, which in its earliest phase focused on heating oil in large distillation units "stills") to get kerosene out of crude oil. The focus on stills that mostly produced kerosene had to change as the internal combustion engine began to power automobiles – especially after Henry Ford began to manufacture the Model T Ford on his massive production lines. By 1900 there were some 8,000 automobiles in the United States, most of them propelled by electricity or coal-generated steam; few used gasoline. By 1910, however, there were 450,000 Model T cars in the United States and the production and sale of gasoline surpassed that of kerosene. Only six years later, that number had risen to 3,367,889 "and the tin lizzie was no longer a luxury, having been recognized generally as a necessity."[97]

By dramatically increasing the amount of gasoline that could come from a barrel of oil, the Burton-Humphreys process provided greater volumes of the fuel needed for tanks, trucks, airplanes, ambulances and the other vehicles so vital in waging war. The strategic benefits were considerable, since gasoline provided greater speed and more efficient use of manpower. Petroleum-hungry Germany couldn't power its military effort with the same finesse and flexibility as the Allies – not only because of short supplies of petroleum, but also because they didn't yet use the Burton still. Germany had invested heavily in railroads as the best way to wage war. From the perspective of Britain and her allies, it was a matter of enormous good fortune that Burton and Humphreys had solved this problem before the war began. America, which had growing supplies of oil, also had ever-larger numbers of Burton stills.

Working together at Standard's Whiting Refinery in northwestern Indiana, Burton and Humphreys had developed the first effective cracking process – one which "cracked" the complex oil molecules of crude oil into smaller, more useful chemicals. This was quite different from the fractional distillation Yale's Benjamin Silliman had tested in 1855. Instead of distilling oil into its fractions, the new stills could split heavier molecules into lighter, more desirable products. So doing, they more than doubled the amount of gasoline refiners could manufacture from light oil, making more available for use in the battlefields.

The Burton-Humphreys still heated crude oil under pressure in a large steel vessel. The vapours from the vessel were piped into a bubble tower, which recaptured the oil while allowing the remaining gases to flow into a condenser coil. That coil led to two separators. A high-pressure separator redirected dry gas, while the low-pressure separator divided the hydrocarbon stream into wet gas and distillate. The engineering problems had been considerable, but the two men had developed the first practical process for producing synthetic gasoline by cracking oil at high temperatures and pressures.

Humphreys sired a clan of oil industry people, many of whom ended up in Canada. His son Claude got petroleum engineering credentials from the University of Chicago in the 1920s, and during his career worked in Imperial Oil's refineries from coast to coast. Indeed, Imperial was the first company to receive a license for the use of this process from Standard of Indiana, in January 1914, as war drums were beginning to beat. As Claude Humphreys' son Bill modestly explained in an interview, the two men "built a steel vessel and started separating petroleum products with it using heat and pressure, and it increased the amount of gasoline off a barrel of oil. That was the basis for most refineries for many years."[98] True, but this description understates the importance of what they had done.

In addition to greatly increasing the output of gasoline from a barrel of oil, the Burton-Humphreys process awakened the petroleum industry to the commercial possibilities of bringing about chemical changes in crude oil and natural gas through industrial research. From a tiny base in the late 1920s, the petrochemical industry grew rapidly because the technological conditions were ripe. By the 1940s, investigations into the value of bitumen evaluated both its potential as a petrochemical feedstock and its value as a source of fuel. According to a 2013 International Energy Agency forecast, by 2035 global oil consumption would only have two uses: transportation fuels (59 million barrels per day) and petrochemical manufacture (14 million barrels per day).

Once the energy potential of petroleum became clear, new applications developed at an astonishing rate. Between 1912 and 1918, crude oil demand in the United States increased by 72 per cent, to 412 million barrels per year as the number of gasoline engines in service multiplied. When the First World War erupted among the European empires, petroleum became an essential sinew of war. Most of the petroleum for the Allied war effort came from the United States, placing a heavy burden upon its petroleum industry. Within the US itself, growing demand for American manufactured goods created an unprecedented domestic demand for fuel oil for industries, railroads, ships and home heating. American fuel oil exports increased from 17 million barrels in 1914 to almost 29 million four years later.

There was a phenomenal increase in demand for fuel for gasoline-powered automobiles and trucks in the United States proper, which saw the number of vehicles in service rise from 950,000 in 1912 to more than six million at Armistice. Besides supplying that vast domestic fleet of vehicles with gasoline, the US was able to increase annual gasoline exports from five million to 13 million barrels. This would have been impossible without the development of new Burton-Humphreys stills.

This development can be credited specifically to Burton, who made a strategically brilliant proposal to Standard of Indiana as soon as the company became independent of the Trust in 1911. By then a company director, Burton proposed that the newly-independent company construct 120 of these stills. The company granted him the full $709,000 appropriation he needed. As construction began, gasoline shortages loomed and prices soared – from 9.5 cents per gallon in October 1911 to 17 cents at the beginning of 1912. In Europe, prices were as high as $1.00 per gallon. Prior to 1897, gasoline's main use had been as a cleaning product. Many refiners had dumped it as a waste by-product. During the First World War, it came into its own.

## A WAVE OF OIL

Winston Churchill had read the signs of war quite wrong when he got into Britain's Lloyd George government. He "decried the scaremongers, those alarmist 'Bismarckian statesmen' who predicted 'hideous and direful wars as imminent'. For him, these war-cries were simply 'nightmare nonsense'. Did Germany, widely perceived as powerful, ambitious, militaristic, unpredictable, set on outbuilding the British navy, constitute a threat to British interests? Churchill's answer was an emphatic 'No!'"[99] Given the benefit of hindsight, and his hawkish stance toward Germany in the mid-1930s, this is ironic.

Britain's Prime Minister appointed Churchill First Lord of the Admiralty in 1911. This appointment took place after McKenna had settled the technical foundations for the Royal Navy's new ships and after 70-year-old Admiral Sir John (Lord) Fisher had resigned from his position as First Sea Lord – but before oil suddenly and dramatically became a political and military commodity across the British Empire. A political crisis developed when Germany's Kaiser Wilhelm II sent a naval vessel into Agadir, on the Atlantic coast of Morocco, to limit French influence and to expand his holdings in Africa. Three weeks later, on July 21st, Prime Minister Lloyd George told a meeting of bankers that he would not countenance his country's being treated "as if she were of no account in the Cabinet of Nations...peace at that price would be a humiliation intolerable for a great country like ours to endure." Until the end of the war, Churchill relied heavily on Fisher's advice and assistance.[100]

A curmudgeon, Fisher's language was picturesque and sometimes brutal. As to those who defied him, he once said "their wives would be widows, their children fatherless and their homes a dunghill." In 1912, he became chairman of a royal commission into liquid fuel, with a view to converting the entire fleet to oil. Throughout the war, he was Churchill's close confidant. "'You must have cheapness & the big gun & speed!'" he said. "The fifteen inch gun 'will stagger humanity'! 'Oil fuel only,' he cried enthusiastically."[101]

According to Lord George Curzon, who sat on Britain's War Cabinet, "the Allied cause floated to victory on a wave of oil."[102]

One of the key players supplying Britain with oil was America's Sun Oil. The president of that company was J. Howard Pew, who was in his thirties. A masterful business tactician, Pew did more than supply oil to Britain during the war. According to the only biography/hagiography of the man, at the end of that war Sun delivered petroleum products to Germany six weeks before any of its competitors. "During the peace negotiations at Versailles, [Pew] quietly assembled a fleet of tankers off Hamburg and Bremen. As word came from Washington that the peace treaty had been signed his waiting tankers steamed into the German ports. When asked how much money he made on the deal he merely smiled and shrugged his shoulders. As always, money was not his motivation – to be the first in service was important to him."[103] Much later in his life, Pew became a towering figure in the oil sands story.

Known at the time as the Great War, the First World War galvanized Canadians like no event before. The trains that had carried an exuberance of immigrants from the east soon began carrying soldiers (especially British-born immigrants) in the other direction.

In the beginning, both sides in the conflict proclaimed that they would see victory by Christmas, so the demand for a place in the forces was particularly strong. Newly-settled Alberta contributed 123,000 men to the Canadian Expeditionary Force, which trained 1.7 million recruits and conscripts. Some 61,000 of those men died in trenches and battles — many of them in 1916 at Vimy Ridge, where the Canadians ended what to that time had been a stalemate among opposing forces on Europe's Western Front. Even though more than half of Canada's soldiers during that war were British-born, one outcome of those battles was the birth of Canadian identity and pride. Worldwide, some ten million people died. To a large extent because of the existence of global empires, the peace conferences that followed redrew the map of the world, with few regions unaffected.

## OIL SANDS FOR THE WAR EFFORT

In a country committed to total war, Bosworth's clients, Messrs. Lowes and Cornwall, were hardly in a position to follow his advice about securing their interests in the north. However, after having his report typed and delivered, the geologist returned to Britain. There, a copy of his manuscript made it into the hands of the brass at Shell Transport Company Ltd.

Toward the end of the war, in 1917, Canada's Interior Minister, William James Roche, received an imperious eight-page letter from Shell. According to Mary Janigan, "The firm wanted exclusive oil and natural gas rights over an enormous swath of the West for the duration of the war and for five years after Armistice." The company asked Ottawa for rights to a 328,000-square-mile parcel – for practical purposes, the land Bosworth had recommended, up to the Mackenzie River delta. Along with other demands, Shell wanted "right-of-way over all Crown lands for pipelines, telegraph and telephone lines, railways and highways; ...land for factories, storehouses, refineries and reservoirs." The company went further, however. Shell Executive R.N. Benjamin said the company "would not pay taxes for the first fifteen years of exploration" and would not begin paying royalties (of three cents per barrel) until January 1, 1930.[104]

The federal government did not cede those rights to Shell – indeed, did not even reply. If Shell's missive rankled in Ottawa, the following year it sparked downright outrage in western Canada, which hosted those petroleum resources. The occasion was an article covering the story in the *Winnipeg Telegram*, dated November 21, 1918 – followed by equally inflammatory newspaper stories in Edmonton and Calgary. Alberta's Legislature promptly passed a resolution describing "the terms of the concession as being oppressive to the people of the province." It continued, "Now be it Resolved in the opinion of this House no such deposition of Pétroleum and or any other Natural Resources should be made."[105]

The drama continued for another year, with a feature story by W.A. McRae submitted in the Toronto-based magazine *Saturday Night*. "Open your mouth and shut your eyes and we'll take your oil land, wherever it lies," blared the headline. It continued, "Shell Transport and Trading Company boldly asks Canadian government for monopoly which might, if granted, make millions of profit for the promoters, and little or nothing for the government. Applicants want 250,000 [square] miles of potential oil lands in the far west and north."[106]

A 1918 meeting of Canada's premiers, in Ottawa, had triggered this storm. The meeting took place in the Victoria Memorial Museum, in the first-floor mineral gallery, which had previously been the Hall of Invertebrate Fossils. The gathering was yet another among Canada's premiers to discuss land settlement and resource ownership, and the occasion was not auspicious. Germany had just signed its Armistice with the Allied Powers, and Prime Minister Robert Borden (1911-1920) was in Europe. Another decade would pass before Ottawa and the central and eastern provinces would agree that the Prairie Provinces owned those resources in their territories that government had not already ceded to others.

In Alberta, this long delay in gaining resource ownership created a unique situation, since it meant the province owned most of the resources – a situation that did not exist in the rest of the country, where landowners generally owned the resources beneath their feet. While some resource ownership was vested in railways and the Hudson's Bay Company, for example, most were eventually owned by the provincial government on behalf of the people of Alberta. In simple terms, the province owns 81 per cent of the province's natural endowment, or 537,000 square kilometres of mineral rights – an area three-quarters the size of Texas. As Gordon Jaremko explained, "If measured by modern energy content rather than geographic extent, the public share of the resource endowment comes even closer to 100 per cent because the provincially owned buried treasure includes the oil sands."[107]

## PROMOTION AND FRAUD

The prospect of building fortunes fuelled the efforts of wildcatters from the beginning, and early explorers were prospecting for light oil instead of bitumen. As we have seen, the Pelican well had been blowing wild since 1898, and early explorers drilled the Athabasca deposit in hopes of finding free oil. Clearly there was oil in the Athabasca region; surely, they thought, there were profitable ways to produce the stuff. Without fail, early investigations of the oil sands describe primitive conditions, remoteness, challenging logistics, unique geology and the chemical composition of bitumen as making it such a stubborn resource to produce.

Early oil sands operators had little success, and in today's world their business practices would have put many of them in jail. For decades, the only business people to make money out of the oil sands were promoters out to fleece investors. However, they added a colourful chapter to oil sands history. Consider the examples of Alfred von Hammerstein and A.F.A. Coyne.

One of the more colourful early promoters was Alfred Hammerstein, who claimed to be an immigrant German count. The balance of this account dispenses with the "von," which suggests noble heritage, because the evidence to support Hammerstein's claim to German nobility is hearsay and almost certainly originated with the man himself. In that era other Europeans in Alberta made false claims about their European lineage, to impress the locals.

Among historians, opinions on this matter are mixed. Ferguson rejects the claim. Other authors either accept it without question or do not express opinions. What is known about Hammerstein's background suggests (to this researcher) that the claim is fraudulent. Before he became involved in the oil sands, Hammerstein tried many different trades, from blacksmithing to trapping. However, he was a talented flautist, which suggests he at least came from a middle-class German home. According to his own account, his father was a military officer. Obituaries in the *Edmonton Bulletin* and *The Albertan* in 1941 refer to him as a "count," as does the 1964 *Edmonton Journal* obituary of his wife (née Dorothy Clark of London, UK), which received the headline "Requiem Mass Set for Countess, 87."

Manfred Prokop's massive *Annotated Bibliography of the German-speaking Community in Alberta, 1882-2000* has about 30 articles, mostly in German, regarding Hammerstein's life. Many of those articles call him a 'count' ['Graf']. One says he raised millions of dollars of oil sands investment money. Several discuss his efforts both in 1914 and 1939 to show that German-Canadians were loyal; in 1939 he proposed raising a German-Canadian military unit to fight the Nazis.

In correspondence for this publication, however, US academic Katharina von Hammerstein said "Every now and then I get an inquiry about [Alfred Hammerstein]. He is actually not part of the aristocratic Hammerstein family. I found this out when I sent an inquiry like yours [from Joyce Hunt] to my uncle Egbert von Hammerstein who is currently head of the von Hammerstein family of 200+ members around the world. He has access to all the old family trees and documents and this was his response." In later correspondence she added, "On the issue of 'count' – there are no counts von Hammerstein, not now and not in the nineteenth century. The von Hammersteins are 'Freiherren,' which corresponds to 'barons.'"[108]

Hammerstein claimed he first saw the oil sands deposit in 1897, on his way to the Klondike gold rush. He subsequently abandoned the more northerly adventure, settling instead in the Edmonton area. He was one of the first to try to extract bitumen from the oil sands commercially, and the first to bring in serious amounts of outside capital. He began his quest for a pool of "free oil" lying beneath the sand formation in 1903. He had drilling equipment and supplies ferried on scows down an 80-mile stretch of the Athabasca River – a stretch which included a series of rapids.

Two years later, Hammerstein went to Ottawa to make a presentation to a Senate committee. Seeking a grant from Ottawa, he gave a glowing report of the mineral wealth to be found in the Athabasca region, a central theme of which was the usefulness of the oil sands to produce asphalt. "It is not straight asphalt," according to the committee report. "It is nothing but oil gum, out of which can be made asphalt. There is a large amount of petroleum in it. He tested it himself, and got some parrafine [sic] out of it. If he could obtain transportation, he could apply it for practical purposes. After it is refined, and all the foreign substances taken out of it, it can be used for road making." In his deposition he said "I have all my money put into it [the Athabasca oil sands], and there is other peoples' money in it, and I have to be loyal. As to whether you can get petroleum in merchantable quantities.... I have been taking in machinery for about three years. Last year I placed about $50,000 worth of machinery in there. I have not brought it in for ornamental purposes, although it does look nice and home-like."[109]

By today's standards, Hammerstein was a scam artist. One early report noted that "when Hammerstein expected someone down to examine the wells, he got Hungenberger [an employee] to empty a barrel of tar into one of them."[110] According to another local resident, Walter Hill, Hammerstein "poured a barrel of oil down a hole, drilled for oil and found it."[111] This was probably part of an effort to secure a lease from the federal government, since before the federal government would grant a lease the prospective lessor had to prove to the Minister that the land could produce oil. With this stringent condition satisfied, the federal government granted von Hammerstein the right to explore 11,405 acres of land.[112]

In 1906 Hammerstein wrote to another employee, Robert Volkoffsky. "Just spread the rumor that you struck a couple of good wells of petroleum. As I told you, I want to have it done on purpose, and trust your conscience will stand it," he said.

"That fellow in the telegraph office is the correspondent for several papers and when you come in and send me a telegraph so I know you be there, and please telegraph like that 'Old petroleum wells still flowing, struck another well,'" he instructed, sounding like an experienced promoter.

"And that will make him jump, and if he asks if he is allowed to give it to the papers, say you don't care as far as you are concerned; but you don't know whether Hammerstein wants it. I do want it to appear, and the only way to do it is to play them. You will understand, I cannot develop an enterprise of such magnitude and difficulties without all kinds of maneuvers, and you will understand."[113]

In 1910 Hammerstein and his group received freehold mineral titles in the oil sands. These mineral rights were granted by the federal government, which still owned all the minerals in what had formerly been the prairies portion of the Northwest Territories. As Darlene Comfort explains, "by 1910 [he] had notified the Department of the Interior that he had struck oil in paying quantities. Under the petroleum regulations that were in effect, this was all that was required in order to purchase the land outright, providing the discovery could be established to the satisfaction of the Minister."[114]

They placed their properties into the Athabasca Petroleum Syndicate, each getting an equal share of the company. However, the *Edmonton Bulletin* reported that Hammerstein also received $1 million from the group for his "previous services."[115] So large a sum at that time is difficult to credit, but some money must have been forthcoming, since he took two trips to Europe over the next three years – in 1913 returning from England with his new bride, Dorothy.

"A smooth-talking, fast-selling artist whose promotional abilities to sell share in his companies and his salt claims was never rivalled," Hammerstein was an elusive figure. He rarely spoke with the media about his oil sands activities, suggesting that any knowledge of the oil sands that he might have gained was actually the property of his syndicate. Not surprisingly, the Alberta government received many complaints about Hammerstein – for example, from a widow concerned about her father's investment. Shortly before Hammerstein died in St. Albert, Alberta in 1941, age 76, he suggested that her 97-year-old father's investment would "soon pay off."[116]

At one point, the *Edmonton Capital* newspaper reported that he had been killed "while engaged in promoting a revolution" in Paraguay. Subsequent editions carried objections from Hammerstein, who said reports of his death had been "greatly exaggerated."[117] Nothing much ever came of Hammerstein's discoveries. Indeed, toward the end of his life he gave a baffling commentary on his search for oil in the Athabasca to a *Calgary Herald* reporter. It is unlikely to have been coincidence that, when he conducted this interview, his oil sands properties were up for sale.

"At the time I drilled there was no object in bringing in a well, as gasoline and fine lubricating oil were not worth anything. In 1905-6-7, automobiles were a joke and aeroplanes not heard of," he said. "Therefore at the least suspicion of oil on the tools or the least bit of gas, I quitted. I drilled 14 wells in all, but looked to the future and had no intention whatever, of advertising the country.... The Dominion Government inspector certified to 8 of 10 barrels of petroleum, which was simply seepage. As mentioned above, I stopped at the first indication of oil, not wishing to bring in a supply which I could not handle. Therefore," he added, "the surface, in light of modern research has value, of a certainty, while the potential value of the under rights may be incalculable."[118]

From the vantage point of contemporary knowledge and experience with the areas where he worked, the suggestion that he stopped drilling to avoid bringing in supply which he could not handle was clearly a fabrication, unless he was talking about the production of brine. There is an early photo of Hammerstein standing near a brine well blowing wild, and he did return to the area in 1925 to help establish the Alberta Salt Company with John Gillespie. That company closed down two years later.

Hammerstein's efforts to cash in on his lands failed miserably. In the 1930s, he offered the properties to both Imperial Oil Ltd. and Royal Dutch Shell – first at $250,000 and later at a "Depression discount" of $110,000. Neither company took him up on the offer. Eventually, executors of the Hammerstein estate sold the 11,000 acres to Sun Oil Company of Philadelphia, but a court case ensued and the properties went instead to Territory Oil Company. In 1995, Suncor Energy – the Canadian descendent of Sun Oil – acquired the freehold lands that had become part of Hammerstein's syndicate so many years before. Given that scholars have found his ventures marked with "wild speculation and fraud,"[119] it is ironic that seven decades later he was inducted into the straight-laced Canadian Petroleum Hall of Fame, with endorsement from the Petroleum History Society.

## THE COYNE AFFAIR

Another questionable character was A.F.A. Coyne, a Scottish immigrant, who took over Great Northern Oil and Asphalt Company (GNOA; founded 1911) in 1915. With that effort began his controversial six-year career as an oil sands promoter. More interesting than his efforts to produce oil were the machinations he used to advance his personal interests.

By 1917 GNOA's financial affairs were such that it could not afford to pay its development costs. Coyne's solution was to transfer its properties for shares in another company he had formed, Northern Production Company. This share exchange gave Coyne the biggest block of shares in the new entity, and GNOA investors soon called foul. Citing a number of irregularities, a group of GNOA investors alleged "that an attempt was being made to plunder the company."[120] There is some evidence that he used forgery as a business tool. On one occasion, for example, he appears to have witnessed a signature which did not quite match that person's normal signature.

After leaving Northern Production in 1919 (probably at the insistence of its shareholders), the company held two meetings to discuss his latest plan for the company. After the second of those meetings the company's new president, John Taylor, wrote to the Minister of the Interior that he "found it practically impossible to carry out the duties of my office owing to the actions of Mr. Coyne and the Secretary-Treasurer who have failed to account for the activities of the Company or for its funds and refuse to produce books and records....The whole scheme of A.F.A. Coyne is to defraud the Public by means of obtaining control of the equipment and changing the name of the Company, when he cannot get any further assistance, after squandering the money entrusted to his care for honest development work which he failed to do."[121]

Coyne was associated with two other companies, which may have included well-heeled investors from Britain. In Canada his last entrepreneurial plan was in 1920, when he proposed to develop a natural gas business for the town of Athabasca. The town went bankrupt before he could achieve his goal. His reputation in tatters, Coyne returned to the UK. He last entered Canada's historical record in 1936 when, in a letter to newly-elected Social Credit Premier William Aberhart, he offered to return to Alberta to develop an oil industry based on the Athabasca oil sands.

Such characters as Hammerstein and Coyne were representative of the boosterism, stock promotion and speculation so common in the newly formed province, which was experiencing considerable growing pains. Orderly development in a rapidly growing place with seemingly endless opportunity was hard to maintain. The greedy enthusiasm that motivated many people made the job more difficult. Outrageous though they may have been, however, Hammerstein's and Coyne's misdeeds took place in a period of progress for the oil sands.

# CHAPTER 3

# Serious investigation

———

*"Greater co-operation is desirable between Government and private*
*investigators and between the private investigators themselves."*

— SIDNEY ELLS, 1926

THE VOLATILITY OF PRICES IN unregulated markets is astonishing, as a pricing table in Ida Tarbell's great work illustrated. She noted that oil averaged $20 per barrel in 1859, but $0.52 two years later. She listed high, low and average prices during the 44 years prior to her book's publication in 1904. In that free-market environment, it was not unusual for a year's highest monthly price to be more than double that of its lowest month. [122] Production costs were low, so producers could make money despite modest demand and ample supply.

That was not true for the oil sands, however. To get to Fort McMurray in the early days, travellers had to go about 150 kilometres north of Edmonton to the Athabasca River. There they would board a scow and ride a dangerous river with many rapids. The return trip was upstream, so for that voyage a team of workers towed the scow from the banks. As winter neared and the river froze, of course, Athabasca became essential inaccessible, except by dogsled.

The only practical solution was to build railways, and in 1906 Alberta proposed to do so. Alberta's early schemes raised cries of scandal, however. The newly-minted province began granting charters for railway construction —

charters which originally included a line called the Athabaska Railway. Within three years, the province had granted 1,761 miles of rights-of-way to three railways, which would eventually become the Alberta and Great Waterways Railway (A&GW), from Edmonton to Waterways.[123]

The provincial government of Alexander Cameron Rutherford, a Liberal, had provided loan guarantees for A&GW that exceeded the cost of construction, had guaranteed interest rates above market, and was accused of exercising insufficient oversight over railway operations.

Opponents spilled tubs of ink and squandered endless volumes of hot air on these issues, but in the 1909 election Rutherford's Liberal party won 37 of the Legislature's 41 seats. Four years later the Rutherford government issued a new charter for A&GW to another promoter, J.D. McArthur. The following year construction began from the central Alberta hamlet of Carbondale. It reached Lac La Biche two years later, the community of Draper in 1922 and its terminus at Waterways in 1925.

## RESOURCE OWNERSHIP

The fact that the Prairie Provinces did not own their resources was the source of much political turmoil and fodder for many premiers' meetings from Confederation until the advent of the Great Depression. In the end, Parliament approved transfer-of-resources legislation for the prairies – to a large extent through the tireless diplomacy of Prime Minister Mackenzie King, but with important feedback from other premiers, including Alberta's John Brownlee, at a final summit in 1929. Once agreed, the documents were signed on December 14, 1929. The legislation, which transferred resource ownership effective October 1, 1930, required Royal Assent, and Britain's Privy Council signed the bill into law on July 10, 1930. [124] Resources within the Prairie Provinces were thus swept out of federal jurisdiction.

Markets continued to gush with oil for a few years after the Great War, as the petroleum industry continued to develop new supplies around the world. And the widespread use of crude oil cracking using the Burton-Humphreys process meant that gasoline production could more than keep up with the increasing numbers of vehicles in use. The result was lowering oil prices and companies felt a need to respond.

The economics of this period were unparalled in Canadian history. A period of high inflation followed the Great War. Soldiers came back to an extremely strong economy with many jobs but commodities and manufactured goods in short supply. The rapid rise in prices made it difficult to do business, and this led to what merchants called the "buyer's strike" of 1920. Prices collapsed and deflation took hold. Firms had to liquidate inventory well below cost, and businesses began to go down. According to historian Michael Bliss, 2,451 companies went under in 1921; 3,695 the following year. Even the Great Depression didn't see so many business failures in a single year. [125]

While we tend to think of the Roaring 20s as a period of economic good times followed by the disaster of the Depression, the reality is that both decades presented economic challenges. It is important to understand activity in the oil sands in the context of two quite different kinds of economic hardship. One was that the world was oversupplied with oil – especially from the United States, Iran and Venezuela. The other was that no one in the world seemed to want primary commodities like grain and lumber. "In wheat, pulp and paper, minerals, and most other commodities, the world was awash in productive capacity," said Michael Bliss. "The buildup had originally been induced by demand during the Great War; it only partially slowed in the early 1920s, and was stimulated again by heavy American lending late in the decade."[126] Thus, experimenters testing early oil sands systems faced technical challenges, but also the economic barrier of markets well-supplied with more desirable, low-cost conventional oil.

In 1928, US oil prices were high but threatened by cheap oil from Iran and Venezuela. Accordingly, in August representatives of Shell, BP, Standard (now ExxonMobil) and other large companies discretely met at Achnacarry Castle in the Scottish Highlands to fix prices. Over a two-week period, they created the "Gulf Plus" system, by which world oil was set at the price in the Gulf of Mexico plus standard freight charges. This eliminated the prospect of BP supplying cheap oil from Iraq to European consumers, for example. Shell, BP and the sixteen largest American oil companies signed on, and the arrangement added greatly to the bottom line. Although modified several times, the system lasted for a decade. "Most of the world's oil resources were in the hands of the big oil companies," wrote Anthony Sampson, "and the agreements succeeded in their main object of maintaining stable prices at the American levels, and of limiting competition inside each country. The Rockefeller monopoly had evolved, with apparent inevitability, into a global cartel."[127]

## SIDNEY ELLS AND THOMAS DRAPER

As we have seen, the federal government's Sidney Ells had begun to investigate the oil sands at the beginning of the First World War when the British Admiralty was seeking to diversify sources of supply for the Imperial Navy. Although involved in oil sands research from the beginning, Ells became an outsider to oil sands research for several reasons.

One was his sometimes off-putting personality. Entrepreneur Thomas Draper, for example, once ordered him to leave his property, accusing him of being "arrogant" and "antagonistic."[128] According to Ferguson, "The considerable uproar surrounding Ells must be seen as an influential factor in the shift in initiative from federal to provincial governments and the relations between research groups in the 1920s."[129] And according to Paul Chastko "Ells never seems to have accepted that his work, though original and important, was sloppy."[130] Also, of course, in the 1920s the federal government agreed to yield resource ownership to the Prairie Provinces, with the result that the oil sands deposit became Alberta's responsibility. As a matter of principle, the province took responsibility for both regulation and scientific research.

Sidney Ells' initial review of the area around Fort McMurray involved only a summer season of tramping around the Peace Country countryside. Working with the Parks Department, he had 580 acres of prime oil sands property just outside the village of Fort McMurray designated the Horse River Reserve. He conducted much of his research on those lands. Ells was a gifted artist, and the maps and sketches he drew during his various expeditions were as important as his field notes. Indeed, his sketches generally give a clearer sense of how oil sands systems worked than did the photographs of the day. During more than 30 years with the Department of Mines, he prepared 26 official oil sands reports and 15 maps of the region.

Historian Earle Gray's brief account of Ells' expedition to the oil sands gave a sense of the difficulties of travel in that period, but also of the energy Ells put into his task. "It was pioneering under conditions as difficult as any fur trader ever faced – travelling by foot with a 70-pound backpack the 250 miles over trackless muskeg and forest between Edmonton and Fort McMurray; camping out under northern stars at temperatures as low as -40°C; hauling on a tracking line 20 hours a day to help pull barges up the Athabasca River," he said.[131]

Ells had set out from Athabasca Landing (north of Edmonton) with a 30-foot scow, a 22-foot freight canoe and a "crew of three white men and an alleged native pilot."[132] It took the party only nine days to cover the 240 miles to Fort McMurray by floating downstream. According to Gray, "in the following three months Ells' party located 247 tar sands outcrops extending over a distance of 185 miles along the banks of the Athabasca and tributary rivers, and collected more than 200 samples from hand-augured holes to depths of five to 17 feet. It took 23 days, with Ells and a 12-man crew of natives pulling 20 hours a day on a track line, on the return trip which brought out the first meaningful tar sand samples."[133] In the early winter months of 1915, Ells shipped out 60 tons of tar sands from McMurray to Edmonton by horse team "in temperatures ranging from 20 to 50 below zero [°F] and without tents for men or horses."[134]

Labs in Ottawa and in Pittsburgh tested Ells' oil sands samples to find ways of extracting and processing the bitumen. "Ells and his associates tried centrifuges, solvents, distillation, and hot water. The most encouraging results were obtained at the Mellon Institute of Industrial Research in Pittsburgh where hot water and varying amounts of acidic and alkaline reagents were used in three types of flotation cells."[135]

To make the oil sands commercial, he proposed using it for road-paving. One notable experiment began in 1916, when Ells shipped tons of oil sand to Edmonton for a road-paving experiment. The pavement survived, without much need for repair, until the 1950s.[136] The following year the Northern Alberta Railway was completed to within 17 miles of Fort McMurray (it was another 10 years before the final stretch was built). This access provided Ells with the opportunity to try out his idea, by making the shipment of large volumes of oil sand to urban areas less expensive and less challenging.

Ells continued the paving material tests in the 1920s, collaborating with entrepreneur Thomas Draper, and saw roads as far afield as Camrose, Jasper and Ottawa getting the oil sands treatment. He also arranged for test drilling – not for production purposes, but strictly to analyse the core. He invested a great deal of time and energy measuring geologic features, mapping terrain and cataloguing oil sands specifications. In a 1926 report he wrote that "commercial development will be possible when, for any reason, the cost of well production and its derivatives reaches a point approximating the cost of production of hydrocarbons from bituminous sands. Such development implies adequate financial resources, and should not be undertaken by men of small capital or by those who desire quick returns on their investment. Meanwhile," he added, "it appears that much duplication of effort exists, and that greater co-operation is desirable between Government and private investigators, and between the private investigators themselves."[137]

Tenacious to a fault, entrepreneur Thomas Draper did make a profit from this business. The scion of an oil equipment manufacturer active in Petrolia, Ontario, he first saw the oil sands in 1920, and received a lease in late 1922. One of the conditions the federal government imposed was that he was to construct and extraction plant within 18 months at minimum cost of $30,000 and promised to operate it continuously for at least six months annually. However, in its first year of operation, 1924, his plant burned to the ground. He rebuilt it over the winter, and the following summer claimed that he was processing oil sands into oil. However, it turned out that he was actually mining the oil sands ore and delivering it for road paving and hot water separation experiments in Edmonton. According to one commentator, "The load had certainly been processed, but not by Draper."[138]

Undeterred, from 1922 to 1926 his McMurray Asphaltum and Oil Company mined more than 1,500 tons of oil sands for Alberta Research Council tests and experiments. In addition, Draper continued to mine and sell ore from his property for road and railway platform construction and for paving roads and streets. He actually supplied oil sand for paving a portion of Parliament Hill and Wellington

Street in Ottawa, as well as for streets in Medicine Hat, Vegreville, and Camrose, Alberta. He received four dollars per ton for this unique paving material.

Of course, Draper had received the lease on condition that he produce oil from it, rather than supply ore to researchers and street pavers. In the end, reflecting advice from Sidney Ells, federal authorities revised his company's lease to allow for the shipment of a certain amount of bituminous sand annually in lieu of the operation of the treatment plant. By the mid-1930s, Draper had had enough. He returned to Port Huron, Michigan, where he became president of the family business, Draper Manufacturing Co. He died there in 1962.

Draper "worked tirelessly in building up a business using the tar sand he quarried for road and sidewalk projects in and around Edmonton and central Alberta," according to Karl Clark's daughter and biographer, Mary Clark Sheppard. "His quarry was of particular interest to Clark because the progress of (Draper's) digging into the cliff face provided opportunities for collecting tar sand samples previously inaccessible."[139]

Sidney Ells had bitumen in his blood, and he stayed on top of research long after retirement in 1954. However, he resented the fact that his contributions received little acknowledgement during his lifetime, and toward the end of his life wrote a self-serving memoir about his years in the field. In that document he quoted another giant from early oil sands history, Max Ball.

"S.C. Ells may well be called the father of the Alberta bituminous sand research and development," Ball said or wrote in 1950. "He made the first – and as yet the only – comprehensive maps of the area in which they lie. He made the first systematic study of the methods for separating the bitumen from the sands. He first developed and demonstrated the principal of hot water separation through pulping the bituminous sands and recovering the separated bitumen in a flotation cell. For thirty-five years in the face of indifference and skepticism, he has been the courageous and unremitting advocate of the value and importance of bituminous sand deposits."[140]

Many historians would argue that Ball is overstating the case. Ells' complex personality notwithstanding, however, he was a man of considerable drive, enthusiasm and talent. His field illustrations were excellent and, as his memoirs illustrate, he was also a careful and sometimes inspired writer.

After retirement, he wrote and published a volume of poetry titled *Northland Trails*. A poem[vi] titled "Epilogue"[141] is a dreamy but plaintive assertion of the value of his life as a northern pioneer.

"Ells was the pioneering geologist, who spent many years studying the characteristics and behaviors of various regions in the deposit," said Clement Bowman, who was himself an oil sands pioneer. By contrast, he said, the Alberta Research Council's Dr. Karl A. Clark "was the experimentalist....His intuitive approach led him to an understanding of the mechanism of the separation process long before corroborating data were collected."[142]

## OIL SANDS SCIENTIST
Ells' pioneering energies were not rewarded with a commercial project during his working career. However, he was a guest of honour at the official opening of the Great Canadian Oil Sands plant in 1967. After years of struggle, GCOS became the first truly commercial oil sands plant. The man who made

---

vi  Here are the verses:
"I asked not stately man-made shaft of stone, / Within some crowded city of the dead, / One of a mighty host, - and yet alone, / While restless feet hurry above my head.
"Out on a wind-swept ridge let me lie, / A rugged twisted pine my marker rude, / Where owls' deep call and loons' sad wavering cry, / Alone will break my peaceful solitude.
"Yet not alone beneath my tree I'll lie, / For all about me furry things will play, / While stately antlered monarchs wander by, / Friends of the long, long trails of yesterday.
"In tugging boughs that toss against wild sky, / The roaring gale will shout an anthem deep, / while whispering winds will croon a lullaby, / and gently lull me fast asleep! Asleep!
"Faint grow the trails my buckskinned feet have trod, / Faint the old landmarks, faint the headlands bold, / Fades afterglow, lengthen the shadows broad, / While flickering camp-fire fades to ashes cold.
"But through the gathering mists I see afar, / Other fair woodlands under cloudless skies, / And in the 'happy hunting grounds' once more, / I'll take the trail, – to greet a new sunrise!"

**Karl Clark**

that first oil sands project possible was Ells' former colleague, friend and rival. Karl Clark didn't make the opening, however; he had died nine months earlier of cancer.

Clark was the foremost "oil sands scientist" — the title his daughter gave to a volume of letters he wrote mostly during his working years. That fat volume includes her excellent biography of the man. A chemist by training and a native of Georgetown, Ontario, Clark invented the hot water separation process which has been in use in mineable sections of the Athabasca oil sands since the 1930s.

Born in 1888, at age 32 he joined the Research Council of Alberta as an engineer. He first successfully separated oil from the oil sands in 1923 in a small plant built on the University of Alberta campus. In a recent volume of popular biographies, Brian Brennan wrote that Clark had "used the family washing machine as part of his experimentation."[143] After publication, however, he received a phone call from Mary Clark Sheppard saying such a thing had never happened. "If true, the tar-like goo would have totally destroyed the washer."[144]

In 1924, Clark established a large test facility at the Dunvegan railway yards in northeast Edmonton. In the 1930s he joined the faculty of the University, but returned to the Research Council from 1943-47. He then became head of the University's Mining and Metallurgy Department. He retired in 1954 and died in Victoria, B.C., in 1966.

Clark was instrumental in developing the design of the Alberta Government Oil Sands Project plant at Bitumount in the late 1940s, and in designing the plant facilities for the Great Canadian Oil Sands Company complex near Ft. McMurray in the 1960s. That innovation was the most important development from the oil sands' early years. Large-scale commercial production would take another 40 years to arrive, but as a young man Clark had created what became a transformational industrial process.

Like Ells, Clark began his career as a research scientist with the federal government's Geological Survey. The lab he worked in was soon transferred to the Mines Branch, with Clark going along with the lab. Still a young man, in June 1917 his boss asked him to make sense of the document on the oil sands Sidney Ells had prepared just before going overseas with the armed forces. With some trepidation, Clark and a more senior colleague, ceramicist J. Keele, prepared the document for publication. That was Clark's introduction to the oil sands.

At that time the federal government was the owner of all mineral resources in the Prairie Provinces and the Northwest Territories, and Ottawa wanted more information about the oil sands. Accordingly, the federal Mines Branch dispatched him to Alberta to investigate whether the oil sands would make a good road-paving material. Only one year after Clark first saw the oil sands, in 1920 President H.M. Tory of the University of Alberta appointed him research professor at the University of Alberta, asking Clark "to find a way of bringing the Athabasca tar sands into utilization."[145]

Clark went on to develop the hot water extraction process which formed the basis of the process utilized by the two large mining/upgrading plants in operation at Fort McMurray. In chemical terms, Clark had created a colloidal suspension – the suspension of a solid in a liquid. According to Mary Clark Sheppard, "this happened in 1919 but he was told to stop the research...the orders 'came down from on high.' She believes that it was because Ells had returned from the war and that Ottawa and Alberta were fighting about [ownership of] the bituminous oil sand resources."[146]

Clark continued work on the oil sands for the Scientific and Industrial Research Council of Alberta (better known as the Alberta Research Council, or ARC), which has since evolved into a group of technical think-tanks known as Alberta Innovates, but throughout this book is represented as ARC. The first such provincial research organization in Canada, ARC's mandate included oil sands research. From this launching point, Clark spent the rest of his career studying the chemistry of the oil sands – beginning with a focus on whether there was a practical way to separate the bitumen from the grains of sand it was attached to. [147]

A year after being hired, Clark wrote to University of Alberta president Dr. H.M. Tory that "I have been more fortunate than there was any reason to expect to have succeeded during one year in bringing to light and correlating the hidden properties of the tar sands and the relations between its constituents and other substances which were needed to block out the various operations, of which I am now making use, to bring about what looks like a very promising separation of the tar sand bitumen from the mineral matter (with) which it is associated."[148]

Such optimism may have reflected a young man's hubris; as the later story of the oil sands illustrates, there were clearly many large obstacles yet to overcome. However, "the value of Clark's contribution to the oil sands effort... is beyond question," according to Paul Chastko. "He systematically investigated many claims made by Ells and remained instrumental in developing and promoting a commercial extraction process. He confirmed that the sands were the physical product that remained after lighter substances – natural gas, for example – escaped leaving behind natural asphalt. Most important, Clark determined that the tar sands were not a direct source of gasoline or kerosene given the state of refining techniques in the 1920s. Through a process known as 'destructive distillation,' tar sand did yield some petroleum products."[149] To get maximum value out of bitumen, it needed to be processed through a Burton still.

## HOT-WATER SEPARATION

In 1922, Clark hired Sidney Blair as his assistant at the University of Alberta. A native of Parry Sound Ontario, Blair was born in 1897. From 1917 to 1919 he was a flying instructor with the Royal Air Force, and received his B.Sc. in Mining from the University of Birmingham in 1922.

On his return to Canada he registered as a graduate student at the University of Alberta, centering his attention on the oil sands at Fort McMurray and working both in the laboratory and in the field with Karl Clark. His Master's thesis was titled "An Investigation of the Bitumen Constituent of the Bituminous

Sands of Northern Alberta." Once accepted in 1924, he became a research engineer working for the Alberta Research Council (ARC). Together, he and Clark produced several papers on the oil sands.[150]

Quite different in character, Clark was a modest intellectual while Blair was "worldly, self-confident and outgoing." They worked well together for three-and-a-half years at the University of Alberta, and built the first bench model of Clark's hot-water separation plant. The following year ARC constructed an experimental oil sands separation plant near the railway yards near Dunvegan, the Edmonton terminus of the Northern Alberta Railway, to give the plant better access to oil sands ore from Athabasca.

The plant processed only 100 tons of raw oil sands in 1924. The following year, an improved facility processed five times as much. Clark's hot water extraction process involved mixing oil sands, hot water and caustic soda in a large rotating drum. This separated bitumen from sand, producing a hot, viscous liquid that could be upgraded into synthetic oil. The following year, the Dunvegan plant was disassembled and reconstructed at a new location along the Clearwater River in 1929 – the same year the Alberta Research Council patented Clark's findings to protect his work. This was the first larger-scale test of Clark's design, although ARC wanted Clark and Blair also to test the oil sands as a paving material. Indeed, in 1927 they co-authored a report which identified them as representing ARC's Road Materials Division.[151]

Blair left Edmonton in 1926, joining the Universal Oil Products Company's laboratories in Chicago to take part in oil-cracking research. He then went to work for a Universal subsidiary company known as Trinidad Leaseholds Limited, working as development manager at an asphalt refinery.[152] He returned to Canada in 1949 as an engineering consultant and vice-president of Canadian Bechtel Limited, a subsidiary of privately-owned Bechtel Corporation – at the time, the world's largest engineering and construction firm. As we shall see, he then played an important role in the later development of the resource.

In 1928 Karl Clark received a patent for his hot water extraction process – a process that is still the basis of surface-mined oil sand projects. The patented process involved mixing oil sands, hot water and caustic soda in a large rotating drum. By steaming the mixture, and maintaining a high temperature, Clark had found that oil readily separates from the sand. To understand hot-water bitumen processing, it is important to understand some of its characteristics. Bitumen is a "semisolid, viscous, dense material that varies in consistency. It is heavier than water and does not flow at room temperatures...An important feature of (oil sands) is the presence of a thin film of water that surrounds each grain of sand separating the bitumen from the sand. This important property facilitates separating bitumen from the sand when hot-water extraction is used."[153]

Clark's system used hot water and a chemical reagent. "The crude bitumen contained about 30 per cent by weight of emulsified water, and 0 per cent of clay and sand," he explained. "The bitumen itself is a very soft form of asphalt. It is too soft at ordinary temperatures for the penetration tests used with pavement asphalts, but too viscous to pour except in the most sluggish fashion. Heated to 100° C it is about as fluid as crude oil is at ordinary temperatures."[154]

Although raw bitumen was usable mostly for roofing tar and water-proofing fence-posts, as the 1920s moved on new technologies began to develop. While Clark's initial effort was to continue seeking a waterproof coating for road construction, he soon realized the importance of the oil sands as a source of refined oil products. In his earliest days as a researcher, refining technology was primitive, and there seemed little hope of commercially getting gasoline or other automotive fuels out of bitumen. Noting that the number of motor vehicles had grown from 17,764 in 1922 to 39,955 in 1928, he said the "conversion of heavy oils into high yields of gasoline is now a matter of every day commercial operations."[155] Therein, he believed, lay the future of the oil sands.

Clark's research continued throughout the Depression, even though most of the research staff at the Council lost their jobs and the province famously defaulted on its debt. However, the provincial government revived the organization in December, 1942, nearly 10 years after it had effectively ceased operations. According to Chastko, "Many other discoveries emerged from [Clark's] long and tireless years of investigation into the sands. He (was) instrumental in developing and promoting a commercial extraction process. He confirmed that the sands were the physical product that remained after lighter substances – natural gas, for example – escaped leaving behind natural asphalt."[156]

Toward the end of his career, in 1949 Clark published six "statements" describing the chemistry of the oil sands. His description noted, for example, that if there is too much clay associated with the oil sand ore, separation "does not take place satisfactorily." A landmark in oil sands chemistry, to this day they are an accurate and valuable chemical description of the oil sands deposits.

Clark was clear that the best way to use the oil was as a separate commodity. Selling bitumen "as an asphalt emulsion should be considered," he said. "The use of such emulsions in construction work is growing rapidly and plants for their manufacture are being established in all parts of the country."[157] While bitumen would be an expensive product to use for this purpose, using it on local materials would be cheaper than large-scale transport of oil sand. He added that the demand for road-building oil emulsions would "make economic and profitable bituminous sand development possible. Preparation of emulsion would be a simple and convenient way of inaugurating development work which would lead on to the larger and more alluring field of gasoline manufacture."[158]

Although no one doubts the importance of Clark's discoveries and contributions, his daughter and biographer noted the irony that "his name is unconnected with any of the patented processes under which the commercial industry operates today, even though hot water separation is employed in all operations that mine oil sand. Syncrude developed a series of its own patents…"[159] She added that Great Canadian Oil Sands – the first large oil sands project, now owned by Suncor – began its operations under a patent clearly based on the work of Karl Clark and awarded to Robert Fitzsimmons in 1932.

## JACOB ABSHER

The earliest efforts to develop underground processes go back to 1910, when a Pittsburgh-based outfit, the Barber Asphalt and Paving Company, drilled a bore hole into a bitumen reservoir and pumped in steam to liquefy the oil. The experiment failed.

In the early 1920s, other *in-situ* experiments also took place, but they were not commercially successful. Jacob Absher was the earliest persistent experimenter with *in-situ* production, and the first important entrepreneur to develop underground processes that could coax oil out of the ground. "Every disappointment and every set-back was met with the incredible good humour of J.O. Absher, " Joseph Fitzgerald wrote. "Again and again he tried, until finally he won the assistance of some of the best of the oil sands scientists. Not even personal injury could stop him from trying to tame the process he believed in."[160] Although this Montana native ultimately failed, he was the first great pioneer behind the technologies that mastered the oil sands 75 years later.

He incorporated the Bituminous Sand Extraction Company in the mid-1920s and began his *in-situ* experiments in 1926. He undertook many experiments and, so doing, drew the interest of Sidney Ells and Karl Clark both. Absher tried using steam to liquefy the bitumen so it could flow to the surface. He also tried igniting fires within his wells. While none of these experiments led to commercial production, Absher was enthusiastic about the results of each of his experiments. According to Clark, Absher was "a persevering, resourceful, enthusiastic worker. He is not a trained engineer or scientist. He is of the intelligent foreman type."

"The general objective Mr. Absher has in view is the winning of the oil from the bituminous sands *in-situ*, or in other words, the avoiding of the necessity of mining the sands," Clark wrote. "First he tried drilling a well into the bituminous sand formation, heating the sands by injecting steam and then recovering the heated bitumen which would flow into the well at the elevated temperature," Clark said. "This scheme did not work and besides, Mr. Absher became convinced that it would be too costly in heat in any case. He then conceived the idea that the heat cost could be avoided by making the bituminous sand supply the fuel. To do this, he would set fire to the bituminous sands and distill oils out of it, the oil vapours escaping up the drill hole to be caught, condensed and collected. Trial of the idea showed that the fire could be started and maintained. But it was such a fierce fire that it burnt up all the casing and pipes in the well."[161]

About Absher's 1926 steam injection experiment, a member of the crew wrote that "with our process we succeeded in bringing up vast amounts of sand and tar which flung itself over the countryside in much the same manner as a gusher."[162] In the end, Absher was unable to produce commercial volumes of bitumen from the oil sands. Whatever the case, his activities ended as the Great Depression raged. This important oil sands pioneer left Waterways "but did not return," Clark said.[163]

It is ironic that the first important oil sands development took place during the Great Depression, when economic activity was awful, oil prices low and oil supplies abundant. Unsurprisingly, the Second World War stimulated government interest in the resource. So did increasing automobile ownership.

CHAPTER 4

# From war to war

———

*"The accessible billion [barrels of oil] can be considered as a reserve*
*of immediate importance, the other billions as a reserve against the*
*day when oil prices are considerably higher than they are now."*

— MAX BALL, 1940

BY 1918, 29,250 CARS WERE rattling along Alberta's unpaved roads; by 1926, that number had reached 65,101 — a number which included 4,362 trucks and 646 taxis.[164] Two years later the United States was home to 8,890,000 registered vehicles. Petroleum had become critical to economic growth, and American production, 443 million barrels of oil per year, dominated global supply.[165]

In the 1930s a number of events that affected petroleum development in Alberta took place in quick succession. First, the federal government's Natural Resources Transfer Act turned over ownership of Crown minerals within their borders to Alberta, Saskatchewan, and Manitoba. Second, the City of Calgary asked the Provincial Utilities Board to cut the cost of household service by giving the city greater access to supplies from Turner Valley. Third, as the newly minted owner of provincial resources, the provincial government — led by the United Farmers of Alberta (UFA) — then levied a 5 per cent petroleum royalty on Turner Valley production, and enacted legislation creating the Turner Valley Gas Conservation Board to control wasteful flaring.

The Conservation Board's mandate was to ration Turner Valley production fairly among its numerous producers. Conceivably, this level of authority could bankrupt individual producers and, ordered to cut production by 95 per cent, one company appealed to the courts. Alberta won the case in the Supreme Court, but the victory was hollow: the court also ruled that production cuts could not be retroactively imposed on mineral leases issued before the 1930 resource transfer.[166] To a large degree this made the new board a toothless tiger. Alberta's first effort to regulate its energy resources went to naught when the federal government rejected Alberta's request for an amendment to the Natural Resources Transfer Act, to meet the terms of the court decision.[167]

## BIBLE BILL

However, during the term of Social Credit premier William ("Bible Bill") Aberhart, in 1938 Parliament passed an act transferring to the Alberta government all federal production licenses that predated the jurisdictional change in 1930. Of particular interest for this history, that included the oil sands leases issued to Hammerstein and others. The provincial government moved quickly to establish Alberta's second oilfield agency, the Petroleum and Natural Gas Conservation Board. The newly-formed board later underwent several name changes —Oil and Gas Conservation Board (1957 – 1971), Energy Resources Conservation Board (1971 – 1995), Alberta Energy and Utilities Board (1995 – 2007), once again the Energy Resources Conservation Board (2008 – 2012)[168] – until it took adopted its present name, the Alberta Energy Regulator.

Officially launched on July 1, 1937 Bill Knode was the chair of Alberta's second conservation board and Charles Dingman, a long-serving senior oil and gas official, was deputy chairman.

A nephew of Calgary Petroleum Products co-founder Archibald Dingman, Charles Dingman was a driller on the Turner Valley discovery well. He later became director of the petroleum and natural gas division of the Department of Lands and Mines and deputy chair of the Petroleum and Natural Gas Conservation Board from its inception in 1929 until he resigned in frustration in 1940, having been passed over three times for the top job.

The third board member was John Harvie, deputy minister of lands and mines. To further free the board from political pressure, the Oil and Gas Conservation Board was set up as a quasi-judicial agency akin to a law court, clearly separate as "a body politic and corporate" in its own right rather than a government department. The head office was located in Calgary rather than in the provincial capital of Edmonton. As the board gradually expanded its authority to coal mining and electricity as well, it established a practise of drawing its budget from equal contributions by the government and the industries being regulated.[169] Although by this time some oil formations at Turner Valley were being developed, it is worth noting that, even though Alberta's main energy commodity was natural gas, one of the regulator's major functions was to maintain oil prices

Policy-makers on the international stage also took steps to control oil prices. The first Lord Beaverbrook – Max Aitken,, an Anglo-Canadian businessman who served as Britain's Minister of Supply – reluctantly agreed during the Second World War to an American-sponsored Anglo-American Petroleum Agreement which "was, in fact, a direct link to the market management of the late 1920s and the 1930s, both to the 'As-Is' [clause] of Achnacarry and the Texas Railroad Commission. Its fundamental purpose was the same: to balance discordant supply and demand, to manage surplus, and to bring order and stability to a market laden with oversupply."[170] America's concern was that new supplies from the Middle East would drive down prices.

This arrangement began to fall apart in 1970, when Libya unilaterally increased its prices. The following year oil exporters signed further agreements on oil pricing in Teheran. The oil pricing system completely crumbled in 1973, when a cartel of national monopolies known as OPEC (the Organization of Petroleum Exporting Countries) became the most powerful player in setting world prices.

## ROBERT FITZSIMMONS AND BITUMOUNT

The most consistent theme in oil sands history is that of collaboration between government-funded science and profit-driven entrepreneurs. As Paul Chastko put it, "The interaction [among] four separate entities – the state, the oil industry, the scientific community, and the world petroleum market – created a dynamic and challenging environment capable of astonishing feats of cooperation and commerce."[171]

Government scientists had done some drilling near Fort McMurray in the late 19th century, but governments did not participate financially in an oil sands project until the 1940s. At that time both the federal and Alberta governments participated, but in different projects. The main focus from Ottawa's side was that the oil sands could be of value to the war effort. Alberta also supported oil sands development, but in the context that the oil sands were a provincial resource.

Karl Clark was conducting research in the Roaring Twenties, but it is unlikely he could have anticipated the importance of a small company incorporated in 1925. Robert Fitzsimmons's International Bitumen was a seminal event for the province. For the man himself it was a business disaster. For the oil sands industry, it was a breakthrough, although closely tied to events of the previous two decades.

Fitzsimmons was the key person in the initial development of Bitumount, and said he selected the site name in 1933. Born in Alberton, PEI, in 1881, he moved west in 1903. He first visited the Athabasca oil sands two decades later, and bought out the Alcan Oil Company's exploration rights – located 89 kilometres north of Fort McMurray – in 1923. Fitzsimmons unsuccessfully attempted to obtain crude oil by drilling, and then constructed a small oil separation plant. He used a hot water process to separate bitumen from the oil sand, making his first sale in 1930. Edmonton was the only city of any size in northern Alberta, so that is where he went to sell raw bitumen for setting pavement, but also as fence post dip and roofing tar.[172]

Bitumount used a process similar to Clark's hot-water separation process, but without the chemical additives and refinements. It was constructed on the cheap, mostly from scavenged parts. In essence, Fitzsimmons' approach was to crush the ore, heat it in hot water, divert it into settling tanks, then skim off the oily gunk that rose to the surface. These efforts were only half as efficient in terms of oil recovery as Clark had achieved with his process. The plant was designed to produce 750 barrels per day, but on a good day produced only 250.[173] However, in the early years the facility did generate a profit. After International Bitumen made its first deliveries, the *Edmonton Journal* gushed that "those shipments of absolutely pure bitumen are the first and second and only shipments in the history of McMurray tar sands to be made for commercial purposes and it certainly (augurs) well for the future development of the much talked of tar sands of northern Alberta."[174]

Fitzsimmons continually improved his hot water separation process and expanded the site in 1936 to include a small refinery – essentially, a refining still using a jerry-rigged version of the Burton-Humphreys process. The long-term significance of his operation and its successors cannot be overstated. As president of the International Bitumen Company (formed in 1927), Fitzsimmons expanded his plant into what, for that day and place, was a significant industrial complex.

He had a passion for the oil sands and he was as stubborn as a mule. Unfortunately for him, two storms were brewing. One was the Great Depression, during which demand and prices for almost every commodity, good and services cratered. The other was a flood of crude oil from Texas and Oklahoma, which drove down prices. In the Dirty Thirties prices were as low as $0.67 per barrel, reflecting lousy markets – too much supply, too little demand.

Sixty years later Tom Morimoto, who worked for a season at Bitumount, described the system as using steam supplied by two wood-fuelled, 50-horsepower boilers. "There was a plentiful supply of fuel," he wrote, "as there was an abundance of fire-killed spruce nearby. [However,] it required a gang of men to cut within the bush, another gang to load it onto wagons, and teamsters to drive the horse-drawn vehicles to the plant site. There, another gang had to saw it into cordwood lengths, using a gasoline-engine-driven power saw. Then, of course, the firemen had to feed the wood into the boilers' furnaces."

As Morimoto described the system, the boilers supplied steam. This "powered a large steam engine that drove most of the separation machinery, he said. "Steam also supplied power to reciprocating pumps for pumping the separated bitumen. Steam and hot water from the boilers were used in the separation process…. The main steam engine drove a huge flywheel, about 10 to 12 feet in diameter. To this flywheel were attached belts, which drove machinery. There were belts going in all directions to drive various machines."

Morimoto provided a detailed description of how the plant worked. "The raw tar sands feed was conveyed by a scoop operated by a dragline, which was powered by a 'donkey engine,' a wood-fired combination steam boiler and engine. The tar sand was dropped into a cold 'grizzly,' which was essentially a coarse screen composed of iron bars to get rid of any rocks," he said. "The tar sand was then mixed with hot water and steam and sent to a mixer – a vessel with paddles – to mix the tar sand and water into a pulp. This pulp was then led by gravity into a separation tank, a steel tank approximately 2.5 feet in length, with a rotating spiral screw about 12 inches in diameter at its bottom. Hot water and steam were injected into the separation tank to supply heat and to separate the bitumen from the sand – the bitumen floating to the top and the cleaned sands sinking to the bottom to be removed by the rotating spiral screw. The bitumen was removed by paddles that continually scraped the surface of the tank, depositing the bitumen in the surge tank from which it was pumped to the refinery. All the moving parts in the system were powered by the belts and pulleys driven by the main flywheel."[175]

By the time he had created this Rube Goldberg system, Fitzsimmons had spent the cash entrusted to him by International Bitumen's shareholders. Bitumen production and sales were slow, and cash flow problems began frustrating his dreams. In the vernacular of the period, his company was a day long and a dollar short. By the end of 1938, the company was insolvent.

Morimoto joined the project in 1937 as an 18-year-old radio operator. "The reason I started working in the plant is that one of the [radio] tubes [had] burned out. I sent out for spares and never got them. When that tube burned out, I didn't have any equipment. So, I started working in the plant." Soon the workers began to realize they weren't going to get paid. Some would "hitch a ride on a boat going north because the mines were starting up." Morimoto didn't leave the project until after freeze-up. He and the other unpaid workers walked across the frozen river to Fort McMurray. Fitzsimmons "was a very nice man," said Morimoto. "I think he was quite an honest man. He thought he was going to make a go of it, but he just got overwhelmed by not being able to finance the project. I think the poor man must've died broken-hearted because he lost everything."[176]

Fitzsimmons sought support in capital markets in eastern Canada and Chicago without success. In a final attempt to succeed, he established Tar Sands Products Limited in 1941 to sell International Bitumen Company products. The strategy didn't help, and he couldn't secure the $50,000 he needed to keep the plant running. Eventually, he applied to the provincial government for either a straight loan or an advance on bitumen for road paving.

## HERE COME THE CHAMPIONS

Fitzsimmons sought support in capital markets in eastern Canada and Chicago without success. In a final attempt to succeed, he established Tar Sands Products Limited in 1941 to sell International Bitumen Company products. The strategy didn't help, and he couldn't secure the $50,000 he needed to keep the plant running. Eventually, he applied to the provincial government for either a straight loan or an advance on bitumen for road paving. The province declined to help, and in 1943 Fitzsimmons sold the failing enterprise to a hard-nosed financier from Montréal, Lloyd Champion, reserving for himself a job as operations advisor. Frustrated, he left that position in 1944. By that time the plant had been sitting idle for five years, so Champion soon hired him back to get the facility in operation. Once Fitzimmons had succeeded at this task Champion fired him once more, with feeling.

As this drama unfolded J.B. Hamilton – a friend of Fitsimmons – published and sold a 24-page booklet describing the situation. Priced at $0.25 (a pricey $5.38 in 2016 funds), he dedicated the manuscript to Fitzimmons who, he said "fought a good fight, solved the problem and kept faith with his fellowman."[177] His focus, however, was to express outrage at the treatment Fitzimmons had received.

Hamilton's booklet provided black-and-white photographs of company facilities and of a bitumen deposit visible along the bank of the Athabaska River. The text reproduced letters on Fitsimmons' oil sands activity from the federal government's C.D. Howe, from Fitsimmons and from the Alberta government's oil controller, G.R. Cottrelle. It also provided a commentary on the profitability of tar and other products that Fitsimmons had already sold.

Most of all, it railed against the perceived unfairness Fitzimmons had received. Hamilton waxed indignant about Fitsimmons' plight, and to correct such wrongs in the future proposed the creation of a "public defenders court" in every province.

These courts would consist of judge and jury, and "deal with questions of the public good." Such a court would be, he wrote, "an instrument of value in the public life of this and any other country in which it is adopted."[178] Since such courts did not exist, he considered the polemics in his pamphlet to be the best substitute he could muster. Little more than a curiosity, his publication accomplished nothing, directly. It is helpful, though, to see it as the histrionics of a man with a reasonable idea, but a limited understanding of how regulation of Alberta's petroleum industry was already evolving.

In 1932 Alberta had created the Turner Valley Gas Conservation Board to prevent wasteful flaring and venting of natural gas. Six years later, the province passed the Oil and Gas Conservation Act, with the regulatory body renamed the Petroleum and Natural Gas Conservation Board. Hamilton did not see that energy regulators were becoming quasi-judicial bodies, with the authority to do just what he was suggesting for his public defenders courts.

The province declined to help, and in 1943 Fitzsimmons sold the failing enterprise to a hard-nosed financier from Montréal, Lloyd Champion, reserving for himself a job as operations advisor. Frustrated, he left that position in 1944. By that time the plant had been sitting idle for five years, so Champion soon hired him back to get the facility in operation. Once Fitzimmons had succeeded at this task, Champion fired him again.

Embittered, Robert Fitzsimmons later wrote and published a document to tell shareholders "what happened to prevent the company's success after it had reached the stage of commercial production of oil…and also to inform them how its accomplishments were nullified by obstructive tactics in government quarters."[179]

The cover page of his pamphlet illustrated the depth of his feelings. Self-published in 1953, its title proclaimed that it was "The truth about Alberta's tar sands" and asked, "Why were they kept out of production? What happened to International Bitumen Co. Ltd.? Who solved the problem of separation and pioneered the production of oil from these sands? Who stood to gain by suppressing their development?"[180]

Fitzimmons died alone in Edmonton in September, 1971. "It is doing great injustice to Canadian initiative, imagination and determination to allow the courage of men like Robert C. Fitzsimmons to be forgotten," wrote Joseph Fitzgerald.[181]

Champion had acquired Bitumount through a company named Oil Sands Limited. With Fitzsimmons out of the picture, in 1944 he transferred most of its assets to a holding company owned by himself and his wife, Ruby. He then arranged province of Alberta financing of $500,000 for a new and larger plant (costs eventually rose to $750,000), with construction to be undertaken by Oil Sands Limited. His pitch was that he would set up a large-scale demonstration project to investigate Karl Clark's extraction methods. Development dragged on until well after the war.

"The government is building a $500,000 fireproof pilot plant at Bitumount that should be in operation next July," the project's operating engineer, William Adkins, wrote in 1946. "Unless I miss my bet, we'll prove to the world that oil can be extracted from the tar sand at less than $1 per barrel, a figure that we believe would warrant a large-scale commercial development."[182] Adkins missed his bet, but his comments reflected the determination and optimism of oil sands pioneers – qualities which continue to characterize the industry.

## Max Ball and Abasand

In those early years pioneers came from many backgrounds. Oil sands historian Barry Ferguson described how an American engineer, James McClave, began working on a prototype hot water separation process for the oil sands in Denver, in 1921. McClave's successes encouraged American businessmen Max Ball, his partner Basil Jones and McClave himself to seek leases and build a commercial plant in the area. All three men had backgrounds in petroleum.[183]

One feature of the McClave process, a diluent mixer, represented an important innovation in the extraction process. "Mild abrasion in warm water breaks the films and gives a pulp of water and sand through which are disseminated particles of oil," Ball wrote. "In a properly designed flotation cell, the oil particles will be picked up by air to form bubbles that float to the surface.

"The froth thus formed is high in mechanically entrained water and mineral matter, which will not settle out because of the high viscosity and specific gravity of the oil," he added. Moreover, that production "quickly settles out if the oil is diluted with naphtha or kerosene, leaving a clean oil that can be pumped through a pipeline. The diluent can be knocked out in a refinery and returned for re-use."[184]

In 1929, Karl Clark received a letter from Ball, who wanted to investigate the possibility of investing in the sands. Given Sidney Ells' estrangement from many oil sands researchers, it is ironic that he went to Denver to meet with Ball to discuss prospects for developing production from the Athabasca deposit.[185] However, he represented Ottawa rather than a provincial government, and at that time the federal government still owned most of Alberta's minerals. After bearing witness to Ells' enthusiasm, Ball secured oil sands properties from the Dominion government – the last leases the feds issued.[186]

Ball and his associates formed Canadian Northern Oil Sand Product Ltd., which later became Abasand Oils Ltd. They received a federal lease on the Horse River and began negotiations with the province to erect and operate a separation plant capable of handling a minimum of 250 tons of oil sand per day. Site clearing began in January 1936. The group's original intention was to invest up to $150,000 in the project.[187]

Sidney Ells played an important role in arranging for Ottawa to issue leases to Abasand. The federal government owned mineral rights in the prairie provinces until 1930, at which time "the care, custody and control of the Alberta tar sands reverted to the Alberta Government, with one exception: The Horse River lease went to Max Ball," according to Robert McClements Jr.[188] The federal government liked the idea of the demonstration plant, and made development of the Abasand plant a condition of Ball's operation receiving Lease 4. "If that was successful then [Ball would also] be granted the six square miles further down. Even after mineral rights had been transferred to Alberta, he "continued negotiating with the province relative to the [six square mile] lease further down the river" — land which he believed his discussions with the federal government entitled him to.

McClements stressed that Ball did more than separate bitumen from sand. "He actually built a relatively sophisticated but small refinery. It produced gasoline, kerosene and, I think, fuel oil. I know that for a fact because I saw them. The druggist at Fort McMurray had samples of that material in his little office up above the drug store. So it is really not right to say that GCOS was the first to produce products from bitumen. It was Max Ball. He sold those products locally; a lot of them went downriver."[189]

Karl Clark's assessment was similar. "Mr. Ball's letter appealed to me at the time as being written by a man who had the ability to deal effectively with a problem of this sort even though he yet knew very little about the bituminous sands. I have learned since that he was on the staff of the U.S. Geological Survey for about six years, was one year with the U.S. Bureau of Mines, was then employed by a number of oil companies and during the last year or so has gone in for private consulting work."[190]

Ball had organized and administered the Western Pipeline Company and the Argo Oil Company, as well as the Glenrock Oil Company, the Marine Oil Company and the Royalty and Producers Corporation. In short, he was a successful businessman. Indeed, the only real failure in his career was his effort to produce bitumen from the Athabasca oil sands. A geologist by training, he had been involved in the industry since just after the turn of the century, when he was in his early twenties.

During his years in Canada he wrote a book titled *This Fascinating Oil Business*, published in 1940, which in its day was a standard petroleum text. His description of the Athabasca oil sands was typically optimistic. "...The oil is heavy, viscous, and asphaltic, but when subjected to a moderate temperature for reasonable time – say 685° [363°C] for 30 min. – it becomes a much lighter, more fluid oil comparable to that found in many oil fields," he wrote.[191]

"The latest United States Geological Survey estimate of the proved reserves of the world's known oil fields is about twenty-five billion barrels. The world's total production to date has been slightly more than thirty-one billion barrels," he wrote. "The oil sands of the Athabaska Valley, according to the Dominion

Mines Branch, contain at least a hundred billion barrels." He continued, "Once recovered, the oil is highly sensitive to refining temperatures and can be converted into all of the conventional products. Out of the hundred billion barrels in the deposit (the United States Bureau of Mines estimate places it at two hundred and fifty billion), perhaps a billion barrels can be easily mined; the remainder can only be won by shafting at considerable expense. The accessible billion can be considered as a reserve of immediate importance, the other billions as a reserve against the day when oil prices are considerably higher than they are now."[192]

Although scheduled to go into operation by September 1936, forest fires and delays in getting needed equipment held up plant construction. The following year, however, the equipment was mostly in place — a fractionating tower, a boiler and a variety of pipelines and other equipment. The products that came off the bubble tower included naphtha, diluent, kerosene oil and heavy asphalt.[193]

"It is hoped that the asphalt, which forms a very large proportion of the products of the operation described, can be sold at profit as high class asphalt and road oils," wrote Karl Clark. "But if and when this is not the case, the asphalt is to be sent to a battery of Burton stills and destructively distilled. The distillation will be sent back through the pipe still and fractionating column."[194]

In his book, Ball observed that mining oil sand was not a new idea. "This has been done in Pechelbronn [France][vii] ...and has been done on a small scale in one or two other places in Europe.... In Czechoslovakia a shaft is being sunk to mine oil sand from two hundred and sixty feet below the surface, and equipment is being installed for extracting the oil from the sand." As we shall see, a similar underground oil mine in the Soviet Union played a key role in transforming production from Canada's oil sands — but not until half a century after Ball published his book.

"The [Abasand] plant now being constructed for mining the famous oil sands of the Athabaska area, often referred to as 'tar sands,' which contain more oil than is known to exist in all the proven oil fields in the world," he continued.

---

vii Begun in the reign of Louis XIV in 1745, the Merkwiller-Pechelbronn oil sands mine continued producing until 1970.

"The part of the sand to be mined, a very small part of the whole deposit, lies in benches along valley walls and can be excavated by open-pit methods with no underground mining. The oil will be washed from the sand by hot water....The writer is too closely associated with the Canadian [project] to be disinterested [so] further discussion had better wait until the next edition of this book."[195]

## The Anglo Albertan Oil Refinery

Other activities were taking place in the oil sands during this period, and the story of the Anglo Albertan Oil Refinery deserves more than a footnote. In 1940 *The Winnipeg Tribune* reported that a company called Anglo-Albertan Oil Refinery would soon be supplying oil products to "the growing settlements of Waterways and Fort McMurray ... as well as in the more northerly mining district of Goldfields."

The newspaper cited Charles Gower, chemist, and president and general manager of the company. Although the company had no oil sands leases and had "acquired" the process in an undisclosed way, Gower seemed optimistic. The *Tribune* described the process as a "solvent procedure" which heated the raw material – presumably an oil sands mixture – to a "softening point." At that point, it dissolved the oil with a "pre-heated solvent." The circulatory solvent process would be one of "continuous operation."

The reporter said the solvent would be reclaimed by evaporation. The system would then introduce the bitumen "to the cracking furnace and refining unit" while the solvent was used to extract more bitumen from oil sands ore. According to Gower and his promotional brochure, loss of solvent from the system would be so small that it would "have little or no effect on the cost of operation and maintenance."[196]

Karl Clark first shed light on this proposal in a letter to L.E. Westman, the editor of a chemical journal. "The bituminous sand is first leached with petroleum distillate such as kerosene," he wrote, with the kerosene dissolving the bitumen from the sands. "The sand tailings from the leaching tank are, of course, saturated with the kerosene-bitumen solution. However, these tailings as they are dragged from the tank car are washed with the clean kerosene that is being constantly added to the tank along with the fresh bituminous sand. The final tailings leaving the tank are wet with practically clean kerosene. This kerosene is recovered from the tailings by a wash in water, the kerosene floating to the surface. The kerosene-bitumen solution, reasonably free from water and mineral matter, goes to a refinery for distillation." Such an operation would recover the kerosene for reuse in the leaching tank.[197]

In 1941, Gower received a patent for his process.[198] The following year, Clark told R.W. Boyle of the National Research Council that Gower's costs "would be higher than those of Abasand." For starters, using distillates would be costlier than using steam, and distilling it out of the process would also be pricier. And since Gower was using solvents, "all his apparatus must be vapour tight to prevent evaporation losses and fire losses, and at that, there would be losses. There is no such necessity in the Abasand process. The extraction apparatus is simple and open."[199]


## WARTIME NEEDS

Because of the wars raging in Europe, the oil sands were once again viewed as a resource with military potential. Mining at Abasand finally began in 1941, and in its first four months of operation the plant processed 18,475 tonnes of oil sand to produce 17,000 barrels of oil. The mining method found to be most effective involved drilling holes in the oil sand where blasting powder was inserted and triggered. The loosened sand was then loaded directly onto dump trucks and hauled to the separation plant. Then disaster struck a second time: a fire broke out in the Abasand power house.[200] This marked the project's end.

By 1942 Lloyd Champion's Oil Sands Limited had acquired International Bitumen, though that project did not contribute to the war effort.[201]

Concerned about potential fuel shortages in the west, in 1943 the federal government took over the plant under the War Measures Act, at one point considering investing $10 million into a project that would produce only 10,000 barrels of oil per day.[202] Because of the need for oil during the war, refining engineer Claude Humphreys was seconded from Imperial Oil to help get the project operating. His son, Bill, was old enough to work at the plant, just as chaotic management was bringing its wartime effort to an end.

Bill Humphreys worked there for a summer as a mechanic's helper, and described a plant with equipment that was huge for its day. "Besides a large diesel-operated shovel," the project used two "Mack dump trucks that had external chain drives...one on each side of the truck. Those chain drives would clog with sand, so periodically they had to be taken off and cleaned." He added that Abasand kept "an old drum out in the field that was full of oil and you'd have to take these chains off them, put them in hot oil to clean them. And then, the mechanics would put them back on again. So, this is a story of all of the equipment up there; the bulldozers that were in there they were always getting jammed up with the sand. You had to go in there with bars and try to clean the sand out...."

The plant used a version of Clark's hot water flotation process. "These trucks would dump [the ore] in an uphill ramp that ran into a hopper. [We also] had a little bulldozer there, the smallest one I've ever seen....We called it Number 22; it was just a little guy," Humphreys continued. The crew used these vehicles to "push the sand up into the hopper. From there it fell down into separation tanks with paddlewheels on sort of a chain drive. [The paddlewheels] would scrape the frothing off into a hopper [and] at the bottom the hopper had a slow moving screw that took the clean sand out. That sand was very clean." Fires at the plant were common. "They had a big cookhouse there and a wood-fired stove and it was sitting on a steel plate," he told me. "But, I guess it got over-heated one day. Then someone decided to pry up the plate and put out the fire," adding oxygen to it. Another time "the roof caught fire and one of the guys climbed up on the roof and put the fire out. But, they found out later that he was the one that set the fire. ...Why he set that fire, nobody knows. But he fell off the roof" and almost killed himself.[203]

Before completion, the Alberta government took over the plant, operated it experimentally in 1948 and closed it in 1949.

The federal government then decided to rebuild the plant but, through gross mismanagement, was successful only in spending large sums of money – about $2 million. Problems included inexperienced and arrogant management, the exodus of knowledgeable employees and their replacement with people with no expertise or background in the oil sands, and the inexplicable decision to sever ties with the few technical experts – Max Ball, Karl Clark and Sidney Ells, mainly – who might have helped the project succeed.[204] The federal government's Minister of Munitions and Supply, C.D. Howe, got so fed up that he made a rather grumpy statement to Parliament. "There seems to be some erroneous idea in the minds of many regarding these tar sands," he said. "Judging by what one hears at times, one would think that oil is running out of these sands, and that all that has to be done is to tap or pipe the oil and this country would overcome its serious oil shortage. [But] the facts do not bear out any such idea."[205]

A year later came the big fire. Bill Humphreys was "sitting in the house on a Sunday when my father got the phone call that the plant had burned down. And, you could hear at his end what it was…. Apparently there was a welder doing some repair work up there" and he sparked a fire. "There was oil residue all over the place. They had this fellow working there as a safety but it did catch fire and they couldn't stop it. So, the whole plant went up."[206] The date was June 16, 1945.

Flames spread to the nearby forest and threatened the bunkhouses and an explosives storage area. The federal government's Minister of Reconstruction C.D. Howe concluded that a new plant should not be built at Ottawa's expense, since the wartime urgency was over. In May, 1946 Abasand Oils announced its willingness to put into reconstruction $350,000 it had received from insurance if the federal government would match that sum. Ottawa refused, and "was prepared to weather the storm which broke out around its head when the decision was announced."[207] The storm broke, indeed.

Alberta politicians became deeply disenchanted with the federal government's efforts, and gave heated speeches in the Legislature. According to the Minister for Public Works, W.A. Fallow, "…not only had there been an apparent waste of public funds, (but the) whole development of the Athabasca oil sands is being systematically sabotaged."[208] He went on at length. "In summing up, Mr. Speaker, may I say that the pathetic flounderings of this gang of pussy-footing amateurs beggars description. In all my experience, I have never seen a more ridiculous attempt to pull the wool over the eyes of the people."[209]

Karl Clark used fewer adjectives. "Our politicians call it sabotage. But I think it is just government ineptitude and petty nonsense running wild."[210] Elsewhere he refers to a newspaper interview in which the president of Abasand said "the bituminous sands were either the world's biggest oil field or biggest flop. If the president of Abasand wished to have the sands turn out a flop, what has been going on is readily understandable."[211]

In later years, Bitumount and Abasand continued to influence the industry through leases they could bring to the table – leases that dated back to the work of Fitzimmons at Bitumount and Ball at Abasand. Like Fitzsimmons before him, Ball used his own money and money he was able to raise elsewhere. In the end, leadership and money were provided by the American firm Sun Oil Co., which at the time was a large integrated oil company. The next chapter tells that story.

Ball returned to the United States, and became special assistant to the Deputy Petroleum Administrator for War in Washington, D.C. In 1947, he was appointed director of the oil and gas division for the Department of the Interior. Max Waite Ball died August 28, 1954 in Washington, age 69. [212]


## ALBERTA GETS INVOLVED

It would be hard to overstate Ernest Manning's impact on Alberta's oil sands. Alberta's eighth premier, he recognized their potential and took steps to spur interest within what would soon become a rapidly-growing petroleum industry. First by providing provincial funding for Bitumount during the Second World War, his government provided political assistance for the embryonic industry during its most critical quarter century.

According to Edward Bell, who wrote a brief biography, "The poor farm boy with little formal education and fundamentalist religious beliefs guided the province's transition to modernity and affluence. He built the province largely by allowing private individuals and organizations to pursue their economic self-interest. Although there was regulation, taxation and substantial government spending, more than any other government in the country Manning's government embraced, albeit belatedly, the policies of market economics and small government. Decades after his retirement, his policies of balanced budgets, moderate taxation, and fiscal restraint became part of the conventional political wisdom in Canada. His critics are mainly those who believe in a more activist role for the state."[213]

In 1943 William Aberhart, then Premier and leader of the Social Credit party, died. Manning succeeded him, and faced a chaotic situation in respect to the oil sands. Nathan Tanner was the province's Minister of Mines and Lands, but Manning became the government's oil sands champion – perhaps not a great turn of phrase, given that he still had to deal with Lloyd Champion on the Bitumount project.

One of his first initiatives as premier had been to finance the experimental project at Bitumount, using a version of Karl Clark's hot-water process. During the war years, the province had agreed to provide $250,000 for a 200-ton-per-day project – later increased to $500,000 for a 500-ton-per day project. In a speech to the Legislature in 1944, Manning said "It has been established beyond question that a successful and efficient simple process exists for the separation of oil from the sands and for its refinement into commercial products. Members of the Government have inspected the plant while in actual operation and producing a sufficient volume of clear sand free of oil to prove the practicability of the process."[214]

Despite (possibly because of) government efforts to promote commercial oil sands development at Bitumount and Abasand as part of the war effort, one disaster followed another at the two pioneering plants. By the end of the war fire had destroyed both, and there was no commercial interest in this seemingly intractable resource. Manning still believed in the oil sands, and took important steps to spur interest within what soon became a rapidly-growing petroleum industry. During his 25-year tenure as premier, he held various other cabinet positions – notably, for this history, serving as Minister of Mines and Minerals from 1952 to 1962.

Behind the scenes, the process still frustrated Karl Clark. "You will understand that the problem at Bitumount is an engineering one," he wrote in a letter to Sidney Ells. "Every plant that has been put together to date has made oil. The widespread notion that there is no feasible process available as yet for taking oil out of the sands is entirely erroneous." There was, however, a serious difficulty.

"Engineers have not yet learned how to design a plant for giving expression to the hot water process which will keep running without getting into mechanical difficulties," he continued "When it comes to designing and building a sizable plant a lot of people become involved and are in a position to have their say."

Operators listened to him on matters of process. "I say how much water is to be put in the pulp, what temperatures are to be established, what flows of water are required, what units of apparatus are to be provided etc. and what I say along that line goes." So far, so good. "But when it comes to just how the separation cell is constructed, what mechanism is to be used to skim off the tar froth, how the tailings are eliminated, what make of pump is to be put here and there, how temperatures and liquid levels are to be controlled, etc. etc. I am told that these are matters of engineering and that I have no particular competence in this field."[215]

In his history of the province, James MacGregor wrote that "with integrity all too rare, Ernest Manning ruled his cabinet with a rod of which he was not sparing as soon as his keen perception detected a departure from the strait and narrow way"[216] After Champion defaulted on the project in 1948, Manning set up a board of trustees for the project that consisted of five men with impeccable credentials. They included Nathan Tanner, Public Works Minister D.D.B. MacMillan, J.L. Robinson, George Clash of the province's crude oil Marketing Board, and William Adkins – formerly a Fitzimmons employee, but then with Born Engineering.[217]

Manning had forty members of the legislature visit the Bitumount plant in 1949, its second year of operation, and the year after the province established Alberta's Petroleum and Natural Gas Conservation Board. Ferguson provided a charming description of the visit. "The little camp entertained this stream of undoubtedly curious politicians in order to show them where and how the best part of $1 million had been spent," he wrote. "The trip imposed a myriad of logistical problems which had pre-occupied George Clash during the summer and which had annoyed a production oriented Atkins. The visit was a success, but it almost proved disastrous. On 26 August, a small explosion occurred in the separation plant. Fortunately, the heater which exploded was repaired on the spot and the MLAs were able to actually witness the plant in operation. The

$1,539.75 that the trip cost the project, then, was money well spent although it might have enabled the visitors to watch the plant's destruction."[218]

## THE BLAIR REPORT AND A GLOBAL CONFERENCE

Because the important Leduc light oil discovery of 1947 was shifting interest to Alberta's light oil potential, interest in the oil sands was waning. It did not die, however. In 1949 Manning asked Sidney Blair, who had once been Karl Clark's assistant at the Alberta Research Council, to prepare a report on the outlook for the oil sands. Released in May 1950, his "Report on the Alberta Bituminous Sands" argued that the costs of mining, separation, upgrading and transporting product to the Great Lakes would total $3.10 per barrel, compared to the light oil price of $3.50.[219]

For that to happen, however, Blair called for further technical studies of geology and of extraction and refining technologies; stressed the need for large-scale projects and stressed the importance of policy – for example, what competitive issues would arise if oil sands development took place while conventional oil production was growing rapidly?

That said, he dismissed the idea that Canadian conventional oil would become an important source of supply in North America: "It is not likely that Alberta oilfields will glut the Canadian, let alone the North American, market in the years ahead."[220]

The Blair report suggested that a project producing 20,000 barrels or more of oil per day would cost $43 million and generate a 5 to 6 per cent annual return on investment. He believed that such an operation could profit in a market where conventional oil was fetching as little as $2.70 per barrel because synthetic oil is such an attractive feedstock. Far more valuable refined products can come from a barrel of synthetic crude than from a barrel of conventional oil. Unlike the early years of oil sands development, the value of bitumen as a petrochemical feedstock was being worked into the economic calculations.

The following year, Alberta sponsored a week-long conference on the oil sands, with participants representing virtually all of the world's large, publically traded oil companies. It began on September 10th, and continued for a week.

The first part of the conference, covering some three and one-half days, took place in Edmonton at the University of Alberta and focused on the technical and administrative aspects of the problem. The second part took place around Fort McMurray, where participants would be able to see in the field both the raw material and the approaches to separating it.

According to consultants who published a study of the oil sands history in 1984, "The SoCred invitation to the largest oil concerns in the world to develop the sands had stemmed from grave insecurities about the lack of economic diversification of Alberta and from a firm belief that no other investors were capable of oil sands exploitation."[221] History certainly bore out these Social Credit concerns about economic diversification, although no government has been able to make headway against the province's lopsided economy. Today more than ever, Alberta's economy is tethered to its resource sector.

Of critical importance, Minister of Mines and Minerals Nathan Tanner outlined provincial policy on oil sands leasing and royalties. To one group of participants he said, "We are quite prepared and anxious to have you come in and spend your risk capital in the development of our natural resources. We want to give you a good run for your money. We want you to know if you are successful in the search, that you will get a profit out of the development and the production. At the same time, we would like you to know that we are going to be at the end of the rainbow to get our share...."[222] Tanner then released the government's oil sands policy which, at fewer than 1,000 words in length, was a masterpiece of brevity and precision.

It began with the declaration that "The Alberta Government is desirous of doing all that is reasonably possible to encourage the orderly development of the enormous oil sands deposits in the interest of the people of the Province and of Canada as a whole, and, further, (for) the security of the continent."[223] It then stressed the need for a licence to do geophysical or subsurface geological exploration.

The policy let companies take out "prospecting permits" of up to 50,000 acres for one-year periods (no more than one permit per company) and renew them for up to two more years. They could then lease enough of the permit area to support an oil sands plant. Initial royalties would not exceed 10 per cent, annual rentals on each lease would be $1.00 an acre, and the remainder of the exploration area would revert to the province.

From Sun Oil's Calgary office, a young land agent by the name of Edward (Ned) Gilbert drafted a memo which nicely captured the terms of the new policy. As written, the regulations "tend to keep the spectator out while encouraging those who are interested in active development," he said. They "allow for an initial 50,000 acre permit or exploratory area and a deposit of $50,000 to guarantee that the company will perform adequate work throughout the three year maximum period of the permit. Rentals for the three years total only forty cents per acre in five cents, ten cent and twenty five cent [increments]…for the maximum permit area they would amount to only twenty thousand dollars to carry the fifty thousand acres for three years."[224]

Gilbert later began circulating the story that he had attended a Sun Oil board meeting in Cincinnati, to formally present this idea to the corporation – then one of the largest oil companies in the world. According to Robert McClements, who succeeded Pew as the company's chair, this could not have been true. The company had begun investigating the oil sands in the 1940s, and such a large corporation would not have invited a 20-something land agent working in a still-obscure operating region to make a presentation to its board. The story remains part of the industry's folklore, however.

Many oil companies participated in the conference, and shortly after its conclusion a dozen took out exploration permits. None of the companies with permits proceeded immediately to the lease stage. The main reason was a government stipulation that the lessee must begin construction of a commercial plant within two years of receiving the lease, and begin operating the plant within five. The government later changed the rule so the lessee's obligation was to build within a year of receiving a government order to do so. The government pledged to be reasonable in making such requests, and several companies took out leases.

In anticipation of policy developments during the Peter Lougheed years, one exchange from the oil sands conference is noteworthy. A participant put this idea to Tanner: "If two companies were to go in with entirely different processes to develop this oil and with different operating costs, would the government set the same dollar royalty on both plants or would it take into account the difference of operating costs?"

"We would not be in a position to take into consideration the operating cost," said Tanner. "We never work on a net royalty, but if we take it on the raw material, then the better operator has the advantage. We never admit that the poorer operator has the disadvantage."[225]

The irony is that in his first negotiations on an oil sands project, premier Lougheed insisted on a royalty based on net profits from the production of synthetic oil. "When Syncrude came along and we got into the negotiations," Lougheed said, "it was clear we could not approach (royalties) from a gross-revenue point of view. It wasn't really fair because of the risk element involved in such a new process."[226]

As the Minister of Mines and Minerals, Nathan Tanner was, at least technically, the point man at this conference. However, from the beginning of his premiership until he retired, Ernest Manning provided much of the energy and drive behind the province's oil sands initiatives. Manning maintained a life-long belief in the importance of the oil sands to Canada, and shared those beliefs in his long friendship with J. Howard Pew, the president, CEO and chair of Pittsburgh-based Sun Oil Company – at the time, the twelfth-largest oil company in the United States and, according to Manning biographer Brian Brennan, long "plagued with the problem of finding enough crude to feed its extensive refining…operations. The Athabasca oil sands seemed to provide a possible solution. Something had to be done, Pew said, to ensure the continuity of North America's petroleum supply and prevent the continent from becoming increasingly reliant on crude imported from Venezuela or the Persian Gulf."[227]

Manning once called Pew "a fantastic man, just a delight to talk to. His grasp of things all over the world was tremendous," Brennan said. "He was a humanitarian, a deeply religious man, an ideal character." For his part, Pew praised the premier's "character and intelligence," and described a religious broadcast on Manning's weekly *Back to the Bible* broadcasts as "One of the greatest sermons I ever heard."[228]

Manning supported funding for the project and the plant went on production in 1948. The entire legislature visited the plant in 1949, its second year of operation. Despite the province's efforts, the plant soon closed. However, operations ended after new wells, including the spectacular blow-out at Atlantic Leduc #3, confirmed that the 1947 Leduc light-oil discovery was not a fluke.

The flurry of effort to develop commercial activity in the oil sands, which had climaxed during and just after the Second World War was over. The reason was Alberta's Leduc oil strike and the other petroleum finds that quickly followed. Bitumen couldn't compete with inexpensively produced conventional light oil.

Though interest waned in those years, it did not die. The Bitumount project made it clear that you could produce crude oil and middle distillates from bitumen, but the economics were still in doubt. To clarify the issue, Manning commissioned an independent evaluation by Sidney Blair. By now a vice president of Bechtel, Sidney Blair was now an oil sands expert who had begun his career as Karl Clark's research assistant. His report concluded, in part, that Athabasca crude could be delivered to Sarnia for $3.10 per barrel.[229] Since that price included transportation costs, it could be competitive in an environment which saw US oil prices set at about $2.50. This report encouraged the Alberta government, which saw bitumen as providing an opportunity to transform the province's agricultural economy.

Blair's study concluded that oil sands development could be economic for projects producing 20,000 barrels or more of oil per day. He envisioned such a plant costing $43 million and generating a 5 to 6 per cent annual return on investment. He believed that such an operation could profit in a market where conventional oil was fetching only $2.70 per barrel, because synthetic oil is an attractive feedstock that can yield more valuable refined products than a barrel of conventional oil.

Blair concluded that the oil sands were "a commercially viable source of crude oil that could compete on the world market." The following year, Alberta sponsored a week-long conference. It began on September 10th, and continued for a week. "The first part of the conference, covering some three and one- half days, took place in Edmonton (at the University of Alberta) and was devoted to the technical and administrative aspects of the problem," he explained in the official proceedings of the conference. "The second part (took place around

Fort McMurray and) was directed to field examinations of the raw material and its possible separation...."[230] In this way, conference participants reviewed oil sands geology, mining, recovery, transportation and refining.

The plant was down, but Lloyd Champion was not out. In 1953 he began forming the Great Canadian Oil Sands consortium, based on his oil sands assets and his business acumen and drive. The Great Canadian Oil Sands consortium, which would later construct the first commercial oil sands plant, included Abasand Oils, Canadian Oils Ltd. and Oil Sands Ltd. That effort lurched from crisis to crisis until J. Howard Pew got into the conversation. The chairman of Philadelphia-based Sun Oil Company, Pew soon became the consortium's primary financial backer.

Lloyd Champion, Sidney Ells, and Robert Fitzsimmons all died in 1971. As for the Bitumount site, it remained a place for oil sands experimentation and testing until abandoned at the end of the 1950s. On December 4th, 1974 the province declared it a provincial historic site, and today it stands as testament to Alberta's oil sands pioneers. Its skeletal remains can be found in eight clusters. These range in interest from Fitzsimmons' small cabin to primitive industrial equipment to garbage dumps and latrines. Bitumount may not look like much, but this is where the modern oil sands industry began.

## COMRADES

While Ells did cause some anxiety and distrust among oil sands entrepreneurs and within the associated scientific community, as their careers ended he and Clark enjoyed a collegial relationship – comrades, after a fashion, in the long struggle to master the oil sands. For example, on November 8, 1948 Ells wrote from Ottawa asking for information about the Bitumount project.

Clark replied that "You folks back in Ottawa seem to have the idea that the Bitumount separation plant is a Research Council of Alberta project and that I am the big official. Actually our Council has no responsibility at all for the project. I am quite closely associated with it and am expected to be helpful. I can only advise.... [However] I am in a free position and I see no reason why I should not tell you, as one with a very real interest in the tar sand situation, what has been transpiring at Bitumount. What I write is between friends and is for your own information...."[231]

Both men remained fascinated by the oil sands throughout their long lives. In another friendly letter — also written in the late 1940s — Clark talked about retiring to the West Coast. "That is where my wife will go and I guess I will tag along. I tell her that I am going to retire down the Athabaska River and I have her a bit worried."[232]

CHAPTER 5

# The atomic age

———

*"There is some good ore in Canada."*

— ALBERTA EINSTEIN, 1939

As STUDIES AND THEN NEGOTIATIONS about the Great Canadian Oil Sands (GCOS)
project were underway, an important change in the petroleum industry's thinking about the oil sands began. Large corporations started looking for ways to
develop bitumen below ground, then pumping the liquid substance to the surface. Today known as *in-situ* techniques, decades passed before effective methods
came into play. As we shall see in another chapter, the solutions were innovative, but the key took another quarter-century to arrive. With this writing,
*in-situ* techniques are responsible for the bulk of Canada's oil sands production.

As in so many things, oil sands scientist Karl Clark was one of the first to
articulate the need to develop this kind of production system. "I am about convinced that there will be no development of the tar sands so long as it is necessary to dig the stuff and put it through a plant," he wrote to Sidney Ells in 1946.
"There are no worthwhile sites for large scale excavating without getting into
too much overburden. The main supply of oil in the sands is unobtainable by
such means. An *in-situ* method of recovery has to be devised before things will
break loose."[233] While, his comment was incorrect insofar as it reflected doubts
about the economics of oil sands mining, on the matter of *in-situ* development
he hit the nail on the head.

For nearly a century, the oil sands business mostly involved surface operations in the Athabasca region. In the earliest days potential entrepreneurs would scoop up oil from surface seeps. As the industry advanced, the bitumen came from open-pit mines. Ever-larger projects would mine oil sands ore – a mixture of sand, water and bitumen – and put it through a process that separated commercial products like bitumen and sulphur from such wastes as sand and other solids. While open-pit systems extract more than 90 per cent of the oil in place, they also present environmental challenges – for example, habitat loss while the mine is in operation, and the production of liquid and gaseous wastes. These and other environmental worries require careful management.

While mining projects were the main focus, a parallel industry was experimenting with ways to recover bitumen from deeper deposits through *in-situ* production. *In-situ* means "in place." In the context of the oil sands, it refers to recovery techniques that apply heat, or solvents and other chemicals to deep reservoirs of bitumen. One of the merits of *in-situ* production was that it could open up the production potential of the resource, since only about 10 per cent of the oil sands deposits were shallow enough for open-pit mining. Another was that it created fewer environmental snags.

## ATOMS FOR PEACE

Although he was a life-long pacifist and supporter of human rights causes, Albert Einstein will ironically be remembered also as the man who convinced US president Franklin Roosevelt to begin the Manhattan Project.

Einstein understood the energy potential of nuclear energy. He worried that German science would develop atomic technology before Britain, and use it on the Allies. In a now-famous letter, Einstein suggested that nuclear chain reactions in large masses of uranium could release "vast amounts of power and large quantities of new radium-like elements." He speculated that "extremely powerful bombs of a new type may thus be constructed." While America had only poor sources of uranium ore, Einstein said, "There is some good ore in Canada."[234]

The United States led the research and development for the Anglo-American atomic weapons effort which produced the first atomic bombs. But within a decade, the United States had taken tentative steps toward a different kind of nuclear age – one based not on fission, but on nuclear fusion. This system smashes together light atoms like those of hydrogen. By turning lighter elements into heavier ones, fusion releases vast amounts of energy. This is the principle behind the hydrogen bomb. It is star power – the fuel that keeps the Sun and the countless other stars alight. Toward the end of 1953, American President Dwight Eisenhower made a speech to the UN in which he famously advocated "Atoms for Peace."

In 1958 Atoms for Peace morphed into Project Plowshares – an American-led effort to find peaceful uses for atomic energy. One of the first companies to respond to Project Plowshares was Richfield Oil Corporation, which in June 1958 suggested detonating a small nuclear device about 1,200 feet below surface in the proposed Pony Creek #3 well. The proposed site was not far from the railway siding at Chard, and accessible by the Northern Alberta Railway.

The explosion would occur in a carbonate deposit just below the McMurray oil sand formation. Priced at about $500,000, the company believed this procedure would liquefy the bitumen, which could then be produced through conventional methods.[235] The concept went through a great deal of thought and research. For example, the US Atomic Energy Agency conducted tests to determine how radioactivity affected oil sands samples.

In theory, the blast would melt the thick, tarry oil so pumps could suck it to the surface. The thermonuclear heat would simultaneously create a large underground cavern which could serve as a collection point for oil the heat was liquefying. As Edward Teller – the Hungarian-American theoretical physicist sometimes called "the father of the hydrogen bomb" – explained, "We would expect the explosion to create a huge bubble in the earth which almost at once would fill up with shattered rock falling from above. We hope that the radioactive products of the explosion will be trapped in the bubble's glassy lining. If the rock in and above this bubble is sufficiently broken up, and if the material does not get compacted and does not resolidify too rapidly, we have opened a passage for a heating fluid to the tar sands and we can thaw out the petroleum. In fact, the heat of the explosion itself might be used." He added, "Ordinary oil wells would then be drilled into the shattered area to pump the liquefied tar to the surface…."[236]

The architect of the idea was Manley L. Natland, a senior geologist with Richfield. He had been travelling in the southern desert of Saudi Arabia and stopped one evening to watch the sunset. The Sun "looked like a huge orange-red fireball sinking gradually into the earth," Natland wrote in his diary. The display of the sun's explosion of heat and light caused him to think about an oil sands lease that Richfield held in partnership with Imperial Oil in the Athabasca region, 85 kilometres southeast of Fort McMurray. "The tremendous heat and shock energy released by an underground nuclear explosion would be distributed so as to raise the temperature of a large quantity of oil," he suggested. This would "reduce its viscosity sufficiently to permit its recovery by conventional oil-field methods."[237]

In the brainstorming behind Project Plowshares, the discussion included using nuclear energy to exploit oil and gas deposits. Natland concluded from Richfield's research that exploding a small device might be the most effective, and perhaps the most inexpensive, way of generating the intense heat needed to release the oil from the Athabasca sands. "The major production problem is the natural viscosity of the oil, which is hundreds of times greater than that of most other oils," he wrote in "Project Cauldron" (later changed to "Project Oilsand,") a proposal his employer reviewed with the Research Council of Alberta.[238] Probably in a moment of hyperbole, Natland said the heat from the blast would remain in the area where the explosion took place for as long as 10,000 years.

Natland suggested that Richfield use a nine-kiloton atomic warhead (a "baby nuclear bomb," as Alberta's then premier, Ernest Manning, called it) to test his hypothesis. His theory was that the heat from the explosion would melt the sands and release liquid hydrocarbons, with little risk to the atmosphere above. The molten sands would solidify into a huge glass bubble, trapping most of the radiation inside. The liquefied oil would then flow into the cavity caused by the explosion, with pumps then bringing it to the surface. If the experiment were successful, Richfield's scientists suggested, the industry would have found a way to "create an oilfield on demand."

Alberta oil industry officials and politicians embraced the nuclear proposal with enthusiasm. After all, according to minutes of a meeting at the time, "the economic feasibility of the proposal is not the concern of the Committee. (A private corporation should be free to spend its own money – so long as there is no hazard to life, property or resources – on research and experiment regardless of the opinion of others on the commercial prospects of the tests."[239]

A former lawyer for Imperial Oil, Gerry Burden recalled that one of his Calgary colleagues, a researcher named Jim Young, had been talking for some years about using nuclear power in the same way. Premier Manning, whose Social Credit administration had been actively seeking bids from oil companies to build the first commercial separation plant in the Athabasca region, said the proposal "makes an awful lot of sense."[240]

A writer for *The Toronto Star*, George Noordhof, was not so sure. A former science producer with BBC TV in London, he concluded that nuclear extraction would be neither cheap nor risk-free. The only practical way to control a nuclear explosion was through a reactor, said one National Research Council official. "Building a reactor is ridiculously expensive for this sort of job, and any oil company would be far better off drilling elsewhere." And while Richfield's Natland believed the radioactivity would be contained if the bomb were detonated in a capsule surrounded by a neutron-absorbing substance such as boric acid, there was no guarantee. If the oil became radioactive, said the NRC official, "safe disposal would present a formidable problem."[241]

In the beginning, this idea had support across the country, especially in Alberta. As Breen explains it, "the old dream of oil-sands development was rekindled despite the current oil glut. In the 1950s, nuclear science held the world in awe, and it was generally believed that mankind was on the threshold of a new age – the atomic age. In this atmosphere, the eagerness of many Albertans to embrace a totally new and exotic technology that held out the promise of sharply reducing the still prohibitive cost of oil-sand separation is hardly surprising." The Oil and Gas Conservation Board studied the idea, and liked it. The board's chair, George Govier, said there was "nothing to be lost and much to be gained from the proposed test."[242]

## First Nations

In the context of recent developments in respect to Canada's Aboriginal peoples, there are many deep ironies in the body of an extensive 1959 report on the project, which discusses in detail the science of the proposed project, and its social implications. Compiled by the Alberta government, the report discusses medical issues related to nuclear energy – for example, how cancer can result from exposure to radiation – but concludes that the project would be perfectly safe. From a contemporary perspective, however, a close reading of the document suggests government neglect toward the province's First Nations.

"The proposed test area is on the southerly portion of the McMurray oil sand deposits, some 65 miles south of the town of McMurray," the authors wrote. The document includes a map showing "the location of hamlets, water courses, railroads, roads and trails within a 10 mile radius of the site."

"The land is gently rolling with muskeg in the low lands and sandy, low to medium grade soil on the hills and ridges. The area is light to heavily wooded with a few timber stands up to 80 feet in height which are too sparse to be considered for commercial logging operations," it continued. After some further brief comments on the land and the vegetation and the mammals that inhabit it, the report gets unintentionally ironic.

In today's terms, it evinces what we would consider old-fashioned attitudes toward local communities. "The area is sparsely populated, with approximately 12 persons at Chard [now part of Janvier South], 25 at Leismar [Conklin] and some 32 others throughout the remainder of the area." The point, of course, is that the people who might possibly have been harmed if something went wrong with the experiment were Aboriginal or Métis people whose livelihoods involved trapping, and hunting and gathering. Thus, "seasonal and vocational fluctuations occur in the population." Almost as though the report wanted to stress the differences between Aboriginals living near the test site and the Caucasians in agricultural Alberta, it said "no farming is carried out in the area, and, except for experimental work on the oil sands, there are no other mineral developments within 50 miles of the site."[243]

Early in 1959, Richfield made a presentation on this project to premier Manning and his cabinet. As evidenced by the Technical Committee/OGCB report, they bought in. Ottawa also liked the idea. Inasmuch as the Conservation Board would soon be holding a hearing on the GCOS project, and since it would also be the Board's job to evaluate Richfield's proposed nuclear test, in 1960 the

Alberta Legislature amended its mandate to include the oil sands. There seemed to be agreement on testing this approach from everyone concerned: American authorities were ready to provide the explosive device; and policy-makers in Ottawa and Edmonton approved the idea in principle; the petroleum industry was ready to foot the bill and conduct the technical operations.

Inventor Thayer Lindsley patented "The Process for Stimulating Petroliferous Subterranean Formations with Contained Nuclear Explosions" in 1959. By Lindsley's estimates, a ten-kiloton device would yield about two million barrels of crude oil, and would do so at a relatively low cost.

A company named Phoenix Canada Oil Co. Ltd. later acquired the rights. A $350,000 nuclear device with 10 kilotons of explosive power would yield two million barrels of oil, said Phoenix, at a cost of $0.75 - $2.00 per barrel. The economics seemed solid, and the idea refused to go away.

However, in 1958 the government of Ireland proposed that the world adopt a nuclear non-proliferation treaty, and politics began rearing its head. Public pressure for an international ban on nuclear testing began mounting, and the following year Ottawa appointed Howard Green as Secretary of State for External Affairs. An advocate of nuclear disarmament, Green believed Canada should play a more aggressive part in the search for an international treaty to limit nuclear testing and the possession of nuclear weapons. Project Oil Sand collapsed in April 1962 with a speech to Parliament by Green. "Canada is opposed to nuclear tests. Period." Richfield unsuccessfully advocated the test until the summer of 1963.'[44]

## DÉTENTE

A decade later, in 1974, the Atomic Energy Control Board received a letter from Phoenix President S. D. Moore seeking approval to detonate a nuclear device in northeastern Alberta.

There were several reasons why it seemed to make sense to reincarnate this idea. Projected oil reserves in North America were worrisome, and the western world was in the midst of the energy crisis related to Israel's Yom Kippur War with the Arab states. This led to fuel shortages in North America and Europe — some service stations in both the US and Europe briefly ran out of fuel, and the West began to worry about its increasing dependence on Middle Eastern supplies.

As Middle Eastern oil exporters began to nationalize their petroleum reserves, the large publically-traded oil companies began to seek ways to develop new reserves. Also, there was a sense of "détente" in the Cold War between the US-led West and the Soviet-led Communist block with its allies in Eastern Europe. Consequently, there was less anxiety about a nuclear experiment in Northern Canada exacerbating international tensions. More to the point, the US government had successfully conducted many underground nuclear tests. However after years of further study and discussion, the Phoenix proposal, like its predecessor, went nowhere.

Twenty years later, in a telephone interview with the then-retired premier, Ernest Manning brought the story up out of nowhere, and told me he really regretted that neither experiment had gone ahead.

Later still, historian Earle Gray would argue that "It was probably a long shot, but there was at least the possibility that it could have unlocked oil sands production without the massive carbon problems. That would have been an enormous game changer. Now we'll never know. With the work that's been done since then on underground thermal release of bitumen [through steam—assisted gravity drainage], the industry might now have a better understanding of what a nuclear explosion might do."[245]

Headquartered in Toronto, at this writing Phoenix still existed. It had small interests in various gas fields in western Canada and, through subsidiary Phoenix International Energy Inc., rights to a patent for generating hydrogen gas. However, its opportunity to become a player in the oil sands had long since passed. While its nuclear test was a no-go, shortly after Phoenix got its last rejection Alberta's Lougheed government took steps to encourage petroleum companies to experiment with other forms of *in-situ* oil sands development by establishing an independent agency called the Alberta Oil Sands Technology and Research Authority.

While the idea of detonating oil sands devices below ground to heat up the oil sands is unlikely to rise again, today the idea of using nuclear has a certain environmental cachet. Consider the work of the Calgary-based Canadian Energy Research Institute (CERI), a partnership among industry, academia, and government formed in 1975. CERI's mandate is to contribute to energy policy through a balance-of-bias advocacy, harmonizing scientific research, economic analysis, and practical experience.

In a technical study released in 2009, the institute suggested that a relatively small Enhanced CANDU 6 reactor using Canadian technology, if located in the oil sands area, could deliver electricity for the province's power grid, and steam to liquefy oil sands reservoirs. "This type of configuration could bring large-scale nuclear power plants into the oil sands to support *in-situ* production," CERI wrote.[246]

CHAPTER 6

# Energy becomes political

———

*"At last the bastards in the big banks, and even the politicians*
*in Ottawa, and even the Premier of Ontario, were getting*
*off their asses and onto planes themselves."*

—MICHAEL BLISS, 1987

AS THE SECOND WORLD WAR drew to a close, most of Canada's energy came from coal, and most of her petroleum from the United States. Turner Valley was still the country's only large domestic oil supply. Its producing life had taken a bad turn during the war, when the federal government had ordered the field pumped without regard for good engineering practices. This had increased the oil available for the war effort – mostly, to fuel aircraft for the British Commonwealth Air Training Plan's training efforts in Alberta. While this contributed to the Allied war effort, it sent the field into steep decline. After the war, Canada's petroleum future looked bleak.

This changed on February 23, 1947. With some fanfare, Imperial Oil brought in an oil discovery just south of Edmonton. Leduc #1 provided the geological key to the most prolific of Alberta's oilfields.

The economic impact of the industry in Alberta was immense. As the province grew, so did the provincial government. Flush with resource revenues and taxes from a fattening economy, provincial spending grew rapidly. Construction and development increased Alberta's municipal tax bases, and infrastructure gradually began to stretch into northeastern British Columbia and the territories. Oil and gas companies built roads into remote forests, and the forestry industry followed. Hamlets became towns or, in the case of Fort McMurray, a small city. As field development created demand for specialized oil and gas equipment, manufacturing facilities set up operations in Edmonton, Red Deer, Calgary, and in other Alberta communities.

The discoveries of oil and gas in the Leduc era were so large that local markets could not begin to absorb the supply. Producers needed pipelines to take western Canadian petroleum to the heavily-populated central region of Canada and or the United States. Construction of the Interprovincial Pipeline (IPL) system from Alberta to Central Canada began in 1950 and began shipping oil to Regina and Wisconsin 150 days later. In 1953, Interprovincial extended the system to Sarnia, and in 1957 to Toronto. Until the completion of the TransCanada gas pipeline, IPL was the longest pipeline in the world. Over the coming decades, Canadian petroleum flowed through a vast system of pipelines, which integrated the energy resources of the enormous Western Canada Sedimentary Basin with those of the numerous, smaller, basins found throughout the mainland United States. Except for localized concerns about pipeline construction – most of them resolved by Alberta's regulatory board and, when they crossed provincial borders, the National Energy Board – the development of these projects proceeded smoothly.

While Leduc took attention away from the oil sands, international events in the mid-1950s directed it back. Political unrest in the Middle East led to the 1956 Suez Crisis. This threatened closure of the Suez Canal, which was one of the principal supply routes for oil from the Middle East. Prices increased temporarily in response to the crisis, but by 1958/1959 international prices were dropping, Soviet oil production was on the verge of flooding the market, dubbed the Soviet Oil Offensive by the Kennedy Administration, and in 1960 the oil companies unilaterally lowered prices with host countries that, in part, sparked the creation of OPEC.

In the Canadian context, the importance of Suez was that Canada helped to fill the gap and exports to the US ballooned. After the crisis, Canada worked hard to achieve an exemption to the 1959 US Mandatory Oil Import Program (MOIP), which limited foreign oil imports to the US.

The 1961 National Oil Policy (NOP) was designed to maintain that access in lieu of building an oil pipeline to Montréal. The US warned Canada that its exemption would be reconsidered if it built the pipeline to Montréal. The reason was that such a move would diminish oil imports from Venezuela and potentially destabilize that country, which suffered somewhat from MOIP. Plus, the Diefenbaker government did not want to risk underwriting the project. Nevertheless, Canada's exemption was not a blank cheque for limitless oil exports. Export amounts were the product of negotiations the NEB and American officials a few times every year. That being the case, it is no surprise that both Manning and the National Energy Board sought to limit oil sands production.

A retired geologist, businessman and politician, Nick Taylor served as leader of Alberta's Liberal opposition during the Lougheed era. Later, he served in Canada's Senate. Taylor commented on another reason Canadian import policy developed as it did. "Companies in eastern Canada wanted to buy overseas oil not so much because it was cheaper," he said, "but because it came from a branch of the multinational company they were part of."

The 1961 National Oil Policy drew a dividing line at the Ottawa River. Within Canada, producers had exclusive rights to sell oil west of the line, while refineries to the east could continue to process imported oil, which at that time was lower-cost. For its part, the Alberta government created policy designed to protect conventional producers by limiting oil sands production to five per cent of total crude. These measures strongly influenced the early pace of development. For the next decade or so, consumers to the West paid between $1.00 and $1.50 above the $3.00 per barrel world price. As a result, they paid higher prices at the pump than Canadians east of the Borden line.

Whatever the reasons for the Ottawa Valley Line, its limits became clear during the brief 1973 OPEC oil embargo and price shock. During the darkest moments of that crisis, the industry piped oil from Alberta to Vancouver, where tankers took the cargo through the Panama Canal and up the Atlantic coast to Montréal.

The members of OPEC realized they were in the driver's seat and soon nationalized oil and gas operations within their own borders. When that happened, Nick Taylor said, for a brief while "there was greater momentum (in Eastern Canada) toward purchasing oil from the West." Infrastructure favoured imports, however, and inertia won the day. Markets east of the Ottawa Valley Line continued to rely on imported oil.[247]

The 1950s in particular were a period of study and experiment in the oil sands. Oilmen – "the petroleum fraternity," as they sometimes called them-selves – saw bitumen resources as a tertiary opportunity, when compared to the discovery and development of many light and medium oil fields. The most remarkable such field was Pembina, which has never been surpassed in size in Western Canada, and in aerial extent was the largest on Earth for decades. In his engaging memoirs, Arne Nielsen described Drayton Valley (population 75) when his team discovered the Pembina structure in 1953. "It was located in an isolated bush and pioneering community," he wrote, "...in a world that still operated in a manner that had become extinct elsewhere in the province, in a world still reliant on kerosene lamps and horses."[248]

Oil does not flow easily through the Pembina Cardium sands. It is a vast, tight sandstone formation. When the company began producing its discovery well, only 132 barrels per day came out of the hole. The company – it was later renamed Mobil Oil Canada, and Nielsen became its president – used hydraulic pumps to force 3,000 pounds of sand in fracking fluid into the zone. Production trebled. In that period it was also common to acidize wells – pumping acid into the formation under pressure to clean out and improve flow channels for oil production.

This treatment transformed the Pembina Cardium oil discovery from what looked like an average play into an elephant of global proportions: it soon became clear that the formation hosted the greatest light oil reserves in Canada – perhaps 8.4 billion barrels of original oil in place. As Pembina developed into one of Canada's great post-war oil booms, "dozens of fami-lies living in vacation trailers were crowded into clearings around Drayton Valley." By 1955, the community's population had shot up to 5,000 – 2,000 people short of its population today.[249]

These riches of low-cost hydrocarbons might have diverted interest from the oil sands, if Mobil Oil of Canada, which operated the field, didn't prevent

Nielsen from telling competitors about the discovery until 1957. In that year he delivered a paper to the Alberta Geological Society on the geological "structure, stratigraphy and lithology of the discovery." This made it clear that large volumes of conventional oil were present in Alberta. The drilling that followed gradually defined the size and extent of the oil sands deposits, which for practical purposes end at Alberta's border with Saskatchewan.

Conventional oil was cheap to produce, and engineers could calculate the amount operators could produce without harming oilfield productivity.

**The major oil sands deposits**

Conventional producers were eager to generate maximum earnings by producing optimal volumes from their wells but if all producers did so, gluts would develop and prices would plunge. To prevent this from happening, the Oil and Gas Conservation Board required conventional producers to "pro-rate" their production. The amount individual wells could produce was restricted under a system known as prorationing.

Prorationing avoided waste, achieved maximum oil recovery, increased competition in the oil patch and helped increase government revenues. Without prorationing, independent oil companies without refineries would have had a hard time staying in business. In times of surplus oil production capacity, large refining companies with substantial reserves, such as Imperial Oil, would use only their own oil. Under prorationing, refiners had to nominate the amount they were going to buy, and this was reported each month in *Oilweek*, the industry's most important business journal. The Pembina oil producers wanted the reserves estimates to be as large as possible because that would increase the rate at which they could produce under the prorationing scheme. Imperial, on the other hand, had little or no Pembina oil. Thus, it wanted a lower figure because that would allow it to produce at higher rates from its more prolific fields, such as Redwater.

These producers had deep worries about competition from the oil sands, since it could conceivably mean stricter pro-rationing. This concern resonated with the province, which therefore would only provide permits for smaller oil sands projects. The first of those projects, Great Canadian Oil Sands, began producing during Canada's Centennial year. Its background illustrated the cooperation between government and industry so often needed to bring the oil sands on stream. However, when it went on stream oil prices were low, and profits, if any, sparse.

## THE CLUB OF ROME

By contrast, decisions surrounding Syncrude development took place in a bullish environment for oil prices. The background is the creation of the Arab Organization of Petroleum Exporting Countries (AOPEC) which, with the later addition of Venezuela and other countries, became the Organization of Petroleum Exporting Countries (OPEC). The background is tied up in the Byzantine politics of the Middle East.

In 1967 a coalition of Arab states led by Egypt and Syria attacked Israel and found themselves quickly defeated in what became known as the Six Day War. The conflict saw the Suez Canal blocked to oil tankers, disrupting European oil supplies and briefly raising oil prices but, more importantly, showing the west's vulnerability. Two years later, revolutionary Colonel Muammar al-Qadhafi overthrew Libya's King Idris and soon forced international oil companies to pay thirty cents more per barrel for his country's oil.

Inspired by his show of strength, OPEC meetings in Caracas (1970) and Teheran (1971) generated agreements on solidarity and joint action. Their stated aims included raising government participation and take from the oil industry, to be achieved through "rational increases in production from the OPEC area to meet estimated increases during the period 1971-75."[250] As global demand grew, the balance between oil supply and demand continued to shift in favour of the producers.

At the same time America – for decades the producer with the capacity to balance supply and demand – reached peak production. Thus, there was no western power with the capacity to stabilize supply. With Britain's withdrawal from the Middle East in 1968, and America's reluctance to take over the job of stabilizing the region, President Nixon and Secretary of State Henry Kissinger came up with the Twin Pillars policy to fulfil the Nixon doctrine, by which regions and countries should fend for themselves, with minimal American involvement. For the Middle East, Nixon looked to Iran – then ruled by the Shah – as the muscle. Saudi Arabia would be the swing producer and guarantor of a stable world oil supply. This policy failed miserably.

Growing worries about world oil prices led to the creation of an international alliance of intellectuals who styled themselves The Club of Rome. In 1972, they published a highly influential book titled *The Limits to Growth*, which quickly became a global bestseller. Using computer-generated feedback loops and other tools which at the time were state-of-the-art, the authors argued that the combination of growing demand for resources would meet rapidly declining supply with tragic consequences. Demographic change and economic growth would exhaust the planet's fossil fuel reserves by the end of the 20th century. This publication gave scientific respectability to concerns about resource depletion, expanding populations, and the impact on the environment of emissions into the air and effluents seeping into lakes, rivers and oceans.

Unknown to the Club as they prepared their publication, oil production in the Lower 48 states had already gone into what seemed like irreversible decline. When the first oil price shock arrived the year after publication, their book appeared clairvoyant.

•

## The Herman Kahn affair

In December 1973 Prime Minister Pierre Trudeau announced that his government would develop a "national oil program designed to reach Canadian self-sufficiency in oil and oil products before the end of this decade."[251]

This policy added fuel to the crude oil firestorm by making royalties a non-deductible expense for corporate income tax calculations and putting price caps – euphemistically called "made-in-Canada prices" – on conventional oil produced and sold domestically. Anticipating steep shortages in oil supply during the winter of 1973/74, Ottawa cut oil exports to the United States by 10 per cent and announced that it would take measures to monitor investment in the petroleum industry by foreign companies. The idea was to "Canadianize" the petroleum industry. The 1974 federal budget made some concessions but retained in principle the right of the federal government to tax provincial resources.

In 1974, definitive estimates confirmed that Syncrude's costs had doubled from the initial estimate to approximately $2 billion. Including the utility plant, originally excluded on the assumption that it would be owned and operated by Alberta Power, anticipated costs now exceeded $2.2 billion. This placed a huge burden on the participants, brought the project almost to a halt and put its future in doubt.

Over a three-year period, global oil prices had more than tripled to $11.50 per barrel. The acceleration of international price increases, coupled with fears of oil shortages, had aggravated tensions among provincial, federal and industry leaders, and policy-makers considered it a matter of national urgency to develop stable, secure energy supplies. Government and industry resolved these issues at a meeting in Winnipeg, covered elsewhere in this book.

Also in 1974, Herman Kahn – a Cold War strategist and founder of the prestigious Hudson Institute, a conservative think-tank now based in Washington D.C. – quickly but briefly caused a stir among oil sands aficionados. According to an article in the *Montréal Gazette* and other newspapers, the idea grew out of a chance encounter between Kahn and Jean-Pierre Goyer, who was then Ottawa's Minister of Supply and Services. In all likelihood, both men were familiar with Alberta's 1972 Athabasca Tar Sands Development Strategy.

Through correspondence and meetings over several months, Kahn and Goyer came up with a draft plan that would conceptually permit large-scale development of the oil sands, and do so in less than five years. "It would involve borrowing virtually all the capital – one third hard cash, two thirds materials and equipment – from the US, Japan and Europe. The loans would be repayable in oil or its cash equivalent." According to the *Gazette*, the idea was to develop 20 plants within a three- to five-year period. Those small-scale plants would collectively manufacture synthetic crude oil at a rate of 2.7 million barrels per day – approximately 1 billion barrels a year. "Thousands of skilled South Korean labourers would be brought in for a large part of the workforce, returning to their homeland after a three-year stint in northern Alberta," wrote a journalist for United Press International. "Technology would be developed on the crash basis to solve ecological and operating problems."

Under this scheme "the debt could be paid off in four to seven years, and the equity and profits would then be entirely in Canadian hands – a drastic change from the 95 per cent foreign ownership of Canadian oil industries at present."[252] Although newspapers and cabinet meetings bandied the idea about, it ultimately went nowhere.

## ENERGY WARS

During Peter Lougheed's premiership, "energy wars" between producing provinces and the federal government were the order of the day. These actually began before the 1973 Arab oil embargo drove oil prices to historically high levels, climaxed with the introduction of the National Energy Program (NEP). in 1980, then tailed off in 1984. So important were these events that an entire volume of a 12-volume history of the province took its name from Lougheed and the energy wars.

Inflation had become a national problem and oil prices were rising, and on September 4, 1973, the Prime Minister asked the western provinces to agree to a voluntary freeze on oil prices. Nine days later, his government imposed a 40-cent tax on every barrel of exported Canadian oil. The tax equalled the difference between domestic and international oil prices, and the revenues were

used to subsidize imports for eastern refiners. At a stroke, Ottawa began subsidizing eastern consumers while reducing the revenues available to producing
provinces and the petroleum industry. This outraged Alberta, which had fought
long and hard for control of its natural resources.

Premier Peter Lougheed soon announced that Alberta would revise its royalty policy in favour of a system linked to international oil prices. His timing
was impeccable. Two days later, on October 6, the Yom Kippur War broke out.
OPEC used the conflict to double the posted price for a barrel of Saudi Arabian
light oil, to US$5.14. Saudi and the other Arab states then imposed embargoes
on countries supporting Israel, and oil prices rose quickly to $12. The price of
imported oil laid down in Montréal rose from an average $2.45 per barrel in
1970 to $10.50 in 1973 to $44.66 by 1980. Domestically, this led to rapid-fire,
escalating moves and counter-moves by Ottawa, western provinces and even
Newfoundland. The atmosphere was one of urgency, alarm and crisis, with
global conflicts adding gravity to the federal-provincial quarrelling.

Alberta, British Columbia and Saskatchewan (the latter two headed by progressive New Democratic Party governments) took steps to increase their revenues from oil and natural gas production and to protect provincial resource
ownership from federal encroachment. The federal government announced a
series of national policies founded on the basic notions of federal/provincial
revenue sharing, made-in-Canada pricing, increasing Canadian ownership of
the industry and a quest for self-sufficiency in oil through development of such
non-conventional resources as oil sands and the frontiers.

As Prime Minister of a minority Liberal government, on September 4,
1973 Pierre Trudeau fired the first shot in what quickly became an energy war.
In response to increased prices for oil imports, he asked Canada's producing
provinces – primarily Alberta and Saskatchewan – to voluntarily freeze prices.
Nine days later, his administration imposed a $0.40 per barrel tax on exported
oil. The tax equalled the difference between Canadian and international oil
prices, and his government used the revenues to subsidize imports by refineries
east of the Ottawa Valley Line.

Outraged that Ottawa would in effect tax a provincial resource, Alberta
retaliated a month later. Premier Lougheed cancelled the Alberta Oil Revenue

and Royalty Plan effective at yearend, eliminated maximum royalty provisions in all leases and introduced a price-related royalty system.

His timing was impeccable. Two days later the Yom Kippur War broke out. The aim of the Arab states was to regain Arab territories lost to Israel in the Six Day War.

With leadership from Libya's al-Qadhafi, AOPEC used the conflict to double the posted price for a barrel of Saudi Arabian light oil to US$5.14 per barrel. When the United States chose to re-supply Israel, OAPEC retaliated by imposing embargoes on countries supporting Israel, and international prices quickly rose to $12. The organization was suddenly aware of its pricing power, and the first energy shock had begun. These events were an eye-opener for the world's oil exporters, many of whom realized they had the power to set prices. For the rest of the 1970s, OPEC sat in the oil price driver's seat.

These distant events further aggravated tensions among provincial, federal and industry leaders. Ottawa responded to widespread fears that higher world oil prices, intensifying American demand for Canadian supplies and suspicions that Alberta and the international oil companies headquartered in Calgary would siphon away inordinate amounts of Canada's wealth.

Higher prices had created a boom in western Canada, and gleaming new office towers in Calgary and Edmonton were symbols of the growing strength of those two cities. "At last the bastards in the big banks, and even the politicians in Ottawa, and even the Premier of Ontario, were getting off their asses and onto planes themselves," wrote historian Michael Bliss. "Easterners were trekking west. Soon they were setting up western offices, moving staff and whole corporate divisions. Westerners were creating their own new institutions to service the boom, ranging from drilling firms and oil supply companies, to restaurants, newsmagazines, and new chartered banks. Make no mistake: the balance in Canada was changing. The West was shifting from hinterland to heartland, and the new urban geography of Alberta showed it."[253] Rents and wages rose rapidly and there were shortages in such specialties as engineering.

In his study of Alberta's history, James MacGregor described the situation in Alberta at that time as quite complicated. "Two problems worried the thoughtful. The first concerned the export of those raw resources which was paying for these fancy cities and for everyone's luxuries and was in truth an export of capital which later generations will sorely need. The time may not yet be economically right to produce all these riches in Alberta, but by the time it becomes so they may well have been exhausted. The second problem is that of pollution. Fortunately Alberta is not yet faced with extensive pollution and, having been warned in time, is taking steps to preserve its ecology and to keep its cities habitable."[254] Prosperity had come for good – or so it seemed.

## THE NATIONAL ENERGY PROGRAM

In 1979/80, further crises in the Middle East led to panic-driven pricing. The Iranian Revolution, in which Islamic militants overthrew the pro-western Shah, came first. War between that country and Iraq soon followed. Markets do not like insecurity, and oil prices more than doubled, to US$36 per barrel.

The energy wars began with the government of Prime Minister Joe Clark. A Progressive Conservative Albertan from High River, as Prime Minister he had an exchange in Parliament's with Liberal Ed Lumley on December 7, 1979. This incident "illustrated the power of political forces with startling clarity," wrote Gordon Jaremko. At the time, Clark led a party that was supposedly pro-business. Given that Albertans had elected him, it would have seemed reasonable to assume that he was also pro-oil and -gas.

During question period, Lumley asked from the floor whether the Tories would respond to reports that the Canadian branches of international oil companies were unfairly raising prices within Canada to enrich their foreign parents. Clark's response showed the power of the consumer in national politics. "We are now actively discussing the mechanism that will be used to ensure that virtually 100 per cent of the revenues that would go to the companies as a result of the increases in energy prices will," he said, "be regained by the Government of Canada for the specific application by the Government of Canada for national energy purposes."[255] In response, the oil and gas index on the Toronto Stock Exchange plummeted 107 points in the day's last four hours of trading.

Within a year, Lumley was Trade Minister in the Liberal government that Western Canadians reviled for introducing the National Energy Program and its gas price regulations, export controls, special taxes and investment rules. Yet clearly Clark was already thinking in those terms the year before.

The higher oil prices of the latter 1970s multiplied the fiscal take the federal government was beginning to covet. Prime Minister Trudeau led the Liberals to electoral victory in 1980, promising vaguely to create a federal energy policy in response to rising oil prices. During the campaign, Jean Chrétien, who had served as Finance Minister in the previous Trudeau Government, hinted at what was to come. "My party fully accepts that the days of cheap and plentiful energy are now over" he told Toronto's Empire Club in a speech at the beginning of 1980. "It will be increasingly expensive to locate and bring on stream the necessary new supplies, he said, because those new supplies must come from distant places like the Beaufort Sea "and because their extraction will require costly new recovery techniques."

The Liberal Party accepted that prices must rise, he said, "but I would suggest that three conditions should govern our pricing formula. First, the amount of the increase should correspond to the needs of the industry. We want a made-in-Canada price, one which reflects the cost of ensuring our energy self-sufficiency, not a price arbitrarily set by a cartel of producers in a far-off part of the world. Second, price increases must be phased in so that they do not cause a gratuitous disruption of the economies of consuming provinces. Finally," he said, "the federal government must get a share of energy revenues adequate to discharge its own commitments in the energy field and to cushion the impact on the national economy."[256]

He was describing the basic elements of what would become the National Energy Program (NEP). —Canada's most controversial federal initiative in peacetime. It ended an era of great prosperity in Alberta.

A year later, his energy minister, Marc Lalonde, made a presentation to an energy conference that showed how this thinking had evolved. The federal government "must have the means available for the sound management of the country's economy," he said. "It must be able to compensate for the vagaries of nature, which has bestowed mineral resources across the land without being overly concerned whether each region received its exact share."[257]

No one could have imagined the rancour that would follow the NEP. In a riveting television broadcast, a fuming Peter Lougheed compared federal actions to those of a rude invader blundering into Albertans' living rooms. The province made plans to cut oil production by 15 per cent over three months, threatened to withhold approval of new oil sands projects and launched court actions. British Columbia and Saskatchewan mounted furious protests of their own.[258]

The NEP pitted vital interests against each other. Supported by eastern consumers, the federal government took one corner of the ring. Supported by regional voters, the western provinces took the other. The petroleum industry was a spectator wishing it could score points against either combatant – or better, both.

In the beginning, compromise seemed impossible. After a year, however, the two levels of government did reach a revenue-sharing agreement – memorialized in the press by photos of Peter Lougheed and Marc Lalonde toasting the deal with Champagne. Left out in the cold, the petroleum industry didn't share in the celebrations. Under the terms of the new deal, the sector could only realize additional revenue if oil prices, which had already begun to erode, continued to rise.

Operating under new rules in a declining oil price environment, corporate cash flows dropped precipitously. In response to federal efforts to "Canadianize" the sector, foreign interests sold their assets and headed home. The Canadian sector became mired in debt – a development that contributed to the bankruptcy of once-mighty Dome Petroleum. Drilling slid into a deep funk, and rigs began a highly publicized exodus across the border. Confidence in the industry plummeted.

As the decade wore on, bankruptcies in Alberta reached new highs and real estate prices crumbled. Although exacerbated in 1982/83 by what was then the worst global slowdown since the Great Depression, the severity of the decline was unique among the world's petroleum-based economies. Norway, for example, boomed throughout the NEP years.

The petroleum industry fought back. The Canadian Petroleum Association – a forerunner to today's Canadian Association of Petroleum Producers, funded by Canada' large, mostly foreign-owned oil companies – took the lead. Its leader, Ian Smyth, expanded the organization to include divisional offices in Regina and Victoria, and then added operations in St. Johns, Halifax and Montréal. "CPA staff often provided access to ministers in Ottawa and the provinces, but we never lobbied in the sense that lobbying is a dirty word," said the organization's leader, Ian Smyth. "We'd do show-and-tells. There would be half a dozen ministers around the table, and we would say: 'Here we are, the industry, and we want to tell you what we're doing. If you have any questions, Minister, we will be glad to answer them.'"[259]

The organization's retired public relations director, newspaperman Jack Gorman, talked about this period with both humour and derision: "The next thing you know they hired Allan Gregg, who had just founded Decima Research, to conduct a nationwide survey to find out what Canadians think about the oilpatch," he said. "I said to Ian, 'I can tell you what the people of Canada think about the oilpatch. They think it is run by a bunch of Yankee fat cats who are exploiting Canadians and making high profits and sending most of the money back to the U.S.' So they launched their campaign and surveyed Canadians and that's exactly what they found out," he said. "Then they decided to let the research drive a campaign to convince the Canadian people that this really wasn't true, that the oil industry was really working in the best interests of the country. So they began this big, expensive advertising campaign, and I don't think it changed a single person's mind."[260]

Hans Maciej was skeptical about the research, but supported Smyth's conclusion that the campaign helped people understand the damage caused by the NEP. "I always questioned the numbers we were getting back from our advertising and polling people," he said. "We would hear that something in public opinion moved by 0.2 percentage points and that was a major improvement. But Allan was an effective snake oil salesman, and it was always interesting to listen to his interpretations."[261]

CHAPTER 7

# Sun Oil and GCOS

———

*"...An exciting adventure — a way of life providing satisfaction in the*
*accomplishment of our goals. So our people have become a great team,*
*welded together by great ideals and purposes accepted by each of us."*

— J. HOWARD PEW, 1956

FROM THE BEGINNING OF HIS premiership until retirement in 1968, Ernest
Manning provided much of the energy and drive behind the province's oil sands
initiatives. Indeed, Manning assumed responsibility for the Ministry of Mines
and Minerals in 1952 after Nathan Tanner quit to return to the private sector,
and he retained the portfolio after the 1955 election, by which time Tanner had
become the first chairman and CEO of TransCanada Pipelines.

It would be "less of a wrench, less of a dislocation, if I took on the portfolio,"
Manning said. "I had worked with Mr. Tanner in the government policy aspects
of the resource development, and probably had more discussions with him on
that, by far, than anybody else in the government."[262]

Lloyd Champion helped form the Great Canadian Oil Sands consortium,
a Toronto-based group which originally included Abasand Oils, Canadian Oils
Ltd. and Oil Sands Ltd. However his group didn't have the expertise needed to
develop the oil sands, nor could it raise the capital required.

The project's promoters selected the name "Great" Canadian Oil Sands to
excite investors in eastern Canada.[263] Their efforts were not successful, so Pew
brought Sun Oil in as the white knight.

## ENTER PEW, CENTRE STAGE

Philadelphia-based Sun Oil owned 75 per cent of the Abasand lease at Mildred-Ruth lakes. Sun had been founded by the Pew family, who also owned and managed it. When GCOS was formed out of the Canadian Oil Sands consortium, Sun's dominant figure was J. Howard Pew, a maverick oilman whose company had developed refining techniques that could turn East Texas heavy crude oil into high-quality lubricating oil. His pioneering and entrepreneurial instincts were of the highest order, and he brought the first large-scale oil sands mine and upgrading facility on production just as real oil prices hit rock bottom, in 1967.

The thumbnail sketch of Pew's life is this: Born in 1882, he graduated from high school at age 14, from university at 18 and became president of Sun Oil at age 30. With his brother Joseph he transformed the Sun Oil Company (founded by his father; later called Sunoco) by introducing new refining, marketing, and distribution techniques and, during the First World War, diversifying into crude oil tankers – and thus playing an important role in supplying Britain during that era. "Tall

**J. Howard Pew**

and broad-shouldered, with bushy eyebrows," a publication celebrating Sun Oil's centenary in 1986 explained, "he was often seen clutching an enormous cigar in his fingers as he moved about Sun's corridors. He was intense, sure of himself and deliberate in his speech even in old age."[264]

He also had extraordinary people skills. I once gave a presentation in which I mentioned Pew, and at the end of my talk a former employee – he had worked in the lower echelons of Sun Oil's global enterprise – stood up to make a few extemporaneous comments. His name was John, and he had worked at a field project in Canada. He had met Pew twice, he said – the first time at a company social gathering of some sort. The second time was several years later at a meeting in the field operation. On that occasion, Pew came up to him and said

"Hello, John. How's your dog, June?" On both names — man and dog — Pew's remarkable memory was correct.

Ernest Manning maintained a life-long belief in the importance of the oil sands to Canada, and shared those beliefs in his friendship with Pew, whom he called "a fantastic man, just a delight to talk to. His grasp of things all over the world was tremendous. He was a humanitarian, a deeply religious man, an ideal character." For his part, Pew praised the premier's "character and intelligence," and described one of Manning's weekly *Back to the Bible* broadcasts as "One of the greatest sermons I ever heard."[265]

A great industrialist to Americans interested in business history, for Canadians he is important because of his insistence that his large, multinational company get behind the oil sands. According to Ernest Manning's son Preston, Pew "was one of the very early proponents of continental energy security, partly because of [his experience during two world wars]. He saw how vulnerable North America was when submarines could destroy tanker traffic and he attached a lot of importance to continental energy security. [This] attracted him to the oil sands. Of course, today the oil sands and continental energy security are inseparably locked up, but this would have been in the 50s...."[266] At the time, private sector commitment for smaller-scale mining projects ranged from shaky to non-existent, and in any case the Alberta Government would only provide permits for small projects.

Conservative in his religious and political views, Pew was passionate about his work. "Working for Sun Company these years has been not merely a job," he said in 1956. "It has been participation in an exciting adventure — a way of life providing satisfaction in the accomplishment of our goals. So our people have become a great team, welded together by great ideals and purposes accepted by each of us."[267]

Pew first took an interest in the oil sands in 1944. His brother, J. Edgar Pew (Sun's vice president of production) began discussions with Lloyd Champion, who was seeking funds to expand Bitumount, and the company sent geologists and lawyers to investigate, but discussions went no further. Two years later, Sun sent engineers to investigate the Athabasca region, but the company decided that "the time for oil sands was not yet ripe."[268]

J. Howard was still concerned about the prospect of North American crude oil shortages, which would make the continent vulnerable to offshore suppliers. Accordingly, in 1949 he instructed George Dunlap, who had just been appointed to head up a new Canadian production division based in Calgary, to always have a significant position in the Athabasca oil sands. When push came to shove, Pew provided the capital and entrepreneurial leadership for the project. In 1960 Premier Manning had the Legislature give the Conservation Board authority to review oil sands projects; he also kept the lobby of conventional oil producers at bay.

This pioneering commercial development involved enormous risk. As costs began to rise, financial difficulties ensued. It was clear that a company with deep pockets needed to lead GCOS. With leadership from the indomitable Pew, who was the company's chairman, Sun took on that responsibility.

Sun was only one member of the consortium which in 1960 applied to the Board for approval to construct Great Canadian Oil Sands, designed to produce 45,000 barrels per day of synthetic oil. In those days the single biggest issue was competition with conventional oil production, and approval was "deferred" until the consortium requested a new hearing – but not until 1962.

Pew also wrote a letter to the Oil and Gas Resources Board saying "I believe in the future of this project and I will put up my own money without reservations if the permit is approved." Read aloud at a meeting of the Conservation Board, that letter carried the day.[269] In addition to putting up the funds, Sun Oil agreed to purchase 10,125 barrels of the oil per day at its Toledo, Ohio, refinery – thereby expanding the market for Alberta oil.

The project is "a great challenge to the imagination, skill and technological know-how of our scientists and engineers," Pew said. "The same group of men who some years ago demonstrated to the world the feasibility of catalytic cracking will be in charge of this work. Unless projects of this kind can be periodically challenged and solved, our organization will become soft and eventually useless. I am convinced that this venture will succeed, and that it will be the means of opening up reserves that will meet the needs of the North American continent for generations to come."[270]

In April, 1964, following a further hearing by the Conservation Board, the Alberta government approved the project. Sun received approval to construct a

45,000 barrel per day plant, on condition that the project be up and running by September 30, 1967. Cost estimates stood at $190 million. By the time GCOS reached completion, the company had invested $235 million in plant and mine construction.

The contractor for the project was Bechtel of Canada, with Clarence Thayer as construction superintendent. Thayer had already retired from Sun, but was called back for this project because of his expertise in plant construction.[271] The engineer representing Sun during construction was Robert (Bob) McClements, Jr., who later became chairman and CEO of Sun Oil. McClements described Pew as "one of the strongest influences on my life."

Pew would visit the construction site and "we would have engineering (and other) discussions," according to McClements. "He would ask 'How much does it cost to feed a man an average twelve hours on a shift?' He was very, very detailed. I still remember: it was six to eight pounds of food per person per day and a little less than $2.00 per person to feed a construction worker... Anyway, there was a side of J. Howard that I don't think has really been widely recognized. I think many people would describe him first perhaps as an industrialist. He was certainly known as the leader of a large corporation. Sun was always in the top 20 of the Forbes list of companies. It was a huge company. But there was also a spiritual side to him. He was a very religious individual. His conversations often included two words, faith and freedom, and they were welded together...."

The Sun Company McClements joined in the 1960s was much different from those in today's oilpatch. "There was no retirement plan, there was no healthcare plan, and there was no sick plan. When you were sick, you took your own time off....You would pay for that time. When you retired – and nobody quit and nobody was ever fired at the Sun Company – you retired at 50 per cent of your pay. There were no documents explaining this in those days."

McClements described the only meeting he attended between Pew and Premier Manning. "I'm telling you I've never been in a business meeting in my life like that. It was like you and me sitting here talking. There were no hard specifics. (There) was a feeling of absolute trust between the two of them. And I remember when I went back to the plant, somebody asked me about it. Without thinking, I said 'Those two men just reeked with honesty.' The relationship they had was unbelievable, exactly the same wavelength."[272]


## BUILDING THE PLANT

Although there were restrictions on development, the notion of developing the oil sands didn't go away. Alberta kept the Bitumount project going until 1955, and the gathering exploration drilling for conventional oil in the province better mapped the oil sands deposits. Soon everyone knew that the sands represented one of the world's largest sources of petroleum. However, the industry still needed to develop those resources economically. During the years following the 1951 oil sands conference, Sun Oil invested just less than half a million dollars in oil sands research.

Then, in 1958, the company signed an agreement with GCOS to construct an integrated oil sands project on the Ruth Lake lease.

Collaboration between government-funded science and profit-driven entrepreneurs has been an important theme in oil sands history. Government scientists did some drilling in the 1890s, but did not again make an attempt to participate in a commercial project until the 1940s – partly reflecting the exigencies of war, but also Alberta's frustration that resource development projects had met so little success. At that time, the easiest and most efficient way to extract bitumen from sand was through a combination of strip mining, hot-water separation and refining or upgrading. The technology quickly developed to the stage that, although capital-intensive, it could recover more than 90 per cent of the bitumen mined. During the late 1940s and throughout the 1950s, the industry learned much about the oil sands. Industrial engineers and chemists improved processes for extracting and upgrading the bitumen, and the petroleum community in general came to a better understanding of the oil sands' business potential.

Pew was the leader of Sun Oil, but it fell to McClements to represent the company during plant construction. As project planning and construction proceeded, an assessment team went to Germany to review some German-made coal-mining equipment for use in the project. "The experiments to use the sands as a source of crude oil were frustrated by problems that almost matched the size of the reserves," according to McClements. "They included the bitter winter weather, the area's remoteness, the handling and disposal of the huge quantities of overburden and the mining of the oil-laden sand beneath it. In addition, there was the critical problem of separating the oil from the sand in sufficient quantities to be economical." His wife, Barbara, had more prosaic interests. When she stayed in Fort McMurray during construction, she said, "diapers froze in the bucket, indoors."

That cold was also a concern when it came to processing the bitumen. To transport as feedstock to a conventional refinery, bitumen needed to be fluid enough for pipeline flow.[273]

The $235 million facility produced oil from a deposit close to the surface. To begin, conventional earth-moving equipment stripped away the overburden from the sand beds, creating an open pit mine. To move the sands from the beds to the separation plant was a huge undertaking in materials handling. To do the job, GCOS used two large, crawler-mounted bucket-wheel excavators "which cut a near vertical face into the tar sand layer," he said. These excavations had ten buckets mounted on the outer rim of a huge wheel which turned at speeds up 7.5 revolutions per minute, with each bucket coming into contact with the tar sand face and digging as much as two tons of material. The two excavators could mine more than 100,000 tons of sand per day. To give those numbers a bite, he converted them into railway equivalents: 2,160 gondola cars, each carrying 50 tons. "That's a railway train 16 miles long." The plant required that much oil sand each day to produce at capacity: 45,000 barrels of light oil per day. The excavators worked throughout winter, when temperature could drop below -40°.

At that point, the excavators would transfer the oil sands ore onto a system of conveyor belts, which transported the sand to the separation plant. There, the oil sands ore was fed into "rotating conditioning drums, 17 feet in diameter and 51 feet long, in appearance – much like kilns used in cement manufacturing." Conditioning consisted of tumbling the sand in the presence of hot water and steam. This conditioning produced "a pumpable slurry which, after screening to remove lumps and debris," was pumped into cylindrical separation cells

44 feet in diameter "with approximately 20 feet of vertical side and shallow cone bottoms."[274]

Inside these cells, most of the bitumen would float to the surface as a froth, where machines would skim it off. The coarser sand would fall to the bottom. There, it would be raked to the center of the cone and removed, along with water and small amounts of oil, and then pumped to a tailings disposal area. "In those days we had no idea how difficult reclamation of those tailings ponds would be," McClements told me nearly half a century later.[275]

From the middle part of these production vessels, equipment would withdraw a stream of fluid that contained oil, water and fine material. Some of this would be returned to the slurry feed pumps, and the rest pumped to air-blown flotation vessels, which removed more froth. After it settled, this froth went into the primary froth. This mixture, which contained oil, water, and minerals, went into intermediate storage.

The physical characteristics of bitumen made further processing mandatory. Below -50°F (-46°C) the substance is almost solid. At ambient temperatures above that, "it is a sticky asphaltic material. It cannot be burned in any but special equipment and it cannot be pumped through a pipeline, even during summer months. Additionally, the market was limited, since refineries in those days could not process bitumen. Thus, GCOS needed to upgrade it into a pumpable, saleable material that could compete with conventional crude oil."[276] To do this, the plant fed bitumen into a coking plant, which cracked it under heat and pressure to produce coke (a high-carbon fuel), natural gas, and raw distillate oils. Burning the coke in boilers produced the steam used to generate power, heat the oil sand and fuel other processes. The oils were upgraded by hydrogenation, a chemical process that adds hydrogen atoms to unsaturated oil. In the case of GCOS, the hydrogen was produced as part of the coker gas. Sulphur was also recovered as a by-product. The refined oil went into storage before being shipped to Edmonton through the company's 266-mile pipeline.

The synthetic oil produced at the original plant made an excellent feedstock for refining. Extremely low in sulphur, nitrogen and oxygen, it flowed easily through pipelines, even in extremely cold weather. At the refinery, it could be refined into gasoline, kerosene, and heating oil. The downside, however, was that for the plant to produce 45,000 barrels per day of synthetic crude, it first needed to extract 65,000 barrels of bitumen from the sand.

As GCOS began staffing up, the company managed employer/employee relations by forming working with employees to create Great Canadian Oil Sands Employees Bargaining Association, with an agreement signed just weeks after the plant opened. According to McClements, "The major issue was scheduling a regular long weekend."[277] The company's agreement with the employee group provided for strong measures to resolve grievances, which quickly went up the chain of command. If there were no settlement within 48 hours, the issue went to the plant manager. If that person were unable to resolve matters within four days, the grievance went to company president McClements, who had two weeks to clear matters up. At that point, the matter went to formal arbitration.[278]

## THE MATTER OF RESERVES

In the case of conventional oil and gas production, over many decades engineers and geologists had developed formulas which enabled them to calculate how much of the resource would come out of a given well, given existing technology. Beginning in the early 1950s the Canadian Petroleum Association (later the Canadian Association of Petroleum Producers, or CAPP) began to prepare a statistical handbook which itemized everything imaginable about the petroleum industry – volumes produced, number of wells drilled, expenditures, reserves and so on. That publication is still available, but it is worth noting that GCOS created a real puzzle for the CPA.

This problem was analogous to the workings of a business balance sheet based on the formula Assets = Liabilities + Shareholders' Equity. These three balance sheet segments tell investors what the company owns and owes, and the amount invested by the shareholders. By contrast, the reserves committee was effectively reporting production from a plant with unknown assets, and therefore had no idea of shareholders' equity. It was as though the oil production were appearing out of nowhere.

One day the CPA's Hans Maciej asked the organization's Reserves Committee "Where the hell is this oil coming from?" The result was "quite the discussion...."

We could have put whatever Great Canadian Oil Sands produced, let's say it produced a million barrels that year, well we could just say we produced a million barrels in reserves, you know, wipe it out. I said, 'Oh, we need to have a process and we can argue about the numbers, we have to put something in the reserves report, and everyone said, 'Okay, hallelujah...but now what?'" he said.

"So after lengthy discussions we decided that we would credit every producing project, and every project that had approval and was reasonably certain to go ahead, with 25 years of production. And we kept that going forward. After all, 25 years was a very conservative estimate as to how long those projects would produce year round. Just to get things going, we agreed on the 25 years, on the producing projects and on those that had approval – we needed to exercise some judgment there."[279]

## LANDMARK

Suncor employed top mining expertise from Canada, the US, UK and Australia. The engineers involved looked at numerous pieces of equipment, ranging from steam to electrical shovels and trucks, and took into account the need for continuous feed tonnages and the near-Arctic digging conditions. The equipment would also have to withstand the abrasive effects of quartz-rich sand, which would contribute to the rapid deterioration of metallic digging heads in winter.

Another possibility would have been to use "mining bogies,' which follow a set of rails driven by chain drives underneath. The full bogies automatically tip and unload their cargo into the main feed bin, then return for another load. Eventually, however, GCOS zeroed in on using bucketwheels manufactured for brown coal excavation in cold war West Germany.

The company ordered two, and had them modified for winter. The equipment's huge wheels needed to be assembled in Germany for testing, disassembled for transportation, and then re-assembled for testing and operation at the mine. Also, of course, they had to purchase spare motors and other vital parts.

GCOS was a landmark in oil sands development. It pioneered technology for bitumen extraction and upgrading, and it was the world's first large-scale commercial plant. Like Syncrude eleven years later, when it began operations, it used bucketwheel excavators to mine the oil sands ore. These vehicles, which stood ten storeys tall, crept forward on two pair of caterpillar tracks, digging out oil sand and depositing it onto a conveyor belt which took it to a plant for processing. Especially during -40° winters, the equipment had constant problems. Buckets broke teeth on large rocks in the frozen ground. Even the conveyor belts split in extreme cold.

There, the sands were conditioned in rotating drums, where they were combined with hot water and caustic soda. Centrifuges removed sand and clay, and the resulting bitumen was moved to a fractionating tower, where it was separated into light gases (used for fuel), naphtha, kerosene, and gas oil. Other impurities were then removed, and the naphtha, kerosene, and gas oil blended for shipment by pipeline to market. This high-quality oil was the first of the synthetic oils pioneered in the Fort McMurray area. McClements was the engineer in charge of plant construction. He also served as MC at the official opening, which he vividly remembered. "It was the end of September in 1967: pouring rain, not a very good day at all."[280] McClements told the audience of about 200 that "synthetic crude is a natural for petrochemicals. I see no reason why the stretch along the Athabasca cannot become an industrial valley in time."[281]

The dedication ceremonies were held in what historian Earle Gray called the "bubble"– a huge fabric structure supported by compressed air and formerly used to cover winter construction at the plant site. The sound of heavy equipment and the shrill siren blast from the excavating machines reverberated throughout the bubble, signifying here was a project so urgent that production couldn't be stopped even...for the official dedication."

He described "a long head-table of company officials and visiting dignitaries and an endless procession of speakers. Sidney Ells was there, a living witness to the 54 years of hopes and frustrations that had passed since that day he had first arrived at Athabasca by river scow to assess possibilities of developing the tar sands."[282] Two others officiated: Premier Ernest Manning and Pew, who was then 85 years old. In his address Manning said that "no other event in Canada's centennial year is more important or significant.... It is fitting that we are gathered here today to dedicate this plant not merely to the production of oil but to the continual progress and enrichment of mankind."[283]

"No nation can long be secure in this atomic age unless it be amply supplied with petroleum," Pew told his audience. "It is the considered opinion of our group that if the North American continent is to produce the oil to meet its requirements in the years ahead, oil from the Athabasca area must of necessity play an important role."[284]

Karl Clark did not live to see plant completion, however. He witnessed the sod-turning in 1963, but died in December 1966, nine months before the plant went into operation. "It affected him deeply to see the landscape of his beloved Athabasca country scarred as the construction gangs began stripping away the overburden for the operation," wrote his daughter Mary in her biography. "Only a few weeks before he died from a cancer he had been fighting for three years, he confided...that he had no wish to return again to the scene."[285]

"When Great Canadian Oil Sands began production in 1967, it represented a remarkable achievement," wrote Chastko. "A Canadian company, backed by the investment capital of a U.S. multinational corporation, used a separation process researched and developed by scientists funded by the governments of Canada and Alberta to produce a synthetic oil capable of competing against conventional Saudi crude in world oil markets."[286]

The first years were extremely difficult. Start-up problems prevented the project from achieving sustained production and seriously affected profitability. The learning curve would be slow and difficult.

Beauty is in the eye of the beholder, however, and McClements recalled the day he gave J. Howard Pew a tour of the plant. "We had visited the mine and were in the refining section of the plant (when) Mr. Pew asked to see a sample of what we were running and I asked an engineer to pull a sample of the product we were making at the moment. Mr. Pew took the bottle and held it up to the light. It was water white. He unscrewed the cap, held one nostril and sniffed the oil. Finally, he stuck his finger in the bottle and tasted the oil. When he did, you could just see his face beam."[287] After Pew's retirement, McClements succeeded him as the chair of Sun Oil.

"Being a pioneer has its glories and rewards," wrote journalist Jim Armstrong in 1975, "but it can also have its hardships and sorrows. Great Canadian Oil Sands Limited is a pioneer in the mining, extracting and processing of the

Athabasca Oil Sands and the difficulties experienced by the company in its first decade of operation have tended to dwarf any glories or rewards the company has achieved."[288]


# OLD OIL, NEW OIL

In 1979, the name Great Canadian Oil Sands became history. Company president Ross Hennigar announced that the three parts of Sun Oil's Canadian operations – GCOS, conventional exploration and production company Sun Oil and the company's downstream operations, which operated under the brand name Sunoco – would merge into a new entity. With these mergers, Suncor Inc. became a fully integrated oil company, with headquarters still in Toronto. Based on an agreement with the federal government, the company began charging world prices for its oil in April 1979 – the same concession on pricing given to Syncrude. However, one of the NEP's goals was to "Canadianize" the oil industry, and Suncor was owned by a foreign company.

During this period of policy turmoil and high energy prices, Canadian petroleum assets were increasingly available as numerous large foreign companies sold their Canadian holdings. In its first year of production the project averaged 15,000 barrels per day – one third of design capacity.

"The company was only kept alive by the faith of Sun Oil Company that poured in tens of millions of dollars to keep the company operating. It was five years before the plant operated to capacity, and seven years before it turned a modest profit," according to another journalist, David Hatter, writing in 1981.

"Not until 1972, five years after start-up, were [the] major problems overcome, and not until 1975 did the plant begin to make money," he continued. "So much cash had to be poured into the plant in the beginning that even today, 14 years after initial start-up, Suncor's economists reckon that, overall, the company is still out of pocket $800 million in 1980 dollars."[289]

The decision to allocate "old oil" prices to Suncor would hit the company particularly hard, according to the *Daily Oil Bulletin*'s first analysis of the new policy. "The real loser in Tuesday's budget appears to be Suncor Inc. While its immediate neighbour Syncrude has not been treated the same way, Suncor has been allotted the Canadian price of $16.75 per barrel for its current production, not the world price of $38 per barrel." Suncor executive vice president William Loar said, with considerable understatement, that "...We will make only 5 per cent on our money. When the Liberal Government estimates that the cost of money is 15 per cent, it seems to me that we are not getting a fair deal."[290]

Fortunately for the oil sands producers, the National Energy Program (NEP) did not touch the prices for expensive-to-produce synthetic oil, which sold at world prices. However, the federal government did expect the company to take steps to increase its Canadian ownership, and the following year Sun sold 25 per cent of its Suncor shares to Ontario Energy Resources (OEC), an Ontario Crown corporation. This development reflected the "Canadianization" goal of the NEP, which used fiscal carrots and sticks to increase Canadian ownership of the industry; the program's aim was to reach fifty per cent Canadian ownership by 1990.

Both partners saw advantages in this deal, according to Jeanne Laux and Maureen Molot. "It gave OEC a 'window' on the oil industry as well as a stake in an integrated petroleum company, and it allowed Suncor to become sufficiently 'Canadianized' to qualify for federal incentive payments that would help defray the costs of exploration on frontier and offshore territory." Because OEC was a taxable subsidiary of the province, Suncor had access to federal grants.[291] Also, Sun was beginning to make a corporate transition away from oil and gas production toward a focus on petroleum refining and marketing. Another attraction for Ontario was that the plant was undergoing a $185 million plant expansion, which would take Suncor production up to 58,000 barrels per day. Under the arcane rules of the NEP, the plant would be permitted to charge world prices for "new oil" from the expansion, while it could still only charge "old oil" prices for output from its original facilities. In 1981, the plant produced its 200 millionth barrel of oil.

That barrel was coincident with the Iran-Iraq War – an armed conflict between the Islamic Republic of Iran and the Republic of Iraq, which lasted from September 1980 to August 1988. At first, oil prices shot into what was then considered the stratosphere – US$30 per barrel. However, within five years prices had plummeted by about two thirds.

Like other oil and gas operators, Suncor sought ways to cut costs. This contributed to a strike/lockout the following year that was one of the most divisive in Alberta history. Suncor had experienced other conflicts between labour and management. For example, in 1969 workers complained about having to pay 10 cents a ride to get on a bus to ride to work. After a few days the company agreed to provide the rides for free. According to a labour historian, Rick Boychuk, in 1978, there was a "bitter, violent" five-week strike at Suncor and there were other, minor conflicts over the years.[292] There is disagreement on the latter. According to Bert McKay, who was a plant supervisor at the time, the only true labour conflict was in 1986.

Suncor was unionized; at the time the labour organization was the McMurray Independent Oil Workers union (which had the acronym MIOW). However, the union proved to be no pussycat. The workers decided to strike over compensation, benefits and shift issues. The company met their efforts with a lockout, and labour/management tensions erupted into a six-month battle. According to a historian of this labour action, Rick Boychuk, the conflict "would shake the city to its foundations. This lockout would last six months and would divide families, skewer neighbourhoods and tear apart friendships. It would drive businesses into bankruptcy, inspire boycotts and provoke mass arrests."[293]

No way, said McKay. There was an injunction to "limit folks on the picket line mainly for safety, and there were some arrests. The record shows that 32 people were cautioned. Thirteen were charged, then released on their own recognizance....Banks gave strikers allowances to minimally pay interest on their mortgages until they returned to work, so few houses were foreclosed In addition when workers went on strike after the lockout, they still had a paycheck to get and many had savings built up in company assets that they freely could cash in."

McKay claimed Boychuk made many factual errors. "We ran the upgrading plant with staff and secretaries and engineers and only called in Sunoco and [other] American folks to help operate the refinery," he said, adding that the refinery was "35 per cent run by local staff, with the balance from outside. Mining, extraction and the powerhouse were run 100 per cent by local Suncor people."[294]

Suncor kept the plant running by setting up a camp at the plant, and bringing in workers from other operations to run the plant; the only access to the plant was by air, because of the picket lines. In the end the two sides reached an agreement. MIOW, which during the strike had received a $1.5 million contribution from the Edmonton-based Energy and Chemical Workers Union, became an affiliate of that union. The Energy and Chemical Workers in 1992 merged with two other labour organizations to form the Communications, Energy and Paperworkers Union of Canada. In 2012 that union merged with the Canadian Auto Workers to become Unifor. At time of writing, a roadside sign decorated with the logos of several dozen unions told those driving into and leaving Fort McMurray that "This is what a union town looks like."

According to Boychuk, years of sour relations between the shop floor and management improved quickly. "Both sides began to trust each other and collaborate in running the plant and mine with greater efficiency and safety....Sick time dropped precipitously and so did overtime. At the same time, production costs began falling and production rates rising." Six months after the workers went back to the job, Suncor calculated that under the new regime, the union would save the company $750,000 in labour costs in the first year. As a sign of appreciation, the company gave each of its thousand union workers a $750 bonus.[295]

# CHAPTER 8

# Syncrude

———

*"Alberta must stand firm in the conviction that the tar sands make up
approximately one third of the known world petroleum reserves."*

— DON GETTY, 1972

IT IS HARD TO UNDERSTATE the importance of Imperial Oil in the oil sands story —
indeed, in the story of Canada's oil industry as a whole. We earlier discussed
the company's pioneering years as a refiner and marketer in the 19th century.
Its pioneering spirit continued through the 20th century — for example, in the
1930s and '40s the company conducted about half of western Canada's oil and
gas activity. According to legend the Leduc discovery was the company's first
successful conventional oil well in Western Canada after a string of 133 dry
holes.

Both Cities Service and Imperial Oil had begun conducting lab tests on the
hot water extraction process. In 1950 Cities Service joined with Royalite and
assumed the majority interest in Bitumount. To run the program, Cities formed
a subsidiary, Cities Service Athabasca, which was joined shortly thereafter by
Imperial and ARCO. In 1960 it constructed a 1,000 ton per day test facility at
Mildred Lake, launching the most comprehensive R&D program undertaken at
the time, and the first trial application of a bucketwheel excavator to mine tar
sand.

## FLUSHED AND AGITATED

As one journalist described the project, it had "an excavator, with a nine-foot diameter bucketwheel, used to gnaw oil and sand loose from the hillside. The oil is separated from the sand in a weird-looking assembly of pipes, tanks and towers called an extraction unit. From 20 to 50 tons of oil sands material per hour is dumped into the unit, flushed with hot water and agitated. A black froth, containing oil, water and some solids is recovered...."[296] This operation, which extracted bitumen at a field facility and upgraded it at a pilot plant, eventually led to the creation of Syncrude.

In 1960, the Cities Service project incorporated as Syncrude, which has since become an oil sands giant. In the same year the GCOS application received approval, 1962, Cities Service Athabasca applied to the Oil and Gas Conservation Board for a license to construct a $356 million project that would produce 100,000 barrels per day of synthetic crude.

As with GCOS, the board had concerns about competition between synthetic oil and conventional oil for limited markets. Edmonton's policy was to limit production from the oil sands to 5 per cent of Alberta's total, however, and rejected the Cities proposal and one from Shell — an *in-situ* project that would have produced 100,000 barrel per day.

As this book makes clear a few chapters hence, Shell's *in-situ* project was quite ahead of its time. It would have injected super-heated steam and a chemical solvent into the sands to emulsify the bitumen, for pumping out of vertical wells.

The one they approved was the 45,000 barrel per day GCOS project. On November 22nd, the day of US president John Kennedy's assassination, the partners in the Mildred Lake project mothballed their test facility. Research continued in Edmonton, where an old oxygen plant was converted into a research lab. To supply a unit capable of processing 120 pounds of the stuff per hour, trucks loaded with oil sand drove over the potholed road to deliver the stuff for experiment.

The four consortium participants in Syncrude — Cities Service, Imperial Oil, Richfield Oil Company and Royalite — still wanted to participate in oil sands development. Accordingly, they formed Syncrude Canada Limited in 1964 to pursue their development interests.

Two Imperial employees, Frank Spragins and Clem Bowman, were assigned to what was then a $16 million project. As research resumed, the participants extended the focus of their research beyond bitumen extraction to include tailings and land reclamation. Later on, they began to investigate lubricants, metals and rubber technology to meet the harsh mining conditions.

Events in Canada and abroad were worrisome. Middle East instability, which had first affected the petroleum industry with the Suez Crisis of 1956, had become a worry again with 1967's Arab-Israeli war – known to history as the Six Day War because that was how long it took Israel to respond to a stealthy, coordinated attack by its Arab neighbours (during a Jewish religious celebration), and defeat them.

Unlike in the glory days of the Leduc and Pembina discoveries, at the time Canada had widespread and growing concerns about Canada's long-term energy supply – not so much because of Alberta's productive capacity, but because of Canada's pipeline network.

Western Canada had given up its potential petroleum markets in Ontario and Québec through the National Oil Policy of 1961. Officially, the federal government's Borden Commission claimed to be promoting Alberta's oil industry by securing for it a protected share of the domestic market. Under the policy, Canada was divided into two oil markets. The market east of the Ottawa Valley (the Borden Line) would use cheap imported oil.

Canadian consumers located west of the Borden Line would use the more expensive Alberta supplies. For the next decade or so, consumers to the West paid between $1.00 and $1.50 more than the $3.00 per barrel world price, and therefore higher prices at the pump than Canadians mostly domiciled in Ottawa and points east.

The Syncrude management committee, the Canadian Petroleum Association and others submitted briefs to Premier Ernest Manning, and Alberta's Legislature tabled a new oil sands policy at the beginning of 1968. In May, Syncrude reapplied to the ERCB – this time, for a license to produce 80,000 barrels per day – only to have external events once again delay approval. Discovered only two months earlier, Alaska's huge Prudhoe Bay oil field raised new concerns that a surplus of conventional oil could develop, threaten oil prices and harm Alberta's crude oil markets. Once again the ERCB deferred the application, but this time only for a year.

Whatever the reasons for the Ottawa Valley Line, it became clear during the 1973 OPEC oil embargo and price shock that it had outlived its usefulness. During the darkest moments of that crisis, the industry piped oil from Alberta to Vancouver, where tankers took the cargo through the Panama Canal and up the Atlantic coast to Montréal.

## BIG GUNS

At that point, according to Syncrude's official account of its history, Imperial Oil and its partners – Cities Service Athabasca, Richfield Oil Corporation and Royalite Oil Company Limited – "called in their top guns to surmount the obstacles.... (Imperial employees) Frank Spragins and Dr. Clement Bowman, men known for their intuitive brilliance and perseverance, were both deeply committed to the success of the project and anxious to see it launched." Spragins became the president of a new entity – an industry consortium named Syncrude. The challenges the two men faced were daunting. The project, in which the participants had already invested $24 million,[297] was on hold, and its sponsors were re-evaluating their resolve. The price of oil never seemed to justify project costs.

Bowman, who later managed the company's research program, tried to develop a new bitumen extraction system based on what he called "sand reduction." As he explained in an interview, this process involved forming bits of sand into a rounded mass – technically, agglomerating them. He developed a tool which then screened these agglomerates away from the sand as a step toward upgrading the bitumen. John Bichard, the inventor, had an important place in some of the early work in the oil sands, according to Bowman, since his invention got rid of 90 per cent of the sand. "I assisted John in developing a pilot plant to test this idea," and in 1962 or 1963 Imperial asked him to be part of the team testing it. It "was an excellent process for handling the course grain tar sands that sit at the base of the formation, close to the valley floor. [However, much tar sand ore is] high in clay and in those areas this sand reduction process was less effective."[298]

Born in Natchez, Mississippi in 1914, Frank Spragins came to Canada in 1943, working for Carter Oil in the Taber area as party chief of a seismic crew. He took a job with Imperial in 1949 and ten years later became involved in what would become Syncrude. Another Imperial Oil veteran, Jack Haston, described him as having "great imagination, tremendous patience in the work he had to do with the participant companies in that project, and a real desire to get as much as he could out of the oil sands. In our spare time, we used to try and think of what could we do [to make it work.] The oil sand holds everything in the world practically [like large quantities of abrasive garnet] and it comes out raw in the bitumen. Frank was desperately pushing the project at that point, because the economics were really, really dicey. The participants were very concerned about proceeding ahead, so Frank was trying to squeeze every nickel he could out of the oil sands in order to justify it."[299]

Spragins was appointed Syncrude's president in 1965, and served as chairman from 1975-1978. Syncrude's account observes that in the 1960s, Spragins urged governments against delay in developing the oil sands. "He warned that if they waited too long, oil sand would be replaced by alternate sources, such as oil from shale in the United States. Spragins predicted that an oil shortage was coming and saw enormous potential in the sticky, oil sands of northern Alberta."[300]

Eric Newell – another Imperial Oil veteran, who served as Syncrude's CEO through the 1990s – described the industry when he took charge. Still dominated by "Frank Spragins and his era's vision, it was draglines and bucket wheels. It was the mining philosophy. You mined for a certain period of time, you mined it out, you shut it down and then you go start a new mine. And in Syncrude's case that meant we could run for 25 years. We could produce about a billion barrels of oil and generate about a billion dollars of royalties for the government. Then we'd be mined out, we'd have to shut 'er down and then we go build another one of these mega-projects. So the vision of the time was mega-projects."[301]

Frustrated at the obstacles to construction of the first mega-project, Spragins sent a blunt message to the province. "We are finding it exceedingly difficult, both individually and jointly, to continue financial support for oil sand development without foreseeable goals. We must emphasize that any additional substantial delay may well have the same effect as a denial of application."[302] The partners reapplied, and in 1969 the consortium received approval to construct an 80,000 barrel per day plant. The consortium proposed a smaller plant in deference to the government's fears about competition between conventional and synthetic oil producers.

With projected labour and construction costs threatening to eat into potential earnings, in 1971 Syncrude asked to have the production capacity of Mildred Lake increased from 80,000 to 125,000 barrels a day.

The ERCB approved this request, but it took another two years for the government of Premier Peter Lougheed to reach a 50-50 agreement with Syncrude on profit sharing. By that time cost estimates were $1 billion. After having the legal documents ratified in September 1973 — just weeks before an oil price crisis began — the premier went on province-wide television to explain the deal. "We feel that profit-sharing is a much more logical way of both evening out the admitted risks for the project, and protecting the ownership rights of the people of Alberta," Lougheed told the province.

"The partners in Syncrude were very reluctant, but we insisted on a 50 per cent share of profits by way of royalty," he continued. "We stayed with this position, and we finally won. It is our estimate that because of this position, the profit-royalties over the twenty-five-year life of the project will exceed one billion dollars."[303] The $960-million Syncrude mega-project would create thousands of jobs for Albertans, Lougheed added. It would also provide a vital backup source of oil for the entire North American continent.

Citizens danced in the streets of Fort McMurray. *The Edmonton Journal* pronounced the deal 'the kind of good news all Albertans can share,'" wrote Brian Brennan. "The *Calgary Herald* and the Calgary *Albertan* echoed the joyous refrain. Alvin Hamilton, a veteran Conservative MP from Saskatchewan, said the deal represented 'economic nationalism at its finest.'"[304]

Chuck Collyer, who began working for Imperial Oil in Sarnia, Ontario in 1952 and 20 years later had an executive role within Syncrude, provided important information on the Syncrude story. Collyer had responsibility for project development and execution, and he held key roles at the company during the

1970s. In the project's early days, he recalled, the Syncrude organization faced important management issues. Prior to 1971, the company was largely research-oriented; many of its staff dated back to the company's formation. Suddenly it was "one of the world's first super-projects, and [had to] transform into an operating company of 3,500 employees."

The company faced intense competition for qualified people. After all, it was in a remote location and until 1975 there were serious uncertainties about whether the project would proceed. Although project participants "provided a small cadre of experienced Canadian senior management, staffing was primarily by external recruitment." He added that "building a company is much more than hiring staff. It also entailed establishing a management philosophy – not easy, considering the diverse backgrounds of even the original executive. What evolved was based on participative management and the team concept."[305]

Syncrude had to define its scope; execute development and construction; and ultimately operate one of the largest and most technically complex projects ever undertaken in Canada, and for which there was no precedent. To put this in perspective, "the mine would be the largest in the world, the mineral processing facilities would be twice the size of the world's second-largest (after those of an open-pit copper and gold mine in Papua New Guinea), and the fluid coker capacity would exceed the total coker capacity worldwide. Given Syncrude's precedent-setting aspects, it was fraught with many risks for the Owners evaluating their investment decision," Collyer said.[306]

"One of the least recognized but most critical challenges was merging cultures, which are so different among the mining, petroleum, and power industries," he added. "Mining personnel joining Syncrude encountered an oil industry culture they didn't easily relate to, and that undoubtedly contributed to frustration. The corporate culture and mutual respect that ultimately evolved have been important contributors to Syncrude's success."[307]

When Suncor started its GCOS plant in 1967, the company mined oil sand with huge bucketwheel excavators which dug directly into the side of the open mine pit. The buckets dug up oil sand and deposited it onto a conveyor belt system, which transported it to the extraction plant. By contrast, the original Syncrude mine used draglines and bucketwheel reclaimers. Draglines scooped up the oil sand, and dumped it into a pile called a windrow. Bucketwheel reclaimers deposited oil sand from the windrow onto vast conveyor belts, which moved it to the extraction plant.


## THE WINNIPEG AGREEMENT

In December 1973, Prime Minister Trudeau announced that his government would develop a "national oil program designed to reach Canadian self-sufficiency in oil and oil products before the end of this decade." Among other measures, this policy added fuel to the crude oil firestorm by making royalties a non-deductible expense for corporate income tax calculations and putting price caps – euphemistically called "made-in-Canada prices" – on conventional oil produced and sold domestically. Alberta responded with plans to implement a 65 per cent surroyalty on oil. The 1974 federal budget made some concessions but retained in principle the right of the federal government to tax provincial resources.[308]

Deeply concerned about global oil supplies, the industrialized nations founded the International Energy Agency toward the end of 1974, just as definitive estimates confirmed that Syncrude's costs had doubled from the initial estimate to approximately $2 billion. Including the utility plant, originally excluded on the assumption that it would be owned and operated by Alberta Power, anticipated costs now exceeded $2.2 billion. This placed a huge burden on the participants, brought the project almost to a halt and put its future in doubt.

Over a three-year period, global oil prices had more than tripled to $11.50 per barrel. The acceleration of international price increases, coupled with fears of oil shortages, had aggravated tensions among provincial, federal and industry leaders, and policy-makers considered it a matter of national urgency to develop stable, secure energy supplies. Ottawa responded by financing subsidies for eastern Canada's oil imports by imposing a tax on western Canada's petroleum exports.

As Canadians in the east worried about living in a country that seemed to be running out of oil, the producing provinces felt hoodwinked and betrayed. In effect, they argued, the feds were arrogating the fiscal benefits of rising oil prices unto themselves and encroaching on provincial resource ownership.

These moves precipitated the bitterest intergovernmental conflicts in Canadian history. The political environment was toxic, and it remained so during the ensuing Syncrude crisis.

When Richfield withdrew from Syncrude, the consortium created two management teams – one to plan ways to deep-six the project; another to find ways to keep it alive. In addition to two top executives from each of the three remaining partners, the life-support team included an executive vice president from Cities Services, Calgary-based Bill Mooney. According to Lougheed, "Everybody knew Bill and he just had a way with him of getting people involved and he's one of the funniest guys I've ever met. He played a major behind-the-scenes role in getting people together."[309]

These men had the task of getting government participation in the Syncrude project despite the toxic political environment. Absent other industry partners, public money was the only alternative to a shutdown. The team of seven made a dozen cross-country trips in 17 days. One breakthrough came toward the end of January, when Mooney walked unannounced into Minister of Energy, Mines and Resources Donald Macdonald's office suite. Hearing that Macdonald was too busy to see him (meetings all day), Mooney decided to wait him out. When Macdonald returned from Cabinet, Mooney accosted him: "I've got to see you." During a brief meeting the minister outlined the concessions the federal government was willing to make. As Mooney was leaving, Macdonald said "If you tell anyone about this I'll call you a goddamned liar."[310]

The Winnipeg Agreement of February 3, 1975 was a thaw in a bitter political climate, but a thaw that did not last. The participants in the 12-hour session convened to reach consensus included many of Canada's key decision-makers.

From the industry's side, top executives included Gordon Sellars of Cities Service, Jack Armstrong of Imperial Oil and Jerry McAfee of Gulf Canada, which had taken over Royalite. Bill Daniel, the chairman and CEO of Shell Canada, was also there to consider taking up Richfield's interest. Each of these leaders was accompanied by a small team of company executives. Spragins, however, was absent.

According to his widow, Nell, "Frank was at home furiously hanging wallpaper. He was not involved in the talks because he was an employee of Syncrude and not of one of the partners... I believe it must have been one of the most trying times of his life."[311]

Three provincial ministers accompanied Premier Lougheed: energy minister Bill Dickie, intergovernmental affairs minister Don Getty, and attorney general Merv Leitch. Ontario Premier Bill Davis also brought key ministers to the negotiations. Federal players included energy minister Donald Macdonald and Jean Chrétien, president of the Treasury Board, and their teams. There was give-and-take from everyone except the Shell delegation, which stormed out of the meetings after an hour. They would have considered taking an equity stake, but first wanted a government-guaranteed base price for production. Daniel and his team went home empty-handed.[312]

The Winnipeg Agreement was a successful effort to replace with government money the 30 per cent equity vacuum created by the departure of Atlantic Richfield: Ottawa took 15 per cent, Alberta 10 per cent and Ontario 5 per cent. The private partners agreed to take a $1.4 billion interest in the project, but Cities Service and Gulf gave Alberta the option to convert a $200 million loan into equity. The province also agreed to construct a pipeline and a power plant, which were risk-free. Particularly innovative was a royalty structure reflecting technological risks. "When Syncrude came along and we got into the negotiations," according to Lougheed, "it was clear we could not approach (royalties) from a gross-revenue point of view. It wasn't really fair because of the risk element involved in such a new process."[313]

At the time a journalist covering Parliament Hill, Gordon Jaremko suggested that there was a clear understanding among Canada's policy-makers – bother federal and provincial – that the oil sands were a critical ingredient if Canada were to become energy self-sufficient. The Winnipeg agreement showed that the understanding that the oil sands were "a national jewel was not just talk. Much of the cost of Syncrude, completed in 1978, two years before the National Energy Programme [sic] arrived, was covered by part-ownership, grants and loans from the Alberta, federal and Ontario governments," he wrote. "At all times the oil sands were exempt from the artificially low made-in-Canada controlled old oil price. The plants received a version of the new oil reference price, which was the deemed international price calculated by officialdom."

"The importance of the oil sands as a priority in the national policy stage was highlighted by one of the two nastiest actions that the Lougheed government conjured up to protest the NEP," he added. "To punish the federal Liberal government and its central Canadian voter base,"[314] Alberta suspended oil sands project approvals, and cut production rates by 15-per-cent.

It took eighteen months to prepare legal documentation for the Winnipeg Agreement, and signing took two days. The second day of signing, for dignitaries, was planned for the Saskatchewan Room in Edmonton's Westin Plaza hotel. For the occasion, Bill Mooney used a pair of table knives to pry off the room's nameplate. He replaced it with the one that said The Alberta Room.

The Canadian Petroleum Association's Hans Maciej summed things up. "The first energy war did not end until 1975, after the federal government introduced price increases for crude oil and natural gas and, most importantly, recognized the role of royalties paid prior to the price upheaval as a legitimate business expense."[315] The first of two political wars had begun. The battles would rage for a decade.


## START-UP

The most influential person at those meetings was probably Peter Lougheed, for whom the oil sands remained a core interest to the end of his long life. "After I left government in '85 I said to my successor, Don Getty, 'Don, I will stay out of most things you're doing…but the one thing I am going to stay involved in is the oil sands, because I am very interested in its evolution and its development.,'" he said. "Things happened quickly [under] Premier Klein. I stayed involved in the oil sands in a public way and I discussed it frequently with Premier Ed Stelmach as well. Perhaps more than any other, that's the one subject I have stayed involved in since I left government."

In addition to getting Syncrude kick-started, Lougheed strongly asserted and ultimately resolved, beyond question, Alberta's ownership of most hydrocarbon and other mineral resources within its provincial borders, and he made it clear to industry itself that the government was in charge. "It was obvious that the oil sands were owned by the people of Alberta," he said. "We consistently and constantly made sure that the industry understood that the Government of Alberta was the owner, and we weren't just there in a supervisory or regulatory way. We were extensively involved because we were the owners."

To a considerable extent, that rescue involved a new way of looking at royalties. Lougheed's interest in petroleum royalties began early in his years in power, before the events of the early 1970s drove prices to historically high levels. "We were in a fairly experimental period with the oil sands," he said, "we had the Great Canadian Oil Sands [project] which was struggling. When Syncrude came along and we got into the negotiations, it was clear we could not approach [the owner's share] from the perspective of gross revenue....We had inherited from [Ernest Manning's] Social Credit government a good system of royalties for the conventional oil and gas system, which was a percentage of gross revenue. We modified it from time to time in government, but the conventional oil and gas business was based on a percentage of gross revenue."

The oil sands were a different kettle of fish. "Right from the start it was clear that it wasn't really fair because of the risk element that came with being involved in such a new process. You know, a lot of people wondered, was it going to work? Would it be economic?" All of those questions led to a discussion between the owner – the Government of Alberta – and Syncrude 'What kind of royalty scheme should we have?' [The discussion] evolved into the whole question of a net profits approach. It was completely different than [the policy used for] the conventional oil and gas industry."[316]

Before Syncrude began operations, the CBC ran a television "docudrama" about the project based on Larry Pratt's book *The Tar Sands: Syncrude and the Politics of Oil.* The slim volume sold 13,000 copies, making it a national bestseller. The book itself is a reasonable analysis of the political events surrounding the development of the oil sands. A professor of political science at the University of Alberta, Pratt was critical of the oil sands, but his work is certainly a reasonable academic study. However, the docudrama was not. It went beyond the facts to portray the personalities involved – including Frank Spragins and Peter Lougheed – as foul-mouthed, cigar-chomping and conniving.

In a statement after it aired, Lougheed said "Such a program is outrageous and immoral. My only remedy is to seek legal redress in the courts. My solicitor sent a message to the Canadian Broadcasting Corporation yesterday cautioning them of the apparently defamatory meaning of such a program. I was instructed by my solicitor to commence an action in my personal name for damages to my character and reputation."[317] In the end, he was awarded $50,000 in an out-of-court settlement, an apology and an agreement from the CBC that the network would never show the program again. This incident graphically captured the gathering political conflict, which increasingly pitted central Canada against the West, with prosperous Alberta shouldering much of the burden. Lougheed didn't find this episode amusing, but it did have a funny side. According to Nell Spragins, The Edmonton Journal's *TV Guide* listed the docudrama "on the TV schedule as *Tarzan* instead of tar sands."[318]

At this writing, the company was the largest industrial employer of Aboriginal people in Canada, with people from Canada's First Nations making up around 8 per cent of its workforce. In addition, the company had conducted more than $1.5 billion in business with Aboriginal companies, most of them headquartered at nearby Fort McKay. By 2011 the company employed 5,500 people directly and an average of 1,000-1,500 maintenance contractor employees. According to the company, Syncrude's operations provided jobs for 14,000 people directly and indirectly across Canada.

Syncrude went into operation in the summer of 1978 and produced 5 million barrels of oil within a year. Inexplicably to most people, the indomitable Frank Spragins – for nearly two decades one of Canada's most vocal and visible proponents of oil sands megaprojects – had resigned his presidency the previous year.

"A number of colossal projects will have to be undertaken and such projects take time," he told a university audience just after leaving the president's office. "Twenty years for the Syncrude project, for example. Therefore, we should waste no time in getting major heavy oil and tar sands projects underway. To do this, it will take complete cooperation between industry and government with a good measure of support by the public. Hopefully the Syncrude Project will be a guide in this direction. Henceforth, if we know the way, the big word is action and that means action now...."[319]

At Syncrude's September 15, 1978 official opening there were endless "tributes and wishes of congratulations between the oil companies and the federal,

Alberta and Ontario governments," according to the *Edmonton Journal's* reporter on the scene. "Lougheed and Syncrude president Brent Scott paid tribute to former Syncrude president Frank Spragins. Scott said Spragins fought for the project and continued to urge Canada to develop its oil sands....[and] after the ceremony, Spragins said he waited for the opening for almost 20 years, which at times 'seemed like a hundred years.'"[320] Spragins received a standing ovation from an audience of seven hundred.

That ovation acknowledged his achievements, of course, but it also reflected concern about his state of health. "He was quite sick," explained Nell Spragins, his widow. "He did speak (at the podium) a little bit, but it was obvious he was very sick. I don't cry easily, but I remember I was in tears. Frank went and lay down and that's where we were after [the ceremonies]. At least he was alive for the opening, but he was terribly sick." She added, "He should've been given painkillers but he wasn't. There [must have been] something they could give him.... I took him [to the hospital] at noon on a Wednesday and he passed away at five the next morning."[321]

Syncrude put the story more glamorously: "The man behind the mission and a visionary of the first order, (he) died six weeks after the official opening of the Syncrude operation."[322]

A big part of that legacy, of course, was keeping Syncrude on the rails. A major investor in R&D, Syncrude made huge strides in improving its mining and processing technology, although not everything went according to plan. The plant had start-up problems and the need for "debottlenecking" was great. And on August 15, 1984 – six years after the plant began operations and just as the consortium was planning a $1.2 billion expansion – Syncrude found itself with a serious problem.

An explosion and fire shut the plant down for four months, and an investigation into the incident soon found the source of the problem. During construction a contractor had installed a piece of pipe, 45 centimetres long and 15 centimetres in diameter, made of the wrong alloy. One outcome was that 11,727,445 barrels of production, which could have fetched up to C$40 per barrel, were lost, and project participants soon found themselves facing claims and counterclaims in court. At one point a ruling from the Alberta Court of Queen's Bench by Chief Justice Kenneth Moore summed up the claims as $240.3 million for damages to property and $916.1 million for loss of profit. The final settlements took place out of court and have never been disclosed. However, the claims from this incident totalled more than the initial projected construction costs, and the case took longer to resolve than the time required to construct the mine and plant.

As these suits were going on, Syncrude began using giant computerized trucks and shovels for overburden removal. Like Suncor, the company later used this system to replace its burdensome and more costly bucketwheel and dragline mining setup. Prior to the development of this system, draglines – each with a bucket the size of a two-car garage – mined the oil sand, placing it in windrows until a bucketwheel placed it onto a conveyor system for transport to the plant.

The use of trucks and shovels only became possible because of improvements in vehicular transport. Today's trucks stand three stories tall. According to Brent Scott, who was then a Syncrude vice president, during the design and planning of the plant one of the big decisions the company had to make was whether to use "truck and shovel versus dragline, or bucketwheel, or conveyer….We started off with the thought that draglines were better…The other option was the one that Suncor used, which was to take bucketwheels up against the face of the thing and mine it there. Now there were advantages to each….The third option was truck and shovel, (but) at that point, trucks were 85 cubic yards or something and it wasn't economic."[323] However, Syncrude soon found that dragline/bucketwheel mining left the sand exposed so long that it would start to oxidize and actually become more difficult to work with. In addition, in some areas of the mine, overburden couldn't support the immense weight of the draglines. Accordingly, the investigation into trucks and shovels took on a new urgency.

The company had to deal with many other start-up problems. Its process systems and equipment were new, with many of them unprecedented in terms of size or application. In addition, the harsh winter conditions in the Fort McMurray area were tough on draglines, bucketwheel excavators, and conveyors. Coming to grips with these issues constrained production in 1979, the first year of operation, to only 18 million barrels (50,000 barrels per day).

The size, financial backing and commitment of the original partners – notably Imperial Oil, which in many ways has always been the project's technical and managerial leader – enabled Syncrude to face down its many challenges, often through innovation. For example, "due to the size of the mining capacity limitations equipment then available, selection of the mining scheme was one of the most critical decisions," according to Chuck Collyer. "Syncrude has remained at the forefront of the suppliers in advanced mining and mineral processing technology – efforts that have led directly to advances such as hydro-transport and 400-ton haul trucks."[324] He added that Syncrude began showing its commitment to environmental preservation in 1969, with the launch of an aggressive environmental research program.

By 2010, Syncrude was producing about 300,000 barrels of synthetic oil per day – roughly equivalent to 15 per cent of Canadian consumption. By this time, the company had undergone three expansions. Between 1996 and 1999, the company invested $470 million to expand the original mine and debottleneck the plant. Starting in 1998, the company invested another $1 billion on a new mine, Aurora, and further debottlenecking. Production from Aurora began in July 2001, with production rising to 90 million barrels per year. The third stage of expansion involved bringing on a second train from the Aurora mine and expanding the Mildred Lake upgrader, and added 100,000 barrels of production per day. This expansion began in 2001, and was quite over budget: $8.4 billion compared to a $5.7 billion estimate. However, good fortune again favoured Syncrude. Its expensive new facilities began operations in 2006, just as oil prices again soared to historic highs.

Ownership in the Syncrude plant changed over the years, as a variety of mergers took over the pieces funded by the original owners. A dramatic change took place at the beginning of 2016, when Suncor added the largest position in the oil sands giant – nearly 37 per cent owned by publically traded Canadian Oil Sands Ltd. – through what initially began as a hostile takeover. The outcome was that Suncor owned about 48 per cent of the giant – almost twice as much as project manager Imperial Oil.

## Oil sands mines multiply

As always a vital player in Canada's oil industry, at the end of 2011 Imperial Oil commissioned a new kind of oil sands mine. The Imperial-operated Kearl oil sands project began processing ore from a mine 70 kilometres from Fort McMurray. At this writing, the owners – Imperial Oil Resources (70 per cent) and ExxonMobil Canada Ltd. (30 per cent) – estimated completion of the first stage to cost nearly $13 billion and a second stage to take construction costs to $28 billion.

When finished, the Kearl project would be huge. At full capacity of 345,000 barrels per day around 2020, it was to become be one of the world's largest sources of crude. From the beginning it would produce low-carbon bitumen, and the company expected it to do so for 40 to 50 years. It would achieve this apparent industrial miracle through advanced oil sand processing techniques and the production of diluted bitumen which did not need to be upgraded.

Unlike the other mine-based projects in the Fort McMurray area, its owners designed the project in such a way that it would not produce high-carbon oil. Indeed, the product flowing into American refineries would produce no more carbon emissions than those produced by the average barrel then refined in the United States. This, of course, was a radical concept, based on a technology known as high-temperature paraffinic froth treatment.

Syncrude did the early fundamental work on this technology. What it does, said Shell VP John Broadhurst, to make bitumen "clean and pipeline-able." To understand the difference, the conventional technologies used at Syncrude and Suncor in the past involved a "naphthenic process. You dilute bitumen still some clays and some water and then you use different mechanisms to physically separate other materials from the bitumen," he said. The outcome is that "you get something that is clean enough to go into a coker, but not clean enough to go into a pipeline. Essentially, you are using mechanical separation."

By contrast, paraffinic froth treatment creates a product "clean enough to put into a catalytic upgrading process, not a coking process." At its Scotford refinery complex, Shell developed an upgrading process based on catalytic hydrogen, and "the paraffinic froth treatment was an absolutely essential component to make the whole thing work. And so, we developed the technology actually in parallel with advancing the project," he said. "It had to work, because everything relied on that plain bitumen product. Similarly, our colleagues over at [Imperial's] Kearl project were able to take the same fundamentals work that had been provided by Syncrude through CONRAD. They developed a paraffinic froth treatment process to get a product that was clean enough to go into the pipeline system. That was a slightly different driver, but the point was the same. You needed something cleaner than the legacy naphthenic processes. This was a critical technology and it's the technology that unlocked our ability to move mineable bitumen to market."[325]

Originally developed by Syncrude in partnership with Natural Resources Canada's CANMET Energy Technology Centre in Devon, Alberta, this froth technology removes only lighter hydrocarbons from oil sands ore, leaving undesirable asphaltenes behind. Asphaltenes carry most of the very fine solid particles "fines") that created tailings pond nightmares for older plants. Asphaltenes contain almost as much carbon as hydrogen, but they also contain nitrogen, oxygen, sulphur, vanadium and nickel. Thus, in the typical refinery, asphaltenes are a low-end product with few uses beyond road pavement and roofing tar. The fewer asphaltenes piped into the refinery, the more high-end products the refiner could ship out after processing. According to Imperial's Pius Rolheiser, through this process "we can return them as waste to the mine."

Although the concept originated in Alberta, Rolheiser stressed that Imperial's relationship with ExxonMobil played an important role in project development. "Imperial has access to global technologies, assets and expertise. They have executed multibillion-dollar projects all over the world. They have an unprecedented research capability. Our affiliation with them gives us a lot." Not only did ExxonMobil bring patents and engineering ideas to the table, he said. "The partnership enabled Imperial to leverage its own expertise."[326]

Syncrude, of course, was still the largest oil producer in Canada. A joint venture operated by seven different oil companies (governments had long since divested their interests) with a management team headed by Imperial, it produced more than 350,000 barrels per day. The other large oil sands mining operation belonged to Suncor Energy, which was Canada's largest energy company. Its base operations include the Millennium Mine and Upgrader, which had been operating since 1967, and the North Steepbank Debottleneck and Mine Extension operation, which went in service in 2007.

Third was Shell's Albian Sands project, which operated the Muskeg River and Jackpine mines. Shell was the operator and majority shareholder of the joint venture among Shell Canada (60 per cent), Chevron Canada Limited (20 per cent) and Marathon Oil Canada Corporation (20 per cent). Besides these mining and extraction operations, the project incorporated Shell's upgrader at Scotford, near Edmonton, and the proposed Quest carbon capture and storage project, north of Edmonton.

The Scotford operation dated back to 1985, when Shell Canada commissioned the first refinery ever designed solely for the processing of synthetic oil from the Athabasca oil sands. Located northeast of Edmonton, this 60,000 barrel per day facility soon became a notable success. Although Shell paid a premium for its feedstock, the company could squeeze more light products from synthetic feedstock than it could from conventional oil. Less waste meant that the refinery got a better return from every barrel of oil it refined.

The fourth oil sands mining and upgrading operation was Canadian Natural Resources' Horizon project, which went onstream in 2008. The project produced about 100,000 barrels per day of synthetic oil in 2013.

# CHAPTER 9

# Policy meets economics

———

*"The decisions relate to energy. They will impinge, however, on almost
every sphere of Canadian activity, on the fortunes of every Canadian and
on the economic and social structure of the nation for years to come."*

— MARC LALONDE, *1980*

THIS STORY HAS ALREADY MENTIONED The National Energy Program, and the global
forces and Canadian political developments that brought it on. To go back to that
time, it is important to understand that Canada was caught up in period of economic nationalism. US industry had long dominated the Canadian economy in
terms of both manufacturing and resource extraction. Canadians worried that
foreign interests – Sun Oil was, after all, a large American oil company – would
continue to dominate what was clearly a vast resource, owned by the province of
Alberta. In 1972 the province developed a strategy clearly focused on this concern.

Led by Intergovernmental Affairs Minister Don Getty, who would later
serve as premier, the authors of this report wrote that "Alberta must stand firm
in the conviction that the tar sands make up approximately one third of the
known world petroleum reserves." Herman Kahn and Jean-Pierre Goyer in all
likelihood were aware of this report, which also worried about land reclamation, which it summarized graphically.

Assuming eight Syncrude-sized plants, an annual production rate of 1
million barrels per day would mean daily water requirements equal to nearly

10 per cent of the minimum monthly average flow of the Athabasca River, and six acres of land would be disturbed daily by mining operations. "Owing to the delay required before tailings ponds can be reclaimed," the report said, "the denuded area may reach as high as 20,000 acres before a balance between newly disturbed and reclaimed areas could be reached. And the volume of waste being disposed to the tailings areas would be in the order of two million cubic yards daily"[327] – an amount equivalent to mining, each day, a volume of oil sand ore equal in volume to 17 Alberta Legislature buildings.

"As demand for energy throughout the world increases, the price per barrel of crude will increase, and the higher the price rises the more economical it will be for the industry to extract, process, and synthesize secondary and tertiary components," the report continued. "Alberta should be able to utilize the tar sands as a lever in the socio-economic development of the province," it said. "In addition to regulating the timing and sequencing, the development of the tar sands will be constrained by insisting on Canadian investment and participation. This should be very definitely spelled out. The province recognizes that the development of the tar sands can only serve the interests of Albertans if Albertans are significant participants in the development. It should be the intent of the province to permit the development of the tar sands only where it has been satisfactorily demonstrated that Albertans and Canadians both will have the opportunity to significantly participate in the development."[328]

In the period leading up to final decisions about Syncrude, concerns about foreign ownership and the environment had become more potent, and costs were rising into the stratosphere. Like other major North American projects in the 1970s, the project's costs began to skyrocket. International concern for energy security prompted widespread positioning for energy-related projects. One result was an unprecedented demand for engineering and manufacturing capacity. This resulted in almost unprecedented levels of price escalation. Frequently contracts only specified cost at time of delivery, and delivery itself was extended and even uncertain. Budgets for practically every aspect of the Syncrude project multiplied – so much so that by the end of 1973 a reassessment of the project, which was already under construction, put its cost at more than $2 billion.

Concurrently, Richfield's parent company found itself with an embarrassment of great places to invest its money – not only Prudhoe Bay, but also in new discoveries in Britain's North Sea. These projects were low-risk, but development costs at Prudhoe Bay were rising. Also, Canada seemed increasingly unfriendly to foreign participants in its petroleum industry. Richfield withdrew its 30 per cent participation, effective December 31$^{st}$, 1974. The remaining partners informed the Alberta government that they were unwilling to invest more than $1 billion. For the project to proceed, they would need to find another $1 billion of risk capital.

At the end of the 1970s, another series of energy shocks began, although not all those shocks took prices skyward. The first came in 1979, when a hodgepodge of leftist, Islamic and student groups overthrew the dynastic regime in Iran – forcing the Shah to flee on January 17$^{th}$. The country's new "Supreme Leader," a cleric named Ayatollah Khomeini, abolished the monarchy and declared Iran an Islamic republic. These developments created a nervous market. Already at their highest real levels in a century, oil prices shot up by another $3, to $15 per barrel. The following year when Iraq's Saddam Hussein, sensing weakness in the neighbouring country, provoked the Iran-Iraq War – the longest conventional war in the 20$^{th}$ century, and one of the bloodiest – oil prices doubled, to $30 per barrel.

"Something has to be done" was the thinking, and governments had already set out to do it. One Canadian response to the volatile oil prices of the 1970s had been to create Crown corporations. The federal government had been the first off the mark in 1973, with a minority Liberal government supporting a New Democratic Party bill to form Petro-Canada. Alberta created Alberta Energy; Saskatchewan, Saskoil.

## A NEW WORLD ORDER

In Canada these institutions have a long and storied history – their main advantage being greater freedom from direct political control than government departments. Canada's first was the Board of Works, established in 1841 to construct a shipping canal system in the Province of Canada. Today they include such enterprises as the Canadian Broadcasting Corporation, VIA Rail, Canada Post and the Bank of Canada. Canada's governments later privatised both the government-owned oil companies of the 1970s and their stakes in Syncrude.

Early successes at GCOS and Syncrude bred enthusiasm for the oil sands, and others wanted to follow. However, there would be no successor to Syncrude for two more decades, for a variety of reasons. In a very real sense, Syncrude was the last of the pioneer oil sands megaprojects. When the next round of plants began to appear, they were part of a new world order.

To understand the background, it is worth noting that there were distinct parallels between Suncor and Syncrude in terms of project development. Both remained in the planning stages until policy-makers began to anticipate conventional oil shortages, and both needed to be large-scale projects to justify the high cost of development. Both received special inducements from government, which included exemptions from the existing pro-rationing system. Effective in 1978, both were also exempt from price controls on crude oil. In addition, both received financing and taxation concessions. By themselves, market forces were not the issue. Governments controlled prices, royalties, taxes and land.

The 1979 turmoil in the Middle East aggravated two problems in Canada. One was a large transfer of wealth from consumers to producers. François Bregha explained it as "a large interregional transfer of wealth from Ontario and Québec (which together accounted for 58 per cent of domestic oil consumption in 1980) to Alberta (which produced 86 per cent of Canada's oil), and an international transfer of wealth from Canada to the US as a result of the high level of American ownership of the oil and gas industry."[329] In addition, the rapid increase in international prices intensified inflation; contributed to the federal deficit; and strained Canada's system of equalization payments.

Ottawa's response came in 1980, with the introduction of the National Energy Program. As the most authoritative study of this policy puts it, this policy was "first and foremost a political act intended simultaneously to change the structure of power between Ottawa and the provinces and between Ottawa and the oil industry," the authors said. "Like most significant national political decisions, it did not result in nor was it primarily intended to produce good economics."[330] Its aims were to increase Canadian ownership of the sector, achieve energy self-sufficiency, and gain a greater share of energy revenues. Created by a small group of mandarins in Ottawa, the NEP was a bewildering mix of policies.

"The energy policies hit the petroleum industry by the discriminatory measures that discouraged the investment of foreign capital," wrote Earle Gray, and "by the 'Canadianization' measures which wound up bankrupting the Canadian-owned firms they were intended to help."[331] In itself, *The National Energy Programme* [sic] book was a masterpiece of persuasion. Such was its silver tongue that it initially won over many readers.

At the time, I worked in Calgary for Gulf Oil Canada and we had a meeting on the policy the day after its launch. Memorably, production manager Dan Motyka said "We think this is good for Gulf and good for Canada." The others in the room — many of them senior people based at the company's headquarters in Toronto — expressed surprise. They were right: the NEP deserved a blue ribbon for being the most ill-timed, counter-productive energy legislation in Canadian history.

Packaged for the electorate as a policy based upon "energy security, opportunity and fairness" in a world apparently facing an energy crisis, the framers of the policy wrote that "We need not face an uncertain supply of oil. Nor do we have to suffer economically as badly as other nations who lack our energy potential. If a way can be found to share more equitably the benefits of Canada's energy resources, it may be possible to insulate Canada from some of the shocks emanating from the world economy, and to build upon this energy strength an industrial base in all parts of Canada that will provide for sustained economic growth."

The policy was based on assumptions about the need for national control over a strategic industry, the critical importance of developing expensive oilfields in the Canadian frontiers, and the virtual certainty of ever-increasing oil prices. In practice, the policy encountered lower oil prices almost from the day Finance Minister Allan MacEachen introduced it as the keystone of the federal Budget. "This is a set of national decisions by the Government of Canada," the policy book said. "The decisions relate to energy. They will impinge, however, on almost every sphere of Canadian activity, on the fortunes of every Canadian and on the economic and social structure of the nation for years to come."[332]

In the beginning, compromise seemed impossible. After a year, however, the two levels of government did agree to a pricing and revenue-sharing agreement, memorialized in the press by photos of Peter Lougheed and Marc Lalonde toasting the deal with Champagne. Left out in the cold, the petroleum sector didn't share in the celebrations. Under the terms of the new deal, the sector could realize additional revenue, but only if oil prices, which had already begun to recede, continued to rise.

The NEP and its successor agreement spilled an alphabet soup of new taxes and incentives on companies within the industry with a significant percentage of foreign ownership. The purpose was to increase tax revenue and influence how and where Canadian exploration and development investment would be spent. In theory, the program would increase general revenues and fund its own programs, which included subsidizing oil imports. Even Canada's domestic oil producers, who might have benefitted from the program, were outraged.

The Independent Petroleum Association of Canada, for example, took out full-page ads addressed five simple messages to the Finance Minister: "Your energy policy will harm Canadians. It will make Canadians more dependent on expensive, insecure foreign oil. It will cost Canadians more for gasoline and heating oil in the long run. It will delay essential frontier exploration, oil sands plants and heavy oil development. It will cost thousands of jobs that could be created by the oil industry across Canada." The ad continued, "Canada must achieve oil self-sufficiency. We are the companies your program was supposed to help – the independent Canadian companies. It doesn't help us – it has stopped us in our tracks. We urge you to reconsider this program for the good of all Canadians."[333]

Compelled by federal law, foreign oil companies sold Canadian assets to Canadian companies at inflated prices – receiving $4.8 billion in 1981 alone. Canadian companies borrowed heavily for the privilege of acquiring overpriced assets, and paid astronomical interest rates for doing so. Petro-Canada was particularly active in the hunt. The company invested more than $7 billion in overpriced assets.

Twenty years later, the privatised corporation's market capitalization was about $9.5 billion, reflecting a poor return on its original investments. Government-funded cash grants encouraged Canadian explorers to spend heavily and fruitlessly in costly drilling in the North and the offshore frontiers. Not a single important frontier discovery took place during the NEP era. Fertilized by government grants, frontier drilling and exploration costs grew dramatically.

Some companies – notably Dome Petroleum, which accrued $8 billion in debt before US-based Amoco came in to acquire its carcass – set up offshore drilling companies. The idea was to drill for grants, rather than drill for oil. The federal government hailed Dome as the Canadian oil industry's great success story, yet it ironically was unable to qualify under NEP rules as a Canadian company. The reason was that its stock was widely held abroad, especially in the United States. As the decade wore on, bankruptcies in Alberta reached new highs and real estate prices crumbled. Although exacerbated in 1982/83 by what was then the worst global slowdown since the Great Depression, the severity of the decline in Western Canada was unique among the world's petroleum-based economics. Norway, for example, boomed throughout the NEP years. The NEP led to the collapse of Syncrude-style oil sands projects.

This policy was a stark contrast to one being developed in the United States for the incoming American president, who had appointed a task force to spell out energy policy. "The Task Force advising President-Elect Ronald Reagan on energy policy is urging him to remove all price controls on oil and natural gas; allow public lands to be explored and developed; to reduce environmental impediments, speed the licensing of nuclear power plants and reprocessing facilities and restructure the Department of Energy. The panel dismissed conservation as an important tool of energy policy and underscored the role of production in solving the energy crisis."[334]

## COLD LAKE

Another important project from the period was Imperial Oil's proposed Cold Lake mega-project. After Athabasca, Cold Lake is the most important oil sands deposit. Imperial had acquired leases in this area in the 1950s, and eventually estimated its bitumen in place at 44 billion barrels. As thick as a 20-story building is tall, the oil sand lies about 1,500 feet below ground. In 1964, the company set up a 4-well pilot plant at Ethel Lake. Eight years later, the company developed a 23-well pilot at May Lake. And in 1975 the company began a 56-well project at Lemming. That plan was so successful the company later increased the number of operating wells to 300.

In 1979 Imperial applied to build a $7 billion, 135,000 barrel per day in-situ plant and upgrader at Cold Lake. "Given the variations in prices and things like that, it took a long time before the company was confident in the production and the thermal production process," according to Howard Dingle, who was a company vice president. However, in the early 80s "we began the process of seeking approval for a combined production process and upgrader. That would have been the Cold Lake mega-project. I was transferred to Cold Lake in 1983 to head up operations," he said. The company decided to go ahead with the production part of the project, but dropped the upgrader. "It got resurrected when we discovered we could sell diluted bitumen to other people who already had upgraders. ...We didn't build the upgrader, but started using other people's upgraders. Well, some of our own in Sarnia. We had a coker with Koch Oil in Minneapolis. So, the project did proceed. It is just that we never ended up building the upgrader onsite."[335]

## THE CRUSHER

Less successful was a plant originally proposed by Shell Canada, Shell Explorer, Amoco Canada, Pacific Petroleum, Chevron Standard, Gulf Canada, Petrofina Canada, and Dome Petroleum. Shell had applied for this Fort McMurray-area plant in 1962, the year of the original GCOS and Cities Service submissions. When first proposed the most ambitious of the original applications, its engineering plans were at a new scale — 130,000 barrels per day, to cost $50 million, with production to begin in 1969. Alberta's policy of restricting oil sands development meant the Shell project, like Syncrude, received a deferral. Unlike the members of the Cities Service consortium, however, Shell did not soon reapply. With Richfield's 1968 discovery of oil at Prudhoe Bay, the decision not to invest heavily in the oil sands seemed prudent. The Alaskan discovery was immense, and there was a chance of similar finds in the Canadian Arctic. Shell came to question the wisdom of investing in high-cost synthetic oil.

When the company did reappear in the oil sands mining scene, the year was 1978, and Shell led a reconfigured consortium proposing the Alsands project. Initially estimated to cost $5.1 billion, the project would produce 137,000 barrels per day of synthetic oil, it would have a 30-year project life, and it would begin operations in 1986. The Conservation Board gave the project the green light in December 1979, and the participants began site-clearing and other preliminaries for project development the following month. However, by then the anticipated cost of the venture – larger than Syncrude – had risen to $6-7 billion. The consortium soon halted construction, reflecting concern about the NEP and costs, which continued to rise.

The project's forecast price tag soon hit $13 billion, representing what at that time was the astonishing investment of $35,000-$40,000 per flowing barrel for capital costs alone. (By way of comparison, the cost per flowing barrel for GCOS had been $7,800.) Capital costs were an important issue, but there were three other reasons the project failed. First, despite high oil prices, the NEP had devastated industry's cash flows; second, prime interest rates were more than 20 per cent; third, oil price forecasts were beginning to decline – a process that would soon accelerate. There would be no profit in the mining venture, but there were other alternatives.

In 1981 Shell "took the investment decision for the Scotford refinery, which is the first and only 100 per cent synthetic crude oil refinery," according to vice president John Broadhurst.

Alsands and Scotford were originally designed to complement each other: Alsands would produce synthetic crude oil and the refinery would process it. Given the economic circumstances in the early 1980s, "the mine to produce the synthetic bitumen didn't make sense," he said. "There was an ample supply of synthetic crude oil from Syncrude and Suncor."

When the company revisited the project again, in the mid-1990s, Shell considered how best to integrate the output from an upgrader into the refinery. "We had to figure about how to transport bitumen 590 kilometres to the upgrader. And then, that drives the process you have to have in place for the upstream. It was a very creative process: you have to look at what assets you have, what assets other people have and then you build out your options to take advantage of that."

The result was Shell's Albian Sands operation, which at this writing included two mines. "The Muskeg River Mine we started up in 2002, the Jackpine Mine on the eastern part of the lease which we started up in 2006," he said.

> We have a significant lease-holding portfolio. We've got pipeline infra-
> structure through a third-party commercial partner. Between the
> mines and the Scotford Upgrader we have a diluent return line as part
> of that pipeline system. And, we have at Scotford a large upgrading
> complex that effectively matches our production. We also have the inte-
> gration with the refineries so that the refinery is taking nearly 100 per
> cent of its feedstock from our existing upgrader. And then, of course,
> you go to market from there with your crude oil products. So, the
> thing that we've always been most proud of is that for Albertans we've
> been able to provide a mine to pump solutions. So, if we go all the way
> from mineable bitumen to gas that is going into your pump, into your
> car, jet fuel that is going in the planes you're flying on. We're the only
> operator that goes all the way from mine face to the tank of your car
> in Alberta.[336]

Despite last-ditch efforts by the Alberta and federal governments to save the project, the economic window had closed and the project went on the shelf.[337] "The day Alsands died was a tough day," said Peter Lougheed. "In fact, one friend of mine said the last day of April 1982 was one of the worst days politi- cally in a rather dismal time because we'd gone through the downturn of the 1981-82 winter and we'd had a [Western] separatist chosen in a by-election in February. Then came the crusher: Alsands collapsed."[338]

The moral is that energy crises can unleash the hounds of bad policy. If another period of panic about oil supplies developed, well-intentioned govern- ments could again create well-meaning but counter-productive energy policy —

for example, invoking the nostrum of protecting consumers (also known as voters) as an opportunity to raise government funds. To cite the example of Jean Chrétien, who had served as energy minister in Pierre Trudeau's last government, proudly proclaimed in 1983 that government policies keeping oil prices low had saved consumers $46 billion.

It took a change of government to rid Canada of the vestiges of the NEP. "To their credit, Brian Mulroney's Conservatives saw what was happening," said the CPA's Hans Maciej. "It took them a long time to rectify all the wrongs of the National Energy Program, but they eventually did" so, after forming a majority government in 1984.[339]

For the petroleum industry, that year was another crusher – one in which two calamities struck. The *Ocean Ranger* tragedy involved a semi-submersible drilling rig going down in a winter storm. She took 84 hands into the frigid sea, and none survived.

The other catastrophe involved a blowout at the Amoco-operated Lodgepole drill site, and involved a high-pressure sour gas well. Out of control for 68 days, it took the lives of two blowout specialists and sent another 16 people to hospital. On days with strong westerly winds, residents of Winnipeg (1,500 kilometres away) could smell the rotten-egg odour of the gas.

Then came the third price shock. Oil prices had averaged $36.83 per barrel in 1980. Over the next five years, however, they declined by about a dollar a year. And in January 1986, annual average prices plummeted by about $13 per barrel in a single month. They averaged $14.43 per barrel for that year, and some global trades actually took place below $5 per barrel.

There were several reasons for this price collapse. People had responded to high oil prices by using less oil and substituting cheaper energy forms like coal, natural gas and hydroelectric. Oil production in the non-OPEC world was increasing and the world economy, badly hammered by the recession of 1982-83 (itself partly induced by high oil prices), was weak. In addition, world oil markets were becoming more sophisticated. Beginning in 1983, commodity markets began trading "paper barrels" of oil for future delivery. Oil quickly became the most heavily traded of all non-financial futures contracts, increasing price volatility.

But the decisive factor was Saudi Arabia's decision to open the taps on its reservoirs, supposedly to re-establish its share of the world oil market. That desert kingdom had held the line on production while other members of OPEC members cheated on their production quotas. Saudi's share of global markets then went into rapid decline, and the country needed revenue from a world that needed less OPEC oil. To compensate for the oversupply coming from other OPEC suppliers, the Saudis cut their own production – to 3.6 million barrels per day in 1985 from 10 million just four years earlier. This kept prices up, but the kingdom lost market share and national revenue. In late 1985, the Saudis had had enough. They announced that they were going to increase market share even if it involved a price war. As they turned on the taps, the markets panicked and prices collapsed.

Syncrude's early success bred enthusiasm about the oil sands, and others wanted to follow. However, there would be no successor for two more decades, for a variety of reasons. In a very real sense, Syncrude was the last of the pioneer oil sands megaprojects. When the next round of plants began to appear, they were part of a new world order.

To understand the background, it is worth noting that there were distinct parallels between the respective developments of Suncor and Syncrude. Both projects remained in the planning stage until conventional oil shortages began to be anticipated, and both needed to be relatively-large scale projects to compensate for the high cost of development. Both received special inducements from government, which included exemptions from the existing pro rationing system. Effective in 1978, both were also exempt from price controls on crude oil. In addition, both received concessions in respect to financing and taxation. Thus, "oil sands development could not have occurred much earlier" than it did, according to historian William N.T. Wylie. Development "required a major change in market forces to become viable."[340]

Several large projects were bandied about in the early 1980s. One was Canstar. A joint venture between Petro-Canada and Nova Corporation, it made a brief appearance as a proposal in 1980 and then quickly faded from view. Sandalta – an *in-situ* mega-project proposed by Gulf for its properties in the Wabasca oil sand deposit – inspired even fewer headlines before biting the dust.

The lingering failures of two mine-based projects, however, illustrate the collapse of the mega-project model, followed by the rapid shift to a new policy framework. By name, the proposed projects were Alsands and OSLO.

# Alsands

In 1962 – the year of the original GCOS and Cities Service proposals – Shell Oil of Canada also proposed a plant near Fort McMurray. The most ambitious of the original applications, Shell proposed a 130,000 barrel per day, $50 million plant; production was to begin in 1969. Alberta's policy of restricting oil sands development meant the Shell project also received a deferral. Unlike the members of the Cities Service consortium, Shell did not soon reapply.

When the company did reappear in the oil sands mining scene, the year was 1978, and Shell was the leader of a consortium of ten companies proposing the Alsands project. Initially estimated to cost $5.1 billion, the project was designed to produce 137,000 barrels per day of synthetic oil; it was to have a 30-year project life; and it was to begin operations in 1986.[341] The Conservation Board gave the project the green light in December 1979 and the participants began site clearing and other preliminaries for project development the following month.

Less than a year later, a consortium concerned about the federal government's National Energy Program (NEP) halted construction. The project's forecast cost was $13 billion, representing what at that time was the astonishing investment of $35,000-$40,000 per flowing barrel for capital costs alone. (By way of comparison, the cost per flowing barrel for GCOS was $7,800.) Capital costs were an important issue, but the project began to fail because, despite high oil prices, the NEP had devastated industry's cash flows, prime interest rates were more than 20%[342] and oil price forecasts were on the decline.[343] In negotiations on fiscal terms, Ottawa offered the plant "a price of $38 per barrel for every barrel of synthetic crude produced – about double the price for conventional oil – with this to rise over the years at the same rate as the Consumer Price Index," according to journalist David Hatter. "The project sponsors argue that, with construction costs going up so quickly, the CPI cannot keep pace sufficiently."[344]

Despite last-ditch efforts by the Alberta and federal governments to save the project, the economic window had closed. The project went on the shelf.[345] Said Lougheed, "The day Alsands died was a tough day. In fact, one friend of mine said the last day of April 1982 was one of the worst days politically in a rather dismal time because we'd gone through the downturn of the 1981-82 winter; we'd had a separatist chosen in a by-election in February – then came the crusher, Alsands collapsed."[346]

## OSLO

The last gasp of the old-style oil sands mining project began in 1981, when a consortium formed to develop the $4-5 billion OSLO (Other Six Lease Operations) oil sands project. The project died in 1992 because of poor economics, the withdrawal of federal subsidies and the consortium's inability to find new partners. Given the tumultuous events of that period, it is astonishing that the project stayed alive for more than a decade.

OSLO's original plan would have literally used Syncrude's blueprints and technology for a 77,000 barrel per day facility. The project would have included a mine and extraction plant 80 kilometres north of Fort McMurray. Its upgrader, however, would have been at Redwater, 60 kilometres northeast of Edmonton.

When the project was first proposed, world oil prices stood at around $30 per barrel, so the economics seemed feasible. However, in 1985 oil prices collapsed to about $10, and the petroleum industry, which was already cash-poor because of high taxes, royalties and price controls from the NEP years, found itself on the ropes. Ironically enough, these developments kept the project alive.

The reasons were political. Heading into the 1988 federal election, the federal government had earmarked several billion dollars for energy projects, from Newfoundland (Hibernia) to Vancouver Island (a natural gas pipeline.) According to one federal civil servant, these projects were motivated by "jobs, regional development, a future election, and pressure to rush things so announcements can be made in time to win votes."[347] For the oil sands industry, the government set aside $1.7 billion for OSLO.

In addition to this federal initiative, Alberta's new Don Getty government (Peter Lougheed retired in 1985) was anxious to help the province – mired in a collapse in real estate prices because of outward migration, high unemployment and a shrinking GDP – recover.[348] "As a capital and labour-intensive operation, oil sands development appealed to the Getty government on many levels," according to Paul Chastko. "Investment drove the Alberta economy in the 1970s, and embarking on a large-scale project like OSLO might bring back investor dollars and confidence in the province. Oil sands projects also employed large segments of the province's workforce, from engineers to tradesmen, and would combat unemployment. Synthetic development also offered the province a way to offset its declining conventional crude stocks. Furthermore, given the energy security component, it just might attract investment from Ottawa or another provincial government...."

Other important policy steps from the 1980s ultimately had a considerable effect on the oil sands industry. In the latter 1980s, the Progressive Conservative government of Brian Mulroney took steps to give the U.S. guaranteed access to Canada's oil and gas resources. After the National Energy Program was dismantled, the federal government deregulated oil and gas exports from Canada to the U.S., opened its doors for direct investment by U.S. oil corporations and removed the "vital supply safeguards" that then required a 25-year domestic supply before oil and gas was to be exported. Then the U.S.-Canada Free Trade Agreement of 1989 incorporated an energy-sharing pact. The provisions of this energy pact were grandfathered, along with the rest of the FTA, into the 1994 North American Free Trade Agreement (NAFTA) among the U.S., Canada and Mexico.

The period of high oil prices also benefitted from cash incentives provided by AOSTRA. During the two decades after 1985 prices were strong enough to support plant expansion, but the economic uncertainties were so great that few commercial developments began ground-clearing for construction.

In the early 1990s the federal government – intent on fighting the country's growing federal deficit – announced that it would withdraw from the project. OSLO consortium members – notably Petro-Canada, which had just been privatized – publically critiqued project economics in what was still a lower-oil-price environment. In 1992 OSLO's partners announced their decision to kill the project.[349]


## EXPANSION

The demise of OSLO coincided with decisions by governments to stop intervening as investors in the energy industry. In future, the success or failure of oil sands projects would depend on basic project economics. Given the widespread gloom of that period, it is ironic that the future would come so soon.

Suncor and Syncrude were soon announcing large expansions. Then, in 1999, the Energy and Utilities Board (a successor to the Energy Resources Conservation Board) granted approval for a Shell-led consortium to begin its Muskeg River Mine oil sands development – better known as the Athabasca Oil Sands Project (AOSP). The project went on stream in 2003.

Construction of Canadian Natural Resources' oil sands mining Horizon project began two years later, with the first phase completed in early 2009. The company plans to eventually expand production of synthetic crude oil rate to 500,000 barrels per day.

As this history explains elsewhere, these developments were a response to a new market-driven oil sands policy developed in the mid-1990s. To a considerable extent, the new environment was a response to the policy vacuum that emerged with the death of OSLO.

So doing, it put paid to the NEP. It freed Canadian oil prices from price controls, which in one form or another had been in place since the National Oil Policy of 1961. This policy eliminated the bureaucracy involved in allocating oil supplies to central Canadian refiners. It also eliminated volume and price restrictions on exports to the United States.

In 1989 the Mulroney government negotiated a Free Trade Agreement with America. One outcome was "free movement of oil between the two countries, without discriminatory trade practices," wrote academics Alan MacFadyen and Campbell Watkins.

"After the long period of government-administered pricing, oil companies found the need to market their oil a novel and, for some, chastening experience," they added. The basic price-setting procedure was "familiar from the post-Leduc days, with the major refiners 'posting' the price they would pay at Edmonton for any oil offered to them."[350] This thorough deregulation of pricing created a competitive market for oil.

Refiners and petrochemical plants bought oil on the open market at a posted price. Under this system the price of Alberta oil in markets where suppliers faced competition from other regions would be highly competitive. Since international oil prices were (and are) denominated in U.S. dollars the commodity's prices would reflect changes in exchange rates. They would go up if the Canadian dollar fell relative to the U.S. dollar, and fall if the Canadian dollar rose.

These events took place under the Alberta's Progressive Conservative party new leader, Don Getty, To sustain industrial growth in Alberta, the Getty government (1985-1992) delivered $250 million worth of royalty cuts and incentives. Before the year was out, it also provided an interest-free, $85 million loan for Syncrude. For its part, GCOS got a nine-month cut in plant royalties, from 12 per cent to a nominal 1 per cent.

Premier Getty also focused on negotiations with Husky Oil to build a heavy oil upgrader near Lloydminster – a project done in conjunction with the Saskatchewan government to take advantage of heavy oil deposits on both sides of the provincial boundary. Desperate to stimulate economic activity, he also urged Syncrude to follow through on plans for a $750 million expansion. The federal government refused to put money into either project, with the result that Alberta provided two loan guarantees – $380 million for the upgrader and $200 million for Syncrude's expansion.

World oil prices stood at around $30 per barrel, so the economics seemed feasible. However, when oil prices collapsed to about $10, and the petroleum industry, which was already cash-poor because of high taxes, royalties and price controls from the NEP years, found itself on the ropes. However, the project consortium had not given up hope. "As a capital and labour-intensive operation, oil sands development appealed to the Getty government on many levels," according to oil sands historian Paul Chastko. "Investment drove the Alberta economy in the 1970s, and embarking on a large-scale project like OSLO might bring back investor dollars and confidence in the province. Oil sands projects also employed large segments of the province's workforce, from engineers to tradesmen, and would combat unemployment. Synthetic development also offered the province a way to offset its declining conventional crude stocks. Furthermore, given the energy security component, it just might attract investment from Ottawa or another provincial government...."[351]

Heading into the 1988 federal election, Brian Mulroney's federal government earmarked several billion dollars for energy projects, from Newfoundland (Hibernia) to Vancouver Island (a natural gas pipeline.) According to one federal civil servant, these projects were motivated by "jobs, regional development, a future election, and pressure to rush things so announcements can be made in time to win votes." For Alberta, the government set aside $1.7 billion for OSLO.

# CHAPTER 10

# Getting steamed

———

*The idea "came from old coffee percolators. You'd put energy*
*in the bottom, it percolated steam and water to the top [where*
*everything condensed]. The water drained through the basket of*
*coffee, and then you produced the coffee out the bottom."*

— BRUCE SLEVINSKY, 2013

DURING THE ERA OF PUBLIC subsidies, energy issues consumed the province, and
by the end of those years Alberta had developed a diverse economy.

The province produced and exported light conventional oil; manufactured
synthetic oil at GCOS; hosted an intricate network of oil, gas and refined product pipelines; and, unusually at that time, was building refining and petrochemical hubs that used natural gas as a feedstock. Gas-based petrochemicals gave
the province an advantage: before deregulation began in 1985, prices in Alberta
were lower than federally regulated prices outside the province and more reli-
able than oil prices set in the Middle East.

In terms of the oil sands, Lougheed took leadership roles in three areas.
In 1975, he played a key role in the Winnipeg Agreement, which saved the
Syncrude project. In a round of bitter struggles over energy with the fed-
eral government, he strongly asserted and ultimately resolved beyond doubt
Alberta's ownership of most hydrocarbon and other mineral resources within
provincial borders.

Taken three years into his mandate as premier, the first of his major achievements was to create the Alberta Oil Sands Technology Research Agency (AOSTRA), and to seed it with $100 million from the new Alberta Heritage Savings Trust Fund. The legislation was formally past in June, 1974. The act originally limited AOSTRA's activities to oil sands, but it was amended in 1975 to include heavy crude oil and was amended again in 1979 to extend its activities to the enhanced recovery of conventional crude oil.

As Clem Bowman described the situation, when Lougheed took office as premier in 1971, work on the deeply buried oil sands reservoirs, which represent about 90 per cent of the resource, had stalled. There had been a little progress on the Cold Lake deposit, but there were no demonstrated technologies that could unlock the oil from the Peace River, Wabasca (now viewed as part of the Athabasca) or deep Athabasca deposits. And there was little likelihood things would improve. Few large, multinational oil companies were actively developing oil sands leases.[352]

A Crown corporation, AOSTRA had the authority to act independently of Edmonton. The act specified that the new institution was to be run by an independent board of directors – no less than three and no more than seven members – appointed by the Lieutenant Governor in Council, and that its chair and vice chair would be chosen from the appointed members. The agency would report to the Legislative Assembly through the Minister of Energy. To cover its first five years of operations and projects, the project received $100 million.

AOSTRA's success arose from what Frank Dabbs called "a remarkable partnership between former Imperial Oil chemical engineer Clem Bowman, the Authority's first chairman, and Alberta Geological Survey geologist Morris [sic] Carrigy, the unchallenged world authority on oil-sands geology." His hyperbole continued. These two men "led a Camelot-like round-table of the brightest men in North America's petroleum community. Over the years, the seven-member governing group included Syncrude president Frank Spragins, the one-time University of Alberta dean of chemistry, Harry Gunning, and Alberta Research Council head Ernie Wiggins who was, after Karl Clarke [sic], probably Alberta's greatest 20th-century petroleum scientist." Through the formation of this government agency, Lougheed created a scientific and technical environment that unlocked the secrets of producing bitumen from deposits too deep for mining "but too shallow for the cyclical steam injection process used at Cold Lake and Peace River,"[353] and fundamentally transformed the industry itself.

Two researchers – Annette Hester and Leah Lawrence – reported in a paper prepared for a United Nations agency that AOSTRA's mission was to convert ideas into commercial technologies. As we have seen, production from mineable deposits – those with minimal overburden – dated back to the 1930s. The technology for developing those projects was adequate, although great improvements would take place at the beginning of the 21$^{st}$ century.

The deeper deposits were problematic, however, and that is where the agency focused its funds – $116 million over 18 years. "The creators of AOSTRA saw that the future would be much more competitive and technology-rich, with investment shifting towards *in-situ* extraction and project budgets accessible and affordable for a diversity of smaller oil companies." Agency programs "facilitated research and development by harnessing the intellectual capital of industry, universities and inventors. It did this through the AOSTRA/industry jointly-funded projects... but also through the funding of universities and other research organizations."[354] In its quest for ideas, the program threw the net wide: An inventors' assistance program provided several hundred thousand dollars a year to inventors with limited means but good ideas. The money was for helping inventors to obtain patent protection for their inventions or to undertake sufficient evaluation work to secure funds for further development from private funding agencies.

## PROJECT ENERGY BREAKTHROUGH

Work on the deeply buried oil sands reservoirs had stalled. Imperial had made progress on the Cold Lake deposit, as had Shell in its shallower Peace River properties, but there were no demonstrated technologies that could commercially unlock deep oil from the Peace River, Athabasca or Wabasca (today seen as an extension of Athabasca) deposits. At the time, there was little likelihood things would improve. Exploration for conventional oil was strong, and few companies were developing oil sands leases outside the mineable area.

Originally called "Project Energy Breakthrough," Lougheed's idea was to speed up the development of new *in-situ* oil sands technologies. AOSTRA spurred the petroleum industry to undertake numerous demonstration projects. During the AOSTRA years, oil companies launched *in-situ* demonstration projects in all the major oil sands deposits. The techniques tested in those years included cyclic steam stimulation (CSS); steam flooding; forward combustion; reverse combustion; and combined forward combustion and water injection (COFCAW).

## THE SAGD TEAM

Roger Butler, who died in 2005, is the best-known among those who patented steam-assisted gravity drainage (SAGD), and he is often given sole credit for the idea.[355] The others were well-construction expert Chic Bombardieri and Bruce Slevinsky.

That said, as a researcher at Imperial Oil's Sarnia research centre, in 1969 Butler developed a SAGD-like process to extract potash from an underground ore-body. The idea "came from old coffee percolators," according to Slevinsky. "You'd put energy in the bottom, it percolated steam and water to the top [where everything condensed]. The water drained through the basket of coffee, and then you produced the coffee out the bottom." This idea ultimately led to thermal melting of bitumen and gravity drainage, which are the key ingredients in SAGD. At age 28 Slevinsky was one of three signatories on the original SAGD patent, and he told me how the notion developed.

Imperial Oil president Jack Livingston had hired Butler to do some work at the Standard Oil of New Jersey (Exxon) research lab, solving some problems of tanker scheduling. Butler then took a job at Imperial's Sarnia research lab. He kept working on heavy oil extraction as an extension of his potash mining expertise, getting his first vertical well patent in 1969. Through his contacts with Livingston – they had developed a friendship – he lobbied for five years before he actually got transferred to Calgary.

Butler had fought hard for the transfer from Sarnia to Calgary, Slevinsky said, "because he had this vision that he could transform Cold Lake. [Livingston] had been complaining that Esso [had been] putting millions of dollars into research at Cold Lake and hadn't made a penny yet. [The people already at Cold Lake] were working full tilt to optimize CSS [cyclic steam stimulation], so it became a head-to-head battle when Roger finally arrived in Calgary."

In production using CSS, the company injected steam into the ground for a period of months, and then produced the heated bitumen. "They just kept cranking the pressures up higher and higher, and eventually they would get to a pressure where suddenly the steam would go away....When I actually did the analysis of the pressure records and the injection records it was pretty obvious that they were actually growing fractures....the process that they'd undertaken to do cyclic steam stimulation at Cold Lake involved fracturing the reservoir," Slevinsky said "People had all kinds of arguments as to what the shapes of those fractures where, whether they were fuzzy, or diffuse, or single planes, but it really didn't matter because basically the only way they were getting contact with the reservoir was to break it open and to generate permeability through the tar sands. Otherwise, nothing would move in there."

Slevinsky had been studying for a Ph.D. in fracture mechanics, so he was asked to investigate. "It was obvious that we were doing something there that wasn't normal," he said. "It wasn't flowing out normally. And so I was able to put some diagnostics together to show that we were actually fracturing the wells, and we were generating vertical fractures. That was pretty easy. Then we measured surface uplift [and found that] the central pads were lifting up a foot or two during each injection cycle. The diagnostics I put together allowed us to actually see, and to map out the growth of the fractures, the extent of the steam zone as a function of time.... It was one of those coincidental things. I happened to have a piece of expertise, and they had a problem that just melded with it."

To put his work into historical context, Slevinsky's connection with Butler began just after the Arab oil embargo. Because of low oil prices, the Cold Lake project had been struggling. First tests at this project began in the 1960s, and over the years Esso (a subsidiary of Imperial Oil) had developed cyclic steam stimulation.[356]

Some years ago K.C. Williams, senior vice-president and director at Imperial, told the World Petroleum Congress how CSS works. "To mobilize the bitumen and provide drive energy," he said, "cyclic steam-stimulation uses periods of steam injection, followed by periods of 'soaking,' followed by periods of production." Thus, the system has three phases - steam injection, the 'soak' period, followed by bitumen production. As the drive provided by injected steam dissipates, production rates decline and the operation begins a new cycle of steam injection. Cycles range from a few months to two years as the company steams reservoir areas increasingly distant from the injection wells. "In simple terms, cyclic steam-stimulation can be viewed as a very large water cycling operation, with associated steam generation and bitumen processing facilities."[357] During production, the heated bitumen and water are pumped to central processing plants where water is separated from bitumen, purified and recycled into gas-fired steam boilers. The bitumen is blended with diluent for shipping.

To a large degree, this is still how things work at Esso's pioneering oil sands plant. However, for 20 years the company's CSS research and experimentation had been a costly money loser. But with higher oil prices and a lot of technical expertise, things were ready to change. Esso decided to develop the Lemming Pilot, which would be a 40- or 50-well expansion. "It was the first time they'd gone beyond single wells and single roads," Slevinsky said. "They were drilling eight wells per pad off central pads – this was very modern in terms of concept. They were drilling them in deviated well arrays, coming out as spiders from central points. Also, they were doing CSS on tight spacing." Esso's Cold Lake project had finally become a profitable enterprise.

In Esso's Calgary production research and technologies services lab, Slevinsky focused on the Cold Lake pilots. He worked "on deviated wells, multiple fractures, injectivity analysis for the steam injectors, the formation of emulsions in the huff-and-puff process – all based on the fracture mechanics at the heart of my PhD work." A year later Butler arrived, joining Slevinsky and completions and well-construction expert Chic Bombardieri. Then the lab went into overdrive. The team researched the fundamentals of the SAGD process – "initially with vertical wells, but within a year we had proven that we would have to use horizontal wells to get adequate processing rates. We worked intensely and filed 140 patent memos in two years – totally overloading Esso's patent processing system."

Started up in 1975, The Cold Lake Project's Lemming pilot was their test facility. "I was hired just at the point where they were starting that up. All the facilities were new; they didn't have oil leaking all over them." Although in today's world they have a familiar ring, the tests they did at Lemming were ground-breaking. The research team tried "taking deviated wells and going in with a frack truck and sand and creating multiple-propped fractures, much like what we're doing in the tight sands and tight oil today. As a matter of fact, I wrote reports in 1975 on that process. We actually did the calculations for how many fractures you could put into a section before it broke the well, and how many you could put in economically." Not exactly bedtime reading, his papers included documents titled "Theoretical Investigation of the Spacing of Multiple Vertical Fractures" and the "Economic Evaluation of the Multiple Fracture Concept, a Preliminary Study."

Of course, SAGD is what this team is famous for. How did that develop? "Within the first six months or so that Roger was in Calgary," Slevinsky said, he and his colleagues "proved that Butler's vertical well concept wouldn't work. Economically it could not compete with what was happening with cyclic steam on the vertical and deviated wells at Lemming." Regrouping, they asked "Well, how could we get higher rates?" That's when they came up with the idea of using horizontal wells.[358]

Thus, Imperial held the patents on both SAGD and CSS. However, the company decided that "CSS was better for Cold Lake than SAGD would have been, so we developed Cold Lake using CSS," according to former VP Howard Dingle. "Based on all the experience I had at Cold Lake that was the right decision. SAGD works in a slightly different reservoir configuration than we experienced at Cold Lake. So, other people had gone ahead and used SAGD elsewhere [but] we've always been happy with CSS in Cold Lake." He added, however, that "as we get into different parts of the reservoir we're beginning to move more and more to a SAGD-type approach."[359]

## Soviet influence

By a piece of good luck, Skov Murray in Esso's Drilling Department had arranged to import the first Russian mud motors for use in Western Canada.

Mud motors use pumps at surface to drive drilling mud into the string. It is that mud which turns everything downhole. "You're just using the pressure and the energy you're putting into the mud to drive the rotary assembly downhole.... We had to learn how to steer them, and that was not obvious, but [the industry] quickly came up with the tools and the techniques to do that. The first application of horizontal drilling in Western Canada was at Cold Lake."[360] These motors worked better in Canada than in the Soviet Union because Canada's mud systems were cleaner and more powerful, and they made horizontal drilling possible, and if the Esso team hadn't been able to drill horizontally, there would be no SAGD. Esso's original test involved steaming bitumen through vertical wells, then drawing it out through a horizontal.

Ironically, the other innovation leading to SAGD also had a Soviet connection. In 1977 a group of Canadian technical people went to a small town called Yarega – about 600 miles northeast of Moscow, near the Arctic Circle, to observe a Soviet "oil mine." When they arrived, they found production literally coming from a mine. The Soviets had constructed vertical shafts and horizontal tunnels into a heavy oil reservoir. Local workers were pumping steam into the reservoir through angled drill holes and production was taking place within the mine. A mining engineer among the Canadians, Gerry Stephenson, described the project: "Wells that were injecting steam were drilled from an upper level of tunnel, which was above the heavy oil reservoir. So the steam injection wells were drilled from above but from tunnels. The recovery wells were drilled from tunnels below."[361]

According to Maurice Carrigy, AOSTRA's vice-chair, "They had a tap, you know like a tap you would see in plumbing, a bathroom tap, and they would turn that on and off to get the oil out."[362] Chronically short of cash, the USSR hoped to sell the technology to the Canadian oil industry. The visit in part reflected a 1972 technology-sharing agreement between Canada and the USSR – one that collapsed in '78 when Canada expelled 13 Soviet officials for trying to infiltrate national security services.

The ultimate proof of the technology came from visits to northern Russia by two Canadian delegations in 1976. What they saw there was an oil mine, like the ones Max Ball had described in his 1940 book about the oil industry.

The Canadians were not impressed with the oil mine, but they were intrigued. According to Carrigy, it led to a "total revolution in the concept of what you could do with bitumen that you couldn't do in a traditional reservoir.... You got (the bitumen) into a form where it was either emulsified or liquefied so that you could produce it."[363]

At least one other group of Canadians had visited a Soviet oil mine. Hugh Lieper, who chaired Canada's petroleum committee for the technology sharing agreement, visited a similar but different operation in 1976. He describes being hoisted 800 feet into the mine in an elevator that swung wildly from side to side. At the bottom of the shaft, he found the oil being collected in a large open pit on the operations floor. "When I asked whether the electrical motors on the site were explosion-proof, no one knew what I was talking about."[364]

AOSTRA's Carrigy put the impact of his group's visit to the Yarega oil mine in perspective. While Canada didn't use the primitive Soviet technology, it gave credibility to "the idea that we could go below (an oil sands reservoir) instead of working from above." That way "we could use gravity as the driver in getting the oil out. That would be natural. It would come down and flow in and then we'd take it from below rather than pulling it up to the surface."[365]

"The system was definitely working, but the mine was very, very primitive," Stephenson said. "The tunnels were tiny. They weren't mechanized at all. When I asked how much it had cost to drive the tunnels I was told they had been driven by prisoners of the State, the implication being no or little cost. The piping systems were not much better than you would find in your garden. But it demonstrated that if you heat heavy oil, it will mobilize, it will be possible then to drain it, and if you put in wellheads below the reservoir, you will get production without pumping."

IDEAL MODEL

To a considerable extent spurred by government, new commercial oil sands developments flourished, although prospects for further development diminished in early 1986 when a precipitous collapse in oil prices once again threatened oil sands development and other high-cost energy projects. While AOSTRA did not have a mandate to undertake projects on its own, it took a significant risk in doing so on one occasion (the Underground Test Facility) and, in doing so, proved steam assisted gravity drainage (SAGD) to be the single most important system for developing deep underground oil sands reservoirs. A few years after the Canadian expeditions to the USSR, Butler and his team began developing the two-well SAGD concept using surface wells, which eventually took the form in use today: injecting steam into a horizontal well and collecting oil through a parallel well below.

One day Gerry Stephenson came into his office and said "The oil companies have got it all wrong. The idea of drilling vertical wells into the oil sands and only contacting the pay zone for the few metres where there's bitumen and having to put multiple wells down in these grid patterns just doesn't make sense. I'm a mining man and the logical thing to do in a mine is to put down a shaft and to drill horizontal wells from that shaft and then every foot of well that's drilled is in the pay zone."[366] Stephenson added that he had gone to the oil companies with this idea without success.

At this point, AOSTRA's first chairman Bowman picked up the story. "And so [Stephenson] came to my office and sat there and made his plea that we should build a facility, put down a shaft and he had worked out what the costs would be," he said. "According to his numbers, drilling a shaft into the deposit is not an expensive operation and the coal companies know how to handle methane in spades. So we put together a concept called the Underground Test Facility. No oil company would put any money into it but [petroleum executives on AOSTRA's board] said they would support it technically and they'd have people help us on it." For the only time in its history, the government agency paid full fare – and for what seemed an unusually speculative idea. Total budget for shafts, tunnels and infrastructure was about $30 million. "It seemed this was the obvious time to test [Roger Butler's] principle of gravity drainage," Bowman said.[367]

Consequently, in 1984, an information presentation was organised by AOSTRA in Gulf Canada Square to which oil companies were invited. It was well attended but not by senior level executives. After an introduction by Bowman and Carrigy, Butler described his SAGD process using two horizontal wells near the base of the pay zone to heat and mobilise the bitumen while forming a steam chamber from which bitumen could be withdrawn. Stephenson described the plan to utilize vertical shafts to access tunnels below the pay zone from which the SAGD well pairs would be drilled, completed and operated with mobilised bitumen being drained by gravity through well heads in the tunnel, thence to a central pumping station in the shaft.

"A great deal of the meeting consisted of extensive – sometimes verging on antagonistic – questioning of Butler's concept of using horizontal well to apply SAGD," according to Stephenson. "AOSTRA then summarised their plan to build the Underground Test Facility and pilot the SAGD horizontal well process and invited oil companies to join this historic venture," he said. "The silence was deafening."[368]

Accordingly, in 1984 AOSTRA decided to go it alone, announcing its intention to spend $42 million (later increased to $80 million) to build the UTF without industry participation. The Alberta government gave AOSTRA lease rights to a tract of land 60 kilometres north of Fort McMurray, and the agency opened the Underground Test Facility (UTF) in 1987.

By this time Roger Butler had left Imperial to become part of AOSTRA, and he was a member of the technical team. Maurice Carrigy was the project executive. Another team member was Chi-Tak Yee, who became a vice president of MEG Energy. "One of the most fortunate things that I was involved with," said Yee, "was the Underground Test Facility project that was essentially the birthplace of SAGD. Think of [the UTF] as the Mac [Macintosh computer] of SAGD development."[369]

"Although we did contemplate going right into the oil sands," Carrigy said, "we thought it would be better to go down below the oil sands, put the tunnels in a secure and safe place" – a layer of limestone – "and then drill upwards" into the reservoir.[370] The magnitude of the UTF is hard to imagine. Stephenson describes the shaft construction procedure. "No shaft had ever been successfully sunk into the oils sands at that time. Sinking the shafts was done with a drill bit almost four metres in diameter weighing 230 tonnes. The two shafts were drilled open hole using a heavy mud to prevent the unstable material in the shaft wall [gravel, Clearwater shale and oil sand] from collapsing. Then a 140 tonne steel liner up to 20 millimetres thick and 3 metres in diameter was floated into the shaft one section at a time, each being filled with water before the next section was welded to it. The liner was then grouted in place using 1,000 tonnes of cement and the water was pumped out of the casing. Three of us were then lowered to the bottom of the shaft at 223 metres to check conditions which were perfect. The lining was secure, the deviation from the vertical was less than 25 centimetres and we had completed the two shafts on budget and ahead of schedule."[371]

Then came the tests. The Phase A pilot involved three well pairs 70 metres in length, each with 40-50 metres of exposure to the McMurray oil sand formation. According to Stephenson, "steam was injected and the first experiment with SAGD wells began. After a year or so, it was obvious the system was working." That was the beginning of a turnaround within the industry, which soon decided to get financially involved. Ten companies contributed $16 million each to the project. That funding enabled the test crew to complete Phase A and to move on to Phase B. It also funded several years of additional experimentation. Phase B involved another three well pairs, 70 metres apart. According to Stephenson, "the effective length in the reservoir was 500 or 550 metres. They resembled a commercial development" despite having only three producing well pairs. Project engineers expected production to reach about 1,800 barrels a day.

"AOSTRA's staff had estimated that the recovery might be somewhere between 30 per cent and 45 per cent of the bitumen in place," Stephenson said. "We actually got 65 per cent recovery. The steam chambers formed by mobilization of the bitumen spread way beyond the area that we'd expected, so obviously we didn't need to drill the well pairs as close together on Phase B as we did on Phase A, so we opened them up. Anyway, on Phase A the figures were 65 per cent recovery – way beyond what we'd estimated. Over the 10-year life of the well pairs, Phase B got a steam/oil ratio, the most critical figure of all, of 2.3 to one."[372] Six years later, AOSTRA announced it was on the verge of the commercial breakthrough now known as SAGD. In fact, SAGD tests were able to recover almost 70 per cent of the bitumen in place. At the time, that was an unheard-of recovery rate.

The petroleum industry soon began to develop SAGD projects from well pads. According to Stephenson, the mining engineer, there are still good reasons to do SAGD from tunnels underground. "You don't disturb the surface to the same extent. You can use gravity to your full advantage." And, he added, surface schemes require a high-capacity, expensive pump for each producing well. They cost a lot to buy and a lot to service. Furthermore, "it costs more to pump through a multitude of 8-inch pipelines than it does through a single 18-inch pipeline in a shaft. Another advantage is that you can drill more accurately from underground, and you get better recovery because you can use lower steam pressures. Your production might not be quite as high, but your recovery of the bitumen is going to be better, because you're allowing a slow process of heat soaking upwards by thermal conductivity."

There may be even more advantages to working in shafts and tunnels. "You're operating in an underground climate in a tunnel. You're doing all your drilling and well completion plus your process manipulation work in a safe working environment at a temperature of 58° F year round and with no snow and ice to hinder and delay your work," he said. "You can operate 24 hours a day, 365 days a year, instead of being confined with your drilling and your completions to those periods when you can drill on the muskeg and so on. You can do all these things in a safe environment that allows you to work all year long."

A visionary but not a dreamer, Stephenson acknowledged that the system also has disadvantages. One is the need for upfront capital: until you've constructed some of the shafts and tunnels you can't do any drilling at all. Also, of course, some reservoirs simply don't have the geological features needed to make the system work. However, as Stephenson points out, the steam-oil ration achieved at a pilot operation in the UTF over a 10 year period was as low as 2.3; a figure which has only been achieved by three or four of more than 20 commercial projects now operating with surface wells.

In the latter 1990s Devon Energy acquired the UTF, and then sold it to Petro-Canada. When Suncor Energy acquired Petro-Canada, it also acquired the UTF – later known internally as its "Devon Project." Petro-Canada developed abandonment plans for the facility, and unconfirmed reports say the ERCB approved them. At this writing the facility was intact, but its future was in question. Stephenson, who almost saw this project as his baby, stressed the immensity of its impact on the oil sands industry. He asked whether the facility should be abandoned "after giving birth to a system which now produces 50 per cent of bitumen and which proved the ability of Canadian engineers to envision and bring into being world-leading systems."[373]

During the active life of that Crown Corporation, it spurred the petroleum industry to invest in nearly $2 billion of research and development. In most cases, the authority essentially agreed to match the amount of money a company or industry partnership was willing to invest in projects that could develop the oil sands.

The 2009 Summit of the Americas held AOSTRA up as an ideal model for energy development. According to the Centre of International Governance Innovation (CIGI), the agency "was an arms-length, government-funded organization that engaged the private sector and the university research community in developing technology related to the oil sands, while the government retained the rights to the technology." A government endowment allowed the organization "to function independently of the electoral cycle. A dedicated expert and respected seven-member board of directors helped secure the private sector's buy-in." In addition, "control by the government helped maintain continuity over downturns in the economic cycle."

CIGI also noted with approval that, before AOSTRA determined its goals, "it conducted two years of extensive consultations with many stakeholders. Only after determining exactly where the technology gaps existed did AOSTRA put out a call for proposals." Furthermore, "aside from successfully developing new technology, AOSTRA fostered and financed a new generation of academic and scholarly expertise in many aspects of oil sands development. The investment in human resources is often discounted, but has been fundamental for the sector's success in Alberta."[374]

Former premier Lougheed got excited when he talked about SAGD. "I think SAGD…should be encouraged by the owner and is being encouraged by the owner," he said in what was probably his last recorded interview. "It's the longer-term asset for the province. Surface mining has its limitations, and involves more environmental and water concerns. So, there is a clear and important distinction when you get into oil sands and that's what the Alberta Oil Sands Technology and Research Authority had been focusing on….Throughout all of our discussions here, let's make sure that we are drawing a distinction between SAGD and *in-situ* [to some extent those words can be used interchangeably] and surface mining."[375] Toward the end of his life, Lougheed served on the board of MEG Energy – one of the first companies to develop a commercial SAGD operation.

## JACOS

Companies from all over the world have developed *in-situ* oil sands production facilities. However, one of the first companies from any country to participate was Japan, which stood on the opposite end of the resource-ownership spectrum from Canada. The country became involved in exploration and production in 1955, when the government founded JAPEX (Japan Exploration). A decade later, the company began to seek overseas opportunities, and in 1970 reorganized as a private company. The company's conventional overseas operations were growing nicely when, in 1978, it created Japan Canada Oil Sands Limited (JACOS) as a wholly-owned subsidiary.

JACOS was an indirect outcome of the 1973 Yom Kippur War. Japan relied on oil for nearly 80 per cent of its energy, most of it imported from the Middle East. According to its president, Toshiyuki Hirata, "because of that embargo the Japanese economy suffered greatly, and all of Japan recognized the importance of energy security for the future." Japan quickly developed a national energy strategy aimed at diversifying its supply to other parts of the world. For example, some companies invested indirectly in Venezuela's Orinoco ultra-heavy oil belt. As part of this global strategy, Japanese firms invested in Brazil, North Africa, Nigeria and Russia's Sakhalin Island. Japan also became one of the world's big importers of LNG, and began switching to nuclear energy from oil for electricity generation.

Many have remarked on a radical difference in perspective between East Asians and North Americans. In Japan, for example, the focus is on the long-term, while North America calls out for short-term gratification. According to Hirata, "shareholders' expectations in North America and Japan (are) different. In the Japanese market, shareholders tend to support industry or the company from a longer term of view. They want the company to grow, so they are patient with their investment." Especially in the early years, patience was a key ingredient in oil sands development.

Soon after incorporation, JACOS joined a consortium investigating the application of cyclic steam stimulation (CSS) in the Athabasca oil sands. Operated by Petro-Canada, the group also included Esso and Canadian Occidental. According to Hirata, "we have to make a profit from this business. (But) as a Japanese company we believe one of our important missions is to build a long-term and stable hydrocarbon supply for the market." The company's oil sands focus, which began in the late 1970s, illustrated its patience. The company became involved when Petro-Canada, Canada's national oil company, invited its Japanese counterpart to join a consortium testing cyclic steam stimulation in the Athabasca oil sands. Petro-Canada operated the project, and other participants included Canadian Occidental (which later morphed into Nexen), Esso and JACOS. The group's initials made it the PCEJ consortium.

Hirata became involved in the project nearly a decade later. After working in Japan's domestic oil and gas fields for seven years, the company seconded him to Petro-Canada for the period 1988-1990 to work on PCEJ — an assignment that coincided with experiments at the Underground Test Facility. "Until '91, we focused on CSS," he said. "We had been working since '84 on CSS, (facing) much difficulty because of the technical challenges. But when we looked at the SAGD process being tested at the UTF we thought, 'Oh, this has to be a technical breakthrough.'" JACOS participated in the UTF tests from the beginning, and its parent company joined in 1992.

Hirata stressed that the original SAGD process needed more than horizontal drilling to become commercial. In the beginning, drillers couldn't drill shallow horizontal wells from the surface — a technology they soon developed. Magnetic guidance systems were another necessary technological breakthrough. They enabled companies to keep horizontal well-pairs parallel even deep below surface.

Hirata spent 1994-97 in the Tokyo office working on a comparative study of CSS and SAGD. "From '92 to '96 we compared those two processes, CSS versus SAGD, to determine which would be better for our future development." In the

Athabasca oil sands, CSS wasn't even the runner-up. "The fractures (used in CSS) cannot be confined within the reservoir. So, we lost a lot of steam outside the reservoir area. That is why in the Athabasca area we could not use it to develop oil sands economically. CSS also had other technical challenges. We used just one vertical well, so productivity was much lower than (from a) horizontal well. Also, because cyclic steam stimulation just repeats injection and production, basically you produce only half a year and half a year you have to inject steam." Also, he added, in the Athabasca area CSS wells often got clogged with sand.

His team concluded that they should use SAGD for future research and project development, and began to construct a pilot project. The company's PCEJ partners were reluctant to participate because of low oil prices. "Most of the Canadian companies were taking a kind of an exit strategy from oil sands research, because they didn't see any economics from oil sands development. There was very little hope about the future commercialization of oil sands business in those days."

## HANGINGSTONE

Focused on the long term, Hirata's team decided to stay the course. According to Hirata, "the Japanese government, Japanese industry and JACOS – we decided to go ahead with an independent pilot test at Hangingstone" – a deposit just south of Fort McMurray. JACOS received operating approvals in 1998, and started up its two well-pairs the following year. The plant went commercial one year after the other pioneering SAGD project – Cenovus' Foster Creek project, which EnCana first developed.

That Hangingstone went on stream so soon was surprising, given the economics of petroleum at the time. It was a wise decision, though. At this writing, JACOS produced 6,000 barrels per day from the project – volumes expected to quadruple with a 2016 expansion. Hirata added, rather modestly, that the company also owned oil sands leases in the Corner and Chard areas of the Athabasca deposit. "In total we have 460 square kilometres of lease holdings. Our current estimate is 1.7 billion recoverable barrels. If we develop all those leases, we should be able to sustain production of 100,000 barrels a day."

Four decades later, Japan's 1970s-era national energy strategy was laden with irony. The original intent was for Japan to diversify its sources of oil away from the Middle East. Yet at this writing, oil production from Canada was still trapped within a North American market. Did it make sense for Japan to be involved in oil sands development? A partial answer to that question lay in a national inclination within Japan to think of its industry as an interconnected whole. By profiting from global oil production, Japanese producers effectively reduced the net cost Japanese industry paid for oil. By contributing to global supply, they offset the cost of energy by slowing upward pressure on prices.

Hirata saw the JACOS effort as part of a sensible national effort. By increasing global oil production, Japanese producers offshore were helping increase global supply. "We will not contribute directly to the Japanese market (in the short term), but combined with other companies' development plans – Japanese trading houses that are also looking for opportunities in oil sands development as well as in sharing with our development in Canada – we can collaboratively contribute to energy security for Japanese industry." He continued, "Our company motto is to secure the long term and stable energy supplies to the market."

He was sure Canada would find ways to supply world markets. "Not only Japan but also Asian countries need more oil because they are growing quickly – Thailand, Singapore, China, and Vietnam. To import Canadian oil they need a pipeline like Gateway. From the Canadian point of view too, I think it is very important to diversify the Canadian oil market to other parts of the world." He added that another Japanese oil company, International Petroleum Exploration Company (INPEX) was also active globally. "They have big projects in Australia and in Indonesia and also in the Middle East and in Canada. They have big activities all over the world."

To help complete his picture of Japan's network of upstream producers, Hirata added that JAPEX was the first oil company in Japan, and was once the largest company. INPEX, which began life exploring offshore Sumatra in 1966, later overtook JAPEX in size. It "merged several companies together and grew into a bigger company."[376]

In natural resource terms, Canada and Japan inherited dramatically different endowments. Japan had capital and a strong sense of industrial integration but was resource poor. Canada had resources but not enough capital to develop its many investment opportunities. JACOS was the first Asian company to participate in the oil sands. It was also the second company to develop an economically viable SAGD project. This international collaboration benefitted nations at both ends of the resource continuum.

Lower oil prices made times tough for Canada's petroleum industry in general and for the oil sands in particular. The last straw, though, was ideological. At the beginning of Ralph Klein's term as premier (1992-2006) he famously described his government as being "out of the business of business" – an early indicator of the economic conservatism that would characterize his term in office.[377] His government and that of Prime Minister Mulroney, a fellow conservative, withdrew financial support from OSLO, which was expecting loan guarantees and tax and royalty concessions to get into business. In 1992, OSLO's partners finally announced their decision to kill the project, marking the end of an era.

# CHAPTER 11

# Inside out

———

*"If you look at a tailings pond, it looks like it is static but in fact it's an operating vessel. You put in fluid tails at the top of the pond, the water goes in, the fines and sands settle and then you withdraw the settled material from the bottom of the pond and you use it to backfill mines."*

— DON THOMPSON, 2014

TO GET BITUMEN OUT OF the ground, you need to understand its reservoirs; the adjacent rock and the soil above; the hydrology of the surrounding land; and the vegetation and wildlife of the boreal forest that covers most oil sand deposits. This kind of information is increasingly technical. It is also increasingly important, because you have to reclaim the land when you close down your oil sands operations.

One of the pioneers in this area of study is Tony Settari. Born during the Second World War in Nazi-occupied Czechoslovakia, the Soviet Union occupied his country at the end of the war. During 1968's Prague Spring, he was able to leave for the University of Calgary. At the U of C, Settari continued his studies in mechanical engineering, receiving a PhD in 1973. When I interviewed him, he held the chair in petroleum engineering once occupied by the legendary Roger Butler. But that came much later. When he joined the work force in the 1970s, he became a pioneer in the use of computers for reservoir simulation. He wanted to go inside the Earth so see what it would reveal.

"My work was always on the technical side of the recovery processes, what we now call down-hole engineering. In the oil sands, way back when, we had difficulties to explain how we can inject fluids into [the reservoir] to provide the heat and steam, and how it would flow back." The reason was that "classical fracture mechanics were built for hard rocks. We know that the oil sands are not consolidated. When you wash all the bitumen out of it, oil sand becomes a pile of sand. So, it doesn't behave the same way. There was a big debate about whether you can actually apply fracturing concepts to the oil sands. And, obviously if you did it without any new concepts then you would be getting very large fractures. It was obviously wrong. So, I got involved in hydraulic fracturing (which is the technique that we use always for stimulating wells in any kind of reservoir), also to oil sands."

Settari became involved with the oil sands in the 1970s. First he worked for a consulting firm known as Intercomp; in the 1980s he started SIMTECH Consulting Services Ltd. "We didn't know very much about how the oil sands behaved," he said, and people from Imperial Oil "got hold of me and said, 'we need to ask you to put some science into all this.'" That was the beginning of an important effort to use computers for reservoir modelling for the Cold Lake oil sands project of Imperial and other projects. Nothing like it had been done in modeling before, but there were also big challenges on other fronts.

Early instigators included Rick Kry and Tom Boone, both with Imperial. Other key players included Norbert Morgenstern – "a very prominent geo-technical guy" – and Don Scott at the University of Alberta. Using specially made mechanical testing devices this team began characterizing the oil sands as they functioned geo-mechanically underground. Soon, "we started to get more of the basic data we needed for better simulations." As research evolved, it grew into a multi-company, multi-year project which was later partly funded by CANMET, a federal agency. "We created the project and we started looking at the modelling issues and understanding the mechanics of what actually happens in the oil sands....We had at one time about 12 companies involved – companies like Imperial Oil, Husky, Petro-Canada, Gulf Canada and the predecessor of Suncor," Sun Oil Canada.

## INSTRUMENTATION

The underground instrumentation used in the field projects played a key role in the evolving understanding of oil sands recovery mechanisms. "What we're trying to do in simulation is build a mathematical model, including equations that describe the physics of the problem," Settari said. "We solve them numerically on computers and that creates a simulation model of the reservoir. Then we run the model and it will create simulated behaviour of that reservoir: How the fluids flow, how the temperature changes as you inject steam and so on. It's much like what the pilots do when they are being trained on simulators."

Developing the model was a long and tedious task. "If you just constructed the model with best information from the geology and geophysics and so on, you could be miles wrong. We need all the information that is being measured in the field because that is known. That is something you can trust. And, then we modify the models and tune them so that they will replicate the existing history of the field," he said. "Sometimes we find that we are missing some physics in the problem."

For example, based on the early understanding of the oil sand behaviour, the steam fractures he was studying appeared to be kilometres in length. "However, we knew from the field that they were only a couple of hundred feet long," he said. "We had to add new physics and tuned these models to the data we collected in the field. And, the primary data is, of course, how much we are producing. In both CSS and SAGD, we are producing some bitumen, hot bitumen; we are producing some water and we might be producing some steam along with that. That's the basic data the model has to reflect."

As research progressed, it became apparent that the largest difference between conventional reservoirs and oil sands reservoirs is their geo-mechanical behaviour. "The geo-mechanics mainly means how the reservoir actually behaves mechanically when you inject [steam] to produce it," Settari said. The system "allowed us to become more realistic in our modelling compared to what we had been doing before."

His group continued to operate these research projects until the mid-1990s, and "it developed our geo-mechanical capabilities," he said. "That's what we're known for now, and we still apply the same modelling techniques. There are some different slants to it – there can be problems like subsidence of reservoirs, fault activation, induced earthquakes.... Geo-mechanics now is actually a rapidly expanding part of reservoir engineering and modelling. So, it sort of echoes the 1970s, 1980s when we were developing techniques for conventional reservoir simulation." That period also saw the rapid expansion of simulation capabilities.

During the decades since this work began, there have been exponential improvements in the accuracy and sophistication of the tools available for geo-mechanical measurement, in the laboratory as well as in the field. As these field experiments began, one of the main tools used was a fairly primitive pressure gauge. Settari contrasts technology then and now and observes: "Today, we have permanent gauges that will measure both pressure and temperature and so on. We have fiber optics that can actually look up and down the well-bore. We have logging techniques that look at saturations of fluids, porosity and permeability. Now we have logging techniques that can look at stresses in the formation."

Excited about the "tremendous development" in these technologies, Settari said "Calgary, especially, is a hotbed of innovators [in this area]. They get one idea and then try to pursue it and try to get it to market and develop it into a business. So, we see new things all the time. Testing the caprock overlying reservoirs, for example, is going through a new phase of re-evaluation, partially because of the Joslyn blowout." The 2006 Joslyn Creek SAGD incident took place when high-pressure steam injected into a reservoir 65 kilometres north of Fort McMurray erupted, sending rocks flying hundreds of metres into the air.

## INNOVATION

On the matter of technological development, Settari argued that entrepreneurs generally develop practical technologies for reservoir management before the science is well understood. "In my view the technology and the science always lag behind business. That's typical of North America. European companies have a tendency to study the problem before they ever touch the oil in the ground. Here it is the opposite. You have an idea and it goes to a point that you patent the idea and then do it in the field and then you worry about how to explain it." He stressed that his team was not the only innovator in the field of oil sands reservoir modelling. While SIMTECH was a pioneer in the field, a company known as Computer Modelling Group was also developed "the forward flow modelling capabilities for the oil sands."

Settari left SIMTECH after Charlotte, N.C.-based Duke Energy acquired the company, but continued to work in reservoir and geomechanical modelling. In addition to teaching at the University of Calgary, he became a principal in TAURUS Reservoir Solutions, a Calgary-based firm that exemplified the changes in the contemporary workplace.

"We have five people in the Calgary office and two who are like full-time contract people but don't live in Calgary," he told me. "One of them lives in the Czech Republic and the other lives in Panama." A few others work as part-timers. "One is a very accomplished mountain climber, and he only works when he isn't climbing. The working environment has changed, as you know."[378]

Indeed. Under Soviet socialism, cynics used to say, "We pretend to work, and they pretend to pay us." As TAURUS illustrated, in contemporary society work, pay and play can find different kinds of equilibrium. It's known as work-life balance.

## BACK TO THE NEOLITHIC

If Settari oversaw a high-tech exploration of the bowels of Alberta to see what was under the land, another group of pioneers began using tools as old as humankind to protect its surface.

Alberta's reclamation rules developed slowly. In 1935 the province passed "The Control of Soil Drifting Act" in response to Depression-era drought. The act required that the occupiers of land – for practical purposes, farmers – be responsible for preventing soil erosion on their own property. It is useful to see this legislation in the context of a Depression-era drought, which had impoverished the very farmers the province expected to control soil drifting.

While the drought could be blamed on nature, newspaperman and historian James Gray described the ensuing "Dust Bowl" as a disaster created by bad farming practices. "Millions of acres were broken to the plough that never should have been broken at all. It was land for grazing and was good for nothing else," he said." The thin dry topsoil began to blow in 1931, and it blew, summer and winter, until 1938. Only after the wind had done its worst, and had blown many thousands of settlers off the land, did the governments take action. In 1935 the Bennett government set up the Prairie Farm Rehabilitation Administration to deal with wind erosion and drouth [drought] as a permanent emergency."[379]

It was in this Dust-Bowl-and-Depression crucible that, in 1938, Alberta passed the *Oil and Gas Resources Conservation Act,* which created the Petroleum and Natural Gas Conservation Board.[viii] The new board began operations with 15 staff, five of whom were assigned full-time to work in Turner Valley, where the board set up an office. Although these rules mostly covered matters aimed at efficient oil and gas production, they also included rules relating to the protection of surrounding lands. For example, producers could not store oil in earthen pits or in any other receptacle the Conservation Board judged to be liable to "cause waste or hazard," and storage tanks or batteries of tanks had to be surrounded by a dike or ditch.

Rules about land and water reclamation grew steadily in Alberta during the 20th century. In 1935, Alberta passed "The Control of Drifting Soil Act" in response to Depression-era drought, which damaged agriculture throughout North America's Great Interior Basin. That act mandated that the occupier of the land was responsible for preventing soil drifting. It was adequate for the time, when the province was poor and there was little industry. After the Second World War, however, rural municipalities began seeking a broader definition of soil conservation, and in 1962 the province replaced the legislation from the Dirty Thirties with the Soil Conservation Act. To a large extent this was because the 1947 Leduc discovery had led to widespread impacts by the

---

viii *Alberta Energy Regulator* (2013 – present) is the name of the oil and gas industry's regulator in Alberta. Previously it was the Petroleum and Natural Gas Conservation Board (1938-1957.) Other names: Oil and Gas Conservation Board (OGCB; 1957 – 1971), Energy Resources Conservation Board (ERCB; 1971 – 1995), Alberta Energy and Utilities Board (1995 – 2007); Energy Resources Conservation Board (2008 – 2013).

petroleum industry on prairie farmers. In response to a public outcry, new laws went into effect in 1963.

In the earliest days of oil sands mining, little thought went into what to do with the sand and other materials (including water) left over after extracting the bitumen. This presented huge challenges to those later responsible for the reclamation of disturbances created by oil sands operations. To appreciate the nature of the problem, consider how the first large-scale open-pit mine functioned.

GCOS employed two operations that disturbed the earth and had an impact upon the environment. The company cleared away the ground cover and overburden on top of the ore body, and then took this material to dumps beyond the mines. In addition, oil extraction operations released mountains of fine uniform tailings sand to a tailings dyke on the Athabasca River. Wind and water eroded both the dumps and the tailings dyke – the latter more than the former. Indeed, 15 - 20 mph winds would generate sand storms; heavy rainstorms would erode deep gullies in the river banks.

Suncor's original concept was to take tailings from oil sands production – an emulsion of clay, bitumen and other chemicals – and spill them over the escarpment into the Athabasca River where a small collector dam would hold the solids, releasing clean water. Unfortunately, this approach did not work according to plan. Instead of cleaning the water for reuse in oil sands operations, the small dyke was releasing these chemicals as an untreatable colloidal suspension into the river.

Reclamation quickly became an issue – not only because of the lack of attention the plant originally paid to its wastes, but because oil sand effectively expands when mined and processed. From each barrel of oil sand processed, the operator ends up with more than a barrel of sand, plus bitumen (about 12 per cent by weight), and waste water. Like a farmer's harrow, equipment used to dig up oil sand would fluff up the materials compacted by the last glaciation, for example, which melted away about 15,000 years ago.

This created many reclamation challenges. For example, if the area needing reclamation was originally a wetland or fen, the reclaimed area is likely to include a mound or hill and a lake, say, but not the original habitat. Given available compaction equipment, plus the changed chemistry of the sand being used as landfill, reclaiming a mine to its original state is difficult or impossible.

In addition, the processed sand was infertile – virtually barren of nitrogen, phosphorus and potassium, which are the three major nutrients for plants. The sand was also alkaline, because oil sands facilities used caustic soda in the extraction process. The overburden clay and muskeg were higher in available nutrients and, mixed with sand, would provide a suitable seed bed by reducing alkalinity and improving water percolation and moisture retention.

Until mixed with clay, peat and fertilizers, it would not support the mix of boreal vegetation that existed before mining began. Indeed, early efforts to reclaim these mined areas, which began in the 1970s, would fail totally during rainless summers in what Robert Fessenden called a "droughty" climate.

Mining companies need to reclaim the land they have disturbed before mine closure. Defined in Alberta as the 'stabilization, contouring, maintenance, conditioning or reconstruction of the surface of land,' reclamation became an essential component of oil sands development. Challenges there were, but Suncor and Syncrude took important steps forward. In 2013, Suncor's reclamation efforts included creating a fen, or wetland.[380]

In 2008 Syncrude announced that it would create a wood bison habitat in a 104-hectare reclaimed area known as Gateway Hill. The person behind that project was Don Thompson, whose job at Syncrude before he retired included a diverse portfolio of responsibilities – environment, safety, loss management aboriginal affairs and so on. The point of creating the bison habitat was to demonstrate that the land could be returned to its previous state – in effect, to disprove suggestions that the soil at a reclaimed mine would "never withstand grazing pressure from the native animals." To Thompson, this was illogical. At first he proposed starting a cattle ranch on the reclaimed land, but the company eventually chose to return the land to what had been there before, "at least in terms of grazing, what could be managed in a research sense was bison. So, we proposed and got approval for the bison ranch."[381] The original stock came from Banff National Park, which was emptying its bison paddocks. The company then sought the approval of nearby Fort McKay, and that aboriginal community became co-managers of the herd.

## MYTH OR REALITY?

Every step in the oil sands story is open to public scrutiny, and the sector has long been subject to public comment by such environmental NGOs as the Calgary-based Pembina Institute. In a 2008 report, Pembina concluded that "the current policies and practices governing oil sands mine reclamation reveals an alarming range of challenges, uncertainties and risks that deserve immediate attention and broader public discussion."[382] For years, the most critical environmental groups suggested that oil sands mines would devastate the province, consuming boreal forest "the size of Florida" in aerial extent.

Not so, according to the University of Alberta's David Lynch; these statements are mostly "myth." The land area of Alberta is 661,185 square kilometres and boreal forest covers 381,000 square kilometres of that area. Oil sands deposits represent 142,200 square kilometres – slightly less than Florida's landmass. However, and this is where these organizations used flawed logic – the mineable oil sands area covered 4,800 square kilometres (0.7 per cent of Alberta's land area) north of Fort McMurray – an area smaller than Prince Edward Island. At time of writing, mines in the Athabasca area represented 715 square kilometres of disturbed land – a number which included 170 square kilometres of tailings ponds. This represented 0.03 per cent of Alberta's land mass, about 9 per cent of which was already under active reclamation.

Because of the cost and complexity of good land reclamation, prevention of unnecessary disturbance has been a consideration since the design of modern mines began, through provincial regulations. Before construction even began, engineers and scientists prepared closure plans outlining reclamation plans for the post-mining period. To prepare the area for surface mining, bulldozers, backhoes, loaders, water trucks, scrapers, side booms and graders removed the overburden (the muskeg and other layers of soil covering the oil sands deposit), and the operator stored those materials for later use. Alberta Environment eventually developed a policy of withholding regulatory approval until it had received and reviewed these plans.


## THE NATURE OF THE PROBLEM

Larry Brocke is one of the people best able to discuss the changes to land reclamation for the petroleum industry. After a year in geology at the University of Alberta (1962), he took a job as a lab assistant at the Research Council, working for Dr. Fred Cook in the agriculture unit. With two years' experience behind him, he returned to the university, graduating in 1970 with a Master's in soil science – a discipline known as pedology. Why? "It interested me; I liked it; it felt good. I had no problem getting up the next day and going back." Brocke's career paralleled recent developments in land reclamation.

Brocke began working with Alberta Environment's Land Use Assignment Section at the end of 1971. The work involved reviewing land use activities, especially where public and private land intersected. Initially, he was assigned to the small community of Fairview in northwest Alberta, north of Grande Prairie, working on soil inventory and land use activities, mainly for public land. "Then all this stuff started," he said. "I started getting calls from various people, coal companies in particular: 'We need our soil inventory and some help with a reclamation plan.' So I had to do these as one-offs on Saturday and Sunday."

In the mid-1970s he left government and, with partners, formed a company named Pedology Consultants. The name comes from the scientific study of soils in their natural environment. "We did get into a little bit of oil sands but not much, because there were only Suncor and Syncrude" and Syncrude was just getting going.

"You can't just drill a well and then walk away. You have to reclaim," he said.[383] That position grew ever-deeper roots because of the unruly growth in the petroleum industry itself. "There was a lot of noise being made about the oil and gas industry. It was growing so fast, well sites everywhere, interrupting the farming, just destroying the space, not doing anything to fix it after they were done."[384]

The 1973 amendments were important for a number of reasons. For one, the Great Canadian Oil Sands plant had gone into operation in 1967, and the earlier reclamation rules did not cover it directly – instead, regulations for gravel pits covered that enormous operation. Nor did the existing rules provide sufficient regulation for the proposed Syncrude project, which would go onstream in 1978.

It was important, Brocke said, to "get them when they're planning their project to plan for reclamation as well."[385] Prior to that time, there were no rules ordering operators to reclaim industrial disturbances. The act enforced minimum standards regarding the reduction of site hazards, cleanup and recontouring, and provided for reclamation certificates.


## CONTEXT FOR OIL SANDS RECLAMATION

While the oil sands underlie 14.2 million hectares in northern and eastern Alberta, the surface mining area is 480,000 hectares.

The total underlain by oil sand is some 142,000 hectares. Of this, about three per cent are shallow enough to be produced using surface mining technology. In practice, this means 20 per cent of the total oil sands resources is squeezed into the surface mineable area located to the north of Fort McMurray while 97 per cent of the surface area of the oil sands, and 80 per cent of the resource, is too deep to be mined and must be produced using drilling or in-situ technology, which does not produce tailings ponds. As of year-end 2012, mining operations in the Fort McMurray area had affected 84,395 hectares. An area of some 8,000 hectares is in some stage of reclamation. Reclamation efforts have included planting more than 12 million seedlings.

Like most surface mines, oil sands projects use "progressive" reclamation. While reclamation is taking place in, some areas, clearing or mining are taking place in others. It is as though a slow-motion assembly line were moving across the landscape. Sometimes it is possible to move the materials (topsoil or overburden) directly from the newly cleared areas to the reclamation site. Called "direct placement," this single-haul transfer saves money and minimizes degradation of topsoil. In many instances, especially in early stages of development, mines cannot avoid stockpiling large volumes of topsoil and overburden. This topsoil storage means more land area is out of service, and adds to the cost and duration of reclamation operations.


## THREE MILESTONES AND AN EIGHT-STEP PROCESS

Syncrude's Don Thompson was much involved in developing and managing land reclamation techniques – in his case, as a company manager. "One of the first things I endeavoured to do was to put more emphasis on that top horizon. I took the opportunity to use what were really just dump trucks to strip that surface layer; we called it direct hauling and capping. All we did was move that top layer and cap it over the top of some overburden material that was to be left in perpetuity at the south end of the Syncrude mine. Obviously, to a biologist or a forester that worked pretty well. In fact, a lot of the vegetation that has subsequently grown there came out of the original material in the form of roots and shoots or seeds or what have you."

According to Thompson, during his years at Syncrude land reclamation went through three milestones. The first was the movement towards more careful, more selective stripping and stockpiling, and better use of the top strata of the soil. "The second area we really focused on was on landscapes; on the creation of landforms, the movement of surface water and groundwater within it and the movement of salts within ground- and surface-water." He described this approach as "holistic landscape planning." The third was planning a mine "so that you can backfill it and turn the land over to reclamation much quicker. If you go back to the original Syncrude mine plan, the east and west pits of the base mine were to be mined out completely before being back-filled and available for reclamation," Thompson said; the original plan involved storing overburden and other soils for 25 years. He added that the move away from draglines and bucketwheels to the more flexible truck and shovel technology had a positive impact on the pace of reclamation. So did the development of ways to dry fine particles out of tailings ponds.[386]

Evolving regulations reflected these technical and scientific findings, and the province required project proponents to apply simultaneously for development and reclamation approval. In 1973, this was quite an innovation, since it meant operators needed soil survey information at the outset. They "had to know what they started with," according to Larry Brocke, because the goal of the new reclamation plans was to have large-scale industrial projects like Syncrude returning the land on which they were constructed to what it had been before. "That's where we fit in," he said, creating "an inventory of the soil resource that was there and what the landscape was and all that." The department also worked "with the company's project plan or mine plan, if it was a mine. It helped them develop their reclamation plan so that it was integrated with their development plan… it makes a lot of sense to do that."

In 1982 Brocke returned to government as chair of Alberta Environments' Development and Reclamation Review Committee. During his tenure "There were amendments to that legislation, particularly in 1983." The revised act had as its objective "the return of land capability as opposed to productivity, which made way more sense to me." He added, "We worked carefully with the companies to see what could be done." Brocke became director of the Land Reclamation Division In the early 1990s, and held that position until "a massive reorganization of the department … regionalized everything" and abolished his role. "I thought, 'Well it's my time to get out of here' – which I did."[387]

In the earliest years, according to Robert Fessenden, "The idea was to return the whole mined area plus the tailings area back to forest, back to the natural forest environment…. The technology that was being used had essentially been brought in from agricultural experience and consisted of simply grasses and legumes." Fessenden, who has a PhD in soil microbiology, worked for Syncrude's Edmonton-based environmental group from 1978, just as operations began, until 1985. Syncrude wanted to "make sure that we had in place the technology to meet the reclamation standards of the day," he added. "The idea was to return the whole mined area plus the tailings area back to forest, back to the natural forest environment." The other kind of area that needed reclamation he called "construction disturbance" – for example, reclaiming water courses diverted to make way for operations.

In the case of water waste now in tailings ponds, the ideal solution would be to store it in non-toxic form, underground. In practice, however, "there's a serious policy issue here. Back when the oils sands first got going, the government's policy was total water containment on site. [But] over time, that policy led to incredible accumulations. Now, a lot of that water does get re-used in the process, so there's a lot of recycling that goes on, but a lot of that stuff really can't be recycled. It's got too much of the colloidal fines in it, and they take forever to settle out. Over time we're going to have to find a way to treat some of that to the point where [we can] reintroduce it into the natural environment in an acceptable way. Otherwise, I don't know physically how you're going to contain all of that material below grade forever."[388]

Don Thompson had a different take on this. "If you look at a tailings pond, it looks like it is static but in fact it's an operating vessel," he said. "You put in fluid tails at the top of the pond, the water goes in, the fines and sands settle and then you withdraw the settled material from the bottom of the pond and you use it to backfill mines with. Now, the more solid that material can be made the less area in your mine pit you need to manage it, because of course when you suck fine material out of the bottom of a tailings pond it is inevitably liquid." To turn tailings into solids for land reclamation, the economics are better if the waste goes into smaller ponds for consolidation. He added that "cyclone treatment of tails, centrifuge tails – that sort of thing facilitates reclamation of mine pits."

This, of course, raised the question of the $2 billion centrifuge was building to quicken the pace for drying tails. "The objective is to use gravity in the form of centrifugal force to squeeze out the water and thereby make the solids dryer when you place them. Really, it's that simple. It's like a large cream separator. You put the material in it. You spin it around. The water goes to the outside. The solids stay on the inside and there you are."

At this point he changed direction. "Now, you mention $2 billion. Remember that taxes and royalties are a key part of oil sands economics. The fact is that for every dollar an oil sands plant spends, about half comes out of the tax and royalty system in the sense of foregone taxes. So, if you spend a billion dollars, half a billion dollars does not go to the Province of Alberta and the Government of Canada and the citizenry as a consequence. So, why are we centrifuging tailings? Well, we're doing that to speed up reclamation, clean up the area disturbed; all those things are good things, no question about it. But, I often wonder if people understand how much cost is really involved. It's not just the oil companies who are spending the money."[389]

For his part, Robert Fessenden did not play a role in the development of reclamation policy. When he left Syncrude he joined the celebrated Alberta Research Council. A few years later he "got kicked upstairs" to a vice president's job and later still, in 1995, became president of the Alberta Science and Research Authority, "a policy shop." Then, he said, he became "an accidental Deputy Minister" – accidental because he didn't apply for the position. "As president of the Alberta Science and Research Authority, I was a senior official so, when they started doing movements of deputies, I got moved into Economic Development, then Sustainable Resource Development, and then Innovation and Science."[390]

The present regulations originated in the department Larry Brocke once worked for, Alberta Environment. They take the form of an eight-step process. Step one is to clear the trees and send them to forestry operations – a business the province regulates as strictly as oil sands development. Government foresters and biologists work alongside forest industry representatives to develop long-term sustainability plans for the forest. Then the operator must remove and store for later use the topsoil, muskeg and mineral material that sits on top of the oil sands deposit. Collectively, these materials are known as overburden and used to best advantage during mine reclamation. The third step in a modern oil sand mine is to use trucks and shovels to remove as much as 720,000 tonnes of material each day. Bitumen mines can be 80 metres deep.

After the mining is done, heavy equipment shifts leftover sand, consolidated tailings and overburden into the mine pit; this is step four. Then a working landscape begins to take shape – one that allows for surface water movement and drainage, and minimal erosion. Once the general shape of the landform is ready, crews cover its surface with topsoil.

The operator is then responsible – this is step six – for planting indigenous grasses, shrubs and trees. The topsoil contains nutrients, as well as seeds and roots, which under the right conditions begin to grow. Frequently, however, to recreate the original habitat the operator needs to blend peat, fertilizers, or other constituents into the soil. Once reclamation is complete, monitoring begins. The soil is tested for various chemical and physical properties, and tree and shrub growth and health monitored. Finally, after a lengthy period of monitoring the oil sands, the operator receives a reclamation certificate.

Fessenden was not involved in the creation of this eight-part regulatory system, and in his view provincial regulation could have been better. He suggested the province should have taken a 'full project approach' to land reclamation. With apologies for being philosophical, he was soon on a roll.

## TURNING POINT

"One of the big issues up there is caribou management," he said, but "there's no way you can take an area that's going to be surface-mined and protect it for caribou." Fessenden's view is that government should have said, "I'm sorry but for the next hundred years this is clearly not going to be an area that's very conducive to caribou. We're going to take another portion of the province and make that really good for caribou. In a hundred years we can introduce caribou back into this area. In the big scale of time, a surface-mined area is a temporary disturbance. "A lot of people have difficulty thinking about 100 or 150 years as a temporary disturbance, but I come out of forestry [where we think] about long rotations."

Historical accounts of Lake Ontario's north shore during the late 17th century described the area as an abandoned, devastated battleground, with English and French fur-traders," thinking of it as an area no longer useful as a major source of furs. "If you read the early journals of Jesuit priests who came over to North America in the 1600-1650 period and their travels across Southern Ontario, they described a deforested landscape. The Indians used to burn the forests so they could plant corn" says Fessenden the history buff, who is now in his element. "In 1649, the Iroquois essentially wiped out the Hurons. Now, this was a result of a period of a hundred years of fur trade wars between tribes, the French and the English, and so on, but the point is that southern Ontario was essentially de-populated of natives between 1650 until the early settlers arrived in the early 1800s. That's 150 years, right? They found what they thought was virgin forest. Well, it had been left alone for 150 years, hadn't been disturbed.

You see, 100 years, 150 years is not a long period of time, really. If you want to think about the use of public land, the access to that bitumen resource right now is the highest and best use of that land," since exploiting that resource helps create a wealthier society.

Indeed, Fessenden saw the reclamation of mining pits as an opportunity to create a better landscape. "The guys who like bogs at the University of Alberta took me to task for saying that. Maybe the politics weren't right at the time. But, relatively speaking the area affected by surface mining is a fraction of the area flooded by the James Bay Hydro Project. Who complained about that?"[391] This enormous project involved flooding 11 per cent of the total area of Quebec – ironically, an area larger than the state of Florida.

The project displaced some 5,000 Cree Aboriginals, and they did complain. "Because the Cree people depend so largely on the natural regime – the forests, rivers, lakes, trees, animals, birds and fish – it is not easy to separate social from environmental impacts. For example, the destruction of a wetland habitat on which moose and beaver depend can have (and in many places has had) a devastating social impact on those who depend on country food," according to the Cree First Nation people's website. "In the Cree villages this includes almost everyone. Not just full-time hunters, but salaried or wage employees who work in the band offices or schools, or operate road maintenance machines, or work in the developing service companies, all hunt after work, weekends or during holidays. They hunt not simply for recreation, or to satisfy some primordial cultural need (although that is a factor, too). The fact is, they depend on moose and beaver and fish for food."[392]

Land reclamation was the original environmental issue for the oil sands, but the number and intensity of those concerns grew steadily, as did the oil sands industry's response. For example, in the 1970s, sulphur emissions from oil sands plants were of deep concern because there was anxiety about acid rain across the continent. The worry in those days was that sulphur and nitrogen emissions from oil sands plants would blow east, acidifying lakes and ponds in the hard rock Canadian Shield, which did not have alkaline rocks like limestone to neutralize the acid. The worry at that time was quite overblown, with suggestions that forests would die and fish would die in acidified lakes. Instead,

Matt Ridley argued, "acid rain was a minor and local nuisance that could be relatively cheaply dealt with, not a huge threat to large stretches of the planet."[393]

Technologies improved to meet growing environmental needs. One such was an innovation known as hydro-transport. This process involved mixing oil sand with water at either 35°C or 50°C, depending upon the mine, and then piping it to the processing plant. "During hydro-transport, the bitumen begins to separate from the sand, water and minerals," explained Peter Madden and Jacek Morawski. "The introduction of the hydro-transport system greatly increased both yields and reliability. Separation continues at the plant where the bitumen forms a thick froth at the top of the separation vessel and the sand settles out to the bottom. Material, including water, from the middle part of the vessel is further processed to remove more bitumen, the water is recycled and the sand is used in mine site reclamation."[394] This illustrates how technological advance frequently contributes to both environmental benefits and economic growth.

## RECLAMATION INNOVATION

For oil sands projects, reclamation meant digging up the overburden, which had gone into an industrial dump, and using it to cover up the clean sand being dumped into mined-out oil sands deposits at Suncor and, later, Syncrude. In the decades since, a lot of science and spending went into reclamation, and tailings became an important issue.

Although the money invested in reclamation bore fruit, development and land disturbance outpaced reclamation by orders of magnitude. At time of writing, certified reclamation – the industry's Holy Grail – was mostly a faint hope. In 2008, the province issued a certificate to Syncrude Canada for 104 hectares of reclaimed land, returned to the province. To put that in perspective, it amounted to about one thousandth of total disturbance by oil sands mining.

Nevertheless nearly 4,000 hectares of land and 1,200 hectares of ponds and wetlands had been reclaimed, but not certified, the amount of land now covered by tailings ponds is daunting – more than 170 square kilometres. Calculating how to reclaim these ponds – lakes, in many cases – has become a head-scratching challenge for the industry. The goal in the end to turn these disturbed areas back into forests and wetlands. So far the two pioneering operators, Suncor and Syncrude, have done the bulk of the reclamation work.

Reclamation rules followed Alberta's 1972 report, and both Suncor and Syncrude took important steps forward. In 2008, Syncrude received a reclamation certification from Alberta Environment for a 104-hectare area known as Gateway Hill, which included wood bison habitat.

The wood bison is the largest terrestrial animal in North America; large males weigh more than 900 kilograms. Both Syncrude and Suncor have undertaken reclamation efforts that included creating a fen, or wetland. Many other oil sands mining sites were in various stages of reclamation, but not yet ready for certification. However, rapid growth in the oil sands industry led to levels of land disturbance rapidly outpacing reclamation by orders of magnitude – a process which is in line with the regulatory findings of the industry but which has concerned some members of the public.

Like the pit mines themselves, reclamation of the oil sands is an enormous undertaking. "Reclamation, as it is applied in the Athabasca oil sands region, involves returning the post-mining landscape to a condition that is capable of meeting the needs of local land users," according to one report. It requires "placing the altered landscape on a trajectory that will result in resilient, self-sustaining, and dominantly native plant associations similar to those existing in pre-disturbance conditions."[395]


## SYNCRUDE'S CENTRIFUGE

"The challenge right now is what we call fluid fines – water containing finer clays and silts," said a Syncrude spokesman, Leithan Slade. Fines are in effect land that needs to be reclaimed. Since those tails are in no hurry to exit the water they are suspended in, tailings ponds grow bigger and bigger, and the industry's reclamation problems mount.

Slade said Syncrude had plans to "apply three main technologies to transform them into a reclamation material." The first was removing water from the tailings pond; second, adding a water treatment material – "a bit like flocculants used in water treatment plants. Then we will basically use centrifuges to spin out" the fluid fines.

Once completed in 2015, this remarkable, $1.9 billion new plant would feature 18 parallel centrifuges. Each centrifuge would be about nine metres long and two metres high, look like a long, steel tube, and spin at approximately 1,700 revolutions per minute – only half the speed of many home clothes driers spinning at full speed. The workforce on the project peaked in 2013 at 1,800 craft workers, making it one of Canada's largest construction projects; and there are still 1,200 workers on site. But what would be the purpose of the plant? It would produce a clay-based tailings cake for use in reclaiming the land. After 12 to 18 months, "that material will become strong enough for use as a reclamation material. It first needs to go through one freeze cycle," he added. "Probably all 18 centrifuges will not be operational at once. Some may need to be kept in reserve for maintenance in the centrifuge plant. Also, we need to be able to manage the amount of tailings cake being produced."[396]

## Suncor's TRO

The oil sands industry created COSIA – the Canadian Oil Sands Innovation Alliance – in 2010 as the coordinator of technology sharing and research efforts and Alan Fair became director of its tailings EPA – an acronym for "environmental priority area." Before joining the organization, he had spent 32 years at Syncrude – his last eight years in research and development. "I retired from Syncrude in order to start the Oil Sands Tailings Consortium which was then integrated into COSIA to become the Tailings EPA," he said. "By background I'm a geotechnical engineer, so I definitely know the tailings thing. I worked on it off and on for thirty-odd years at Syncrude."

To stress how important the tailings file had become, he offered a few statistics: In 2013, alliance members invested about $80 million in environmental research and development – a number which illustrated that "significant dollars are being spent by the companies to develop these technologies. That's strictly R&D. So, there's considerably more money being spent in commercially implementing these technologies, for example. We've got a substantive project portfolio on the go now – about 48 projects that various companies are working on."

"All de-watering technologies to some degree rely on gravity," Fair explained, "and they also rely on some form of polymer." These chemicals bind to clay particles, with each polymer becoming a complex molecule connected to many clay particles. Once a molecule has taken on its load of clay, it will settle more quickly. That, he said, was the first step. From that point on there were only a few ways to separate solids from the water. "You can use thermal energy – heat it up and boil it off – or mechanical energy" like centrifugal force.

"You can also use evaporation, like what naturally occurs, and that is what thin-lift drying does. In that particular technology you add the polymer or the flocculent and then spread the resulting slurry in very thin layers, typically 23 centimetres thick. And, by doing that you create a large surface area that's exposed to the atmosphere." Given that Fort McMurray is surrounded by wetlands, at first it seemed surprising that these layers would dry out if left to themselves, but it was clear that the moisture would evaporate from the reclaimed material. "Granted, it only occurs about five or six months of the year," Fair said. "In the winter months there's very little evaporation. It's a seasonal effort to dry them with evaporative forces."

Suncor's most important contribution in this field is Tails Reduction Operations, a patented technology. According to Suncor, TRO enabled the company to cancel plans for five additional tailings ponds at existing operations. And in the years ahead, the company expected it to play a role in reducing tailings ponds at its mines from eight to two, and reduce the land area covered by ponds by 80 per cent. "Although people don't generally understand it this way, in reality it's their overall tailings management system," said Fair. "It's essentially thin-lift drying."

When he began describing the process of using thickening technology, he quickly gave a sense of the scale of these operations. The vessels the industry uses for tailings reclamation were big and essentially horizontal. "In diameter, they're about 90 metres, even as big as 100 metres. So, they're large vessels. The aspect ratio, height to diameter, it's usually four to five times bigger in diameter than it is in height. So, if it's 100 metres in diameter, it might be 20 metres in height." By contrast, vessels used to clarify process water for reuse were more vertical in shape – only twice as wide as they were tall. By adding the flocculent to the vessel, he said, "you create an environment where the solid particles will settle from the bottom of the vessel and of course the water rises to the top." Inside the vessel "you use a number of rakes within the thickener that slowly go round and round. These rakes are sections of a picket fence. They create a path for the water to move upwards in the thickener vessel."[397]

## Shell's AFD

Shell's version of this technology held a patent for Atmospheric Fines Drying. Another technology aimed at accelerating the pace of tailings reclamation, the technology was developed for the Shell-led Athabasca Oil Sands Project (AOSP), which included participation by Chevron Canada and Marathon Oil Sands Canada.

The original test of Atmospheric Fines Drying involved pumping mature fine tailings from the tailings pond into a large barge, which transferred them to a drying area which covered 75 acres. The mature fine tailings were then mixed with flocculants – chemical thickeners like the ones Alan Fair described – and the concoction spread on a sloped surface. This allowed sun and gravity to extract the water from the grayish goop. The released water went back into the bitumen extraction process, and the deposits of particles dried further to make sure they were strong enough to use in reclamation. Conducted in 2010, this early test delivered 250,000 tonnes of reusable soil.

By combining it with non-segregated tailings, the system could create a fine-tails mixture which contained 40-45 per cent solids and has the consistency of motor oil. "Then they pump it to the disposal site," said Fair, "and often add another chemical or even spike it with additional fines to create slurry. Canadian Natural does much the same, but they have an added piece. They treat all of their tailings with $CO_2$. The carbon dioxide changes the pH of the slurry, making it more basic so the particles, the fine clays they drop out. They precipitate out more easily in a basic environment than in a neutral or acidic environment."[398]

# COSIA

The hydro-transport system was an excellent example of environmental collaboration among 14 of the largest oil sands producers, representing almost 90 per cent of oil sands production. This partnership took an important step forward in 2012, when those companies agreed to share their environmental innovations, to advance reclamation and other conservation issues.

"There are many good news stories to tell regarding the industry's performance in air, water and land management, including the formation of Canada's Oil Sands Innovation Alliance (COSIA), one of the largest collaborative groups in industrial history, anywhere," said *Oilsands Review*'s Deborah Jaremko. COSIA focused on four areas of environmental performance, she continued, "with the goal of accelerating significant improvements: tailings, water, land and greenhouse gases. To date, its member companies have shared 560 distinct technologies and innovations that cost over $900 million to develop – numbers that are increasing as the alliance matures and expands."[399] In the beginning, its members did not share information about tailings because it might have given their competitors proprietary knowledge about the processes they used to extract bitumen at their plants.

COSIA originated with the Canadian Association of Petroleum Producers. Formed at the request of the CEO Council, which includes CEOs of oil sands companies belong to CAPP, it reflected the industry's desire to share environmentally significant technology. A metallurgical engineer by training, Canadian Natural Resources, vice president Joy Romero has been an eloquent spokeswoman for this project. She joined Canadian Natural Resources in 2001 to participate in the development, construction, commissioning and operation of CNRL's Horizon project, which produces about 114,000 barrels of oil per day.

A research cooperative, COSIA replaced a number of other research organizations, two of which were CONRAD (Canadian Oilsands Network for Research and Development) and OSLI (the Oil Sands Leadership Initiative.) "We had several other places in which technology development was being done," said Romero, and when that happens it's diluted. You can't focus. So, we brought the entire industry together under one umbrella. We put in more money, more people and more resources to make sure that we are progressing in these issues even faster. We needed to gain a social licence to move our product." The industry needed to offset the view that bitumen is 'dirty oil.' That said, Romero acknowledged that there was no defense against the view, "No fossil fuels, period."

The point of COSIA was to focus research. "If there is a gap in our greenhouse gas intensity [compared to] conventional oil, what do we need to do to close that gap?" Romero asked. "With respect to water usage, even though we're within regulatory requirements, what does it take to reduce that yet again? What can we do to reclaim tailings ponds faster, to reclaim land sites faster?"

"If you don't believe that we want to improve the environment because it's the right thing to do," she said, shifting her focus from COSIA to CNRL. "Just look at the economic benefit good environmental practice brings. [CNRL's] tailings pond is half the size of a conventional tailings pond because reducing the amount of water we take in reduces the amount of water we have to treat and recycle. You don't have to be a rocket scientist to figure out that it is good business to have a smaller tailings pond. [Developing] heat integration between our upgrader and our extraction plant means that facility won't use gas. It'll use waste heat from the upgrader."

"When you look for flares on-site you basically can't see them," she said. "We use fuel gas to fire our furnaces. We recycle all of that." These environmental innovations were possible, of course, because recent technological innovations simply weren't available to earlier oil sands plants. But a key benefit for CNRL was that they lower the company's operating costs. Romero then added a new element to the discussion: "You can't create a strong oil sands project that isn't focused on the environment and on building human capacity. COSIA is the vehicle where I have an opportunity to influence the social licence so that there won't be those restrictions with respect to the pipelines. So, it's the place that Canadian Natural can turn to, that Shell can turn to and that all of the other operating companies can turn to; where we put all of our efforts together to improve the technologies that we're using to bring every member level of the best performer. We work in a way that is truly collaborative. When the technical teams are working together you can't tell which company somebody is from."[400]

Unlike the earliest days of oil sands mining, a tremendous amount of thought went into what to do with the sand, tailings, waste water and other left-over materials when the bitumen was gone.

CHAPTER 12

# Profitable years and their collapse

————

*"We picked Petro-Canada off at the low point of the market, or pretty*
*close to that…putting the assets together, particularly their downstream*
*with our upgrading and our upstream, made a lot of sense."*

— RICK GEORGE, 2011

IN 1991, THE WEST WAS back at war in the Middle East, and the first war of the
Post-Cold War era was about protecting oil supply. The Gulf War began when
Iraq used tanks and infantry to invade tiny Kuwait — a conquest which took a
single day. "With the possession of Kuwait, Saddam Hussein controlled 22 per
cent of the world's exportable oil," Walter Youngquist wrote. "If he could also
take Saudi Arabia, as there were indications that he might, he would control 44
per cent of the oil [available] for export."

Concerned about security if the Iraqi regime controlled so much of the
world's oil supply, US President George Bush assembled an alliance of countries to wage war against Iraq. In late February 1991, before battle was joined,
Hussein boasted, "The Mother of all battles will be our battle of victory and
martyrdom." A week later, the American Secretary of Defence, Richard
Cheney, laconically observed, "The Iraqi forces are conducting the Mother of
all retreats."[401]

The United States and its allies quickly defeated Saddam's forces in a high-
technology, highly public military and media event. After winning the battle,

however, Bush and his allies chose simply to stop the war. The armies did not take Baghdad and overthrow the government. They expected a spontaneous uprising in Iraq to do the job for them. Although weakened, Saddam's regime lived to fight another day. UN sanctions and other forms of pressure were placed on Iraq, and the country's oil exports were briefly taken out of the world market. This contributed to an upward bulge in the price of oil. According to President Bush, the Gulf War was signalling a "New World Order." From then on, noble alliances of countries would band together to do the right thing for the world, as they did by liberating Kuwait. It soon became clear, however, that it was just another episode in 1,300 years of conflict between the West and the Middle East.

As Samuel Huntington put it, "At stake was whether the bulk of the world's largest oil reserves would be controlled by Saudi and emirate governments dependent on Western military power for their security or by independent anti-western regimes which would be able and might be willing to use the oil weapon against the West. After the war the Persian Gulf was an American lake."[402] That lake today is anything but secure, and that insecurity is a source of great vulnerability. The good news is that the events of the 1990s and the following decade laid the groundwork for Canada's oil sands to become a petroleum powerhouse.


## THE KLEIN LEGACY

Alberta's premier from 1992 until 2006, Ralph Klein oversaw the oil sand sector's period of greatest growth yet, when he took over from Don Getty, Klein had inherited "a bloated bureaucracy and an angry electorate."[403] The province faced large and growing deficits and was desperate for a more balanced budget. Ottawa was also desperate for more jobs across Canada and Prime Minister Jean Chrétien (1993-2003) had just handily won an election. Oil prices were in the tank and the industry was desperate for investment opportunities. This set the stage for the industry's great surge forward – one that at this writing is two decades in duration. Call it the Klein legacy: it has been a period in which financial responsibility for oil sands development has lain entirely with the private sector. It has already been the longest-lasting of the major periods of oil sands policy, and in the near future seems unlikely to change.

Soon after Klein took office, the Edmonton-based Alberta Chamber of Resources handed him a report from the Task Force on National Oil Sands Strategies. The task force included mostly technical people representing a broad spectrum of organizations, government agencies and corporations. Comprised of subcommittees representing marketing and transportation, science and technology, environment and regulation, government and communications, fiscal and socio-economic issues, and "materials/services and coalition building," Erdal Yildirim chaired the group.

Turkish-born with a doctorate in engineering science from Columbia, Yildirim had proposed the task force in August 1982, when he put together "a one- or two-page write-up about the concept of improving business environment, tackling the PGRT, the resource allowance" and the other irrational features of the National Energy Program. "Time passes," he said, "and in 1983 we have a brand new energy minister, John Zaozirny, and three people from Alberta Chamber of Resources – two board members and the general manager – are going to visit with Zaozirny and [they] propose my little text, now cast into some kind of slide. They had one slide with four or five points."[404] The energy minister bought the idea, but the task force did not begin deliberations until after he left politics in 1986.

The Chamber led the project. Government, the petroleum industry and other stakeholders appointed representatives to a variety of technical committees. Eighteen months later the task force issued a report titled *The Oil Sands: A New Energy Vision for Canada*. In clear and compelling prose, the summary outlined eight areas where players in the emerging oil sands industry could help the industry grow – by developing new markets, for example, a pipeline system that better served areas where bitumen was being produced. One key to growth was a better fiscal regime. In addition, "The Federal and Alberta governments... should develop a generic set of harmonized tax and royalty measures based on economic profits. Such a system will provide a consistent fiscal framework for all oil sands projects and result in a balanced sharing of profits. These common fiscal terms are necessary for the future development of Canada's oil sands."[405]

After the release of the task force report, Klein's government began look-ing for ways to implement its suggestions. In cooperation with Jean Chrétien's Liberal government in Ottawa, in September the two governments approved a generic oil sands royalty and tax regime that would apply to all new projects.

New projects would pay the province a 1 per cent royalty on production until net project revenue had paid out all start-up costs. At that point, the royalty would rise to 25 per cent, although all capital costs, including operat-ing, research and development, were fully deductible in the year they were incurred. This was radical, and the free-market Klein government stepped up to the plate without hesitation. The outcome was a flood of oil sands spending in the province. Suncor began a series of mining and *in-situ* expansions that made it Canada's largest petroleum company. Syncrude also announced large expansions. Both companies introduced technologies and operations that led to huge reductions in the cost of production.

Development went ahead in these years for three main reasons. First, the industry had enjoyed technical successes in its pilot projects, and relatively small-scale plants were less risky and quicker to bring on stream than mega-projects. Second, Alberta and the federal government devised a fiscal regime to encourage *in-situ* development. Third, some companies saw this technology as being economic over the long term. Together, these factors led to a dramatic flurry of oil sands activity. Cenovus (formerly a unit of EnCana) and the Japan Canada Oil Sands Corporation were first off the mark. As the new millennium dawned, both completed commercial SAGD projects, and soon followed by multiple others. *In-situ* production now exceeds mining volumes by a consider-able volume.

During the Klein era there was a land rush that made the post-conference land registrations of the 1950s look like a non-event. Oil sands companies popped up like mushrooms – indeed, there were so many that this chapter can't do them justice. In 1999, a Shell-led consortium began its Muskeg River Mine oil sands development – better known as the Athabasca Oil Sands Project. The project went on stream in 2003. Others included Cenovus, an offshoot of the huge gas producer EnCana, and Canadian Natural Resources Limited, which began building its vast Horizon mining and processing project toward the end of Klein's term, completing the first phase in 2009. Nexen Energy – then independent but later a wholly-owned subsidiary of China National Offshore Oil Corporation, began constructing its Long Lake facility, which at this writing produced more than 112,000 barrels of synthetic oil a day.

## DROWNING IN OIL?

To many people these developments seemed misplaced. As 1999 began, world oil prices dropped below $10. In inflation-adjusted terms, oil prices were near historic lows.

Forgetting the cyclical nature of the petroleum business, many pundits were proclaiming a world of low oil prices well into the foreseeable future. Twenty years earlier, many of the same pundits had been forecasting high oil prices into the foreseeable future. So pessimistic was opinion in the investment community that a highly respected business magazine, *The Economist,* issued a special supplement about crude oil. The magazine's leader described "A world drowning in oil" and, with spectacular bad timing, argued that prices could drop to US$5 because of a glut in world supplies. Nothing could save the price of oil, even OPEC. The magazine despaired that the cartel could work its traditional magic, because OPEC's members continued to cheat shamelessly on their export quotas. Furthermore, the cartel was no longer the only game in town: increasingly large volumes of oil were flowing into world markets from such non-OPEC countries as Norway and Russia. The authors' grim conclusion: surplus oil supplies would continue to depress world prices.[406]

As the magazine hit the newsstands, OPEC announced that it would bring new discipline to world crude markets. Members would cut production, and they would keep their exports low. In addition, the cartel negotiated coordinated cuts with Russia, Mexico, Norway and Oman. The cartel and its co-conspirators (except Russia) stuck to their guns, and a new bull market began.

What the magazine's writers failed to consider was that, when conditions are right, oil can be a weapon of great power. If unconstrained and if conditions are favourable, cartels tend to grow in power. By using diplomacy to bring

Norway, Mexico and Russia on side, OPEC strengthened itself by orders of magnitude. Bragging rights for the first major work to predict a new bull market in oil stocks go to Michael Economides and Ronald Oligney, both academics. In a commentary on the global energy industry, they wrote that "now is the time to buy energy stocks. They will escalate in value substantially in the early 2000s. The wise investor buys for the long-term because energy is the world's biggest business, and it continues to move unstoppably forward."[407]

During Ralph Klein's term as premier, the growth of one company stands out. When Sunoco was near the top of its game its chairman, Bob McClements, asked American-born lawyer Rick George to take charge of the company's Canadian subsidiary, Suncor Energy Inc.

With degrees in both law and engineering, George was in charge of Sunoco's North Sea development and production, and had overseen construction of Europe's first purpose-built offshore production platform. "I flew over to London and asked him whether he would give up his position with an established operation in the UK and move to a totally different environment in Canada After only a day, he agreed," said McClements. "You have never met a more unassuming, low-key but brilliant executive in your life. He's quiet, but when he speaks you listen. He knows what he's doing because he came up the ranks. He was given increasing responsibilities and he did well in every one of them."[408]

## SUN RISE

George became Suncor's president and chief operating officer in 1990, taking up residence in the company's Toronto head office. The following year the board appointed him chief executive officer. Also in 1991, McClements retired and Sunoco began a policy of divesting upstream assets so it could focus instead on refining and marketing. Accordingly, it spun off Suncor as an independent entity. For Rick George this represented a great deal of opportunity. When he took over, Suncor's primary assets included the money-losing oil sands plant, some service stations and a small refinery in Ontario. The oil sands business "really struggled with return on capital well into the mid-1990s [because of] high costs relative to low oil prices," he said. "There were 20–25 years of real struggle between when this industry got its first plant online and when it actually started to make enough money to make sense."[409] George assembled a high-powered executive team and together they set out to make changes.

Dee Parkinson-Marcoux was the company's oil sands executive vice president, and in 1991 it became her job to alter the fortunes of the money-losing plant. A mining engineer by training, Parkinson-Marcoux had a background in mining and refinery management, and she also had exceptional business instincts. "I knew the mine should be run by a miner," she said. Petroleum engineers are "a different creature," she said. "They thrive on problems, they know that Mother Nature's going to throw them a curve ball every day and they just get up and say, 'Well, what's today's problem going to be?' So I hired a miner" — Cliff Britch by name.

She had read about Britch in a newspaper article, and the story had convinced her that "he was of the breed that was tough and fair." Britch was one of a number she interviewed for the job, and he was "absolutely the man. I tell you, when you've got people you can rely on who have high principles, you know they're fair, they know where we're headed, they know what has to be done, you can relax at night."[410]

Oil prices were low and declining, and Suncor was not making money. According to Britch, who came from a coal mining background and became a vice president in 1992, the company had to arrange a massive layoff — "a third of the hourly people and half of the staff" — conducted over two or three days. "We brought everybody in and told every person, 'You are going tomorrow [or] 'You are going in three years; here's the progression.'" He added, "I was quite impressed with Suncor's attention to social issues and people and work equity. They put a lot of money into making it right, issuing severance packages and so on."[411] Then the company turned to mechanizing the operation in totally new ways — transforming the operation.

As Parkinson-Marcoux's team began to analyze the mine's operations, they identified many problems. For example, "we were processing tonnes of sand that had no bitumen in it," she said; this meant "huge costs." Bucketwheels were another problem. "The downtime had become incredible, and maintenance costs in this harsh, harsh environment" were huge. "You wouldn't run your car that way and there just had to be a better way." The solution here team came up with was to replace bucketwheels, which are unselective, with a system of trucks and shovels. This was "more efficient in a thousand different ways. It can selectively mine, so we became much more sophisticated at dealing with the ore body the way miners do. You don't mine stuff that's lean; you mine the stuff that's fat."[412]

The company brought in "trucks, shovels, all of this miscellaneous stuff," said Britch. "They were the biggest shovels in the world, biggest trucks in the world, everything was big" – indeed, the wheels on the trucks "cost $30,000 to $40,000 each, and there were six of them." This conversion was expensive, but it offered flexibility. "The key is, if you lose one truck, big deal. You've got a fleet of 50, right? So, it's not the end of the world. If you lose one shovel, it's a little more serious. But, you've got eight or nine of them, so it's not the end of the world." By contrast, when the company was using two bucketwheel reclaimers, if one went down the company would lose half of its production.

"What we really did was replace the front-end," he continued, elaborating on Parkinson-Marcoux's explanation. "We changed the whole mining scheme. The bucketwheels and the belt conveyers running up into the plant, the long conveyer going out to the mine with all the laterals coming off it – that whole business we replaced." This new system was transformational. "All of a sudden you could take advantage of your knowledge of the ore body," he said. "Now, we could do the geology and use the information to decide almost shift by shift, where we wanted the shovel and what kind of material we needed to get maximum through-put and maximum recovery in the plant."[413]

Don Thompson acknowledged the importance of what Suncor did, but was adamant that Syncrude president Jim Carter had introduced truck-and-shovel mining into the oil sands – a system Carter had learned in the iron ore business. "We used 170-tonne trucks and smaller shovels – initially in overburden and then in the North Mine. We used trucks and shovels in what I'll call small operations to prove them out prior to our North Mine opening. Suncor had to revise their mine plan to become as efficient as ours or, frankly, go out of business.[414]

The other area Parkinson-Marcoux looked at was "our product and our product quality. It was one size fits all." The plant would combine its three refined products – diesel, gasoline and synthetic oil – into a single blend to transport to its refinery customers. "I had produced as a refiner from my days at Esso," she said, "and I understood a lot about crude oil, so I asked, 'Well, why aren't we blending? Can't we blend to meet the customer's need?' So instead of them buying or not liking our crude because its one-third, one-third, one-third, some people actually want a bit more of this and a bit less of that and some other people want it the other way around. So we started to create synthetic blends that actually were more valuable to the customer. That wasn't rocket science."[415]

When George, Parkinson-Marcoux and Britch took over, the plant was still small. They and the others on the new executive set out to restructure what was still a 60,000 barrel per day plant. They developed plans to deploy truck-and-shovel technology for mining, make major improvements to the processing plant, and expand capacity to 130,000 barrels per day by 2001. Then, in 1998, the company filed a regulatory application for Project Millennium, comprised of mining capacity increases and a new upgrader. The project was a dramatic expansion, designed to increase production to 210,000 barrels per day.

George picked up the story, referring to *The Economist's* classic miscalculation of the oil price outlook in an issue that came out just as Suncor's board approved the Millennium Project. "I think what [*The Economist*] lost track of is that this industry moves through cycles and it will continue to roll through cycles as we invest, as we try to figure out where the next investments should be." Millennium was a good investment, he added. "We started the project when there were low oil prices. When we got the project done in 2002, oil prices rose and it was obviously a great win for our shareholders. Oil companies are big deployers of capital. And I think the management and leadership of oil companies is really about making right choices at the right time."

In 2001, Suncor announced its Voyageur growth strategy, a multi-pronged approach targeted to bring oil sands production to 500,000 barrels per day by 2012. The plan included a mine extension, third upgrader, and *in-situ* expansions at its Firebag SAGD project. George said the upgrader should reduce business volatility. "It should improve reliability. It's going to be a project that will be online for 50 to 100 years...you've got to take a very long-term view of this business."

And that long-term view rests a lot on *in-situ* development. In 2009, George announced a \$19.1-billion bid to take over Petro-Canada. With the merger's success, Suncor suddenly had the biggest refining and marketing presence in Canada, light oil and gas properties around the world and significant additional oil sands properties. In addition to undeveloped leases and the MacKay River SAGD project acquired through the acquisition, George considered its Firebag assets to be a key piece of the future. "Firebag is in the middle of a lease we hold that has 9 billion barrels of recoverable oil," he said. "So this is again an asset base that will be on production for the next hundred years in some form or another."

"If you look at it in a historic sense, we picked Petro-Canada off at the low point of the market, or pretty close to that," he said. "I'd thought for a period of time about putting the assets together, particularly their downstream with our upgrading and our upstream made a lot of sense. The opportunity to drive to drive costs out the system – all of that was there in spades. I think it was a great move, made at the right time. And, you know, most mergers actually don't drive shareholder value. This is one that did."

George believed that even though he had been at the helm of Suncor for 20 years, the real excitement was yet to come. "I think the next ten years in this industry are going to be some of its best," he said, pointing specifically to technology around reducing the environmental footprint of operations. "It is going to astound people how quickly this happens and how well it happens." The step-changes will come particularly in the *in-situ* area, he told me. "The important thing to remember about SAGD is that is still a very, very young industry. [You're going to see] a real take-off because of the critical mass of investment in technologies that will rapidly change how we do this. It will reduce water use. It will reduce energy intensity. It will make wells more productive. As wells get to the end of their life, we'll figure out ways to extend that and recover more."

"Listen, industry is looking at all kinds of ways to [improve efficiency], whether it's use of solvents, surfactants, better downhole pumps, whether you eventually, once you get these caverns, use fire-flood," George continued. "There are so many technologies out there that are being looked at, being researched, being tried in the field, you're going to see this thing change rapidly, particularly over the next decade or so. It's actually quite exciting."

Suncor's production grew dramatically under George's leadership – knocking Imperial off its perch as Canada's top oil producer, for example. In the longer term, he said, the company would "have production coming in from Fort Hills, eventually Joslyn, but also from Firebag, from MacKay River, from our two base mines. And this will feed this large upgrading complex that includes upgrader number one [constructed in 1967], upgrader number two (from the Millennium Project) and upgrader three which is Voyageur. The total capacity of that upgrading facility will be somewhere in the 550,000-barrel-a-day range."[416] In practice, however, Suncor cancelled Voyageur mid-construction.

Suncor's market capitalization at this writing was more than $51 billion. In a recent Forbes list of the 2000 biggest companies in the world, the company ranked 149th. By contrast Sunoco – once the mighty Sun Oil – had a market cap of $4.31 billion and ranked 1,258[th]. Based on decisions taken after Bob McClements left the board, the company no longer produced oil or refined it. It sold refined fuels, including gasoline, from a large fleet of service stations.

## TEARFUL FAREWELL

The question of how to book reserves from the oil sands was an issue for the Canadian Petroleum Association in the 1970s and 1980s. However, the question emerged again just after the turn of the century. On that occasion, the result was an eye-opener.

The ERCB was then responsible for estimating reserves in Alberta. According to Neil McCrank, who was chair at the time, when the staff began asking hard questions about oil sands reserves they realized that "what we were booking was that which was underneath the actual mining permit that we had approved – so, for Syncrude and Suncor, and nothing beyond that. We weren't even going beyond the boundaries of the mining permit, and we were booking absolutely zero for *in-situ*." He added that the board's failure to book *in-situ* may have been more than "a failure to understand that we should be booking more oil sands reserves. The economics of the time indicated that *in-situ* was never going to be developed." However, the board started to recognize the economics of SAGD production and "the fact that we should book beyond the specific mine approval that we had," and "overnight we went from I think it was 25 or 30 billion barrels to 170 billion barrels of reserves.... We knew that we would be attacked. We knew there would be an attack on the calculations that we came up with, so we needed government to believe in what we were doing."

Knowing he would need political support to dramatically increase the province's reserves, McCrank explained the situation to provincial energy minister Murray Smith, whom he described as being "a quick study on anything, and understands the oil and gas business very well." He continued that Murray "immediately saw the merit of what we were talking about, not just from the point of view of technically, but of course what it means to Alberta. So he took on the role of being a great supporter within government so that we didn't get our hands slapped by government. We did go public, and we were attacked" – notably by an editorial in *The New York Times*, which said "these cowboys up there think they have all this oil but it's really just a joke. I responded in a letter to the editor, which they didn't print, but they quit talking about it."[417]

Oddly enough, as he completed his term as one of the most popular premiers in Alberta's history, Klein held a news conference in which he essentially proclaimed himself a failure. On the matter of oil sands development, he was partly responding to general criticism by Peter Lougheed, who had called for more limited oil sands development. "What's the hurry?" Lougheed had asked. He was concerned about the environmental and social impacts of oil sands development. "Why not build one plant at a time? I hope the new government in Alberta will reassess this and come to the conclusion that the mess, and I call it a mess, that is Fort McMurray and the tar sands will be revisited." Lougheed didn't stop there. "The government of Alberta, with its acceleration of oil sands operations, will in my judgment be seen as the major villain in all of this in the eyes of the public across Canada, he added. "My surmise is that we're into this constitutional legal conflict soon," he said. "And my surmise is that – and this is strong stuff – national unity will be threatened if the court upholds federal environmental legislation and it causes major damage to the Alberta oil sands and our economy."[418]

In his sometimes tearful farewell, Klein said he couldn't have imagined how forcefully the industry would respond to the royalty and tax changes of the mid-1990s. Thus, his government didn't have a plan for how to deal with the spectacular growth that followed. Of course, any other premier would have basked in the glow of leaving behind an economic boom. That Klein didn't have a plan more or less characterizes the man himself. According to one biographer, a "certain irrationality had entered Alberta's political life – irrationality in the sense that facts, arguments and political debate itself no longer counted – when he entered politics."[419]

After introducing technologies and operations that led to huge reductions in the cost of production, and reflecting the work of the National Oil Sands Task Force, both Suncor and Syncrude announced large mining expansions. Then, in 1999, the Energy and Utility Board (a temporary, Klein-era successor to the Energy Resources Conservation Board) granted approval for a Shell-led consortium to begin its Muskeg River Mine oil sands development – better known as the Athabasca Oil Sands Project, which went on stream in 2003. Shell's Neil Camarta led the construction of that project. At the time this publication went to press, Camarta continued to be an optimist on the oil sands. "If I was asked to place my money on where in the world the industry is going to make progress, resolving environmental issues, I'd bet on the Canadian industry," he said. "I wouldn't be placing my money on Iraq or Saudi Arabia or Nigeria or Venezuela. I'd be putting my money here."[420]

Given the gloom of that period in the petroleum industry, it is ironic that the future would come so soon. What made this new era a period of solid growth for Alberta is that during the Klein era conventional oil prices rose from about $19 when he began his term to $63.43 on the day he retired. Gas prices also more than tripled, from $2 to $7. Driven by the 2003 US-led invasion of Iraq, these price spikes pulled bitumen along, and ever more investment went into the oil sands. Indeed, construction of another leviathan project began toward the end of Klein's term, and went into operation in 2009. Located on leases initially covering 14.3 billion barrels of bitumen in place, at this writing Canadian Natural Resources Limited's Horizon project produced about 112,000 barrels of synthetic oil per day.

At the beginning of Klein's term, in 1994, the province merged AOSTRA into the Provincial Ministry of Energy's Oil Sands and Research Division. The corporation was dissolved in 2000, with its assets and liabilities vested in the Alberta Science and Research Authority. According to Clement Bowman, AOSTRA funds eventually stimulated $1 billion in public/private sector investment. During its years of influence, the industry launched *in-situ* demonstration projects in all the major oil sand deposits. These evolved into multiple commercial projects over subsequent decades. SAGD proved to be a wildly successful technological advance, and this initiative helped develop scientific, engineering and entrepreneurial expertise for the oil sands.

These pages have often referred to Clement Bowman, who kindly offered a great deal of information and advice to the author. Formerly an executive with Imperial Oil Ltd., he was also AOSTRA's first chair.

Some years ago, Bowman shared the $1.3-million Global Energy International Prize for his work on the development of highly efficient processes for oil extraction. As Bowman observed in some of our discussions, Canadian energy is now an integrated system with the oil sands, coal, hydro, nuclear and renewable energy all performing key roles. Each of those energy resources has its own environmental and economic challenges, and all of those challenges need to be addressed. In the case of oil sands, he said, the challenges include the need for new processes to minimize water use, and emissions into the atmosphere must be reduced.

In an article in *The Globe and Mail*, he described his vision of Canada as "a sustainable, environmentally sound energy superpower," but added that "a vision without a plan is but a dream." Canada cannot walk "away from fossil fuels and (close) down coal plants," he said. "It's about learning to work with what nature has given us, without using the environment as a dump for waste products."

"Canada has an opportunity to provide global leadership in addressing the collision between energy and the environment, the dominant issue facing our planet in this century," he wrote. "We lack only one ingredient - the national will. In the past, our big achievements have been conceived and led by champions. The railway across Canada, the construction of our airport system in the midst of the depression, the massive James Bay generating facility, the unlocking of the deeply buried oil sands - in each case, there was a champion who provided the leadership and who created a sense of public purpose. Where is Canada's champion to lead our energy vision?"

"Nature has bestowed an enormous gift on Canada – the Alberta oil sands," he said. "But without the addition of hydrogen, the full value of this resource will not be realized. Hydrogen and bitumen will forever be joined at the hip, and the challenge will be to install the capacity to upgrade the bitumen (cracking it into smaller molecules via hydrogen addition) in Canada. There are many routes to producing hydrogen, two of which fit well with other energy resources in Alberta – natural gas and coal. Production of hydrogen from natural gas is a well demonstrated technology in which Alberta is a world leader. Gasification of coal is an alternative technology which produces hydrogen, electricity, and a concentrated stream of carbon dioxide that can be recovered and stored underground."[421] Using coal gasification as a source of hydrogen would make coal and oil sands an integrated resource.

"Greenhouse gas capture, transportation and storage are natural pathways for Canada," according to Bowman. "We are already injecting carbon dioxide into conventional oil reservoirs to promote enhanced oil recovery. We have almost unlimited future storage capacity in deep underground saline aquifers. The carbon dioxide is not stored as a high-pressure gas, in danger of sudden release. It is stored as a liquid in the pore space, just like the original petroleum."[422]

Some years after Bowman began promoting these ideas, an academic named Richard Marceau had begun studying and promoting his ideas. A vice president at Memorial University and president of the Canadian Academy of Engineering, Marceau was quoted as saying, "We've built our country through big projects, massive undertakings that have stretched our resources to the limit." Constructing Suncor and Syncrude were mega-projects that fit this bill, but in its day so did the nation-building Canadian Pacific Railway.

The successful completion of these immense transportation, energy and communication projects is a testament to the strength of the Canadian innovation strategy, Dr. Marceau told a journalist for *The Globe and Mail*, adding that big projects are at the foundation of today's prosperity. According to Bowman, "We have the capability to generate enormous quantities of electricity, way beyond our own needs." Canada could conceivably triple it hydroelectric power production and increase nuclear energy production by a factor of 10. Since both forms of energy generate low greenhouse gas emissions, Bowman proposed "a national grid that connects from east to west across Canada and is linked to the U.S., we could provide electricity to the States." This would have a substantial impact on America's greenhouse gas emissions, but it would also generate economic spinoffs. Such efforts would be national projects, serving Canada's long-term national interest by realizing the country's potential to be an energy superpower.

As this book has shown, leaders who enabled the oil sands to flourish have represented business, science and government, all three. Of particular significance, in recent decades many players have emerged from anonymity in the petroleum industry to create substantial oil sands businesses. To appreciate the importance of these developments, consider the interlocking stories of Sir John Browne of BP and Amoco on the one hand, and Bill McCaffrey's MEG Energy, which he created with a dollar and a dream.

Having risen to the top of BP, Browne received a knighthood in 1998 and a life peerage in 2001. In his memoirs, he said almost nothing about Canada – only that in the late 1970s he got an assignment in Alberta (he almost got an assignment in China instead) to investigate opportunities in the oil sands. Specifically, he looked at BP's project at Wolf Lake. His conclusion? The oil sands were "too inefficient" to produce. "It was a viewpoint I continued to hold, for economic and environmental reasons, during the rest of my time at BP."[423] Browne rose quickly through the ranks of BP, and sold off its Canadian operations as soon as he could. In the end, the company's Wolf Lake property went to Amoco Canada for a nominal fee.

His view about the oil sands profoundly affected operations at Amoco when BP took the company over. Amoco had tested many approaches to oil sands production. In 1958, the company began a pilot project near Fort McMurray at Gregoire Lake – one of the early experiments with *in-situ* production. Partly as a result of this work, Amoco patented the COFCAW ("combination of forward combustion and waterflood") production process. This technique involved simultaneously injecting air into the underground reservoir and igniting some of the bitumen with a chemical catalyst. The air would keep the fire burning and the resulting heat would increase the reservoir formation's temperature to 93° C. When the formation reached these temperatures, operators injected water into the reservoir. This produced a complex set of drives, including forces from heat, gas and water that drove the hot, fluid oil into production wells, and early results were promising. Amoco Corporation's 1968 annual report said the company had applied for approval to expand production rates to 8,000 barrels per day. In addition, said the report, "We contemplate expanding the project to about 60,000 barrels of oil per day after improving the production technique further."[424] One of the first modern *in-situ* pilot plants in Canada, the project did not reach those levels of production, but it was an important source of technological innovation.

Amoco Canada's first commercial heavy oil production came from the Elk Point project near Lloydminster, on the Alberta/Saskatchewan border. This reservoir is a source of conventional heavy oil, since it is light enough to flow to the wellbore without *in-situ* production techniques. Begun as a primary heavy oil facility in 1984 (when production was selling for $33.50 per barrel,) the plant closed down briefly in 1986 when its heavy oil fetched as little as $6.36 per barrel – less than a third its operating costs. The Elk Point properties were 100 per cent Amoco owned. Through the Dome acquisition of 1988, Amoco acquired an additional 140 sections of land at nearby Lindbergh. The following year the company experimented unsuccessfully with steam flood – part of an effort throughout the petroleum industry to bring costs down in the wake of the previous year's oil price crash. Companies had to shift their thinking on the economics of heavy oil recovery. Primary production rather than thermal recovery became the goal.

Then field engineers and operators noticed that the more sand that came out with oil produced through primary recovery, the greater the oil production. The next step was stunningly simple: Operators removed sand control screens from the wells and otherwise modified the production system. Strange concepts such as "foamy oil" and "wormholes" explained the otherwise impossible (with traditional fluid flow concepts) producing rates and recovery factors that resulted from this change. This and other process changes enabled the company to take production from 2,140 barrels per day in 1988 to 4,500 barrels per day in 1991. More importantly, production costs declined to only $5.56 per barrel – a 73 per cent reduction.

But change was in the wind, with the biggest oil companies getting much bigger through mergers. The years 1998 to 2002 were a period of consolidation, with the world's energy giants combining to form six super-majors. Browne was the first off the mark. With cooperation from Amoco's chairman, Larry Fuller, he engineered BP's $110 billion take-over of Amoco – when the regulators gave their approval, the biggest industrial merger of all time. The following year, BP acquired ARCO – a descendent of Richfield Corporation, whose 1975 departure from the Syncrude consortium triggered crisis followed by the Winnipeg agreement – in a separate $26.8 billion deal.

This started a stampede. Exxon merged with Mobil to form ExxonMobil. French major Total absorbed Elf-Aquitaine, and then took over Belgium's Petrofina to create a European giant. Chevron and Texaco merged, also consuming Gulf Oil. The final union came when Conoco and Phillips joined forces. Only Royal-Dutch Shell, with its complex head office structure, stayed clear of the fray. The purpose of these mergers was to create companies with complementary geographic and strategic assets. During his term as chair and CEO, BP became the world's second-largest non-state oil company by market capitalization. At this writing, it was number 17 on the Forbes magazine list of the 2000 biggest publically-traded global companies. Only three oil companies – ExxonMobil, PetroChina, and Shell – are bigger.

As Browne put it, "What appealed to us was that Amoco was very much a US business and it would give us access to great US refining and marketing operations and US natural gas production."[425] Not a word about its oil sands assets.

"The deal will place it in the top three of international oil producers but 6,000 people worldwide will lose their jobs as a result," wrote the BBC when the Amoco deal received regulatory approval.[426] Indeed: No one could have predicted the impact these deals would have on human lives, of course, but neither could anyone have imagined what an impact they would have on the petroleum industry itself. I knew McCaffrey at Amoco, which might have been a leader in oil sands development. That storied company was not, but McCaffrey was.

# A DOLLAR AND A DREAM

With consummation of the BP/Amoco merger, corporate employees in Canada received generous severance packages as they were walked out the door, and McCaffrey was one of them. A 16-year Amoco veteran and an engineer by training, the layoffs didn't faze him. After getting his package he joined with two friends to form McCaffrey Energy Group – it later became MEG Energy – which had market capitalization of more than $8 billion within ten years.

McCaffrey had joined Amoco straight out of university, and the new U of A graduate went through a typical training progression. "I started off as a facility engineer, then a production engineer then an operations engineer. I became a reservoir engineer over time. I was involved with developing technologies that would advance the oil sands – specifically Primrose. It had been using cyclic steam in those areas before and my job as a reservoir engineer was to find something that would work, that would be economic. After developing that technology I was in charge of actually developing the fields.... And for a period of about three years we were drilling horizontal wells day in, day out, non-stop in the Air Weapons Range. We had perhaps two hundred horizontal wells. What that taught us is that you could drill wells horizontally from surface in a commercially viable way and ... could count on the production from it."

McCaffrey was at Amoco during "D-Day" – corporate slang for September 1 1988, when the company formally acquired Dome Petroleum for $5.8 billion. For more than a decade, that was the largest cash acquisition in Canadian history. The merger was "a pivot point" for his employer, according to McCaffrey. For one thing, there were two Dome employees for every one employee from Amoco, so there was a change in corporate culture. "Amoco had been a fairly rigid company; Dome was more entrepreneurial, had been pursuing the oil sands and had a portfolio of [assets] that was truly great. Primrose was a major project. At one point I was responsible for the commercial development of up to 80 billion barrels of resource. That's a massive number on any scale, but it was a prize that came to Amoco as a result of that merger. At the time of the merger they really had no appreciation for the sheer magnitude of what they had acquired with Dome...."

"There were other properties," McCaffrey said enthusiastically. "We acquired Wolf Lake for a dollar from Petro-Canada and BP," and that gave the company a production facility the company could tie into its nearby Primrose property. "It spawned development of the property that Canadian Natural Resources, (CNRL) has today." He described other properties that came with the deal. There was one "called Mic Mac which is now [CNRL's] Horizon. There was Kirby and that's now in partnership between BP and Devon." Dome assets at Gregoire Lake became part of the OPTI/Nexen Long Lake project. "Burnt Lake, which is in the Air Weapons Range, was later owned by Suncor and now by CNRL. It was one of those unique points in time where you had that kind of size of resource being identified and Amoco had control of it all, they had one hundred per cent, except for the Burnt Lake stuff."

McCaffrey was also one of the project engineers involved with the Underground Test Facility, "working worked shoulder-to-shoulder to advance a technology that had been developed by Roger Butler. This is a great technology and it forms the basis of the majority of the *in-situ* technology used in the province today." Even though Amoco had all these assets and this experience in the oil sands, however, when BP took the company over, the new management dropped them all. The reason, according to McCaffrey, was at the top of the organization. Chairman and CEO John Browne's earliest experience with the oil sands had been as a junior reservoir engineer at Wolf Lake, which was not a high quality reservoir. "He came to dislike the oil sands, and believed that it wasn't something that you should have in your business. We all make our decisions from our experiences, and his experience was with old technology and a lower-quality reservoir. That's what shaped his thinking. After the BP-Amoco merger, he decided to divest. It didn't fit into his strategic model. There are different thoughts and different strategies and at that time, for Sir John, it didn't fit into the BP portfolio."

McCaffrey got a package from Amoco at the end of 1998, and within months world oil prices were about ten dollars a barrel. On St. Patrick's Day he set up a company; "I'm Irish," he said, "so that's a good thing." He had told his wife Janice, an Olympic-calibre race-walker, that he was going to do something "crazy:" buy swampland (a reference to the muskeg covering much of the oil sands) and start a company. He asked, "Are you okay with this?" She said, "Go for it."

McCaffrey, his brother-in-law Steve Turner and Vancouver-based entrepreneur Dave Wizinsky put $100,000 each into the company. McCaffrey then bought their first property – nine sections (each section is one square mile) – at Christina Lake for $150,000. "There was about a billion barrels in place at the time and we were able to compete with industry because industry believed that the oil price was going to stay down in the $10 per barrel range for a long time. 'Who cares about oil sands?'" was the prevailing sentiment. For the oil in place on that property, about 1 billion barrels, they paid roughly 1.5 cents per barrel.

For the first four years of operations, McCaffrey Energy Group focused on quietly acquiring oil sands leases; the company gave little thought to actually building an oil sands operation. The conventional wisdom at the time was that only a super-major could have the resources to do so. But McCaffrey became intrigued by the idea of doing so himself. "To me it was really three things you needed: quality assets, people with experience and quality investors. And if you could put those three legs of the stool together you could compete favourably with the majors." The first two legs of the stool were in place, but he needed investors.

For a while, McCaffrey walked around the streets of Calgary, hat in hand, looking for investors – "anybody who would put in money." It was a time-consuming process, because most people were only investing, say, $25,000. But in 2004 McCaffrey came upon a New York-based investment group called Warburg Pincus – "a class, class organization. They're private equity. They have a long-term value-focused orientation and they bet on the people. So when they invest they go through every detail about you, they dig up information about you, but because they're going to count on you I think that's fair."

After Warburg Pincus, he was able to find investors like Toronto-based Wellington Financial, Chinese insurance companies and pension funds, and endowments and sovereign wealth funds. "From 2004 to maybe even the end of 2009, the company was able to bring in thirty blue chip investors. We were able to raise more money privately [$3.2 billion] than any other company in any industry in the world ever. That's a huge statement but it has been backed by five different banks. They have done the research and they cannot find another one like that." He added, "All money is not equal. We could only deliver a product that we thought would have enormous value over time, but it did take time. You needed to make sure that the dollars that you were going to bring in were well aligned with what you could deliver."

Raising money became an obsession, and he found himself doing enormous amounts of travelling because "in the private equity in the world you do one-on-ones. You sit down in meetings of three of four people and you just tell your story and you work with them to understand it. We were doing laps of the Earth. We got it down where you could go around the earth in five days. Three nights sleep, two in airplanes, on top of that you get three continents. When you leave, you go east. You come back from the west five days later."[427] McCaffrey lived up to his promises, and production from the company continued to grow. In 2013 MEG produced, on average, 35,317 barrels per day. That represented a 23 per cent increase over the previous year.

In that year, the company was testing a refinement on SAGD, which it called – given its predilection for acronyms – eMSAGP, which stands for "enhanced modified steam and gas push." At its Christina Lake operation, MEG drilled two infill wells and injected non-condensable gas with steam between three well pairs in early stages of production – a technique normally applied in late phases of SAGD production. The technology lowered steam rates by 30 per cent without decreasing the production trend. The system, the company said, was "driving expectations of further efficiencies and incremental production increases."[428]

## DOING BETTER

As chair and CEO of Suncor, Rick George was competitive when it came to production systems and oil sands technology, but collaborative on environmental issues. As one of the founders of the Oil Sands Leadership Initiative, he said the industry should share "anything to do with safety, the environment, environmental improvement, anything on reducing our air, land and water footprints. This is important, very important."[429]

If George saw the environmental picture from the executive offices, Deborah Jaremko had the view as a working journalist. She became the editor of *Oilsands Review* at the magazine's inception, in June 2006. The publication carries the tagline "The heavy oil authority," although its focus has always been the oil sands. I asked for her thoughts on what is next.

Her main points were environmental. "As the world began to pay attention to the scale and potential of the oil sands industry, people also became more aware of the environmental challenges that developing this resource presents," she said. "The biggest challenge the oil sands sector has faced in recent years – expanding market access – is inextricably tied to its environmental performance, both in terms of misguided perceptions and real areas for improvement."

In a note, Jaremko quoted David Collyer – formerly the president of CAPP, and, ironically, the son of Chuck Collyer, whose name appears so many times in these pages. "The way the world sees us is defined by our performance. The linkages between stewardship and the reputation of the energy sector have never been more clear," he said. "This is not at all about communicating our way out of a problem. It never has been and it won't be in the future. We certainly need to focus on communications to improve awareness and understanding, but it is essential that this be underpinned by ongoing improvement. In a world that is always moving and changing, we can't stand still. We have to do better, and we will."

To a large degree because of the oil sands, North America has essentially been self-sufficient in energy for some years. At this writing, however, new pipelines were essential for increasing supply in Canada to gain greater access to international markets, and thereby to become a global energy superpower.

"For major projects, the gap is now closing between the regulatory process and shovels in the ground," Jaremko wrote, adding that "oil sands producers, mainly majors with lots of internal cash flow, have seen this turn in the road coming and have continued to push forward. That's why there is still so much capital going into the oil sands. And as the positive transportation infrastructure dynamic plays out, financial markets will have that clear view too." Like others with a professional background in the oil sands, she was positive about the outlook, but not blind. The petroleum industry was undergoing rapid change.

"The rise of tight oil production in the United States has caused Canada's main existing market for crude oil, the U.S. Midwest, to become saturated," she said, summing up the industry's major anxieties. "The corresponding drop in revenues has hit hard producers, their supply chains, and government royalty programs. Efforts to build large new export pipelines continue to face regulatory delays, stymied by public opposition largely due to the real and perceived environmental impacts of the oil sands industry." Yet she was optimistic about the outlook for pipelines despite what seemed to be endless delays in getting regulatory approval for such critical routes as Northern Gateway, Keystone and Energy East.[430]

## POLITICAL WILL

As US President Barack Obama looked toward the legacy he would leave to a politically fraught America, on November 6, 2015 his administration declined Canada's application for the Keystone XL pipeline – approval of which Canada's previous Prime Minister, Stephen Harper, famously called a "no-brainer."

Until ignominiously defeated in October 2015, Canada's Conservative government led a government that boosted economic growth at the expense of environmental change – toward the end of its last mandate, arrogating unto Cabinet decisions which in previous years had been the responsibility of the National Energy Board.

On the matter of reducing greenhouse gas (GHG) emissions, Harper repeated endlessly to Parliament that the Canadian government was "waiting for the Americans to catch up" before it would enact legislation in this area. "This government's position has been clear: that we want to see oil and gas regulations on a continental basis, given the integrated nature of this industry. With the current conditions in the oil and gas sector, this government will not consider unilateral regulation of that sector."

"Frankly, Mr. Speaker," he said on another occasion, "under the current circumstances of the oil and gas sector, it would be crazy, it would be crazy economic policy to do unilateral penalties on that sector. We're clearly not going to do that." Ironically, these comments came just as environment ministers from British Columbia, Manitoba, Ontario and Québec signed an international agreement to combat climate change in Lima, Peru.[431]

Harper's defeat in the 2015 election coincided with new political environments both in Alberta and nation-wide.

## NOTLEY IN EDMONTON

In Alberta, Rachel Notley — a rookie leader who spent a 28-day election campaign promising to deliver hope despite the economic downturn — was the New Democratic Party's not-so-secret weapon on the trail. Her victory on May 5th was a landslide, to the surprise of most of her party's candidates and possibly the leader herself. How long will the NDP now stay in power?

Barely six months after taking office, Notley's government announced an ambitious "climate change action plan" that will undoubtedly affect the oil industry in Alberta. It included tough regulations covering greenhouse gas emissions within the province — notably in respect to the oil sands. "This is the day we start to mobilize capital and resources to create green jobs, green energy, green infrastructure, and a strong, environmentally-responsible, sustainable and visionary Alberta energy industry with a great future," Notley said.[432]

While this announcement came as a surprise across the country, it was consistent with thinking within Alberta Innovates: Energy and Environment Solutions, a provincial think-tank, and the Carbon Capture and Emissions Management Corporation, which this document introduces elsewhere. On its website, the think-tank describes itself as the province's lead agency for advancing energy and environmental technology innovation.

Shortly after Notley's electoral win, Richard Dicerni — the head of Alberta's public service — received a report adamant that "existing and emerging technologies are capable of reducing the environmental footprint of oil sands, including GHG emissions." It said "strong leadership, investment in new ways of moving technologies from the lab into commercial application, removal of barriers and transformative technologies will be needed to extract the oil sands resource while also protecting the environment." It represents a fundamental change in policy.

"As a major exporter of energy products, Alberta needs to ensure that our products are GHG competitive and trending toward being the lowest in the world," it said. "Alberta can be and should aspire to be an international leader in meeting intensity-based targets. In a world moving into a low-carbon economy, to gain international credibility, Alberta needs also to address its absolute level of carbon emissions."

This brief argued that there were many ways to reduce GHG emissions from oil sands operations through improvements to energy efficiency. There could be "energy efficiency improvements of at least 20 per cent in *in-situ* thermal recovery by 2020." Looking farther out, co-generation technologies that "capture $CO_2$ offer the greatest opportunity to reduce GHGs," it said. "There are also millions of tonnes of $CO_2$ in highly concentrated form (ranging between 40 per cent and 90 per cent) in bitumen upgraders and petrochemical plants." This gas, it added, could be used for enhanced oil recovery. At present, carbon capture technologies "face significant cost barriers, [but] new technologies promise to reduce costs by about 50 per cent and are advancing to the pilot stage."[433]

This is the advice Notley received as she prepared her climate change announcement, and her action plan was a strong endorsement of the information Dicerni had received. "The oil sands sector accounts for roughly one-quarter of Alberta's annual emissions," her policy document said. "Large oil sands facilities pay a levy based on each individual facility's historical emissions, irrespective of how intense or efficient that operation has been." These are the funds allocated to the Carbon Capture and Emissions Management Corporation book. While oil sands operations emit some 70 megatonnes of $CO_2$ emissions per year, "there is currently no limit on oil sands emissions, either by facility or industry-wide." The new regulations were to set a 100-megatonne limit. All else being equal, this would allow for new projects to proceed, but it would tie the ultimate size of the sector to the development of GHG-reduction technology.

Details, however, were scant. Alberta would transition to an oil sands-based performance standard, it would increase the price of carbon on large emitters, and it would set a limit to GHG emissions from the oil sands. This would "create the conditions for the oil sands sector to innovate and become more globally competitive." The policy would drive technological progress, while giving industry the time to "develop and implement new technology that takes more carbon emissions out of every barrel." This would "bend Alberta's overall emissions trajectory downward."[434]

Four oil sands leaders – Murray Edwards, the billionaire oil investor and chairman of Canadian Natural Resources Ltd.; Steve Williams, president and CEO of Suncor Energy Inc.; Lorraine Mitchelmore, president of Shell Canada; Brian Ferguson, president and CEO of Cenovus Energy Inc. – shared the stage with Notley as she announced her climate change plan, thereby giving her plan a virtual endorsement. In addition to imposing a $3-billion a year economy-wide carbon tax, it would phase out coal-fired electricity generation in the province. However, leaders of competing companies – including Imperial Oil Ltd. chairman and CEO Rich Kruger and MEG Energy Corp. president and CEO Bill McCaffrey – apparently expressed outrage at the plan. They "worry the deal is unenforceable," wrote *The Financial Post*'s Claudio Cattaneo, "and that it is premature to support a policy whose details and financial implications remain unknown."[435]

## TRUDEAU IN OTTAWA

Voters threw out the government of Stephen Harper's Conservatives – nearly ten years in power – with equal abandon. Only Saskatchewan and Alberta remained faithful to the Conservative Party. The others gave at least a plurality of seats to the Liberal Party of Canada's Justin Trudeau, with Atlantic Canada electing only Liberal members. In part, this probably reflected the genealogy of the Liberal Party's leader, Justin Trudeau, who was the scion of Prime Minister Pierre Trudeau – still infamous in Alberta for the implementation in 1980 of the National Energy Program.

Born three years after his father began his first term as PM, the younger Trudeau lived his early years at 24 Sussex Drive – the Prime Minister's official residence in Ottawa. Justin Trudeau's Liberals ran on a political platform which was long on environmental policy.

An early indication of the Trudeau government's intentions came with the announcement of a moratorium on crude oil tanker traffic along BC's north coast. This could result in the cancellation of the Northern Gateway pipeline, which Alberta producers once hoped would give them tidewater access to overseas markets.

Six weeks after the new Trudeau government's swearing in, the oil sands industry got news which did not really come as a surprise. Speaking from the White House, US President Barack Obama gave a formal speech which was of great interest to Canada oil sands sector. "Several years ago, the State Department began a review process for the proposed construction of a pipeline that would carry Canadian crude oil through our heartland to ports in the Gulf of Mexico and out into the world market," he said. However, "the State Department has decided that the Keystone XL Pipeline would not serve the national interest of the United States. I agree with that decision." Within the United States, this decision was pure environmental politics. However, it also probably reflected a certain disdain within America for the attitudes of Canada's Harper Government, which was "waiting for the Americans to catch up" on the climate change file.

The news from Washington was not all bad, however. Obama had "had the opportunity to speak with Prime Minister Trudeau of Canada" on this matter. "And while [Trudeau] expressed his disappointment, given Canada's position on this issue, we both agreed that our close friendship on a whole range of issues, including energy and climate change, should provide the basis for even closer coordination between our countries," he said. "In the coming weeks, senior members of my team will be engaging with theirs in order to help deepen that cooperation."[436]

As part of his management system for the new government, Trudeau provided each of his new ministers with a "mandate letter," which defined the job and explained the government's expectations of the minister in question. When he appointed Jim Carr as Natural Resources Minister, his mandate letter made no direct reference to resource development. Rather, it said the minister's "overarching goal will be to ensure that our resource sector remains a source of jobs, prosperity and opportunity" – but qualified that injunction with reference to "a world that increasingly values sustainable practices and low carbon processes."[437]

Trudeau gave Carr seven priorities. One was to "protect Canada's energy security; encourage energy conservation; and bring cleaner, renewable energy onto a smarter electricity grid." The next three were to work with other

ministries to invest in clean technology producers, to tackle "pressing environmental challenges and create more opportunities for Canadian workers."

In addition, Carr was to work with other ministries to review Canada's
environmental assessment processes "to regain public trust and introduce new,
fair processes" that would provide "robust oversight and thorough environmental assessments of areas under federal jurisdiction, while also working with
provinces and territories to avoid duplication." This oversight would include
procedures to make sure decisions were based on evidence. This would involve
creating procedures by which experts, Indigenous groups, and other interested people could participate in the review and monitoring of major resource
development projects. Carr's mandate also included modernizing the National
Energy Board and, for good measure, providing assistance to other ministries
working in partnership with the United States and Mexico "to develop an ambitious North American clean energy and environmental agreement."[438]

Since Canada's constitution ascribes the regulation of resource development
to the provinces, the only way the federal government can affect the system is
by contributing to technological development, collaborating with provinces and
cities, and signing international treaties. Clearly, Carr's remit will cover those
areas, writ large.

In a sense, these political events represent the end of an era for the world's
oil industry. As this manuscript went to press, the petroleum industry – the oil
sands sector in particular –found itself facing new and challenging problems. In
terms of severity and duration, this period might turn out to be comparable to
the partially self-inflicted 20-year downturn that began with Canada's National
Energy Program.

## WILDFIRES

A few per cent of Canada's boreal forest, which stretches from Newfoundland
through the northern zones of Canada to Yukon and the northeastern tip of
British Columbia, burns every year. So statistically speaking, 100 per cent of
the boreal forest burns at least once every century. Put another way, wildfires in
areas around the oil sands are hardly new. As a headline in a May 1919 issue of

the *Edmonton Bulletin* proclaimed, "Lac La Biche Village in Ashes; Entire District Is Homeless; Condition of People Perilous."

"Swept away in the maelstrom of a raging forest fire which descended upon the place like a furnace blast on Monday afternoon," the newspaper wrote.

> The little village of Lac La Biche is today a mere smouldering mass of ruin and desolation, and its entire population is homeless and bereft of all personal effects, save scant articles of clothing which could be worn through the nerve-wracking struggle the people were forced to make to preserve their lives. The absence of a death toll in the catastrophe is due to the heroic measures taken by the citizens, who rushed into the waters of the lake and defied suffocating heat and smoke by means of wet blankets. Only such measures saved many of the women and little children, the intensity of the fire being shown by the burning of the very reeds along the shore and surface of the lake.[439]

It burned about two million hectares of forest, including homes, villages and farms. Like most fires in Canada's boreal forest, that one was the product of human activity. So, perhaps, was the one that roared toward Cenovus's Foster Creek project in May 2015.

The company immediately took the precaution of evacuating 1,800 employees from the site, according to company spokesman Reg Curren. "The big challenge was that it was threatening to cut off the road in and out of the facility," he said. "We couldn't take the chance of having people stranded, and provincial forest fire officials asked us to get ready for a potential evacuation." The company decided to evacuate. Most people left in the large buses already on-site to transport workers, while those with personal vehicles drove to safety.

"We thought we might be able to continue to operate, with reduced staff, so about 140 people stayed behind to continue operating the plant," he said. "When it became clear that we couldn't do that, we brought helicopters into play. Over a period of a few hours, we were able to get the last people off-site." The facility was down 11 full days, and "we returned to full operations on June 11." Operations quickly returned to normal.[440]

The company was lucky. So was Canadian Natural Resources, which needed to close down its Foster Creek and Kirby South operations at the same time. The reality, however, is that the both the number and the extent of the forest fires in Alberta's boreal forest are increasing. The risk of forest fire disruptions to oil sands operations is on the rise.

That is the view of Dr. Mike Flannigan, who is director of the University of Alberta's Western Partnership for Wildland Fire Science. Global warming and climate change are real, he said, and they affect the way the oil sands business operates.

Warming up to the topic of climate change, he said it was no coincidence that Earth's hottest ten years have all taken place in the 21st Century. Indeed, the meteorological winter from December 2014 through February 28th 2015 was the warmest Earth had seen since record keeping began, more than 135 years earlier. Another piece of evidence: Alberta's official fire season now starts March 1 – a full month earlier than only five or 10 years ago.

That year the province's fires were less destructive than in some years past, and they had a curiously positive impact on the bottom line of oil sands producers as a whole. By closing access to oil sands facilities, they reduced supplies to the booming downstream sector, accelerating increases in Western Canada Select oil prices after nearly a year of declines. These bottom-line impacts reduced production by more than 8 per cent of the province's total oil output. There were 917 fires, compared to the average over the previous five years of 690.

Designed with fire barriers to resist the dangers of this frequent occurrence, most oil sands projects find themselves surrounded by boreal forest. Careful planning notwithstanding, fire does disrupt operations. Events in 2015 demonstrated clearly that fire could lead to evacuations from field camps – sometimes by helicopter, when fire made rural roads impassable. Smoke could close airports, complicating helicopter rescue. In addition, people with respiratory ailments were especially susceptible to injury from smoke inhalation.

For rural communities in particular, big fires can lead to the destruction of property. In 2011, for example, a bush fire torched the Town of Slave Lake, with 40 per cent of its structures going up in smoke. During that time there was another "huge fire, 600,000 hectares—it was a huge fire" – near Fort

McMurray, several hundred kilometres away.[441] Insurance companies paid \$742 million to settle claims related to those fires[442] — small change compared to what was to come.

## THE FORT MCMURRAY FIRE

Five years later, at the beginning of May 2016, fires struck the beating heart of the oil sands, forcing evacuation of Fort McMurray itself. Wildfire destroyed entire neighbourhoods, took its toll on the energy industry and forced as much as a quarter of Canada's oil output offline. The province and the petroleum industry were already suffering from the lowest oil prices in more than a decade.

The city gave its name to the McMurray geological formation, the one which hosts most of the Athabasca oil sands deposits, and the fire put the city in deep trouble. It forced the evacuation of 90,000 people, including the citizens of Fort McMurray and the nearby communities of Anzac, Gregoire Lake Estates, and Fort McMurray First Nation. It burned neighbourhoods to the ground, consuming or damaging beyond repair 1,595 homes and buildings.

Although oil sands projects take countless precautions to avoid fire, whether in processing plants or from encroachment from the boreal forest, 14 plants around Fort McMurray went into closure or partial closure mode. This was partly in response to the labour shortage that arose in response from the fires, partly as a safety measure.

The wildfires continued to burn, however, and soon the province issued a mandatory evacuation order for work camps and facilities north of Fort McMurray and south of Fort McKay. Nineteen camps and some 8,000 workers came under this evacuation order. Then flames destroyed a 665-room work camp north of the city.

Although the 2016 wildfire in and around Fort McMurray covered an area approaching the size of Prince Edward Island, its spread was far smaller than that of the monster fire of 1919. The recent fire was far more important, however, because of the gathering expansion of Alberta's population and economic importance. The growth in the city's population, in particular, reflected the evolution of oil sands into Canada's foremost resource industry.

Two months after the fire hit, the Insurance Bureau of Canada released an estimate of the cost of the Fort McMurray wildfire, which it called "the costliest insured natural disaster in Canadian history." Catastrophe Indices and Quantification Inc., which provides detailed analytical and meteorological information on Canadian natural and man-made catastrophes, estimated the damage to insured property at $3.58 billion.

The company said there were more than 27,000 personal property claims, with an average $81,000 per claim. There were 12,000 auto insurance claims, at $15,000 each, on average. In addition, there were some 5,000 commercial claims at about $227,000 apiece. In addition to this insured damage, the company said, "The community, its residents and businesses have suffered incalculable losses not typically covered by insurers. [They continue] to work to help the community rebuild."[443]

# CHAPTER 13

# Maelstrom

———

*"Construction of the projects that we are working on won't even start until 2019. They won't be going on production until 2023, and then they'll produce for maybe 40 years. What you care about is the median price, maybe three decades forward."*

— BILL GWOZD, 2014

SINCE HER EARLIEST DAYS, CANADA has prospered from natural resources and geography. In his magisterial history of the fur trade, Harold Innis suggested that geography created the map of Canada, and also many of its institutions. The country did not become what she is despite her geographic structures, but because of them.

His work describes how the struggle for control of the fur trade influenced more than Canada's borders, of course. It also puts in context "aboriginal goals and strategies, mercantilist economic thought, European imperial struggles on a global scale, the changing economic fortunes of England and France, and Canadian entrepreneurship," as Arthur Ray summed matters up.[444]

Innis wrote that the trade in staple products like fish and fur, then timber and mineral resources, characterize "an economically weak country." One outcome — clearly apparent in the 1920- was that Canadian businesses consisted to a large degree of exporters focused on selling resources to Europe and the United States. Besides encouraging business to develop around the export market, these developments led to "various peculiar tendencies in Canadian development," he wrote. "The maintenance of connections with Europe, at first with France and later with Great Britain, has been a result. The diversity of institutions which attended this relationship has made for greater elasticity in organization and for greater tolerance among her peoples. This elasticity of institutions facilitated the development of the compromise which evolved into responsible government and the British Empire."

"The fur trade permitted the extension of the combination of authority and independence across the northern half of the continent," he continued. "Moreover, the business structure shifted from the elastic organization characteristic of the Northwest Company along the St. Lawrence from the Atlantic to the Pacific, to the more permanent organization from Hudson Bay. The diversity of institutions has made possible the combination of government ownership and private enterprise which is been a further characteristic of Canadian development."

Countless hats and fortunes came from the beaver pelt, which played a key role in the development of Canada's history and even her borders. "The importance of staple exports to Canadian economic development began with the fishing industry but more conspicuously on the continent with the fur trade," he wrote. Canada's borders were "a result of the dominance of furs. The exploitation of lumber in the more accessible areas followed the decline of furs."

The geographic unity of Canada which resulted from the fur trade became less noticeable with the introduction of capitalism and the railroads. Her economic development has been one of gradual adjustment of machine industry to the framework incidental to the fur trade. The sudden growth occasioned by the production of wheat and the development of subsequent staples in the Canadian Shield have been the result of machine industry."[445]

But, according to economics writer David Parkinson, the resulting "staples" economy was overly dependent on export markets. It led to "skewed economic decision-making, and impeded the development of a more robust, self-sustaining domestic economy. We have remained prone to booms and busts that periodically whipsaw our well-being and re-divide our nation between haves and have-nots."

Parkinson's commentary references a 1963 paper titled "A Staple Theory of Economic Growth,"[446] in which economist Melville Watkins termed this phenomenon Canada's "staples trap." The idea is that economic policies have often reflected support of one in-demand staple or another. This would leave the economy struggling when the staple fell out of favour in export markets.

In his study, Watkins argued that the staples trap within Canada had waned since Innis's day. "The staple theory can fruitfully be limited" to the case of a young country with a relatively small population, he wrote, and "an absence of inhibiting traditions." Many kinds of staple commodities – petroleum is a good contemporary example – can lead to industrial linkages. "A staple with potent linkage effects can create extraordinary economic success, whereas the wrong kind of staple – or a resource base not conducive to industrialization – can cause the economy to be caught in a 'staples trap' and to exhibit the characteristics, and face the difficulties, of the conventional overpopulated, tradition-ridden underdeveloped country."[447]

"Some modern economists would dismiss Watkins' staples theories as quaint historical artifacts in a Canadian economy that has grown more mature and complex over the past five decades," Parkinson said. But Canada's recent "love affair with oil – and its heartbreaking, economy-shaking end – raises some profound questions about our economic future."[448]

In a recent commentary on Watkins' work, labour economist Jim Stanford described his "long-time interest in more sustainable and sensible policies for managing Canada's resource wealth." Given the "lucrative but fleeting nature of resource booms," he said, policy-makers continually seek ways to "leverage Canada's resource wealth in a manner that stimulates a more diversified, inclusive, and sustainable economy." Strengthened free trade deals "including, in particular, the still-unprecedented energy-sharing provisions of [the North American Free Trade Agreement's] market-driven approaches" typically lead to a "skewed, polarized, fragile, and unsustainable resource-addicted economy."[449]

## CLOSE ENCOUNTERS

Bitumen is an industrial material, ownership of which belongs to the people of Alberta through its government. In that context, the story of Alberta's oil sands will be important as long as hydrocarbons provide fuel and petrochemical feedstock. Its presence has contributed greatly to the growth of scientific and technological leadership within the province and also, of course, to industrial growth. Also, it sometimes spills.

Although rare, spills can be a problem for the oil sands industry as well as for light oil producers. When they happen, however, bitumen spills are more problematic to clean up. The year 2010 was a watershed for industry people who specialize in oil spill prevention and recovery. BP oversaw management of the biggest blowout in history in the Gulf of Mexico. Well control and cleanup of its Deepwater Horizon catastrophe cost BP US$54 billion, plus US$18.7 billion to settle other claims.[450]

These events coincided with an Enbridge pipeline spill. Though a far smaller disaster, that spill became history's most expensive oil spill clean-up operation. The accidental release of diluted bitumen into a tributary of Michigan's Kalamazoo River from a two-metre rupture in an Enbridge pipeline took two years to clean up, at a cost of US$765 million. US authorities later imposed a US$61 million fine and other penalties on the company.[451]

Also in that year, the National Energy Board gave conditional approval for Enbridge to construct its Northern Gateway pipeline. As one of its conditions, though, the regulator instructed the company to establish a research program into the behaviour and cleanup (including recovery) of oils spilled in watery environments. This reflected the newsworthiness of the two big spills, which are now hot-button issues in both traditional and online media. Because Alberta hosts, produces and transports such large volumes of hydrocarbons, we have certainly not seen the last oil spill in the province.

Since oil became a serious business in the 19th century, petroleum busts have always followed petroleum booms, and vice versa. Indeed, in tough times people in the oil patch always trot out the old joke that "to make a small fortune in oil and gas, you have to begin with a large fortune." In recent years, many investors and producers have created smaller fortunes from larger ones. The process began in 2008, when natural gas prices collapsed. On the surface, this seemed to reflect an industry flush with shale gas produced through fracking. After all, West Texas Intermediate oil soon jumped over the jaw-dropping hundred-dollar-per barrel mark again.

Another take-away from this richness of discovery is that, at least from an air emissions perspective, the province's hydrocarbon wealth creates internal conflict within provincial conversations about global warming. These resources contribute enormously to the scientific, technical and industrial wealth of both the province and its people; and to Edmonton's ability to provide infrastructure and services.

They also release greenhouse gases during the production process – although most of those emissions are released at the other end of the pipeline, from the stacks of refineries and petrochemical plants and, farther downstream, from the tailpipes of vehicles and from furnaces for home heating. Increasingly, these emissions are a matter of global anxiety.


THE BUST

After hitting its US$145 per barrel peak in 2008, oil prices declined steeply, and by 2016 the drop sometimes felt like a freefall. This development reduced new development in the oil sands. It led to thousands of lay-offs in the petroleum industry and the petroleum service sector. It greatly reduced tax and royalty revenue for Canadian governments. To some degree consumers benefitted from cheaper fuels, but not enough to offset the damage done by these price declines. The crash in Alberta's economy was the worst since the bad old days of 1986. It created a geopolitical maelstrom that profoundly affected oil sands development.

In a presentation to the 2014 World Petroleum Congress, BP economist Christof Rühl explained why world oil prices had, in real terms, been extremely high for a number of years. The main reason was that there had been supply disruptions throughout the developing world but concentrated in North Africa and the Middle East. "Cumulative supply disruptions since the advent of the 'Arab Spring' from these countries have reached an extraordinary 3 million barrels per day," he said. "We are now in a better position to return to the question of why oil prices were so stable the last three years," despite "violent shifts" in production.

The main reason was the application of horizontal wells and underground fracturing to source rocks discussed in some detail in this book. The first

impact of those technologies was to bring on enough oil supply to offset supply disruptions elsewhere in the world stage. Reflecting on the near-perfect
balance between new supplies and supply disruptions, Rühl said "the match is
sheer coincidence. Higher prices may induce more shale production. But virtually nothing else of logic or substance connects the two developments. And so
markets will remain on edge – or eerily calm – until one side gains the upper
hand."[452]

Who had the upper hand soon became clear. So effective was fracking in the
United States in particular that, in December 2015, America lifted a 40-year-old
oil export ban; producers and shippers responded quickly. By the first quarter
of 2016, American exports totalled 416,000 barrels per day. The top customers
included Canada – exempted from the ban on exports in 1985 – and Curaçao,
where Venezuela's national oil company, Petróleos de Venezuela, has a refinery.
In the second quarter, total US exports rose to 547,000 barrels per day.[453]

So effective have tight oil technologies been that, for the first time in
more than 40 years, in 2014 the United States began to talk about exporting
oil again – something it hadn't done for 40 years. If that country were to do
so, where would it find a market? Every oil-producing region in the world is
seeking export markets.

In 2015 the world's super-majors – BP, Shell, Statoil, TOTAL, Chevron,
ExxonMobil and ConocoPhillips – cut their capital expenditures by 27 per cent
from 2013 levels. These dramatic reductions could mean that within a few years
world oil supplies would struggle to keep pace with consumption, thus driving
prices upward again. Did this mean the oil sands industry would soon regain the
momentum it enjoyed at the beginning of the 21st Century? Maybe not.

Writing in the *Harvard Business Review*, economists Bernhard Hartmann and
Saji Sam argued that "countries and companies should prepare for oil to hover
around $50 per barrel for the foreseeable future. Historically this wouldn't be
shocking at all." Using the 2014 US dollar as their baseline, they calculated that
the average price of oil for since oil production began to develop as an important industry has been $35 per barrel. "In fact," they said, the prices we now
consider "low are actually near the real average price of a barrel of oil for the
last 150 years."

"What is surprising," they continued, "is the fundamental shift we think is happening. The current low oil price environment is not an 'oil bust' that will be followed by an 'oil boom' in the near future. Instead, it looks as if we have entered a new normal of lower oil prices that will impact not just oil and gas producers but also every nation, company, and person depending on it."[454]

That said, at this writing, global investment has dropped by 45 per cent since 2014. This was a disaster for the capital-intensive business that relies on steady development to keep supply available. Whatever grade of oil is in question – light oil, heavy or bitumen – equilibrium cannot occur until the price of the commodity equals the cost of bringing the last barrel consumed out of the ground. Supply cannot respond as fast as demand, so the two sides do not react to prevailing price signals in real time. The result has been "the mother of all market share battles," according to ARC Energy's Peter Tertzakian. "Expect many years of ups and downs," he said: "steep price recoveries followed by destabilizing price wars that weaken prices."[455]

## THE BIG PICTURE...

At this writing, oil prices were in the tank even though demand was growing at the highest levels since the Great Recession of 2008-2009 – an event brought on by a sudden jump in the price of light oil to an eye-popping US$145 per barrel.

Growing demand was more than offset by growing supplies from outside OPEC. The world was awash with oil. Reluctantly, producers everywhere were hoarding record stockpiles. Petroleum reserves – by definition, the recoverable portion of resources available for use based on current knowledge technology and economics – had been on the rise for 20 years, world-wide.

Were the price declines transitory or longer term? According to David Russum, a geologist working for Deloitte, an accounting firm, "I think the petroleum industry is going through a period with few precedents in its history. It is reasonable to expect prices to bounce back on a global supply/demand basis at some point," he said. "However, my concern is that Canada could easily miss the boat. We don't have the ability to market our gas or oil to the global market, so even when prices do begin to recover we may not be able to benefit."[456]

An International Energy Agency (IEA) report said "stockpiles of oil at a record three billion barrels are providing world markets with a degree of comfort"[457] – unprecedented protection against geopolitical shocks and unexpected supply disruptions. This may have been comfortable for consumers, but for the petroleum producer those "comforting" inventories were disruptive.

How much should the sector worry? Global oil reserves had been increasing for more than 20 years, as demand growth slowed. Global reserves increased 52 per cent between 1994 and 2014, compared to 31 per cent increase in consumption.

Based on past performance, the conventional wisdom is that prices will rebound and prosperity will return to the sector, including the oil sands. Remember: after each bust comes a boom. Furthermore, according to that same wisdom, the rebound would lead to a boom which would again enable investors to make larger fortunes out of smaller ones. The crash of 2015-2016 was the worst in recent memory, however. Over a two-year period, Alberta's economy would decline by some 6.5 per cent, compared to a 5.5 per cent decline during the Great Recession of 2008-2009.[458]

## ... AND THE LONGER VIEW

How would this reality play out in Alberta? There were two bits of good news. One was the practice of pricing oil in US dollars, which meant producers got more per barrel (in Canadian dollars) than their American counterparts; the other was that operating costs in the oil sands dropped, as companies took severe measures to reduce staff and in other ways reduce expenditures.

The offsets were greater, however. Synthetic production – described as Western Canadian Select oil – fetched less on the market than West Texas Intermediate (WTI) and Brent oil, the global marker crudes. Also, the discounted Canadian dollar made imported goods and services (whether from Europe or the US) more expensive.

Times became really tough. In terms of raw statistics, some 72,000 oil industry workers lost their jobs. Also, there were secondary impacts that wouldn't be top of mind for most people. For example, the Calgary United

Way's Lucy Miller noted a 300 per cent increase in the use of Calgary's Women's Emergency Shelter and a 91 per cent increase in calls to the Calgary Counselling Centre, both of which her organization funds. Also, of course, there was greater demand at food banks across the province.

Another business shows how tough the downturn has been. In 1997, Steve Austin founded Energy Service Accounting in Calgary. The company provides accounting services for fifty or so of oil and gas companies – "the smallest of the small," he called them. His clients ranged from two-person start-up operations to somewhat bigger operations. The one characteristic they had in common is that they are too small to hire in-house accounting staff. "They are cutting everywhere they can," he said. "I have never seen conditions so bad."[459] The drop in oil prices created an environment in which projected revenue from new petroleum developments did not justify the investment.

"I have not found one person still working in the oil industry who is making the same money as previously" said geologist Russum. "Wage roll-backs and reduced hours of work are also having a severe negative impact on the economy."[460] Over the next five years, oil sands production would likely be 800,000 barrels per day higher, reaching 3.3 million barrels per day in 2020, with *in-situ* production responsible for most of the increase. Production from mining operations would also increase, the organization said. This would reflect another 220,000 barrels per day at Imperial's Kearl mine and the start up in 2017 of the Fort Hills project under development by Suncor Energy and partners. That project's initial production would total 160,000 barrels per day.

The industry cancelled other projects – for example, Shell's 80,000 barrels per day *in-situ* project at Carmon Creek – and deferred some expansions. In addition, companies revised their plans for capital spending in the oil sands. The good news was that some of this decrease reflected improved process and operational efficiencies. That said, 2015 investment in constructing and expanding major oil sands projects is likely to be $15 billion – 30 per cent lower than the previous year.

Others, however, took the longer view. "The current price is irrelevant," said Bill Gwozd, then a vice president with Calgary-based Ziff Energy. "What is really important is the price over the next several decades." Active in most of the world's petroleum basins, his firm helped exploration and production firms by forecasting energy prices to the year 2050. "Construction on the projects that we are working on won't even start until 2019," he said. "They won't be going on production until 2023, and then they'll produce for maybe 40 years. What you care about is the median price, maybe three decades forward."[461] Most of the seasoned hands in the industry agreed. Suncor showed that it did, through its actions.


## SUNCOR'S EXPANSION

Already the largest energy company in Canada, the energy giant used a combination of historically low interest rates and the oil price crash for rapid and fundamental expansion during the 2016 bust. The company began by making a takeover bid for Canadian Oil Sands, the only piece of the Syncrude giant to trade directly on the stock market.

Reflecting a rapid drop in oil and gas stocks, the company began by trying to buy COS shares on the open market. COS fought back, however. In the end Suncor CEO Steve Williams – he had been promoted from chief operating officer in 2011 when Rick George retired – signed an amalgamation agreement with COS. In February, a friendly $6.6-billion cash and stock deal gave Suncor control of the COS asset, with Suncor holding a majority of COS shares through a subsidiary. Two months later, Suncor bought Murphy Oil Corp's 5 per cent interest in the project for $937-million. This acquisition gave the company majority control of Syncrude, the largest single source of oil in Canada.

While consumption growth was tepid, reserves growth was strong. Notably, the US recorded the world's largest volumes of growth in production (1.6 million barrels per day), and was the first country in history to increase production by a million barrels per day for three years running.

One outcome of these developments is that, for the first time on record, the oil sands represented a smaller share of global reserves. During the ten years ending in 2014, they declined from 11 to nine per cent.

The price collapse shook the confidence of investors and management. In the new environment, commitment to an oil sands project with a 10-year lead time which would require a minimum $60 oil price to be profitable involved too much risk. Instead, the industry was more likely to expand existing projects where marginal costs were lower.

One reason is that local cost inflation can be volatile In Alberta, rising quickly in response to local conditions. Perhaps the effort needed to rebuild after fire devastated so much of the city of Fort McMurray would trigger such a response.

Prices for fossil fuels fell in 2015, around the world. In US dollar terms, oil prices recorded the largest decline on record and the largest percentage decline since 1986. Yet oil remained the world's leading fuel, accounting for about one-third of global energy consumption. Although emerging economies continued to dominate the growth in global energy consumption, growth in these countries, at 1.6 per cent, was well below its 10-year, 3.8 per cent average.[462]

## Fundamental change

Old-timers in the sector are well aware that energy is a boom-and-bust industry. The career of CAPP vice president Greg Stringham illustrates that reality. During his 30-year in the oil sector – first with the ERCB, and for 20 years with CAPP – the 55-year-old saw four royalty reviews, numerous pipeline battles and three industry downturns. "Nothing in this industry stays the same very long," he said.

After joining CAPP he quickly became a senior voice for the industry, and his work took him to high places. "Being in this job has been a wonderful experience. CAPP has had so many great leaders that I've been able to learn from. I've worked with government, I've worked with ambassadors, I've met with Congressmen, and I've met with all the Prime Ministers. Where else," he asked, "could you find a job providing that much opportunity?"

"CAPP is the epicentre of the industry," he said. "In this organization you are constantly shaking, rocking and rolling. You are in the midst of the most important things that are happening in the industry." Organized as an association of member companies, CAPP to a large degree is about policy development. "It is our member companies that come up with the ideas," he said. Staff members help them get things done. "We have a board of directors and ten executive policy groups, and literally hundreds of subcommittees. Once the directors tell us 'This is the way to go,' then we can really get things done."

In some ways, the industry when he left was no different from when he began. Hydrocarbon prices were in the tank, there was another royalty review in the offing, and the industry was struggling for new pipe to take more production to market. "When I started here, oil prices were just over $20 a barrel and natural gas was about a dollar a GJ," he said. "I've seen oil go all the way up to [WTI's all-time peak of US$145 per barrel in 2008] and now it sits at about $30. Gas was $14 during [the 2005] Katrina Hurricane; now it's about $2." On the pricing front, at least, the only constant is change.

Prices began to seriously drop in 2014, and the process sometimes felt like a freefall. This development reduced new development in the oil sands. It led to extensive lay-offs in both the petroleum industry and the service sector. And it greatly reduced tax and royalty revenue for Canadian governments. To some degree consumers have benefitted from cheaper fuels, but those benefits hardly offset the collateral damage caused by the crash.

According to CAPP, by year-end 2015 100,000 workers directly and indirectly tied to the oil-and-gas sector had lost their jobs, with the blue-collar workforce sustaining a disproportionate share of the pain. While this was the third bust Stringham experienced during his career, it was different from the others because Canada's petroleum industry had fundamentally changed, he said.

"Just about the time I got started [at CAPP], the oil sands kicked in," and that added a lot of stability to the provincial economy, since production operations in the oil sands are so much like manufacturing operations. "Even though we're suffering right now and it's a hard time for the industry, the momentum would be much different if we didn't have the oil sands as a stabilizing influence." Without them, "we would be in a much deeper trough right now."

## A REMOTE PROVINCE

When Stringham joined CAPP, the industry association was overwhelmingly Canada-focused, but as the oil sands developed that had to change, since the sector needed new markets. The industry needed to develop a North American focus, and it did.

"Increasingly," he said, "we are becoming an international player. We are aware of the impact of the globe, which is hitting us on all sides. The pace at which things are happening is speeding up – things are moving faster and faster. Not just from pricing, but from the perspective of demand, public perception of what's going on, the need for us to draw from our resources – whether it be labour or steel, for example."

Going back to his earliest years in the industry, Stringham cited the bust of 1986, when oil cratered at $10 a barrel – partly in response to high inflation and high interest rates. "People were abandoning their houses," he said. So inflated had prices become that owners would sell them for a dollar, leaving their mortgages unsecured and banks taking the hit.

While its severity was similar to the bust of 2016, that was fundamentally different from the bust of 2016. "Back then the industry was really focused in Alberta. There was a little activity in Saskatchewan and British Columbia, and some on the East Coast, but for the most part, people only felt the impact of low oil prices here in Alberta."

By contrast, the most recent crash echoed across Canada. "Premiers across the country are talking about how much it is affecting their economies, and jobs," he said. "People who came to Alberta to work, lost their jobs and have gone back East can't find employment there." That was fundamentally different from what happened during the crashes of '86 and '98 – two localized crashes. The change reflected the growing importance of energy within the Canadian economy. As the recent crash illustrated, Canada had become a nation in which every province benefited when the industry was healthy, and hurt when it was ailing.

"Technology is making it possible for us to provide that resource not only to Canadians, but also to the world," he said, arguing that Canada had become a world leader in petroleum production because of both its growing technological know-how and its top-of-class resources. "We have the third-largest petroleum resources in the world," he said. "Our technology and our ingenuity are the keys to our ability to sell our resources around the world." This seemed a bit far-fetched, since oil sands production doesn't yet have access to tidewater.

"It is astonishing how reluctant Canada was to turn from our comfort zone in North America to trading with other countries," he said. Increasingly, though, "we are realizing the importance of trading on the global stage. We have talked about our role in the global economy for a long time, but it only began to come to life in the last couple of years."

Over the previous five years, tight oil had changed that. During that period America increased its tight oil production by 4 million barrels per day. The US thus became Canada's "biggest competitor, in addition to being our biggest market," and bountiful tight oil began displacing demand for Canadian exports.

For that reason Canada began to recognize a need to begin shipping oil around the globe. Of course, the question was whether tidewater pipelines would ever become reality. "I'm very positive that export pipelines are going to be approved, and we're going to need many of them," Stringham said. He believed Canada would soon construct pipelines going both east and west, to extend its reach to global markets around the world. "Canada is one of the few countries in the world that really has the capacity to increase its production, and that's mostly because of the oil sands."

Environmental concerns are why approval has been slower than in the past, "but it is going to happen. Part of the reason is that Canadian environmental standards are world-class – I have travelled around the world, and I can confirm that – but it is government that has to make the decision whether we want to continue to be North American or whether we want to be a global player." The oil sands industry's future is global, he said, "but to get there the industry needs access to tidewater."[463]

Calgary-based economist Peter Findley, however, had a different perspective. Although oil sands production growth "has been impressive and robust since 1999," he said, "it seems that the more production barrels that come online from the massive heavy oil basin, the more headwinds arise that operators must overcome to deliver a return to increasingly impatient investors." Operators had little to show from their investments, he said, "even before the oil price rout."[464]

In this bust a "lacklustre" job market elsewhere in Canada (except B.C.) contributed to Alberta's pain, added economist Todd Hirsch. In effect, the work force voted with its feet, by going nowhere. "The nasty recessions of the 1980s saw tens of thousands of people pack up and leave Alberta, resulting in a drop in the size of the work force," he said. And "during the darkest days of 1987, the province saw more than 1.2 per cent of its workers leave or drop out of the labour market. This repeated itself during the recessions of 1992 and 2009-10."

One reason was that those earlier busts coincided with stronger economies elsewhere in Canada attracting the province's unemployed. Alberta's pain this time around got no such assistance — indeed, new international immigration made matters worse.[465] Unemployment reached 8.6 per cent, the highest since 1994. Gradually, though, things got better. After touching US$26 per barrel in February 2016, West Texas oil prices doubled within a year. At this writing, the worst of the bust seems behind us.

## By Clint Tippett

THE HISTORY YOU HAVE BEFORE
you has a complex geneal-
ogy. It is obviously based on
Peter McKenzie-Brown's long
involvement with the Canadian
oil and gas industry as an author,
journalist and historical ana-
lyst. These have been supple-
mented by the roles played by
the Calgary-based Petroleum
History Society (PHS), its
related oral history projects and
its other activities.

McKenzie-Brown played
important parts in this organization almost from the beginning.
The importance of oral history
in this setting was brought to the
fore by a well-known scribe of
the Canadian oil patch, Aubrey
Kerr. During the research for
his series of self-published books

Recently retired, Clint Tippett worked as
a geologist at Shell Canada for more than
30 years. At Shell, he made it his niche to
pursue the corporation's history in Canada.
His interest in this field comes naturally,
since his father worked for North Star Oil
in Winnipeg and, following North Star's
takeover by Shell in 1960, Clint became
part of the Shell family of companies. His
pursuits have included research for anniversary
celebrations of Shell's natural gas discoveries
in the Rocky Mountain Foothills at Jumping
Pound in 1944 and at Waterton in 1957.

and related journal articles, Kerr interviewed many of the key players in the industry, recording their observations on reel-to-reel tapes. To further this process, he worked with the nascent Petroleum History Society in the 1980s to establish a system for preserving these transcripts and recordings at the Glenbow Archives, where they are available for researchers of many kinds — those who want to know about relatives, for example, and those who want first-hand information about life in Alberta.

Kerr was instrumental in the related fundraising that was required to support his work, which became known as the Petroleum Industry Oral History Project. The execution of this initiative took place in several stages over the subsequent decades and involved multiple interviewers. The resulting transcripts and recordings have been bequeathed to the Glenbow Archives in Calgary.

In 2010, McKenzie-Brown and other writers, detailed in the text, realized that the petroleum industry in Canada had crossed a threshold with regards to the importance of the oil sands sector. Although some of the people related to the oil sands had been contacted in earlier phases of the oral history project, we agreed to make a concerted effort to preserve the historical underpinnings of this rapidly growing sector. The research team established under the aegis of PHS undertook a significant fundraising effort that was well-received by most of the major industry players, which contributed several hundred thousand dollars. With the support of that funding, the research team undertook 117 interviews, which they delivered to the Glenbow Archives. In some situations, the interviews were videotaped as well for future audiovisual projects. McKenzie-Brown was the major instigator of the Oil Sands Oral History Project (OSOHP), and he is to be congratulated on its success.

This volume is based on a combination of previous research, material gathered through OSOHP, and McKenzie-Brown's experience. The story is complex, but several major themes emerge when we stand back and consider the big picture.

First is the primary importance of economics, the recognition of monetary risks and the ways in which those risks can be mitigated. Many early initiatives had some limited technical success but were simply not robust enough to navigate through the shoals of low price, oil oversupply, industry politics, costly logistics and difficult access to capital markets. The sector only started to move forward in earnest once somewhat higher prices, market availability, infrastructure, equipment reliability and the emergence of a corporate willingness to take a chance on this massive resource were in place.

Second were the multiple roles of technology. In surface mining, that involved the machinery used in the mining operations, techniques for the basic separation of bitumen from sand and the minimization and ultimate disposition of tailings. For subsurface operations it was the identification of the optimum approaches for the injection of steam and the recovery of the bitumen. For upgrading and refining it was the invention of the processes that could most efficiently transform the heavy hydrocarbons in the bitumen into the lighter products more sought after in global markets. All of these aspects were tackled with a combination of theoretical work and field experimentation. All involve components of environmental stewardship. Some companies stand out in technology advancement – for example, Imperial Oil and its related companies. Others have honoured the philosophy that it is best to simply copy what you know is working and have found their success in that way. In either case, technology is essential.

The third theme is people and the difference that they can make. There are several individuals in this oil sands story that can be characterized, for at least part of their careers, as being arrogant and hard to work with – in other words some people who worked alongside them saw them as a pain in the ass. However for people who passionately believed in what they are doing and were pursuing a dream of transforming an otherwise useless resource into a viable economic venture, that abrasive reputation was probably a small price to pay. One has to ask where the oil sands would be today if not for the work and commitments of Ells, Clark, Pew, McClements and Spragins. Perhaps also often downplayed is the visionary roles played by some politicians like Ernest Manning who made the choice to not do the easy thing, like ignoring the oil sands in a time of oil surplus, but to see farther into the future when these vast accumulations might provide a massive bounty for Alberta and Canada. Surely these are lessons for everyone in similar roles today.

Unfortunately there are still major hurdles ahead if we are to truly fulfil the promise of the oil sands. Extracting the bitumen and upgrading it are intensive both in terms of energy use and of greenhouse gas generation. Transportation and market access continue to be challenges. It remains to be seen whether the Canadian oil sands sector will be nimble enough to avoid becoming roadkill, or at least become significantly restricted, in either a fundamental economic sense or through the global controversy concerning greenhouse gases and global warming.

The Petroleum History Society is a volunteer organization that has, for the last quarter century, been involved in the preservation, analysis and communication of the history of the petroleum industry in Canada. We publish a monthly newsletter titled *Archives*. We also sponsor a range of activities and programs including luncheons with a guest speaker at the Calgary Petroleum Club, field trips and historical walking tours. You are welcome to join us.

ACKNOWLEDGEMENTS

———

THIS HISTORY DEVELOPED FROM MY personal interest in the oil sands – one that goes back four decades. More importantly, it echoes the work of many experts in the field.

Driven by enthusiasm and dedication, uncountable men and women from science, business and government turned the oil sands into a resource giant. Many of those people shared with me their time and knowledge, as I pieced together the fragments of this long and complex story. They included both individuals and organizations. The Alberta Historical Resources Foundation provided funding for my early research, much of which involved a study of the best-known oil sands histories. The foundation also helped fund an oral history project managed by the Calgary-based Petroleum History Society under Clint Tippett's, presidency. The society has more than three decades' experience in making oral history available to researchers.

Oral history is a rich resource for historians, who need to tap the memories of others in order to breathe life into their writings. Industry leaders R.W. (Bob) Taylor and Eric Newell championed the project to potential funders within the industry. Athabasca Oil Sands Corp., Canadian Natural Resources Limited, Canadian Oil Sands Limited, Connacher Oil and Gas Limited, Imperial Oil Limited, MEG Energy Corp., Nexen Inc., Suncor Energy and Syncrude Canada contributed to the project financially, without placing any constraints on the project itself.

My colleagues in the oral history research project were Robert Bott, Brian Brennan, Adriana Davies and Gordon Jaremko. Collectively, our efforts created transcripts of the memories of 116 individuals, each of whom played a role in shaping the oil sands sector. By preserving their stories, our efforts contributed to a deeper understanding of how the industry developed and how it functions.

Other historians, researchers and educators have access to project records. Stored at Calgary's Glenbow Museum archives, the files include original recordings (both audio and video) and digitized transcriptions. I would be remiss not to mention Judith Wrigglesworth-Stevens, an inimitable transcriber; and the ever-helpful Doug Cass, director of the Glenbow's Library and Archives.

Especially when using material from oral history interviews, for stylistic reasons I frequently edited and condensed the text, although I took care not to change its meaning.

A number of people reviewed and commented on all or portions of this manuscript. One was Earle Gray – a legend in the petroleum industry because of his many excellent histories, but also because of his long career as editor of the industry magazine *Oilweek*. Early encouragement also came from freelance editor Peter Enman. Robert McClements, Jr., who chaired Sun Oil when it was an industry giant employing 70,000, patiently answered my questions. Bert McKay, who worked for GCOS when it started up, shared material from that era I would have been hard-pressed to find elsewhere. Another was geologist Clint Tippett.

In many discussions, personal friends with depth of thought and experience about the oil industry often challenged my views, making me dig deeper. They included Robert Bott, Anil Jain, Bob James, Dave Russum, and Chris Saunders. Juliette Champagne provided a number of French-language documents which helped round out the story. My wife Bernie was unfailingly supportive as I went through the countless ups and downs of preparing and editing the manuscript.

To these people and organizations, I offer my thanks. For the errors in fact and interpretation that probably exist, I extend my regrets.

# ABOUT THE AUTHOR

---

A Calgary-based author, editor and writer, Peter McKenzie-Brown has worked for several corporate clients and for industry and business publications. He has written many articles for energy-related magazines and was coordinator and an interviewer for the Petroleum History Society's *Oil Sands Oral History Project*.

British by birth, he is American by upbringing and Canadian by choice. He began his writing career with the Reuters news agency in London, UK, in 1971. In Calgary he has worked for Gulf Oil Canada, the Canadian Association of Petroleum Producers, and Amoco Canada.

His other books include *Footprints: The Evolution of Land Conservation and Reclamation in Alberta* (2016, with Robert Bott and Graham Chandler); *Barbecues, Booms and Blogs: Fifty Years of Public Relations in Calgary* (2008; co-editor and contributor); *In Balance: An Account of Alberta's CA Profession* (2000, with Stacy Phillips); *The Richness of Discovery: Amoco's First Fifty Years in Canada* (1998); and *The Great Oil Age: The Petroleum Industry in Canada* (1993, with Gordon Jaremko and David Finch.) In 2006, he contributed a five-part series on the history of Canada's petroleum industry to *Wikipedia*.

Prior to serving as a coordinator and interviewer for the Petroleum History Society's *Oil Sands Oral History Project*, he was a recipient of that society's Lifetime Achievement award. In 2011 he was one of several recipients of the society's Article of the Year award for a series on the oil sands, published in the *Oilsands Review*.

He has completed the Ironman Triathlon eleven times — twice in Hawaii, the other times in Penticton, B.C.

SOURCES

PUBLICATIONS

Adelman, Morris Albert. The genie out of the bottle: world oil since 1970. MIT Press, 1995.

Alberta Oil Sands Technology and Research Authority. AOSTRA: A 15 year portfolio of achievement. Edmonton, 1990.

Alberta Technical Committee. "Report to the Minister of Mines and Minerals and the Oil and Gas Conservation Board with respect to an experiment proposed by Richfield Oil Corporation involving an underground nuclear explosion beneath the McMurray oil sands with the objective of determining the feasibility of recovering the oil with the aid of the heat released from such an explosion." August, 1959.

Anonymous. "J. Howard Pew proved his point with personal test." Sun News, Sun Oil Company; June 13, 1981.

Anonymous. "Company claims new process of extracting oil." Winnipeg Tribune, October 23, 1940.

Anonymous. "MEG reports low SOR in SAGD pilot." Oil and Gas Journal, April 24, 2013.

Anonymous. "Nodding donkeys: Oil companies and climate change; some oil majors are still ducking the issue of global warming"; The Economist, November 14, 2015.

Anonymous. "Oilsands outlook" – an interview with Glen Schmidt, Neil Camarta and Bob Dunbar; in Our evolving industry: celebrating the diamond anniversary of the Daily Oil Bulletin; 2013.

Anonymous. "POLAR SOVEREIGNTY Claims Utilization of New Lands Likely to Govern Nationality," The New York Times, April 2, 1926.

Anonymous. "Sept. 15, 1978: Syncrude opens $2.2-billion oil sands plant," Edmonton Journal, Saturday, September 15, 2012.

Anonymous. "Social impact on the Crees of James Bay project," Grand Council of the Crees website, http://www.gcc.ca/archive/article.php?id=38; accessed 30 May, 2014.

Anonymous. "The Alberta Salt Company Ltd." At Oil Sands Research and Information Network, http://www.osrin.ualberta.ca/en/Resources/ DidYouKnow/2010/September/TheAlbertaSaltCompanyLtd.aspx; accessed November 28, 2013.

Anonymous. "The men at the helm," Our Sun: Special GCOS issue: The dawn of a new age of energy; Sun Oil Company; autumn, 1967.

Anonymous. "The next shock? The price of oil has fallen by half in the past two years, to just over $10 a barrel. It may fall further—and the effects will not be as good as you might hope," The Economist, March 4th, 1999.

Anonymous. Agreement between Great Canadian Oil Sands Limited and Great Canadian Oil Sands Employees Bargaining Association; October 17, 1967.

Anonymous. Information on the Athabasca Tar Sands and the Great Canadian Oil Sands Limited Project; written by Public Relations Department, Sun Oil Company; September 1967.

Anonymous. Statistical review of world energy, "End-use oil product prices and average crude oil import costs"; International Energy Agency. file downloaded as a spreadsheet March 30, 2014.

Anonymous. Syncrude: One billion [barrels for Canada]. Fort McMurray: Fort McMurray Today, 1998.

Anonymous. The Daily Oil Bulletin, October 29, 1980.

Appenzeller, Tim. "The end of cheap oil," National Geographic, vol. 2, 05. No. 6, June 2004, 98-99

Armstrong, Jim. "First oil sands plant a true pioneer," Energy Processing Canada; October 1975

Armstrong, Warren; Atlantic Bridge, from Sail to Steam to Wings: A Diverse Record of 100 Years of North Atlantic Travel; Muller, 1956

Babad, Michael. "Alberta hit by one of worst recessions ever, recovery to lack 'punch': TD," The Globe and Mail, July 18, 2016.

Back, Captain George "Account of the Route to be pursued by the Arctic Land Expedition in Search of Captain Ross"; Royal Geographical Society, The journal of the Royal Geographical Society of London, Volume 3, 1833

Ball, Max. This Fascinating Oil Business; Bobbs-Merrill Company, 1940.

Barnett, Douglas E. From Fur King to Oil King: A history of the Athabasca oil sands, Edmonton: D. Barnett, 2006.

Barrie, Doreen, "Ralph Klein 1992" in Rennie, Bradford James, ed. Alberta Premiers of the Twentieth Century. Vol. 10. University of Regina Press, 2004. ISBN 0920897835.

BBC, "BP and Amoco in oil mega-merger," Tuesday, August 11, 1998; http://news.bbc.co.uk/1/hi/business/149351.stm; accessed May 16, 2014.

Bell, Edward. "Ernest Manning: 1943 – 1968" in Rennie, Bradford James, ed. Alberta Premiers of the Twentieth Century. Vol. 10. University of Regina Press, 2004. ISBN 0920897835.

Blair, Sidney M. The Development of the Alberta Bituminous Sands. Government of Alberta, Edmonton, 1951.

Blair, Sidney Martin Fonds Finding Aid; Anonymous, "Biography of Sidney Martin Blair" http://archives.library.ualberta.ca/FindingAids/SMBlair/85-53.html; accessed 27 November, 2013.

Bliss, Michael. Northern Enterprise: Five centuries of Canadian business. McClelland and Stewart, 1987.

Boorstin, Daniel J. The Seekers: The story of man's continuing quest to understand his world; Random House, New York, 1998.

Bosworth, T.O., "The Mackenzie River between Old Fort Good Hope and Fort Norman; the Tar Springs District on the Great Slave Lake; and in the Tar Sand District on the Athabasca River", unpublished document, 1914; available at the Glenbow Archives, Calgary, reference number M-8656, 69 pages.

Bott, Robert. "Tar sands plan global in scope," The Montreal Gazette, Feb 16, 1974.

Bott, Robert, David M. Carson, Jan W. Henderson, and Shaundra Carvey. Our Petroleum Challenge: Sustainability into the 21st Century. Canadian Centre for Energy Information, 2004.

Bott, Robert, Graham Chandler, and Peter McKenzie-Brown. Footprints: The Evolution of Land Conservation and Reclamation in Alberta. Kingsley Knowledge Publishing, 2016.

Bowman, Clement. "Energy superpower?" The Globe and Mail, Published Monday, May. 26 2008; last updated, Thursday, September 30, 2010.

_____. "Six Visionaries," http://www.Clementbowman.info/Visionaries.html (audio).

Boychuk, Rick. River of Grit: Six months on the line at Suncor. Edmonton, Duval House Pub., 1996.

BP. "Statistical review of world energy," 64th edition; June 2015. https://www.bp.com/content/dam/bp/pdf/energy-economics/statistical-review-2015/bp-statistical-review-of-world-energy-2015-full-report.pdf.

BP. "Statistical Review of World Energy," 65th edition; June 2016. https://www.bp.com/content/dam/bp/pdf/energy-economics/statistical-review-2016/bp-statistical-review-of-world-energy-2016-full-report.pdf.

Breen, David H. Alberta's Petroleum Industry and the Conservation Board. Edmonton, University of Alberta Press, 1993.

Bregha, François. "Energy Policy." The Canadian Encyclopedia, McLelland and Stewart, Toronto, 1999.

Brennan, Brian. "Project Oilsand: Alberta's Brush with the H-bomb;" Oilsands Review, June, 2012.

_____. "Oilsands Apostle: Frank Spragins, Syncrude and North American Energy Survival." In Oilsands Review, December 2012.

_____. The Good Steward: The Ernest C. Manning Story. Fifth House, 2008.

_____. Alberta Originals: Stories of Albertans who made a difference. Fifth House, 2001.

Browne, Sir John. Beyond business: an inspirational memoire from a visionary leader. Wiedenfeld & Nicolson, UK, 2010.

Brunner, Paul, editor. Lougheed and the war with Ottawa. Volume 11 of a 12-volume series, Alberta in the 20th Century; 2003; ISBN 0-9730760-1-1.

Butler, Roger. Practical applications for horizontal wells in petroleum production, text book for non-credit short course. University of Calgary, Department of Chemical and Petroleum Engineering, Department of Continuing Education, 1993.

Canadian Energy Research Institute (CERI), Green bitumen: the role of nuclear, gasification and CCS in Alberta's oil sands. 2009

Careless, J.M.S. Canada: a story of challenge. Toronto: MacMillan of Canada, 1963

Carlyle, Thomas. Critical and miscellaneous essays. Philadelphia, A. Hart, late Carey & Hart, 1852, 57. Accessed online.

Carrigy, M. A. Bibliography of the Athabasca oil sands. Alberta, Alberta Research Council. Preliminary report 62-7 (Alberta Geological Survey REP) 1962.

Cattaneo Claudia. "Secret deal on Alberta's oilsands emissions limits divides patch." Financial Post, December 1, 2015.

CCEMC and Alberta Innovates. "Briefing note for Richard Dicerni: Technological innovation and climate change." June 8, 2015.

Champagne, Juliette. Langue du pays et langue du travail: Le français dans le Nord-Ouest du XIXe siècle; Colloque sur les droits linguistiques dans l'Ouest. Presentation to l'Association des juristes d'expression française de la Saskatchewan, 19 and 20th of February, 2010, Regina, Saskatchewan.

_____. "Mission Notre-Dame-Des-Victoires, Lac-la-Biche, 1853-1963: Entrepôt et Couvent pensionnat."

_____. Souvenirs d'un missionnaire breton dans le Nord-Ouest canadien, Septentrion, Sillery, 1997.

Chastko, Paul. Developing Alberta's oil sands: from Karl Clark to Kyoto. Calgary: University of Calgary Press, 2004.

Chrétien, The Honourable Jean. "The challenge of Canadian federalism in the 1980s," address to the Empire Club of Canada. http://speeches.empire-club.org/61471/.

Clark, James A. "The energy revolution," in History of Petroleum Engineering; Boyd Printing Co., Dallas; 1961.

Clark K. A. and S. M. Blair, The bituminous sands of Alberta. Scientific and Industrial Research Council of Alberta, Report No. 18, Edmonton, Alberta: W. D. McLean, Acting King's Printer, 1927.

Collyer, C.R. (Chuck). "The beginnings of the oil sands of Alberta," November 10, 2004. Unpublished presentation to a gathering of Syncrude Canada employees.

Comfort, Darlene J. The Abasand fiasco: The rise and fall of a brave pioneer oil sands extraction plant, Friesen Printers: Edmonton, 1980.

Dabbs, Frank. "The brains behind the oil-sands breakthrough," in Lougheed & the War with Ottawa, edited by Don Baron; United Western Communications, Edmonton, 2003.

Davenport, Coral; New York Times, "Large companies prepared to pay price on carbon," December 5, 2013.

Das, Satya Brata. Green oil: Clean energy for the 21st century? Sextant, 2009.

Davies, Adriana A. "Saving money with monster trucks: retired Syncrude COO Jim Carter and an oilsands mining technology revolution" Oilsands Review, January, 2012.

_____. "Gone crazy over sand" Oilsands Review, July, 2013

_____. "Jacob Masliyah on the evolution and future of oilsands R & D" Oilsands Review, May, 2012.

_____. "Mary Clark Sheppard on her father – Karl Clark – and the quint-essential oilsands research breakthrough" Oilsands Review, September, 2011.

_____. "Overcoming the early geotechnical challenges of the oilsands" Oilsands Review, April, 2013

Dawson, George. "The progress and trend of scientific investigation in Canada," Proceedings & Transaction of the Royal Society of Canada 12 (1894), LII-LIII; report reprinted in No Ordinary Man: George Mercer Dawson 1849-1901 Lois Winslow-Spragge (Author), Bradley Lockner (Editor); 1993.

_____. Beneath my feet: The memoirs of George Mercer Dawson, McClelland and Stewart; copyright 2007 by Phil Jenkins.

De Mille, George. Oil in Canada west: The early years, Calgary: Northwest Printing and Lithographing Ltd., 1970.

Deane, Phyllis. The first industrial revolution, Cambridge University Press, 1965.

Department of Energy. The National Energy Programme, Ottawa: Queen's Printer, 1980.

Doern, G. Bruce and Jeffrey S. Kinder. "The CANMET energy technology centre – Devon and Alberta's oil sands" in Strategic science in the public interest: Canada's government laboratories and science-based agencies. Toronto: University of Toronto Press, 2006.

Doern, G. Bruce, and Glen B. Toner. The politics of energy: the development and implementation of the NEP. Methuen, 1985.

Economides, Michael and Ronald Oligney. The color of oil: The history, the money and the politics of the world's biggest business. Katy, Texas: Round Oak Publishing Company, 2000).

Ells, Sidney Clarke. Recollections of the development of Athabasca oil sands. Vol. 139. Department of Mines and Technical Surveys, Ottawa, Mines Branch, 1962.

_____. Bituminous sands of northern Alberta: Occurrence and economic possibilities; Ottawa, 1926.

_____. Preliminary report on the bituminous sands of northern Alberta, Mines Branch Report 281. Ottawa: Department of Mines, 1914.

Enbridge. "Enbridge Energy Partners L.P. settles with the U.S. Department of Justice and U.S. Environmental Protection Agency on Marshall and

Romeoville incidents," http://www.enbridge.com/media-center/news/details?id=2072418&lang=en&year=2016; accessed July 21, 2016.

Energy Information Agency, http://www.eia.gov/todayinenergy/detail.cfm?id=27532

Executive Council, Government of Alberta Conservation and Utilization Committee. "Athabasca tar sands development strategy." Edmonton, Alberta, August, 1972.

Ferguson, Barry G. Athabasca oil sands: northern resource exploration, 1875-1951. Edmonton, 1985.

Ferris, Timothy. The science of liberty: democracy, reason and the laws of nature. HarperCollins; 2010.

Findley, J. Peter. "The future of the Canadian oil sands: growth potential of a unique resource amidst regulation, egress, cost, and price uncertainty." Oxford Institute for Energy Studies. ISBN 978-1-78467-051-1, 2016. http://www.oxfordenergy.org/wpcms/wp-content/uploads/2016/02/The-Future-of-the-Canadian-Oil-Sands-WPM-64.pdf; accessed February 10, 2016.

Fitzgerald, J. Joseph. Black gold with grit: the Alberta oil sands, Gray's Publishing Ltd., Sidney, British Columbia, 1978.

Fitzsimmons, Robert. "The truth about Alberta oil sands," privately published in Edmonton, 1953.

Forrest, Jackie. "Oil sands, greenhouse gases and US oil supply: getting the numbers right—2012," Cambridge Energy Research Associates; http://www.api.org/~/media/files/%20oil-and-natural-gas/oil_sands/cera_oil_sands_ghgs_us_oil_supply.pdf.

Franklin, Lady Jane, and Erika Behrisch Elce. As affecting the fate of my absent husband: selected letters of Lady Franklin concerning the search for the lost Franklin expedition, 1848-1860. Vol. 56. McGill-Queen's Press-MQUP, 2009.

Freeman, James Morton. Biggest sellout in history: foreign ownership of Alberta's oil and gas industry and the oil sands. Edmonton, 1966.

Fumoleau, René. As long as this land shall last: a history of Treaty 8 and Treaty 11, 1870-1939. University of Calgary Press, 2004.

Geological Survey of Canada; Report of Progress, Annual Report – 1875-76; published by authority of Parliament, 1877.

Giddens, Paul Henry. Standard Oil Company (Indiana): oil pioneer of the Middle West. Appleton-Century-Crofts, 1955.

Gilbert, E.E. (Ned). Letter to George Dunlap; 21 September, 1951.

Gough, Barry M. First across the continent: Sir Alexander Mackenzie. Vol. 14. University of Oklahoma Press, 1997.

Gould, Ed. Oil: the history of Canada's oil and gas industry; Hancock House Publishing, 1976.

Government of Alberta. "Climate leadership plan: capping oil sands emissions," http://alberta.ca/climate/oilsands-emissions.cfm; accessed December 17, 2015.

Government of Alberta. "Soil conservation act," Revised Statutes of Alberta 2000, Chapter S-15, Current as of November 1, 2010 http://www1.agric.gov.ab.ca/$Department/deptdocs.nsf/all/rsv13634/$FILE/2013_Module_5_January_2013.pdf.

Government of Alberta. Alberta energy, http://www.energy.alberta.ca/oil-sands/791.asp.

Government of Alberta. Proceedings: Athabasca oil sands conference, 1951.

Government of Canada. Office of the Prime Minister; "Minister of Natural Resources mandate letter" http://pm.gc.ca/eng/minister-natural-resources-mandate-letter; accessed December 18, 2015.

Grant, Jennifer; Simon Dyer; Dan Woynillowicz, Fact or fiction? Oil sands reclamation. The Pembina Institute; May 2008; introduction.

Grant, Shelagh D. Sovereignty or security? Government policy in the Canadian north, 1936-1950. University of British Columbia Press, 1998.

Gray, Earle. About Canada: my God, this is a great country, Toronto: Civil Sector Press, 2012 ISBN: 9781895589955,

Gray, Earle. "Gesner, Williams and the birth of the oil industry," Oil-Industry History, volume 9, 2008. Petroleum History Institute, Oil City, Pennsylvania.

Gray, Earle. The great Canadian oil patch: The petroleum era from birth to peak, second edition, (2004).

Gray, James Henry. The winter years: The depression on the prairies, Macmillan of Canada, 1973.

Great Plains Research Consultants. The Athabasca oil sands, 1951-1983; prepared for Historic Sites Service, Alberta Culture; 1 March, 1984.

Grun, Bernard. The timetables of history. Based on Werner Stein's Kulturfarplan Simon and Schuster, third edition, 1991

Gulley, John R. Vivienne R Wilson, and Ian B Mackenzie, "Oil sands reclamation," in Masliyah, J., J. Czarnecki, and Z. Xu. Handbook on theory and practice of bitumen recovery from Athabasca oil sands. (2010), vol. 2.

Hall, Capt. Charles Francis. Life with the esquimaux: a narrative of Arctic experience in search of survivors of Sir John Franklin's expedition, 1864; republished in 1970 by M.G. Hurtig, Edmonton. George Swinton, "Introduction to the New Edition."

Hamilton, J. B. "Evidence on the tar sands for the public defenders' court." Unpaginated privately published booklet. Edmonton, 1942(?).

Hatter, David. "Alberta's tar sands in the energy perspective," Canadian Geographic, April/May 1981.

Hendry, Anthony. The journal of Anthony Hendry, 1754-55: York Factory to the Blackfeet country; edited by Lawrence J. Burpee; Canadiana House, 1973.

Hester, Annette, and Leah Lawrence. "A sub-national public-private strategic alliance for innovation and export development: the case of the Canadian province of Alberta's oil sands." CEPAL (2010).

Hirsch, Todd. "Alberta's economy is dipping, but its labour force is staying put." The Globe and Mail, Thursday, August 11, 2016.

Hopwood, Kate. "Dinosaur skull (Albertosaurus) discovered in Alberta," The Globe and Mail, August 12, 2016.

Hopwood, Victor G., ed. David Thompson: travels in western North America, 1784-1812. Macmillan of Canada, 1971.

Houston, C. Stuart "John Richardson (1787-1865)"; 1983 pubs.aina.ucalgary.ca/arctic/Arctic36-4-376.pdf

Houston, C. Stuart, editor, Arctic ordeal: the journal of John Richardson, surgeon-naturalist with Franklin, 1820-1822, 1984.

Hunt, Constance D. "Environmental regulation: its impact on major oil and gas projects: oil sands and Arctic," Calgary: Canadian Institute of Resources Law, 1980.

Hunt, Joyce e. Local push, global pull: the untold history of the Athabaska oil sands 1900-1930: PushPull Ltd., 2011.

Huntington, Samuel P. The clash of civilizations and the remaking of world order, New York: Touchstone, 1997.

Innis, Harold Adams. Peter Pond: fur trader and adventurer. Toronto: Irwin & Gordon, 1930.

_____. The fur trade in Canada: an introduction to Canadian economic history. New Haven, Yale University Press, 1930.

Insurance Bureau of Canada. "Northern Alberta wildfire costliest insured natural disaster in Canadian history – estimate of insured losses: $3.58 billion," http://www.ibc.ca/on/resources/media-centre/media-releases/northern-alberta-wildfire-costliest-insured-natural-disaster-in-canadian-history.

Isaacson, Walter. Einstein: his life and universe. Simon and Schuster, 2007.

James, William. The will to believe and other essays in popular philosophy. Longmans, Green, and Company, 1912.

Janigan, Mary. Let the eastern bastards freeze in the dark: The west versus the rest since Confederation. Random House LLC, 2012.

Jaremko, Gordon. Steward: 75 years of Alberta energy regulation; 2013; isbn 978-0-9918734-2-5 (bound).

Jevons, William Stanley. The coal question: an inquiry concerning the progress of the nation, and the probable exhaustion of our coal-mines. Macmillan, 1906. http://oilcrash.net/media/pdf/The_Coal_Question.pdf

Klein, Naomi. This changes everything: capitalism vs. the climate. Simon and Schuster, 2014.

Knight, James. The founding of Churchill: being the journal of Captain James Knight, Governor-in-chief in Hudson Bay, from the 14th of July to the 13th of September, 1717. Edited by James Francis Kenney. JM Dent and sons Limited, 1932.

Kutney, Gerald; Sulfur: history, technology, applications & industry ISBN 978-1-895198-37-9; 2007.

Lalonde, Marc, "Introduction," The National Energy Programme, Department of Energy, Ottawa: Queen's Printer, 1980.

Lambton, John George, Earl of Durham; The report on the affairs of British North America; http://eco.canadiana.ca/view/oocihm.32374/3?r=0&s=1; accessed November 22, 2013.

Laux, Jeanne Kirk, and Maureen Appel Molot. State capitalism: public enterprise in Canada. Cornell Univ Pr, 1988.

Laxer, James. Oil and gas: Ottawa, the provinces and the petroleum industry. Lorimer, 1983.

Lewis, Jeff. "Suncor Reaches $4.2 billion deal with Canadian oil sands: friendly deal signals end of public feud between companies," The Globe and Mail; Tuesday, Jan 19, 2016.

Lisac, Mark. The Klein revolution. NeWest Press, Edmonton, ISBN 0920897835 1995

Lisac, Mark. "Don Getty, 1985 – 1982" in Rennie, Bradford James, ed. Alberta Premiers of the Twentieth Century. Vol. 10. University of Regina Press, 2004. ISBN 0920897835

Lorenz, Andrea. "Battlefield: 30 years ago Suncor's oil sands pioneers took on raw nature with untried gear and won – eventually." Oilweek, volume 48, number 40, October, 1997.

Lucas, Alastair R. "Canada's role in the United States oil and gas supply security: oil sands, Arctic gas, NAFTA, and Canadian Kyoto protocol impacts" Energy Law Journal, volume 25, 2004.

MacFadyen, Alan J., and G. Campbell Watkins. Petropolitics: petroleum development, markets and regulations, Alberta as an illustrative history. University of Calgary Press, 2014.

MacGregor, James Grierson. A history of Alberta (revised), Hurtig Publishers, 1981.

_____. Vision of an ordered land: the story of the Dominion Land Survey. Saskatoon: Western Producer Prairie Books, 1981.

Mackenzie, Alexander. Voyages from Montreal, on the River St. Laurence, Through the Continent of North America, to the Frozen and Pacific Oceans; in the Years 1789 and 1793: With a Preliminary Account of the Rise, Progress, and Present State of the Fur Trade of that Country:

Illustrated with Maps. T. Cadell, Jun. and W. Davies. Cobbett and Morgan and W. Creech, at Edinburgh, 1801.

MacMillan, Margaret. Paris, 1919: Six months that changed the world; Random House, New York; 2003.

Macoun, John. Autobiography of John Macoun, MA, Canadian explorer and naturalist, assistant director and naturalist to the Geologic Survey of Canada. A memorial volume published by the Ottawa Field-Naturalists' Club, 1922.

Madden, Peter B. and Jacek D. Morawski. "The Future of the Canadian oil sands: engineering and project management advances;" presentation at AMEC Oil Sands conference, 2010-001

Mair, Charles. Through the Mackenzie Basin: an account of the signing of Treaty No. 8 and the Scrip Commission, 1899. Edmonton, University of Alberta Press, 1999.

Makin, Kirk. "Clash over oil sands inevitable: Lougheed," The Globe and Mail, August 14, 2007.

Mann, Charles C. 1491: A New revelation of the Americas before Columbus. Second edition; Vintage Books, A Division of Random House, Inc. New York, 2011.

Marchildon, Gregory P., and Duncan McDowall. Canadian Multinationals and International Finance. Routledge, 2013.

Marsden, William. Stupid to the last drop: how Alberta is bringing environmental Armageddon to Canada (and doesn't seem to care). Vintage Canada, 2010.

Martin, Don. "Black Gold," in 100 Days That Changed Canada, Canada's History Society, HarperCollins, 2012.

Masliyah, Zhenghe Xu, and Marta Dabros, editors: Handbook on Theory and Practice of Bitumen Recovery from Athabasca Oil Sands; Volume II: Industrial Practice; Kingsley Knowledge Publishing, 2011ISBN 978-1-926832-16-6 [v. 2]

Matar, Sami. Synfuels: hydrocarbons of the future. Tulsa: PennWell Publishing Company, 1982.

May, Gary. Hard oiler! the story of Canadians' quest for oil at home and abroad. Dundurn, 1998.

McClements, Robert Jr. "The Athabasca tar sands," in Dusters and gushers: the Canadian oil and gas industry; Pitt Publishing Company, Toronto; 1968.

McDiarmid, Margo. "Regulating oil and gas industry would be 'crazy' under current oil prices: Harper." CBC News. http://www.cbc.ca/news/politics/stephen-harper-says-oil-and-gas-regulations-now-would-be-crazy-1.2866306.

McGeer, Dudley and Victor T. Reynolds. Suncor Inc.: an account of the first seventy years. Toronto, 1987; privately published.

McGoogan, Ken; How the Scots invented Canada, HarperCollins Publishers, Toronto, 2010.

McKenzie-Brown, Peter and Hans Maciej. "Canadian oil and gas: the first one hundred years," Canadian Petroleum Association, 1989.

McKenzie-Brown, Peter; Gordon Jaremko and David Finch. The great oil age, Calgary: Detselig Enterprises, 1993.

McKenzie-Brown, Peter and Stacey Phillips. In Balance: An Account of Alberta's CA Profession, 1910-2000; ISBN 0-9691132-1-8; Institute of Chartered Accountants of Alberta Accountants of Alberta, 2000.

McKenzie-Brown, Peter, The Richness of Discovery: Amoco's First Fifty Years in Canada, 1948-1998; published by Amoco Canada, 1998; ISBN 0-9684022-0-8.

_____. "Centre of a storm: The Canadian Petroleum Association during the energy wars" in Barbecues, Booms & Blogs: 50 Years of Public Relations in Calgary; edited by Peter McKenzie-Brown and Jim Rennie; Detselig Publishers, 2008.

_____. "How Public Money Saved Syncrude"; Oilsands Review, August 2011.

_____. "In-situ Step-change: How underground shafts and tunnels changed the future of the oil sands"; Oilsands Review December 2011.

_____. "New gas mega-wells threaten to strain contractor fleet"; Alberta Oil magazine, April 2009.

_____. "Six visionaries who built the modern oil sands." An address to the Canadian Association of Lifelong Learners. Calgary; January 22, 2013

_____. "The Bosworth expedition: an early petroleum survey." In The Frontier of Patriotism: Alberta and the First World War, edited by Adriana A. Davies and Jeff Keshen. Calgary: University of Calgary Press, 2016.

_____. "The Carbonate Question." Oilsands Review, November 2008.

_____. "The Visionaries: A history of Alberta's oil sands, bitumen carbonates and heavy oil." Report prepared for Historic Resources Management Branch, Energy Resources Heritage Website Project, March 2013.

_____. "Water wisdom: Royal Society report reviewing how spilled oil reacts in water is helping enhance industry's water knowledge," Oilweek, March 2016.

McRae, W.A. "Open your mouth and shut your eyes and we'll take your oil land, wherever it lies," Saturday Night, March 15, 1919.

McRory, Robert E. Energy heritage: oil sands and heavy oils of Alberta. Energy and Natural Resources, Edmonton, Alberta, 1982.

Moberly, Henry John, and William Bleasdell Cameron. When Fur was King. Dutton, 1929.

Morimoto, Tom. Breaking Trail: from Canada's Northern Frontier to the Oil Fields of Dubai; Fifth House Publishers, 2007.

Murphy, Peter J., Cordy Tymstra, and Merle Massie. "The Great Fire of 1919: People and a shared firestorm in Alberta and Saskatchewan, Canada," Forest History Today, Spring/Fall 2015; http://foresthistory.org/Publications/FHT/FHTSpringFall2015/GreatFireof1919.pdf

Myers, Steven Lee. "Arctic Council adds 6 nations as observer states, including China." The New York Times, May 15, 2013

National Energy Board. Canada's oil sands: a supply and market outlook to 2015. Ottawa, October 2000.

National Task Force on Oil Sands of the Alberta Chamber of Resources, "Comprehensive report. The oil sands: a new energy vision for Canada," 1995; online at http://www.acr-alberta.com/Portals/0/projects/PDFs/The%20Oil%20Sands%20A%20New%20Energy%20Vision%20for%20Canada.pdf?ver=2015-07-15-164525-940.

Neatby, Leslie H. "Swan," in Dictionary of Canadian Biography, vol. 2, University of Toronto/Université Laval, 2003–, accessed November 21, 2013, http://www.biographi.ca/en/bio/swan_2E.html.

_____. Introduction to John Franklin, narrative of a second expedition to the shores of the polar sea in the years 1825, 1826 and 1827; appendix by Richardson, xxxvi; edition published by M.G. Hurtig, Edmonton, 1971.

Newman, Peter Charles, and Max Samples. Company of adventurers. Vol. 1. Markham, Ont.; New York: Viking, 1985.

Nielsen, Arne. "Canada's New Energy Regime," in Tax Treatment of the Petroleum Industry under the National Energy Program, published by the Canadian Tax Foundation, 1981.

_____. We gambled everything: the life and times of an oilman. University of Alberta, 2012.

Nikiforuk, Andrew. Tar sands: dirty oil and the future of a continent. Greystone Books Ltd, 2010.

Notley, Rachel. "Climate leadership plan," Government of Alberta, Edmonton, November 22, 2015.

Obama, Barack. "Statement by the President on the Keystone XL Pipeline, "The White House, November 06, 2015, https://www.whitehouse.gov/the-press-office/2015/11/06/statement-president-keystone-xl-pipeline.

Parkinson, David. "A seismic shift," The Globe and Mail, July 1, 2016, http://www.theglobeandmail.com/report-on-business/economy/canada-economy-shift-resources/article30715265/.

Patel, Sanjay. The future of oil: a straight story of the Canadian oil sands, Creativentures Publishing, 2012.

Potyondi, Barry. The Athabasca oil sands, 1951-1983: a history; unpublished study prepared for Historic Sites Service, Alberta Culture, 1984.

Pynchon, Thomas. Gravity's rainbow. 1973. Random House, 2013 edition.

Raffan, James. Emperor of the north: Sir George Simpson and the remarkable story of the Hudson's Bay Company; a Phyllis Bruce Book, HarperCollins, 2007.

Ray, Arthur J. "Introduction" to Harold Adams Innis, The fur trade in Canada: an introduction to Canadian economic history. University of Toronto Press, 1999.

Richardson, Sir John. Arctic searching expedition: a journal of a boat-voyage through Rupert's Land and the Arctic Sea, in search of the discovery ships under command of Sir John Franklin. With an appendix on the physical geography of North America.

Ridley, Matt, The rational optimist: how prosperity evolves. London: Fourth Estate, 2010

Rister, Carl Coke. Oil! titan of the southwest. Univ. Oklahoma Press, 1949

Robinson, J.M.A. and Jessup, J.M. The Alsands project. Calgary: Canadian Major Projects Association, 1988.

Rose, Norman. Churchill: the unruly giant; Simon and Schuster, 1994.

Russell, Loris S. "Gesner, Abraham." Dictionary of canadian biography, vol. 9. University of Toronto/Université Laval, 2003, accessed February 12, 2014, http://www.biographi.ca/en/bio/gesner_abraham_9E.html.

Sampson, Anthony. The seven sisters: the great oil companies and the world they shaped. (New York: The Viking Press, 1975).

Schmidt, John. Growing up in the oil patch. Dundurn, 1989.

Sennholz, Mary, ed. Faith and freedom: a biographical sketch of a great American, John Howard Pew. Sowers Printing Company, 1975.

Sharma, Prakash, Allen Brown, David Weiner "Canada: drawers of water, hewers of wood and dangers of other myths" Department of Foreign Affairs and International Trade, Trade and Economic Policy Paper No. 96/07, Ottawa, Government of Canada, 1996.

Sheppard, Mary Clark. Athabasca oil sands: from laboratory to production: the letters of Karl A. Clark, 1950-66. Edmonton, Alberta: University of Alberta Press, 1989.

Sidney Martin Blair Fonds Finding Aid; "Biography of Sidney Martin Blair" http://archives.library.ualberta.ca/FindingAids/SMBlair/85-53.html; accessed 27 November, 2013.

Silliman, Benjamin Jr., "Professor Silliman's Report on Petroleum," April 16, 1885. Reproduced in Ida Tarbell, History of the Standard Oil Company, appendix 1, volume 1; copyright 1904 by The MacMillan Company. Reprinted 1950, by special arrangement with Sarah A. Tarbell and John N. Trainer.

Simpson, Jeffrey. "Why Jim Carr will be the loneliest cabinet minister," The Globe and Mail, December 17, 2015.

Spragins, Frank. "The tar sands position in Canada's future energy requirements," November 4, 1977. Speech in Spragins fonds, Glenbow Archives.

Spragins, Nell. "F.K. Spragins," brief biography in Spragins fonds, Glenbow Archives.

Stanford, Jim, ed. The staple Theory@ 50: reflections on the lasting significance of Mel Watkins' "A staple theory of economic growth," Centre for Policy Alternatives, 2014.

Sun Oil Company. Centennial celebration: the story of Sun Company, 1986.

Sun Oil Company, Philadelphia, autumn, 1967. Our Sun [corporate newsletter] "Special GCOS issue" [Contents: "Profiles in Pioneering [Dr. Karl A. Clark, Clarence H Thayer]," 2; "GCOS: the way it works," 3-8; "GCOS is people at work," 9-13; "The men at the helm [Robert McClements Jr]," 14-15; "Ft. McMurray up to date," 16-18; Dougherty, James P. "Alberta: patterned for progress," 19-23; "The making of Athabasca," 24-25; Reynolds, Victor T. "Sun in Canada," 26-28.]

Sweeney, Alastair. Black bonanza: Canada's oil sands and the race to secure North America's energy future; John Wiley & Sons Canada; 2010

Syncrude. A billion barrels for Canada: the Syncrude story. Edmonton, 2000.

Syncrude. The Syncrude story: in our own words. Edmonton, 1990.

Tarbell, Ida. History of the Standard Oil Company, Appendix 1, Volume 1; copyright 1904 by The MacMillan Company; reprinted, 1950, by special arrangement with Sarah A. Tarbell and John N. Trainer.

Teller, Edward. "We're going to work miracles," Popular Mechanics, Volume 113, number 3, March 1960, 101

Tertzakian, Peter. "The nature of the oil beast." ARC Energy Charts, March 10, 2015

_____. "A case of oil rig arrythmia." ARC Energy Charts, February 24, 2015

_____. "Oil price outlook: The view from the bar." ARC Energy Charts, May 17, 2016.

Pratt, Larry. The tar sands: Syncrude and the politics of oil; Hurtig, 1976

Tupper, Allan. "Peter Lougheed, 1971 – 1985." Rennie, Bradford James, ed. Alberta premiers of the twentieth century. Vol. 10. University of Regina Press, 2004. ISBN 0920897835.

Viscount Milton and W. B. Cheadle, The north-west passage by land, sixth edition, London, Cassel, Petter and Galpin, Ludgate Hill, E. C., originally published in 1865, facsimile edition, Toronto, Coles Publishing Company, 1970.

Vodden, C. E. "No stone unturned: the first 150 years of the Geological Survey of Canada;" Energy, Mines and Resources Canada, Ottawa, 1992.

Waiser, W. A. "Bell, Robert (1841-1917)." Dictionary of Canadian biography, vol. 14, University of Toronto/Université Laval, 2003–, accessed October 10, 2013, http://www.biographi.ca/en/bio/bell_robert_1841_1917_14E. html.

Waiser, W. A. "Macoun, John." Dictionary of Canadian biography, vol. 14, University of Toronto/Université Laval, 2003–, accessed October 10, 2013, http://www.biographi.ca/en/bio/macoun_john_14E.html.

Watkins, Melville H., "A staple theory of economic growth." Canadian journal of economics and political science/Revue canadienne de economiques et science politique 29, no. 02 (1963): 141-158.

Wells, John W. "When was petroleum first noticed in United States?" GEOLOGICAL NOTES." AAPG Bulletin 46, no. 4 (1962): 551-552.

Wiens, J., C. McKnight, A. Taguinod, and W. Schiewe. "Feed-monitoring strategy improves hydrotreater reliability." Oil and Gas Journal, Vol. 114.1 (January 4, 2016), pp. 68-73.

Williams, K.C.. "Technology Evolution and Commercial Development at Cold Lake." Presentation to the World Petroleum Congress, Calgary; June 14, 2000.

Winchester, Simon. Atlantic: great sea battles, heroic discoveries, titanic storms, and a vast ocean of a million stories. Vintage, 1991.

Wood, David. The Lougheed legacy, Key Porter Books, 1985, Toronto; ISBN 0-919493-48-3

Wylie, William N.T. The history of the petroleum industry in Alberta: A study prepared for the Historic Sites and Monuments Board of Canada. 1990. Unpublished.

Yerbury, J. Colin. "Protohistoric Canadian Athapaskan populations: an ethnohistorical reconstruction." Arctic Anthropology (1980): 17-33 http://www.jstor.org/stable/40315976; accessed December 25, 2014

Yergin, Daniel. The prize: the epic quest for oil, money and power, Simon and Schuster, 1991.

_____. The quest: energy, security, and the remaking of the modern world, The Penguin Press, 2011.

Youngquist, Walter. GeoDestinies: the inevitable control of earth resources over nations and individuals, Portland, National Book Company, 1997.

## CORRESPONDENCE AND INTERVIEWS

Correspondence with Jaremko, Deborah. Various dates, 2014. Peter McKenzie-Brown.

Correspondence with McKay, Bert. December 9, 2013. Peter McKenzie-Brown.

Correspondence with von Hammerstein, Professor Katharina. January 31 and February 10, 2012. Peter McKenzie-Brown.

Correspondence with Brennan, Brian. November 13, 2015. Peter McKenzie-Brown.

Correspondence with Russum, Dave. January 2, 2016. Peter McKenzie-Brown.

Interview with Andries, Kirk. July 16, 2015. Peter McKenzie-Brown.

Interview with Barr, John. Oil sands oral history project; July 13, 2011. Robert Bott

Interview with Bowman, Clement. Oil sands oral history project, June 28, 2011. Robert Bott.

Interview with Broadhurst, John. Oil sands oral history project, September 24, 2012; Peter McKenzie-Brown

Interview with Brocke, Larry. Oil sands oral history project, January 22, 2013. Adriana Davies

Interview with Burden, Gerry. Oil sands oral history project, Monday, March 19th, 2012. Brian Brennan

Interview with Carrigy, Maurice. Oil sands oral history project, September 17, 2011. Peter McKenzie-Brown

Interview with Collyer, C.R. (Chuck). Oil sands oral history project, June 25, 2013. Peter McKenzie-Brown.

Interview with Dingle, Howard. Oil sands oral history project, December, 2012. Peter McKenzie-Brown

Interview with Fessenden, Robert. Land reclamation project, May 20, 2014. Peter McKenzie-Brown

Interview with George, Rick. Oil sands oral history project, August 2, 2011. Peter McKenzie-Brown

Interview with Gwozd, Bill. October 20, 2014. Peter McKenzie-Brown

Interview with Haston, Jack. Oil sands oral history project, August 1, 2013. Peter McKenzie-Brown

Interview with Humphreys, William. Oil sands oral history project, February 27th, 2013. Peter McKenzie-Brown

Interview with Hyndman, Alan. Oil sands oral history project, Adriana Davies

Interview with Lougheed, Peter. Oil sands oral history project, April 13, 2011. Peter McKenzie-Brown

Interview with Maciej, Hans. Oil sands oral history project, March 22, 2012. Peter McKenzie-Brown

Interview with Manning, Preston. Oil sands oral history project, October 21, 2011. Peter McKenzie-Brown

Interview with McCaffrey, Bill. Oil sands oral history project, December 22, 2011. Peter McKenzie-Brown

Interview with McClements, Robert Jr. Oil sands oral history project, March 27, 2012. Peter McKenzie-Brown

Interview with McClements, Robert Jr., (telephone). October 30, 2011. Peter McKenzie-Brown

Interview with Miller, Lucy. Calgary United Way; October 07, 2015. Peter McKenzie-Brown.

Interview with Morgenstern, Norbert. Oil sands oral history project, Adriana Davies.

Interview with Morimoto, Tom. Oil sands oral history project, August 27, 2012. Peter McKenzie-Brown.

Interview with Newell, Eric. Oil sands oral history project, May 25-26, 2011. Robert Bott.

Interview with Romero, Joy. Oil sands oral history project, February 22, 2013. Peter McKenzie-Brown.

Interview with Scott, Brent. Oil sands oral history project, July 14, 2011. Robert Bott.

Interview with Settari, Professor Antonin (Tony). Oil sands oral history project, November 29, 2012. Peter McKenzie-Brown.

Interview with Slevinsky, Bruce. Oil sands oral history project, July 31, 2013. Peter McKenzie-Brown.

Interview with Spragins, Nell. Oil sands oral history project, June 7, 2012. Peter McKenzie-Brown.

Interview with Stephenson, Gerry. Oil sands oral history project, September 2, 2011. Peter McKenzie-Brown.

Interview with Stringham, Greg. January 14, 2016. Peter McKenzie-Brown.

Interview with Yee, Chi-Tak. Oil sands oral history project, June 22, 2011. Peter McKenzie-Brown.

Interview with Yildirim, Erdal. Oil sands oral history project, July 28, 2012. Gordon Jaremko.

## NOTES

### FOREWORD

1.  Clement Bowman, "Energy superpower?" *The Globe and Mail*, Monday, May 26, 2008. http://www.theglobeandmail.com/report-on-business/energy-superpower/article4389657/

### INTRODUCTION

2.  Phyllis Deane, *The First Industrial Revolution,* Cambridge University Press, 1965, 254-275.

3.  Jackie Forrest, "Oil Sands, Greenhouse Gases, and US Oil Supply: Getting the Numbers Right—2012," Cambridge Energy Research Associates; http://www.api.org/~/media/files/%20oil-and-natural-gas/oil_sands/cera_oil_sands_ghgs_us_oil_supply.pdf, 16.

4.  Thomas Carlyle, "On History" in *Critical and miscellaneous essays*, Philadelphia, 497; A. Hart, late Carey & Hart, 1852; 57. Accessed online.

5.  William James, *The Will to Believe: And Other Essays in Popular Philosophy.* Longmans, Green, and Company, 1912.

6.  William N.T. Wylie, "The History of the Petroleum Industry in Alberta: A study prepared for the Historic Sites and Monuments Board of Canada, 1990;" unpublished manuscript, 57-58.

7.  Deborah Jaremko, email communication with Peter McKenzie-Brown, May 9, 2014.

8.  Government of Alberta, Alberta Energy, http://www.energy.alberta.ca/oilsands/791.asp

9. Peter McKenzie-Brown, "The Carbonate Question," *Oilsands Review*, November, 2008.

10. Kirk Andries interview with Peter McKenzie-Brown, July 16, 2015.

11. Joseph Fitzgerald, *Black Gold with Grit: The Alberta Oil Sands*, Gray's Publishing Ltd., Sidney, British Columbia, 1978, 182-189.

12. William Shakespeare, *Hamlet*, Act 2, Scene 2.

13. Peter McKenzie-Brown, "The Carbonate Question," *Oilsands Review*, November, 2008.

14. Glen Schmidt, Neil Camarta and Bob Dunbar, "Oilsands Outlook," in *Our Evolving Industry: Celebrating the diamond anniversary of the Daily Oil Bulletin*; 2013, 54.

15. Prakash Sharma, Allen Brown, David Weiner, "Canada: Drawers of Water, Hewers of Wood and Dangers of Other Myths." *Trade and Economic Policy Paper No. 96/07*, Ottawa, Government of Canada, 1996.

16. Matt Ridley, *The Rational Optimist: How Prosperity Evolves,* London, Fourth Estate, 2010, 245.

17. William Stanley Jevons, *The Coal Question: An inquiry concerning the progress of the nation, and the probable exhaustion of our coal-mines*, Macmillan and Co. 1866; accessed 26 December 2014; Internet. http://oilcrash.net/media/pdf/The_Coal_Question.pdf.

## Chapter One: Revolution

19. Matt Ridley, *The Rational Optimist: How prosperity evolves.* London: Fourth Estate, 2010, 11.

20. Michael Bliss, *Northern Enterprise: Five Centuries of Canadian Business*, McClelland and Stewart, 1987, 8.

21. C.R. (Chuck) Collyer, "The beginnings of the Oil Sands of Alberta," November 10, 2004; text for presentation.

22. Charles C. Mann, *1491: A New revelation of the Americas before Columbus*, second edition; Vintage Books, A Division of Random House, Inc. New York, 2011; 176-180.

23. J. Colin Yerbury, "Protohistoric Canadian Athapaskan Populations: An Ethnohistorical Reconstruction." Arctic Anthropology (1980), 17-33.

24. Carl Coke Rister, *Oil! Titan of the Southwest,* University of Oklahoma Press, 1949; 3.

25. Wells, John W. "When Was Petroleum First Noticed in United States? GEOLOGICAL NOTES." AAPG Bulletin 46, no. 4 (1962): 551-552.

26. Leslie H. Neatby, "SWAN," in *Dictionary of Canadian Biography, vol. 2*, University of Toronto/Université Laval, 2003; http://www.biographi.ca/en/bio/swan_2E.html.

27. Harold Innis, *The Fur Trade in Canada: an introduction to Canadian economic history.* New Haven, Yale University Press, 1930, 388.

28. Joseph Fitzgerald *Black Gold with Grit: The Alberta Oil Sands*, Gray's Publishing Ltd., Sidney, British Columbia, 1978, 11.

29. Victor G. Hopwood, ed., *David Thompson: Travels in Western North America, 1784-1812.* Macmillan of Canada, 1971, 59.

30.   Harold Adams Innis, *Peter Pond: Fur Trader and Adventurer.* Toronto: Irwin & Gordon, 1930, 10.

31.   Harold Adams Innis, *Peter Pond*, 125.

32.   Juliette Champagne, "Langue du pays et langue du travail: Le français dans le Nord-Ouest du XIXe siècle; Colloque sur les droits linguistiques dans l'Ouest; presentation to l'Association des juristes d'expression française de la Saskatchewan, 19 and 20th of February, 2010, Regina, Saskatchewan, 20.

33.   Barry M. Gough, *First Across the Continent: Sir Alexander Mackenzie.* Vol. 14. University of Oklahoma Press, 1997, 66.

34.   Victor G. Hopwood, *David Thompson*, 152.

35.   Barry M. Gough, *First Across the Continent*, 66.

36.   Alexander Mackenzie, *Voyages from Montreal, on the River St. Laurence, Through the Continent of North America, to the Frozen and Pacific Oceans; in the Years 1789 and 1793: With a Preliminary Account of the Rise, Progress, and Present State of the Fur Trade of that Country: Illustrated with Maps.* T. Cadell, Jun. and W. Davies. Cobbett and Morgan and W. Creech, at Edinburgh, 1801, lxxxiv.

37.   Timothy Ferris, *The Science of Liberty: Democracy, Reason, and the Laws of Nature.* New York: Harper, 2010, 4-5.

38.   John Franklin, *Narrative of a Second Expedition to the Shores of the Polar Sea in the Years 1825, 1826 and 1827;* appendix by Richardson, xxxvi; edition published by M.G. Hurtig, Edmonton, 1971, 77.

39.   Captain George Back, "Account of the Route to be pursued by the Arctic Land Expedition in Search of Captain Ross," *Royal Geographical Society, The Journal of the Royal Geographical Society of London,* Volume 3, 1833 69.

40. John Franklin, *Narrative of a Journey,* xxxvi.

41. C. Stuart Houston, "John Richardson (1787-1865)", 1983 pubs.aina.ucal-gary.ca/arctic/Arctic36-4-376.pdf.

42. C. Stuart Houston, editor, *Arctic Ordeal: The Journal of John Richardson, Surgeon-Naturalist with Franklin,* 1820-1822, 1984.

43. John Franklin, *Narrative of a Second Expedition to the Shores of the Polar Sea in the Years 1825, 1826 and 1827,* 81.

44. Leslie H. Neatby, in introduction to *John Franklin, Narrative of a Second Expedition to the Shores of the Polar Sea in the Years 1825, 1826 and 1827,* xxxvi.

45. C. Stuart Houston, "John Richardson – First Naturalist in the Northwest," *The Beaver* 315 (1984): 10-15.

46. Earle Gray, *The Great Canadian Oil Patch: The Petroleum Era from Birth to Peak,* second edition (2004), 564

47. Lady Jane Franklin and Erika Behrisch Elce, *As Affecting the Fate of my Absent Husband: Selected Letters of Lady Franklin Concerning the Search for the Lost Franklin Expedition, 1848-1860.* Vol. 56. McGill-Queen's Press-MQUP, 2009, 23-24.

48. Ken McGoogan, *How the Scots Invented Canada,* HarperCollins Canada, 2010, 92.

49. George Swinton, in Hall, Capt. Charles Francis. *Life with the Esquimaux: A Narrative of Arctic Experience in Search of Survivors of Sir John Franklin's Expedition,* 1864; republished in 1970 by M.G. Hurtig, Edmonton. "Introduction to the New Edition," xxi.

50. Anonymous, "POLAR SOVEREIGNTY Claims Utilization of New Lands Likely to Govern Nationality," *The New York Times*, April 2, 1926.

51. Steven Lee Myers, "Arctic Council adds 6 nations as observer states, including China," *The New York Times*, May 15, 2013.

52. Timothy Ferris, *The Science of Liberty*, 1.

53. John George Lambton, *Lord Durham's report: an abridgement of a Report on the affairs of British North America*. Vol. 1. McClelland and Stewart, 1963, http://eco.canadiana.ca/view/oocihm.32374/3?r=0&s=1.

54. Ida Tarbell, *History of the Standard Oil Company, Appendix 1, Volume 1*; copyright 1904 by The MacMillan Company; reprinted, 1950, by special arrangement with Sarah A. Tarbell and John N. Trainer, 5.

55. Earle Gray email communication to Peter McKenzie-Brown, February 12, 2014.

56. Earle Gray, "Gesner, Williams and the birth of the oil industry," *Oil-Industry History*, volume 9, 2008. Petroleum History Institute, Oil City, Pennsylvania.

57. Loris S. Russell, "Gesner, Abraham," Dictionary of Canadian Biography, vol. 9, University of Toronto/Université Laval, 2003.

58. Earle Gray, "Gesner, Williams and the birth of the oil industry."

59. Earle Gray, *ibid.*

60. Benjamin Silliman, Jr., in Ida Tarbell *"Professor Silliman's Report on Petroleum," April 16, 1885; reproduced in Ida Tarbell, History of the Standard Oil Company, Appendix 1, Volume 1*, 265-275.

61. Earle Gray, "Gesner, Williams and the birth of the oil industry."

62. George de Mille, *Oil in Canada West: The Early Years,* Calgary: Northwest Printing and Lithographing Ltd., 1970, 161.

63. Juliette Champagne, "Mission Notre-Dame-Des-Victoires, Lac-la-Biche, 1853-1963: Entrepôt et Couvent pensionnat," Interpretative Matrix and Narrative History, an occasional paper for the Lac-La-Biche Mission Historical Society and Historic Sites Services, Alberta Culture and Multiculturalism, July 1992, 111.

64. Juliette Champagne, *ibid.*, 115.

65. Juliette Champagne, *ibid.*, 73.

66. Juliette Champagne, Souvenirs d'un missionnaire breton dans le Nord-Ouest canadien, Septentrion, Sillery, 1997, 279

67. Christy Vodden, "No Stone Unturned: The first 150 years of the Geological Survey of Canada: Energy." Mines and Resources Canada (1992).

68. Kate Hopwood, "Dinosaur skull (Albertosaurus) discovered in Alberta," *The Globe and Mail*, August 12, 2016.

69. James G. Macgregor, *Vision of an Ordered Land: The story of the Dominion Land Survey.* Saskatoon: Western Producer Prairie Books, 1981, 87.

70. John Macoun, *Autobiography of John Macoun, MA, Canadian Explorer and Naturalist, Assistant Director and Naturalist to the Geologic Survey of Canada. A memorial volume published by the Ottawa Field-Naturalists' Club, 1922,* 119.

71. Geological Survey of Canada, *Report of Progress, 1875-76*; published by authority of Parliament, 1877, 170.

72. W. A. Waiser, "Macoun, John," in *Dictionary of Canadian Biography*, vol. 14, University of Toronto/Université Laval, 2003, accessed October 10, 2013, http://www.biographi.ca/en/bio/macoun_john_14E.html.

73. W. A. Waiser, "Bell, Robert (1841-1917)," in *Dictionary of Canadian Biography*, vol. 14, University of Toronto/Université Laval, 2003, accessed October 10, 2013. http://www.biographi.ca/en/bio/bell_robert_1841_1917_14E.html., "Bell, Robert."

74. Earle Gray, "*The Great Canadian Oil Patch,* 334.

75. Joyce Hunt, *Local Push Global Pull: The Untold History of the Athabaska Oil Sands 1900-1930*, PushPull Ltd., 2011, 32.

76. W. A. Waiser, "Bell, Robert (1841-1917)."

77. George Mercer Dawson, *Beneath my Feet*, 307-309.

78. George Dawson, "The Progress and Trend of Scientific Investigation in Canada," Proceedings & Transaction of the Royal Society of Canada 12 (1894), 195.

79. Joseph Fitzgerald, *Black Gold with Grit*, 60.

80. Henry John Moberly and William Bleasdell Cameron, *When Fur was King*, Dutton, 1929,142.

81. Tom Morimoto, *Breaking Trail: From Canada's Northern Frontier to the Oil Fields of Dubai*; Fifth House Publishers, 2007, 40-41.

82. Joseph Fitzgerald, *Black Gold with Grit*, 41.

83. Tom Morimoto, Interview with Peter McKenzie-Brown.

84.     Joyce Hunt, *op. cit.*, 33.

85.     Joseph Fitzgerald, *op. cit.*, 30.

86.     George de Mille, *Oil in Canada West*, 40.

87.     Charles Mair, *Through the Mackenzie Basin: An Account of the Signing of Treaty No. 8 and the Scrip Commission, 1899*, University of Alberta Press, 1999, 121.

88.     René Fumoleau, *As Long as this Land Shall Last: A history of Treaty 8 and Treaty 11, 1870-1939*. University of Calgary Press, 2004, 92.

## CHAPTER TWO: THE WAR TO END WAR

89.     Warren Armstrong, *Atlantic Bridge, from Sail to Steam to Wings: A Diverse Record of 100 Years of North Atlantic Travel;* Muller, 1956, 18.

90.     Simon Winchester, *Atlantic: Great Sea Battles, Heroic Discoveries, Titanic Storms, and a Vast Ocean of a Million Stories.* Harper Collins, 2010, Vintage, 1991, 300-301.

91.     Simon Winchester, *ibid.*, 260-261.

92.     *Mary Clark Sheppard, Oil Sands Scientist: The Letters of Karl A. Clark 1920-1949, Edmonton, Alberta: University of Alberta Press, 1989*, 15-16.

93.     Barry Glen Ferguson, *Athabasca Oil Sands: Northern Resource Exploration, 1875-1951,* Edmonton, 1985, 24.

94.     Joyce Hunt, *Local Push Global Pull: The Untold History of the Athabaska Oil Sands 1900-1930*, PushPull Ltd., 2011, 238.

95.     Volo, James M.and Volo, Dorothy Denneen , *Daily Life on the Old Colonial Frontier.* Westport, Connecticut: Greenwood Press, 2002, 176 -177.

96. T.O. Bosworth, "The Mackenzie River between Old Fort Good Hope and Fort Norman; the Tar Springs District on the Great Slave Lake; and in the Tar Sand District on the Athabasca River;" unpublished manuscript available at the Glenbow Archives, Calgary, reference number M-8656, 69 pages.

97. James A. Clark, "The Energy Revolution," in History of Petroleum Engineering; Boyd Printing Co., Dallas; 1961.

98. William Humphreys, interview with Peter McKenzie-Brown, February 27th, 2013.

99. Norman Rose, *Churchill: The Unruly Giant*; Simon and Schuster, 1994, 104.

100. Norman Rose, *ibid.*, 105.

101. Norman Rose, *ibid.*, 122.

102. Margaret MacMillan, *Paris, 1919: Six Months that Changed the World*; Random House, New York; 2003, 395.

103. Mary Sennholz, ed., *Faith and Freedom: A Biographical Sketch of a Great American, John Howard Pew*, Sowers Printing Company, 1975, 31.

104. Mary Janigan, *Let the Eastern Bastards Freeze in the Dark: The West Versus the Rest Since Confederation*, Random House LLC, 2012, 202-3

105. Joyce Hunt, *op. cit.*, 261-262.

106. W.A. McRae, "Open your mouth and shut your eyes and we'll take your oil land, wherever it lies," *Saturday Night*, March 15, 1919.

107. Gordon Jaremko, *Steward: 75 years of Alberta energy regulation*; 2013; isbn 978-0-9918734-2-5 (bound), 3.

108. Katharina von Hammerstein, email correspondence with Peter McKenzie-Brown.

109. *Joseph Fitzgerald, Black Gold with Grit: The Alberta Oil Sands*, Gray's Publishing Ltd., Sidney, British Columbia, 1978, 38-9.

110. Joyce Hunt, *Local Push Global Pull*, 90.

111. Darlene J. Comfort, *The Abasand Fiasco: The Rise and Fall of a Brave Pioneer Oil Sands Extraction Plant, Friesen Printers*, Edmonton, 1980, 46.

112. Paul Chastko, Developing Alberta's Oil Sands: From Karl Clark to Kyoto, Calgary: University of Calgary Press, 2004, 5.

113. Joyce Hunt, *op. cit.*, 89.

114. Darlene J. Comfort, *The Abasand Fiasco*, 46.

115. Joyce Hunt, *op. cit.*, 100.

116. Darlene J Comfort, *op. cit.*, 46-47.

117. Joyce Hunt, *op. cit.*, 107.

118. Joyce Hunt, *op. cit.*, 106-7.

119. Barry Glen Ferguson, *Athabasca Oil Sands*, 21.

120. Joyce Hunt, *op. cit.*, 279-297.

121. George de Mille, *Oil in Canada West: The early years,* Calgary: Northwest Printing and Lithographing Ltd., 1970, 55.

## Chapter Three: Serious investigation

122. Ida Tarbell, *History of the Standard Oil Company,* Appendix 1, Volume 1; copyright 1904 by The MacMillan Company; reprinted, 1950, by special arrangement with Sarah A. Tarbell and John N. Trainer, 383.

123. James Grierson MacGregor, *A History of Alberta* (revised), Hurtig Publishing, 1981, 209.

124. Mary Janigan, *Let the Eastern Bastards Freeze in the Dark: The West Versus the Rest Since Confederation*, Random House LLC, 2012, 328.

125. Michael Bliss, *Northern Enterprise: Five Centuries of Canadian Business*, McClelland and Stewart, 1987, 384-5.

126. Bliss, *Northern Enterprise*, 414.

127. Anthony Sampson, *The Seven Sisters: The Great Oil Companies and the World They Shaped*, New York, The Viking Press, 1975, 77.

128. Darlene J. Comfort, *The Abasand Fiasco: The Rise and Fall of a Brave Pioneer Oil Sands Extraction Plant,* Friesen Printers, Edmonton, 1980, 28.

129. Barry Glen Ferguson, *Athabasca Oil Sands: Northern Resource Exploration, 1875-1951,* Edmonton, 1985, 28.

130. Paul Chastko, *Developing Alberta's Oil Sands: From Karl Clark to Kyoto,* Calgary: University of Calgary Press, 2004, 13.

131. Earle Gray, *The Great Canadian Oil Patch: The Petroleum Era from Birth to Peak.* Second edition (2004), 336.

132. Sidney Ells, *Preliminary Report on the Bituminous Sands of Northern Alberta*, 8.

133. Earle Gray, *The Great Canadian Oil Patch*, 337.

134. S.C. Ells, Preliminary Report on the Bituminous Sands of Northern Alberta, 1914

135. Earle Gray, *The Great Canadian Oil Patch*, 337.

136. Joseph Fitzgerald, *Black Gold with Grit: The Alberta Oil Sands*, Gray's Publishing Ltd., Sidney, British Columbia, 1978, 48.

137. S.C Ells, *Bituminous sands of northern Alberta*, 236.

138. Darlene J. Comfort, *The Abasand Fiasco*, 35.

139. *Mary Clark Sheppard, Oil Sands Scientist: The Letters of Karl A. Clark 1920-1949, Edmonton, Alberta: University of Alberta Press, 1989, 24.*

140. Sidney Clarke Ells, *Recollections of the Development of the Athabasca Oil Sands*, Vol. 139. Department of Mines and Technical Surveys, Ottawa, Mines Branch, 1962, 26.

141. Sidney Clarke Ells, *Recollections of the Development of the Athabasca Oil Sands*, 32.

142. Clement Bowman interview with Robert Bott, June 28, 2011.

143. Brian Brennan, *Alberta Originals: Stories of Albertans Who Made a Difference*, Fifth House, 2001, 68.

144. Brian Brennan, Email correspondence with Peter McKenzie-Brown, November 13, 2015.

145. National Energy Board, *Canada's Oil Sands: A Supply and Market Outlook to 2015*; Ottawa, October 2000, 17.

146. Adriana Davies, "Mary Clark Sheppard on her father – Karl Clark – and the quintessential oilsands research breakthrough" *Oilsands Review*, September, 2011.

147. Paul Chastko, *Developing Alberta's Oil Sands: From Karl Clark to Kyoto*, Calgary: University of Calgary Press, 2004, 12-13.

148. Sheppard, *Oil Sands Scientist*, 117.

149. Paul Chastko, *Developing Alberta's Oil Sands*, 14.

150. Sidney Martin Blair Fonds Finding Aid; "Biography of Sidney Martin Blair" http://archives.library.ualberta.ca/FindingAids/SMBlair/85-53.html; accessed 27 November, 2013.

151. K. A. Clark and S. M. Blair, *The Bituminous Sands of Alberta*. Scientific and Industrial Research Council of Alberta, Report No. 18, Edmonton, Alberta: W. D. McLean, Acting King's Printer, 1927.

152. Sidney Martin Blair Fonds Finding Aid, "Biography of Sidney Martin Blair" http://archives.library.ualberta.ca/FindingAids/SMBlair/85-53.html; accessed 27 November, 2013.

153. Sami Matar *Synfuels: Hydrocarbons of the Future*, 48.

154. Sheppard, *Oil Sands Scientist*, 33.

155. Sheppard, *ibid*, 2.

156. Paul Chastko, Developing Alberta's Oil Sands, 14

157. Karl Clark and S.M. Blair, *The bituminous sands of Alberta*, Scientific and Industrial Research Council of Alberta, Report No. 18, Edmonton, Alberta: W. D. McLean, Acting King's Printer, 1927, 16.

158. Karl Clark and S.M. Blair, *The Bituminous Sands of Alberta*, 2.

159. Sheppard, ed., *Oil Sands Scientist*, 75.

160. Joseph Fitzgerald, *Black Gold with Grit*, 92.

161. Sheppard, ed., *op. cit.*, 215.

162. Joseph Fitzgerald, *Black Gold with Grit*, 93.

163. Sheppard, ed., *op. cit.*, 216.

## CHAPTER FOUR: FROM WAR TO WAR

164. James Grierson MacGregor, *A History of Alberta* (revised), 250.

165. Bernard Grun, *The Timetables of History*, based on Werner Stein's Kulturfarplan Simon and Schuster, third edition, 1991, 477.

166. Peter McKenzie-Brown, Gordon Jaremko and David Finch, *The Great Oil Age: The Petroleum Industry in Canada*, Calgary: Detselig Enterprises, 1993, 132.

167. Gordon Jaremko, *Steward: 75 years of Alberta Energy Regulation*, 2013; isbn 978-0-9918734-2-5 (bound), 159.

168. Gordon Jaremko, *Steward*, 159.

169. McKenzie-Brown et. al., *The Great Oil Age*, 133.

170. Daniel Yergin, *The Prize: The Epic Quest for Oil, Money & Power*, Touchstone (1991), 402.

171. Paul Chastko, *Developing Alberta's Oil Sands: From Karl Clark to Kyoto*, Calgary: University of Calgary Press, 2004, xiv

172. ERCB: http://www.ercb.ca/portal/server.pt/gateway/PTARGS_6_0_ 309_0_0_43/http;/ercbContent/publishedcontent/publish/ercb_home/ public_zone/oil_sands/history_of_oil_sands_development/

173. Barry Glen Ferguson, *Athabasca Oil Sands: Northern Resource Exploration, 1875-1951*, Edmonton, 1985, 200.

174. *Joseph Fitzgerald, Black Gold with Grit: The Alberta Oil Sands*, Gray's Publishing Ltd., Sidney, British Columbia, 1978, 75.

175. Tom Morimoto, *Breaking Trail: From Canada's Northern Frontier to the Oil Fields of Dubai*, 98-99.

176. Tom Morimoto Interview with Peter McKenzie-Brown, August 27, 2012.

177. J. B. Hamilton, "Evidence on the Tar Sands for the Public Defenders' Court;" unpaginated privately published booklet, 1942(?); dedication on inside cover.

178. J. B. Hamilton, 3.

179. Ed Gould, *Oil: The history of Canada's oil and gas industry*; Hancock House Publishing, 1976, 115.

180. Fitzsimmons, "The Truth about Alberta Oil Sands," cover page.

181. Joseph Fitzgerald, *Black Gold with Grit*, 80-81.

182. Joseph Fitzgerald, Ibid., 86.

183. Barry Glen Ferguson, *Athabasca Oil Sands*, 85.

184. Ferguson, *ibid.*, 90.

185. Ferguson, *ibid.*, 69

186. Ferguson, *ibid.*, 71.

187. Paul Chastko, *Developing Alberta's Oil Sands*, 21.

188. Robert McClements Jr., telephone interview with Peter McKenzie-Brown, October 30, 2011.

189. McClements Jr., *Ibid*.

190. Mary Clark Sheppard, *Oil Sands Scientist: The Letters of Karl A. Clark 1920-1949*, Edmonton, Alberta: University of Alberta Press, 1989, 198.

191. Max Ball, *This Fascinating Oil Business*, Bobbs-Merrill, 1940, 51.

192. Max Ball, *Ibid.*, 373.

193. Darlene J. Comfort, *The Abasand Fiasco: The Rise and Fall of a Brave Pioneer Oil Sands Extraction Plant*, Friesen Printers, Edmonton, 1980, 70.

194. Mary Clark Sheppard, *Oil Sands Scientist*, 264.

195. Max Ball, *op. cit.*, 171.

196. Anonymous, *Winnipeg Tribune*; October 23, 1940.

197. Mary Clark Sheppard, ed., *Oil Sands Scientist: The Letters of Karl A. Clark 1920-1949*, 281.

198. Mary Clark Sheppard, 427.

199. Mary Clark Sheppard, 289.

200. Darlene J. Comfort, *The Abasand Fiasco*, 74.

201. Robert McClements Jr, "The Athabasca Tar Sands," in *Dusters and Gushers: The Canadian Oil and Gas Industry*; Pitt Publishing Company, Toronto; 1968, 169.

202. Paul Chastko, *Developing Alberta's Oil Sands*, 31.

203. William Humphreys interview with Peter McKenzie-Brown, February 27th, 2013.

204. Paul Chastko, *Developing Alberta's Oil Sands*, 40 ff.

205. Darlene J. Comfort, *The Abasand Fiasco*, 88.

206. William Humphreys interview with Peter McKenzie-Brown, February 27th, 2013.

207. Darlene J. Comfort, *The Abasand Fiasco*, 126.

208. Darlene J. Comfort, *ibid.*, 94.

209. Paul Chastko, *Developing Alberta's Oil Sands: From Karl Clark to Kyoto,* 49.

210. Darlene J. Comfort, *op. cit.,* 94.

211. Mary Clark Sheppard, *Oil Sands Scientist: The Letters of Karl A. Clark 1920-1949*, 329.

212. Provincial Archives of Alberta http://www.archivescanada.ca/english/search/ItemDisplay.asp?sessionKey=1149011692062_206_191_57_196&l=0&lvl=1&v=0&coll=1&itm=253411&rt=1&bill=1

213. Edward Bell, "Ernest Manning: 1943 – 1968," 177.

214. *Joseph Fitzgerald, Black Gold with Grit*, Gray's Publishing Ltd., Sidney, British Columbia, 1978. Gray's Publishing Ltd., Sidney, British Columbia, 81.

215. Mary Clark Sheppard, ed., *Oil Sands Scientist: The Letters of Karl A. Clark 1920-1949*, 438-439.

216. James Grierson MacGregor, *A History of Alberta*, Hurtig Publishing, 1981, 302.

217. Barry Glen Ferguson, *Athabasca Oil Sands*, 130.

218. James Grierson MacGregor, *A History of Alberta,* 302.

219. Barry Glen Ferguson, *Athabasca Oil Sands*, 141.

220. Paul Chastko, *Developing Alberta's Oil Sands,* 82.

221. Great Plains Research Consultants, *Athabasca Oil Sands, 1951-1983*, 34.

222. Government of Alberta. *Proceedings: Athabasca Oil Sands Conference*, 1951, 173-174.

223. *Ibid.*, 174-175.

224. E.E. (Ned) Gilbert, letter to George Dunlap, September21, 1951, Glenbow Archives.

225. Government of Alberta, *Proceedings, op. cit.*, 181.

226. Peter McKenzie-Brown, "How Public Money Saved Syncrude," August 2011, *Oilsands Review.*

227. Brian Brennan, *The Good Steward: The Ernest C. Manning Story,* Fifth House, 2008, 112.

228. *Ibid.,* 112-113.

229. C.R. (Chuck) Collyer, "The beginnings of the Oil Sands of Alberta," November 10, 2004.

230. Government of Alberta, *Proceedings: Athabasca Oil Sands Conference*, iii.

231. Mary Clark Sheppard, *Oil Sands Scientist,* 438.

232. Mary Clark Sheppard, *Oil Sands Scientist*, 442.

## CHAPTER FIVE: THE ATOMIC AGE

233. Mary Clark Sheppard, *Oil Sands Scientist: The Letters of Karl A. Clark 1920-1949*, Edmonton, Alberta: University of Alberta Press, 1989, 391.

234. Walter Isaacson, *Einstein: His Life and Universe*, Isaacson, Walter. Einstein: His life and universe, Simon and Schuster, 2007, 474.

235. David Breen, *Alberta's Petroleum Industry and the Conservation board*, Edmonton, University of Alberta Press, 1993, 450-1.

236. Edward Teller, "We're going to work Miracles," *Popular Mechanics*, Volume 113, Number 3, March 1960, 101

237. Paul Chastko, Developing Alberta's Oil Sands: From Karl Clark to Kyoto, Calgary: University of Calgary Press, 2004, 97.

238. David Breen, *op. cit.*, 450.

239. Alberta Technical Committee, "Report to the Minister of Mines and Minerals and the Oil and Gas Conservation Board with respect to an experiment proposed by Richfield oil Corporation involving an underground nuclear explosion beneath the McMurray oil Sands with the objective of determining the feasibility of recovering the oil with the aid of the heat released from such an explosion." August, 1959, 6.

240. Gerry Burden interview with Brian Brennan, Monday, March 19th, 2012

241. Brian Brennan, "Project Oilsand: Alberta's brush with the H-bomb," 2012.

242. David Breen, *op. cit.*, 446-455.

243. Alberta Technical Committee, *op. cit.*, August, 1959, 12.

244. David Breen, *op. cit.*, 453.

245. Earle Gray, email correspondence with Peter McKenzie-Brown, April 22, 2014.

246. Canadian Energy Research Institute (CERI), "Green bitumen: The role of nuclear, gasification and CCS in Alberta's oil sands," 2009.

## CHAPTER SIX: ENERGY BECOMES POLITICAL

247. Nick Taylor interview with Peter McKenzie-Brown, August 2014.

248. Arne Nielsen, *We Gambled Everything: The Life and Times of an Oilman*, University of Alberta, 2012, 76-77.

249. Arne Nielsen, *We Gambled Everything*, 93.

250. Morris Albert Adelman, *The genie out of the bottle: World oil since 1970*, MIT Press, 1995, 64.

251. Alastair Sweeney, *Black Bonanza: Canada's oil sands and the race to secure North America's energy future*, John Wiley & Sons Canada; 2010, 113.

252. Robert Bott, "Tar sands plan global in scope," *The Montreal Gazette*, Feb 16, 1974.

253. Michael Bliss, Northern enterprise: Five centuries of Canadian business. McClelland and Stewart, 1987, 537.

254. James Grierson MacGregor, *A History of Alberta*, Hurtig Publishing, 1981, 314.

255. Peter McKenzie-Brown, Gordon Jaremko and David Finch, *The Great Oil Age: The Petroleum Industry in Canada*. Calgary: Detselig Enterprises, 1993, 127-128

256. The Honourable Jean Chrétien, "The Challenge of Canadian Federalism in the 1980s," An address to the Empire Club of Canada, http://speeches. empireclub.org/61471/data

257. James Laxer, *Oil and Gas: Ottawa, the Provinces and the Petroleum Industry*, Lorimer, 1983, 144.

258. Peter McKenzie-Brown, *et. al., op. cit.,* 140

259. Ian Smyth Interview with Peter McKenzie-Brown, "Centre of a Storm: The Canadian Petroleum Association during the energy wars" in *Barbecues, Booms & Blogs: 50 Years of Public Relations in Calgary*; edited by Peter McKenzie-Brown and Jim Rennie; Detselig Publishers, 2008, 22.

260. Jack Gorman interview with Peter McKenzie-Brown, "Centre of a storm: The Canadian Petroleum Association during the energy wars," ibid., 25.

261. Hans Maciej interview with Peter McKenzie-Brown in "Centre of a storm: The Canadian Petroleum Association during the energy wars," 27.

## CHAPTER SEVEN: SUN OIL AND GCOS

262. Brian Brennan, *The Good Steward: The Ernest C. Manning Story,* Fifth House, 2008, 126

263. Robert McClements Jr., telephone interview with Peter McKenzie-Brown, March 7, 2014.

264. Sun Oil Company, *Centennial Celebration: The Story of Sun Company*; 20.

265. Brian Brennan, *The Good Steward*, 113.

266. Preston Manning interview with Peter McKenzie-Brown, October 21, 2011

267. Sun Oil Company, *Centennial Celebration: The Story of Sun Company*; frontispiece.

268. Dudley M. McGeer and Victor T. Reynolds, *Suncor Inc.: An account of the first seventy years,* Toronto, 1987; privately published, 59.

269. Clement Bowman, online audio presentation.

270. Dudley M. McGeer and Victor T. Reynolds, *Suncor Inc.*, 68-69.

271. Bert McKay email correspondence with Peter McKenzie-Brown, December 9, 2013.

272. Robert McClements Interview with Peter McKenzie-Brown, March 27, 2012

273. Robert McClements, Jr. "The Athabasca Tar Sands," in *Dusters and Gushers: The Canadian Oil and Gas Industry*; Pitt Publishing Company, Toronto; 1968, 169.

274. Robert McClements, Jr. "The Athabasca Tar Sands, 170-173.

275. Robert McClements, Jr., email communication with Peter McKenzie-Brown, March 7, 2014.

276. Robert McClements, Jr. "The Athabasca Tar Sands," 170-173.

277. Robert McClements, Jr., email communication with Peter McKenzie-Brown, June 19, 2014.

278. "Agreement between Great Canadian Oil Sands Limited and Great Canadian Oil Sands Employees Bargaining Association," dated October 17, 1967, 26-27.

279. Hans Maciej Interview with Peter McKenzie-Brown, March 22, 2012.

280. Robert McClements, Interview with Peter McKenzie-Brown, March 27, 2012.

281. Anonymous, "The men at the helm," *Our Sun: Special GCOS issue: The dawn of a new age of energy; Sun Oil Company*, autumn, 1967.

282. Earle Gray, *The Great Canadian Oil Patch: The Petroleum Era from Birth to Peak,* second edition (2004), 246.

283. Don Martin, "Black Gold." *100 Days That Changed Canada*, Canada's History Society, HarperCollins.

284. Earle Gray, *The Great Canadian Oil Patch*, 246.

285. Mary Clark Sheppard, *Oil Sands Scientist: The Letters of Karl A. Clark 1920-1949*, Edmonton, Alberta: University of Alberta Press, 1989; 89-90.

286. Paul Chastko, *Developing Alberta's Oil Sands: From Karl Clark to Kyoto*, Calgary: University of Calgary Press, 2004, xiv-xv.

287. Anonymous, "J. Howard Pew proved his point with personal test," 3.

288. Jim Armstrong, "First oil sands plant a true pioneer," 24.

289. David Hatter, "Alberta's tar sands in the energy perspective," *Canadian Geographic*, April/May 1981.

290. *The Daily Oil Bulletin*, October 29, 1980.

291. Jeanne K. Laux and Maureen A. Molot, *State Capitalism: Public Enterprise in Canada*, Cornell University Press, 1988, 166.

292. Rick Boychuk, *River of Grit: Six months on the line at Suncor* (Edmonton, Duval House Pub., 1996,) 18.

293. Rick Boychuk, *ibid.*, 12.

294. Bert McKay email communication with Peter McKenzie-Brown, December 9, 2013.

295. Rick Boychuk, *op. cit.*, 147.

## CHAPTER EIGHT: SYNCRUDE

296. Syncrude, *A Billion Barrels for Canada: The Syncrude Story. Edmonton, 2000,* 14.

297. Syncrude, *A Billion Barrels for Canada,* 19.

298. Clement Bowman interview with Robert Bott, June 28, 2011.

299. Jack Haston interview with Peter McKenzie-Brown, August 1, 2013.

300. Syncrude, *A Billion Barrels for Canada,* 19.

301. Eric Newell interview with Robert Bott, May 25-26, 2011.

302. Letter in Spragins fonds, dated January 14, 1967; Glenbow Archives.

303. David Wood, *The Lougheed Legacy,* Key Porter Books, Toronto; ISBN 0-919493-48-3; 113.

304. Brian Brennan, "Oilsands apostle: Frank Spragins, Syncrude and North American energy survival."

305. C.R. (Chuck) Collyer," The beginnings of the Oil Sands of Alberta," November 10, 2004.

306. C.R. (Chuck) Collyer correspondence with Peter McKenzie-Brown, January 13, 2014.

307. C.R. (Chuck) Collyer, "The beginnings of the Oil Sands of Alberta."

308. Paul Chastko, Developing Alberta's Oil Sands: From Karl Clark to Kyoto, Calgary: University of Calgary Press, 2004, 152.

309. Peter Lougheed interview with Peter McKenzie-Brown, April 13, 2011.

310. Bill Mooney interview with Peter McKenzie-Brown, April 3, 2012.

311. Spragins, Nell, "F.K. Spragins" in Spragins fonds, Glenbow Archives.

312. Bill Mooney interview with Peter McKenzie-Brown, June 6, 2011.

313. Peter Lougheed Interview with Peter McKenzie-Brown, April 13, 2011.

314. Personal correspondence with Gordon Jaremko, November 10, 2015.

315. Hans Maciej interview with Peter McKenzie-Brown, March 22, 2012.

316. Peter Lougheed interview with Peter McKenzie-Brown, April 13, 2011.

317. David Wood, *The Lougheed Legacy*, 120-121.

318. Nell Spragins interview with Peter McKenzie-Brown, June 7, 2012.

319. Frank Spragins, "The Tar Sands Position in Canada's Future Energy Requirements," November 4, 1977. Speech in Spragins fonds, Glenbow Archives.

320. Anonymous, "Syncrude opens $2.2-billion oil sands plant," *Edmonton Journal,* Saturday, September 15, 2012.

321. Nell Spragins Interview with Peter McKenzie-Brown.

322. Syncrude, *A Billion Barrels for Canada*, 22-23.

323. Interview with Brent Scott, Oil sands oral history project; 14th July 2011.

324. C.R. (Chuck) Collyer, "The beginnings of the Oil Sands of Alberta."

325. John Broadhurst interview with Peter McKenzie-Brown, September 24, 2012.

326. Pius Rolheiser interview with Peter McKenzie-Brown, May, 2012.

## CHAPTER NINE: POLICY MEETS ECONOMICS

327. Conservation and Utilization Committee, "Athabasca Tar Sands Development Strategy," Government of Alberta, 4.

328. Conservation and Utilization Committee, "Athabasca Tar Sands Development Strategy," 46.

329. François Bregha, "Energy Policy," *The Canadian Encyclopedia*, McLelland and Stewart, Toronto, 1999.

330. G. Bruce Doern and Glen Toner, Politics *of Energy: The development and implementation of the NEP.* Methuen, 1985, 1.

331. Earle Gray, "The Great Canadian Oil Patch: The Petroleum Era from Birth to Peak," second edition (2004), 449.

332. Lalonde, Marc, "Introduction," *The National Energy Programme,* Department of Energy, *Ottawa: Queen's Printer, 1980.*

333. Paul Brunner, *editor, Lougheed & the War with Ottawa; volume 11 of a 12-volume series, Alberta in the 20th Century; 2003; ISBN 0-9730760-1-1,* 231.

334. Arne Nielsen, "Canada's New Energy Regime," in *Tax treatment of the petroleum industry under the National Energy Program*, published by the Canadian Tax Foundation, 1981, 24-25.

335. Howard Dingle Interview with Peter McKenzie-Brown, December, 2012.

336. John Broadhurst interview with Peter McKenzie-Brown, September 24, 2012.

337. Paul Chastko, *Developing Alberta's Oil Sands: From Karl Clark to Kyoto,* Calgary: University of Calgary Press, 2004, 191.

338. David Wood, *The Lougheed Legacy*, Key Porter Books, 1985, Toronto; 123.

339. Hans Maciej interview with Peter McKenzie-Brown, Barbecues, booms & blogs, 27.

340. William N.T. Wylie, *op. cit.,* 67.

341. J.M.A. Robinson and J.M. Jessup, The Alsands Project, 12.

342. J.M.A. Robinson and J.M. Jessup, Ibid., 20-21.

343. Wood, 122.

344. Hatter, David. "Alberta's tar sands in the energy perspective," Canadian Geographic, April/May 2001, 14.

345. Chastko, 191.

346. Wood, 123.

347. Chastko, 202

348. Chastko, 202-3

349. Chastko, 212

350. Alan J. MacFadyen, and G. Campbell Watkins, Petropolitics, 126-7.

351. Paul Chastko, Developing Alberta's Oil Sands: From Karl Clark to Kyoto, 203

## CHAPTER TEN: GETTING STEAMED

352. Clement Bowman interview with Robert Bott, June 28, 2011.

353. Frank Dabbs, "The brains behind the oil-sands breakthrough," 37.

354. Annette Hester and Leah Lawrence, "A sub-national public-private strategic alliance for innovation and export development: the case of the Canadian province of Alberta's oil sands," CEPAL (2010), 15-27.

355. Alastair Sweeny, *Black Bonanza: Canada's Oil Sands and the Race to Secure North America's Energy Future;* John Wiley & Sons Canada; 2010, 135-138.

356. Bruce Slevinsky interview with Peter McKenzie-Brown, July 31st, 2013.

357. K.C. Williams, "Technology evolution and commercial development at Cold Lake," a presentation to the World Petroleum Congress, Calgary; June 14, 2000.

358. Bruce Slevinsky interview with Peter McKenzie-Brown, July 31st, 2013.

359. Howard Dingle interview with Peter McKenzie-Brown, December 7, 2012.

360. Bruce Slevinsky interview with Peter McKenzie-Brown, July 31st, 2013.

361. Gerry Stephenson interview with Peter McKenzie-Brown, September 2, 2011.

362. Maurice Carrigy interview with Peter McKenzie-Brown, September, 17, 2011

363. *Ibid.*

364. Hugh Lieper communication with Peter McKenzie-Brown, September 2011

365. Maurice Carrigy, *op. cit.*

366. Gerry Stephenson interview with Peter McKenzie-Brown, September 2, 2011.

367. Bowman interview with Peter McKenzie-Brown, June 28, 2011.

368. Gerry Stephenson correspondence with Peter McKenzie-Brown, May 4, 2014.

369. Chi-Tak Yee interview with Peter McKenzie-Brown, June 22, 2011.

370. Maurice Carrigy Interview with Peter McKenzie-Brown, September, 17, 2011

371. Gerry Stephenson correspondence, *ibid.*

372. Gerry Stephenson interview with Peter McKenzie-Brown, September 2, 2011.

373. Gerry Stephenson correspondence, *ibid.*

374. Annette Hester and Leah Lawrence, "A Sub-national Public-private Strategic Alliance for Innovation and Export Development: The Case of the Canadian Province of Alberta's Oil Sands," 38.

375. Peter Lougheed interview with Peter McKenzie-Brown, April 13, 2011.

376. Toshiyuki Hirata interview with Peter McKenzie-Brown, October 24th, 2012.

377. McKenzie-Brown, Peter, "The Way We Were" in *Oilsands Review*, March, 2013.

## Chapter Eleven: Inside out

378. Tony Settari interview with Peter McKenzie-Brown, November 28, 2012

379. James Henry Gray, *The winter years: The depression on the prairies*, Macmillan of Canada, 1973, 213.

380. Robert Fessenden Interview with Peter McKenzie-Brown, May 21, 2014.

381. Don Thompson interview with Peter McKenzie-Brown, June 25, 2014.

382. Jennifer Grant, Simon Dyer and Dan Woynillowicz, *Fact or fiction?* Introduction.

383. Larry Brocke interview with Adriana Davies, January22, 2013

384. Larry Brocke interview with David Finch, January 10, 2013

385. Adriana Davies interview with Larry Brocke, January 22, 2013

386. Don Thompson interview with Peter McKenzie-Brown, June 25, 2014.

387. Larry Brocke interview with Adriana Davies, January 22, 2013

388. Robert Fessenden interview with Peter McKenzie-Brown, May 20, 2014.

389. Don Thompson interview with Peter McKenzie-Brown, June 25, 2014.

390. Robert Fessenden interview with Peter McKenzie-Brown, May 20, 2014.

391. *Ibid.*

392. Anonymous, Grand Council of the Crees website, "Social Impact on the Crees of James Bay Project," http://www.gcc.ca/archive/article.php?id=38; accessed 30 May, 2014, 1.

393. Matt Ridley, *The Rational Optimist: How Prosperity Evolves,* London, Fourth Estate, 2010, 306.

394. Peter B. Madden and Jacek D. Morawski, "The Future of the Canadian Oil Sands: Engineering and Project Management Advances," presentation at AMEC Oil Sands conference, 2010-001.

395. John R. Gulley, Vivienne R. Wilson, and Ian B. Mackenzie, "Oil Sands Reclamation," in J. Masliyah, J. Czarnecki, and Z. Xu, editors, *Handbook on Theory and Practice of Bitumen Recovery from Athabasca Oil Sands* (2010), vol. 2, 477.

396. Leithan Slade interview with Peter McKenzie-Brown, July 14, 2014

397. Alan Fair interview with Peter McKenzie-Brown, July 17, 2014.

398. Ibid.

399. Deborah Jaremko email communication with Peter McKenzie-Brown, May 9, 2014.

400. Joy Romero interview with Peter McKenzie-Brown, February 21, 2013

## Chapter Twelve: Profitable years and their collapse

401. Walter Youngquist, *GeoDestinies: The inevitable control of earth resources over nations and individuals,* Portland: National Book Company, 1997, 68-69.

402. Samuel P. Huntington, *The Clash of Civilizations,* 251-2.

403. Paul Chastko, Developing Alberta's Oil Sands: From Karl Clark to Kyoto, Calgary: University of Calgary Press, 2004, 212.

404. Erdal Yildirim interview with Gordon Jaremko, July 28, 2012.

405. National Oil Sands Task Force, 46.

406. Anonymous, "The next shock? The price of oil has fallen by half in the past two years, to just over $10 a barrel. It may fall further—and the effects will not be as good as you might hope," *The Economist*, March 4th, 1999.

407. Michael Economides and Ronald Oligney, *The Color of Oil, Katy,* Texas: Round Oak Publishing Company (2000), 25.

408. Robert McClements Jr. interview with Peter McKenzie-Brown, March 27, 2012

409. Rick George interview with Peter McKenzie-Brown, August 2, 2011.

410. Dee Parkinson-Marcoux interview with Robert Bott, October 18, 2011.

411. Cliff Britch interview with Peter McKenzie-Brown, August 15, 2012.

412. Dee Parkinson-Marcoux interview with Robert Bott, October 18, 2011.

413. Cliff Britch interview with Peter McKenzie-Brown, August 15, 2012.

414. Don Thompson interview with Peter McKenzie-Brown, June 25, 2014.

415. Dee Parkinson-Marcoux interview with Robert Bott, October 18, 2011.

416. Rick George interview with Peter McKenzie-Brown, August 2, 2011.

417. Neil McCrank interview with Peter McKenzie-Brown, May 9th, 2013.

418. Kirk Makin, "Clash over oil sands inevitable: Lougheed," *The Globe and Mail*, August 14, 2007.

419. Mark Lisac, *"The Klein Revolution,"* NeWest Press, 1995, 210

420. Anonymous, "Oilsands Outlook" – an interview with Glen Schmidt, Neil Camarta and Bob Dunbar; in *Our Evolving Industry: Celebrating the diamond anniversary of the Daily Oil Bulletin*; 2013, 50.

421. Clement Bowman "Energy superpower?" *The Globe and Mail*, May 26, 2008; updated, September 30, 2010.

422. *Ibid.*

423. John Browne, *Beyond Business: An Inspirational Memoir from a Visionary Leader,* Weidenfeld & Nicolson, 2010, 44.

424. Peter McKenzie-Brown, *The Richness of Discovery: Amoco's First Fifty Years in Canada, 1948-1998, Amoco Canada, 1998; ISBN 0-9684022-0-8.*34

425. John Browne, *op. cit.*, 70.

426. BBC, "BP and Amoco in oil mega-merger," Tuesday, August 11, 1998.

427. Bill McCaffrey interview with Peter McKenzie-Brown, December 22, 2011.

428. Anonymous, "MEG reports low SOR in SAGD pilot," *Oil and Gas Journal,* April 24, 2013.

429. Rick George interview with Peter McKenzie-Brown, August 2, 2011.

430. Deborah Jaremko email correspondence with Peter McKenzie-Brown, March 10, 2015.

431. Margo McDiarmid, Environment Reporter, "Regulating oil and gas industry would be 'crazy' under current oil prices: Harper," *CBC News,* http://www.cbc.ca/news/politics/stephen-harper-says-oil-and-gas-regulations-now-would-be-crazy-1.2866306

432. Government of Alberta, "Climate Leadership Plan: Capping oil sands emissions," http://alberta.ca/climate/oilsands-emissions.cfm; December 17, 2015.

433. CCEMC and Alberta Innovates, "Briefing Note for Richard Dicerni: Technological Innovation and Climate Change," June 8, 2015.

434. Government of Alberta, "Climate Leadership Plan."

435. Claudia Cattaneo, "Secret deal on Alberta's oilsands emissions limits divides patch."

436. Barack Obama, "Statement by the President on the Keystone XL Pipeline," The White House, November 06, 2015, https://www.whitehouse.gov/the-press-office/2015/11/06/statement-president-keystone-xl-pipeline.

437. Jeffrey Simpson, "Why Jim Carr will be the loneliest cabinet minister," The Globe and Mail; December 17, 2015.

438. Office of the Prime Minister, "Minister of Natural Resources Mandate Letter." Government of Canada, http://pm.gc.ca/eng/minister-natural-resources-mandate-letter; accessed December 18, 2015.

439. Peter J. Murphy, Cordy Tymstra, and Merle Massie, "The Great Fire of 1919: People and a shared firestorm in Alberta and Saskatchewan, Canada," *Forest History Today*, Spring/Fall 2015; http://foresthistory.org/Publications/FHT/FHTSpringFall2015/GreatFitymstrareof1919.pdf.

440. Peter McKenzie-Brown interview with Reg Curren, July 2015.

441. Peter McKenzie-Brown interview with Mike Flannigan, July 2015.

442. Jeff Lewis and Shawn McCarthy, "Crisis in the Oil Patch," Report on Business, *The Globe and Mail*, May 5, 2015.

443. Insurance Bureau of Canada, "Northern Alberta Wildfire Costliest Insured Natural Disaster in Canadian History - Estimate of insured losses: $3.58 billion," http://www.ibc.ca/on/resources/media-centre/media-releases/northern-alberta-wildfire-costliest-insured-natural-disaster-in-canadian-history.

## CHAPTER THIRTEEN: MAELSTROM

444. Arthur J. Ray in "Introduction" to Harold Adams Innis, *The fur trade in Canada: An introduction to Canadian economic history.* University of Toronto Press, 1999.

445. Harold Innis, *The Fur Trade in Canada: an introduction to Canadian economic history.* New Haven, Yale University Press, 1930, 407-8.

446. Melville H. Watkins, "A staple theory of economic growth," *Canadian Journal of Economics and Political Science/Revue canadienne de economiques et science politique* 29, no. 02, 1963, 141.

447. Melville H Watkins. "A staple theory of economic growth," 142.

448. David Parkinson, "A Seismic Shift," *The Globe and Mail*, July 1, 2016 http://www.theglobeandmail.com/report-on-business/economy/canada-economy-shift-resources/article30715265/

449. Stanford, Jim, ed. *The Staple Theory@ 50: Reflections on the Lasting Significance of Mel Watkins' "A Staple Theory of Economic Growth,"* Centre for Policy Alternatives, 2014.

450. Peter McKenzie-Brown, "Water Wisdom: Royal Society report reviewing how spilled oil reacts in water is helping enhance industry's water knowledge," *Oilweek*, March, 2015.

451. Enbridge, "Enbridge Energy Partners L.P. settles with the U.S. Department of Justice and U.S. Environmental Protection Agency on Marshall and Romeoville incidents," http://www.enbridge.com/media-center/news/details?id=2072418&lang=en&year=2016; accessed July 21, 2016.

452. Christof Rühl, "Energy in 2013: Taking stock Christof Rühl World Petroleum Congress, Moscow 16, June 2014; http://www.bp.com/

content/dam/bp/pdf/speeches/2014/energy_in_2013_taking_stock.
pdf

453. Anonymous, "Daily chart: Where America exports its oil," *The Economist,*
August 11, 2016.

454. Bernhard Hartmann and Saji Sam. "What Low Oil Prices Really Mean,"
*Harvard Business Review,* March 28, 2016. https://hbr.org/2016/03/
what-low-oil-prices-really-mean?utm_source=twitter&utm_
medium=social&utm_campaign=harvardbiz

455. Peter Tertzakian, "Oil Price Outlook: The View from the Bar," *ARC
Energy Charts,* May 17, 2016.

456. Dave Russum email communication with Peter McKenzie-Brown.
January 2, 2016.

457. International Energy Agency, Oil Markets Report, November 13, 2015.

458. Michael Babad, "Alberta hit by one of worst recessions ever, recovery to
lack 'punch': TD," The Globe and Mail, July 18, 2016.

459. Steve Austin interview with Peter McKenzie-Brown, October 6, 2015.

460. Dave Russum email communication with Peter McKenzie-Brown.
January 2, 2016.

461. Bill Gwozd interview with Peter McKenzie-Brown, October 20, 2014.

462. BP, "Statistical Review of World Energy," 65th edition; June 2016.
https://www.bp.com/content/dam/bp/pdf/energy-economics/sta-
tistical-review-2016/bp-statistical-review-of-world-energy-2016-full-
report.pdf

463. Greg Stringham interview with Peter McKenzie-Brown, January 14, 2016.

464. J. Peter Findley, "The Future of the Canadian Oil Sands: Growth potential of a unique resource amidst regulation, egress, cost, and price uncertainty." Oxford Institute for Energy Studies. ISBN 978-1-78467-051-1, 2016. http://www.oxfordenergy.org/wpcms/wp-content/uploads/2016/02/The-Future-of-the-Canadian-Oil-Sands-WPM-64.pdf; accessed February 10, 2016, 8.

465. Todd Hirsch, "Alberta's economy is dipping, but its labour force is staying put," *The Globe and Mail,* Thursday, August 11, 2016.

# INDEX

74761727R00209

Made in the USA
Columbia, SC
05 August 2017